AN UNDERGROUND HISTORY OF EARLY VICTORIAN FICTION

How does the literature and culture of early Victorian Britain look different if viewed from below? Exploring the interplay between canonical social problem novels and the journalism and fiction appearing in the periodical press associated with working-class protest movements, Gregory Vargo challenges long-held assumptions about the cultural separation between the "two nations" of rich and poor in the Victorian era. The flourishing radical press was home to daring literary experiments that embraced themes including empire and economic inequality, helping to shape mainstream literature. Reconstructing social and institutional networks that connected middle-class writers to the world of working-class politics, this book reveals for the first time acknowledged and unacknowledged debts to the radical canon in the work of such authors as Charles Dickens, Thomas Carlyle, Harriet Martineau, and Elizabeth Gaskell. What emerges is a new vision of Victorian social life, in which fierce debates and surprising exchanges spanned the class divide.

Gregory Vargo is Assistant Professor at New York University. His published essays have appeared in *Victorian Studies* and *Victorian Literature and Culture*. He has held fellowships from the Fulbright program, the American Council of Learned Societies, and the Mrs. Giles Whiting Foundation. With Rob Breton, he is the creator of *Chartist Fiction* (http://chartistfiction.hosting.nyu.edu/), a bibliographic database of several hundred reviews and stories that appeared in more than 25 Chartist periodicals.

CAMBRIDGE STUDIES IN NINETEENTH-CENTURY LITERATURE
AND CULTURE

General editor
Gillian Beer, *University of Cambridge*

Editorial board
Isobel Armstrong, *Birkbeck, University of London*
Kate Flint, *University of Southern California*
Catherine Gallagher, *University of California, Berkeley*
D. A. Miller, *University of California, Berkeley*
J. Hillis Miller, *University of California, Irvine*
Daniel Pick, *Birkbeck, University of London*
Mary Poovey, *New York University*
Sally Shuttleworth, *University of Oxford*
Herbert Tucker, *University of Virginia*

Nineteenth-century British literature and culture have been rich fields for interdisciplinary studies. Since the turn of the twentieth century, scholars and critics have tracked the intersections and tensions between Victorian literature and the visual arts, politics, social organization, economic life, technical innovations, scientific thought – in short, culture in its broadest sense. In recent years, theoretical challenges and historiographical shifts have unsettled the assumptions of previous scholarly synthesis and called into question the terms of older debates. Whereas the tendency in much past literary critical interpretation was to use the metaphor of culture as "background", feminist, Foucauldian, and other analyses have employed more dynamic models that raise questions of power and of circulation. Such developments have reanimated the field. This series aims to accommodate and promote the most interesting work being undertaken on the frontiers of the field of nineteenth-century literary studies: work which intersects fruitfully with other fields of study such as history, or literary theory, or the history of science. Comparative as well as interdisciplinary approaches are welcomed.

A complete list of titles published will be found at the end of the book.

AN UNDERGROUND HISTORY OF EARLY VICTORIAN FICTION

Chartism, Radical Print Culture, and the Social Problem Novel

GREGORY VARGO

New York University

CAMBRIDGE
UNIVERSITY PRESS

CAMBRIDGE
UNIVERSITY PRESS

University Printing House, Cambridge CB2 8BS, United Kingdom

One Liberty Plaza, 20th Floor, New York, NY 10006, USA

477 Williamstown Road, Port Melbourne, VIC 3207, Australia

314-321, 3rd Floor, Plot 3, Splendor Forum, Jasola District Centre, New Delhi - 110025, India

79 Anson Road, #06-04/06, Singapore 079906

Cambridge University Press is part of the University of Cambridge.

It furthers the University's mission by disseminating knowledge in the pursuit of education, learning and research at the highest international levels of excellence.

www.cambridge.org
Information on this title: www.cambridge.org/9781107197855
DOI: 10.1017/9781108181891

First published 2018

A catalogue record for this publication is available from the British Library

Library of Congress Cataloging in Publication data
NAMES: Vargo, Gregory, author.
TITLE: An underground history of early Victorian fiction : Chartism, radical print culture and the social problem novel / Gregory Vargo, New York University.
DESCRIPTION: New York : Cambridge University Press, 2017. | Series: Cambridge studies in nineteenth-century literature and culture | Includes bibliographical references and index.
IDENTIFIERS: LCCN 2017030747 | ISBN 9781107197855 (alk. paper)
SUBJECTS: LCSH: English fiction – 19th century – History and criticism. | Social problems in literature. | Working class in literature. | Chartism in literature.
CLASSIFICATION: LCC PR878.S62 V37 2017 | DDC 823/.7–dc23
LC record available at https://lccn.loc.gov/2017030747

ISBN 978-1-107-19785-5 Hardback
ISBN 978-1-316-64791-2 Paperback

To Kim, Clara, Jonah, and Nalo

Contents

Figures

Acknowledgments

In an 1841 essay, critical of a proposal to establish a literacy test for the right to vote, the radical activist Peter Murray McDouall outlined a labor theory of knowledge, which elaborated how a network of craft occupations (such as papermaking and bookbinding) underwrote literacy itself. With McDouall's expansively social view of the conditions for the production of knowledge in mind, I am keenly aware of how my research and writing depend upon the labor of countless persons, many of whom I will never meet. I would like particularly to thank the librarians whose efforts acquiring, cataloging, and shelving books; answering queries; staffing circulation and information desks; arranging interlibrary loans; and performing many other jobs make academic research possible. Special thanks to Charlotte Priddle, Rosa Monteleone, and Amanda Watson at NYU and to the librarians and archivists at Columbia University, especially in the Rare Book and Manuscript Library, which houses a wealth of radical print in the Seligman collection; the Fales Library, the Tamiment Library, and the Robert F. Wagner Archive at NYU; the People's History Museum, Manchester; John Rylands Library, University of Manchester; the Working Class Movement Library, Salford; and the Cambridge University Library. Thanks also to the staff in the English Department and Gallatin for much support and guidance, especially Alyssa Leál, Lissette Florez, Patricia Okoh-Esene, Shanna Williams, Mary Mezzano, Taeesha Muhammed, and Bennett Williams.

At NYU, numerous friends and colleagues have provided encouragement and support, which have enriched this project as well as my life as a scholar and teacher. Elaine Freedgood, who read and commented on the whole manuscript, has been deeply generous with advice and critique, mentorship and comradeship. Catherine Robson has offered support and excellent feedback at key moments. Sonya Posmentier, John Maynard, and Jeff Spear provided helpful commentary and suggestions on various chapters. I would like also to thank Hannah Gurman, Patrick

Deer, Julia Jarcho, Anne DeWitt, Jini Kim Watson, Pacharee Sudhinaraset, Wendy Lee, Nick Boggs, Peder Anker, Crystal Parikh, Simón Trujillo, John Waters, Joseph Alban, Eugene Vydrin, Gianpaolo Baiocchi, Dara Regaignon, Millery Polyné, and Maureen McLane for their friendship and engagement. My research also profited from conversations with colleagues at many conferences, especially gatherings sponsored by the British Women Writers Association, the Research Society for Victorian Periodicals (RSVP), and the Northeast Victorian Studies Association. At RSVP in particular I have been fortunate to have the chance to speak with many wonderful scholars of radicalism and working-class print culture, and I have deeply appreciated the sense of community among people working in these areas. Despite my best efforts, my footnotes and bibliography cannot do justice to the immense debts I owe to the scholars I've met and many I haven't. Thanks also to colleagues for invitations to speak at the Rutgers British Studies Center, Chartism Day, and the CUNY Victorian Seminar. The latter seminar has been an important institution in my academic life, and I greatly value the mentorship Anne Humpherys has given me there and elsewhere. I greatly appreciate, too, my exchanges and friendship with Tanya Agathocleous and Nick Birns. At City College, where I worked as an adjunct faculty member for three years, the camaraderie of my colleague Harold Veeser and my colleague and office mate Brendan Costello cut against the isolating aspects of contingent academic labor.

This book comes out of a doctoral thesis I wrote at Columbia University. My teachers there helped shape my project with feedback and criticism while teaching me much about research and writing. In particular, I thank Nick Dames for his encouragement and insightful commentary, Bruce Robbins for his prompt to investigate Chartist internationalism, and Amanda Claybaugh for her meticulous comments about the craft of writing and argumentation. A course with Martin Meisel sparked my interest in melodrama and seminars with Robert Scally (at NYU) and Susan Pedersen encouraged my desire to bring the questions and perspectives of social history to the study of literature. Ellen Rosenman, John Plotz, Ryan Suda, and Josh Welsh also read and commented on sections of the dissertation. Ryan and Josh are dear and longtime friends; Ellen and John generously provided assistance and encouragement to someone who was a virtual stranger. Anne Humpherys and John Plotz served as outside readers at the dissertation defense and offered very helpful feedback.

I have been fortunate to receive institutional support for this project in a variety of contexts. I thank Chris Cannon as chair of the English

Department and Susanne Wofford as dean of the Gallatin School of Individualized Study for the substantial aid they have provided. At Columbia, a Mrs. Giles Whiting Foundation Fellowship and Mellon Summer Research Fellowships granted financial support. An American Counsel of Learned Societies New Faculty Fellowship allowed time to research with a reduced teaching load at NYU. An NYU Center for the Humanities Faculty Fellowship provided time to work on final manuscript preparations while beginning a new project. A generous grant from the Abraham and Rebecca Stein Faculty Publication Fund of the NYU department of English helped defray costs of the book's production. I am very grateful to have been able to work with two excellent research assistants, Proma Chowdhury and Charline Jao, who both made important contributions for which I am very grateful. Proma aided in researching Chapters 2 and 7 by combing microfilm reels and digital databases for newspaper reports about the New Poor Law and political refugees in Britain. Charline joined at a later stage and helped with diverse tasks, including creating the index and taking photographs for several of the book's illustrations. I gratefully acknowledge permission from the British Library Board to reproduce Figures 1 and 3; and from the Rare Book & Manuscript Library, Columbia University in the City of New York, to reproduce Figures 5 and 6 (both from the Seligman collection).

Portions of the book have appeared as articles in various journals. Earlier versions of Chapters 3 and 4 appeared in *Victorian Literature and Culture*; a portion of a version of Chapter 6 was published in *Victorian Studies*; and a short section of Chapter 1 appeared in *Nineteenth-Century Gender Studies*. My thanks to the editors of (and anonymous readers for) these journals for their excellent suggestions on those articles, both stylistic and substantive, and to Cambridge University Press and Indiana University Press for permission to republish.

At Cambridge University Press, I have been lucky to have Linda Bree and Tim Mason as editors. I thank them for their support for and work on my project. Thanks also to my anonymous readers of the book manuscript for their helpful and insightful commentary. And thanks to my copy editor Linda Benson for her careful attention to the manuscript.

Finally, I would like to thank my family, upon whose love and support I depend every day. I thank my parents for helping foster my love of reading and research, my sister for her support and friendship, and my brother for encouraging my enjoyment of political argument. Conversations with Benin Ford and Jesse Phillips-Fein have enriched my thinking on many subjects; I am deeply grateful for their love and friendship. My in-laws,

Charlotte Phillips and Oliver Fein, who have spent their lives in struggles for peace and social justice, inspire me. My children, Clara Beulah and Jonah Albert, are inspirations, too. I especially thank Clara for sharing parts of the project with me, and I admire her sense of justice, enjoyment of good stories, and love of chants. And, finally, Kim Phillips-Fein has accompanied me during every stage of the writing of this book, reading multiple drafts of every chapter, discussing ideas, and lending love and support. Along the way, on a bright spring day in London a decade ago, we visited sites of nineteenth-century protest, touring Trafalgar Square, shaking our fists at Somerset House (the headquarters of the Poor Law Commission), and enjoying the sun as it shone down on the park that was formerly Kennington Common.

Abbreviations

CWH   *Champion and Weekly Herald*
NP   *Notes to the People*
NS   *Northern Star*
PMG   *Poor Man's Guardian*

Introduction: Can a Social Problem Speak?

Tens of thousands of readers encountered Charles Dickens's *Nicholas Nickleby* and Benjamin Disraeli's *Coningsby* in a context that might surprise contemporary critics. The Chartist weekly the *Northern Star* reviewed and republished portions of the novels in the spring of 1838 and the winter of 1844–45, excerpting the first nine numbers of Dickens's work and adapting the first volume of *Coningsby* to an abridged serial format. As the *Star* boasted a circulation around 10,000 and a readership several times that, a significant portion of the books' audiences read them in this fragmentary form, inflected by the preoccupations of the preeminent working-class radical periodical of the late 1830s and 1840s and surrounded by the *Star*'s running commentary on contemporary literature and politics.[1]

Yet this context for the novels remains largely unknown, in part because literary historians have too readily accepted middle-class writers' description of the gulf separating "the two nations" of rich and poor, assuming that the cultural world of the Victorian middle class remained isolated from working-class print culture until the rise of a new mass culture in the 1860s and later. Disraeli's own account of a fractured social universe appears early in his 1845 novel *Sybil*, when the Owenite journalist Stephen Morley describes the division of the country into classes "between whom there is no intercourse and no sympathy; who are as ignorant of each other's habits, thoughts, and feelings, as if they were dwellers in different zones, or inhabitants of different planets" (65–66). Though Disraeli ultimately ironizes Morley's description (Gallagher, *Industrial* 203), similar pronouncements appear in writing across a wide spectrum, including by Thomas Carlyle, Charles Dickens, Elizabeth Gaskell, Douglas Jerrold, Charlotte Tonna, and Henry Mayhew. But although these and other authors adopted the guise of brave anthropologists entering a subterranean world when they wrote about the working classes, the cultural reality of social division was different, characterized on both sides by argument, contest, parody, and appropriation as much as separation and ignorance. Radical writers closely followed the development of reform-minded fiction; they used popular literary forms for their own ends and recontextualized familiar genres in an oppositional print culture. Middle-class authors learned in turn from experimental writing that appeared in the radical press. Indeed, much of what was most innovative in social problem fiction of the 1830s, 1840s, and 1850s had its origin in the intersection and collision of these two literary nations.

Realist fiction that raised the debate about the "Condition of England" in the age of industrialization contained within itself a host of stylistic innovations. It expanded the domain of fiction to encompass new aspects of everyday life and a host of topical problems; it pursued an ever more difficult dynamic of formal and social inclusiveness; and it interrogated different forms of allegiance – to class, to community, to nation – even as it moved to view society from a distant, outside perspective (Buzard 171). Each of these aspects can best be understood by examining the complex interplay between middle-class reforming novelists and the print culture successive protest movements fostered. The transaction between the working-class radical press and reforming novelists was complex and contradictory, characterized by violent denunciations and significant borrowings. Popular protest was more than a theme to be analyzed as part of the Condition of England. Radical writers, rather, were treated as social commentators in their own right, sophisticated interlocutors who demanded substantive engagement on both formal and thematic axes.

This introduction explores the cultural resonance of political protest in the early Victorian period from a variety of angles. I begin by outlining some of the most important conflicts of the 1830s and 1840s, particularly the Chartist movement and the struggle against the New Poor Law. Next, I turn to the literary sides of these movements by offering an overview of the experiments in fiction found in the radical press, focusing on revisions to the crucial Victorian genres of melodrama and the *Bildungsroman*. Third, I examine the publishing conventions, consumption patterns, and political context of radical periodical culture. Next, I consider how Chartist periodicals responded to middle-class novelists' efforts to describe social protest movements. Finally, I explore the impact of popular protest on middle-class writing and publishing, examining the way radical writers influenced the development of Condition of England fiction. Throughout, my focus is on the mutual engagement of middle-class and radical writers, the generative exchange that shaped the work of each group.

"*Our* French Revolution"

Chartism, a movement that extended from the late 1830s to the 1850s, sought the expansion of democratic rights as a way to redress social, economic, and political wrongs. It emerged from a variety of other struggles, including the movement for union rights and factory reform; the effort to rescind taxes on the press, which constrained working-class publishing and reading; and the anti-New Poor Law movement. The latter agitation challenged the program of social retrenchment instituted by the 1834 Poor Law Amendment Act and contested the world view of an increasingly hegemonic political economy. Besides critics of the New Poor Law, Chartism enrolled under its banner republican internationalists, Owenites, unionists, and many other stripes of radicals. It convulsed British society for more than a decade and became a touchstone for describing political upheaval for the rest of the century.

By the 1850s, a Whig version of the recent past had become conventional wisdom. This narrative distinguished Britain from its European neighbors by emphasizing how constitutional freedoms ensured peaceable movement toward reform, avoiding revolution. But only retrospectively did this interpretation take hold. Following the defeat in 1848 of revolution on the continent and Chartism at home, concerted efforts were made to erase the radical past (Haywood, *Revolution* 218–42). These efforts took two main forms: the ironic dismissal of the upheavals of the 1830s and 1840s and broader melioristic accounts of social and political change, both of which can be found in an array of writing from Macaulay's historical opus to *The Times* and *Household Words*. This context rendered it unlikely that the literary culture of (partially) defeated political movements would be transmitted to posterity, especially given the noncanonical nature of their writing, much of which appeared in short-lived journals or in cheap book editions that went quickly out of print.[2] As Margaret Oliphant remarked in 1858 of working-class periodicals, their "flimsy pages [seemed] made to kindle fires withal to-morrow" (202).

Nevertheless, the omission of the radical canon from much modern criticism has had the effect of projecting backward the highly contingent stability of the 1850s onto the whole early Victorian period (and sometimes onto the nineteenth century writ large). Building on groundbreaking work by Louis James and Martha Vicinus, recent scholarship on nineteenth-century radicalism has enlarged our sense of the range of Victorian literature. Ian Haywood, Rob Breton, Margaret Loose, Mike Sanders, and others have investigated the experimental and formally capacious nature of writing affiliated with working-class social movements. This volume contributes to this growing body of scholarship by taking up the still largely unexplored question of the relationship between the radical canon and more familiar writing by authors such as Gaskell, Dickens, Carlyle, and Martineau.[3]

If commentators in the 1850s congratulated themselves on the stability of British political institutions, the recent past looked different to contemporary observers, who were confronted with successive protest movements forcibly inserting themselves into the public sphere. Abolitionism, the campaign to end the Stamp Acts, the struggle for the Reform Bill, the anti-New Poor Law movement, the agitation to repeal the Corn laws, campaigns against militarism and war, the factory movement, and Chartism, each reshaped British society as they mobilized thousands of participants for sustained periods and won widespread popular support. The mass mobilization of working-class people in the anti-New Poor Law, factory, and Chartist movements appeared particularly troubling to many middle-class observers. Although no Chartist convention declared an alternative Parliament and British sans-culottes only presented petitions when they marched on Westminster, Thomas Carlyle could remark in 1839 that "these Chartisms, Radicalisms, Reform Bill, Tithe Bill ... are *our* French Revolution" (*English* 192). In the same year as Carlyle's essay, James Kay, the secretary of the Committee of the Privy Council on Education, struck an equally apocalyptic note: "The consequences of permitting another generation to rise, without bending the powers of the executive government and of society to the great work of civilisation and religion, for which the political and social events of every hour make a continual demand, must be a social disquiet little short of revolution" (Kay-Shuttleworth, "Recent" 85) The actions of the state during these tumultuous years further belie *ex post facto* celebrations of consensus and gradualism. The 800 newsvendors and journalists imprisoned in the war of the unstamped; the 1500 people jailed in the Chartist strike wave of 1842; and the nearly 100,000 police, troops, and special constables mobilized to ensure public order in London in April 1848 eloquently testify to how threatening working-class radicalism appeared. Kay, who saw education as the only means to return to rule by moral suasion rather than repressive power, put it grimly: "At this hour military force alone retains in subjection great masses of the operative population, beneath whose outrages, if not thus restrained, the wealth and institutions of society would fall" (Kay-Shuttleworth, "Recent" 88).

Advancing and receding in successive waves, Chartism had three high-water marks. In 1839, 1842, and 1848, the movement presented massive petitions to Parliament that demanded suffrage rights. These documents, each registering more than a million signatures – and more than three million in 1842, gathered by 50,000 people – enunciated the Six Points of the Charter: universal male suffrage, equal electoral districts, annual parliaments, a secret ballot, no property qualification for members of Parliament, and the payment of members. These demands remained central, rendering cohesive a movement that put forward diverse critiques of the British economy and social structure. Although petitioning Parliament was an eminently constitutional strategy, this tactic was supplemented by "auxiliary measures," which sometimes verged on insurrection, most notably the Newport rising of November 1839 in which several thousand armed miners marched on Newport, Wales, and suffered more than twenty casualties at the hands of infantry troops; the 1842 strike wave that involved a half million workers, engulfed the Potteries and Black Country, stilled Lacashire mills, and inspired the riot scenes in *Sybil*; and an alliance with revolutionary Irish Republicans in 1848.

While the planks of the Charter outlined a platform of reform recognizable from the 1770s, the movement was fed by diverse ideological currents. The Chartists asserted the right to the vote was customary, a legacy of freeborn Britons usurped by Norman conquerors. To stake the claim of suffrage rights, however, they also turned to Paineite first principles, braiding universalist and constitutionalist discourse in complex patterns (Epstein, *Radical* 17–20). Always eclectic, the movement accommodated patriotic rhetoric side-by-side with strident internationalism. A single issue of a Chartist periodical might recount histories of the lost Saxon democracy and offer a biographical sketch of a Jacobin orator. This ideological diversity led to conflicts, which were heightened by the group's geographic and social breadth. Polemical debates over political violence, the place of culture in a protest campaign, and the role of women in the economy played out in the movement's press and its literature.

Yet Chartism's strength lay in its ability to subsume a variety of grievances – over the New Poor Law, economic inequality, the repression of unions, the persecution of the press, Irish coercion, and expanding police powers – into a unified vision of democratic rule, which adherents believed would enable a fundamental restructuring of society. The scope and ambition of this program separated Chartism from earlier movements, which advocated specific reforms within the context of the established political structure. As Malcolm Chase has pointed out, the term "Charter" quickly became "shorthand for a whole new political order" (*Chartism* 19). An economic agenda remained entwined with Chartism's explicit demands. The anti-New Poor Law movement lent the Chartists their millenarian rhetoric and commitment to militant direct action (Epstein, *Radical* 12). From the anti-austerity politics of the 1830s through the strike wave of 1842 to the immensely popular Land Plan, which resettled urban operatives in model agricultural communities, economic issues remained constituent.

Chartism, however, was never simply a political or economic movement. On the contrary, its cultural front nourished artistic, educational, and literary activity that sustained the struggle in times of defeat and propelled it forward in periods of resurgence. These endeavors demonstrated the depth of the Chartist critique, how it grappled with questions of alienation and self-realization as well as those of inequality and oppression. Radical reformers organized hundreds of democratic chapels, temperance societies, schools, reading groups, lending libraries, and theatrical clubs as provisional embodiments of the more open and participatory culture they hoped to create (Epstein, "Some" 221–22). In these institutions, the movement drew attention to an array of issues beyond wages and suffrage rights, including the flawed assumptions in current educational provision and the way hierarchy marred art, culture, and worship.

Finally, Chartism was a movement which spawned an extensive literature. Its leaders called openly for the creation of a canon that would reflect the interests of and belong to the working classes. Writers such as Thomas Cooper proclaimed their ambition to "create a literature of [our] own."[4] The Chartists published more than 120 newspapers and journals, ranging from the local *Midland Counties Illuminator* to the regional *Chartist Circular*, which reached most of Scotland, to the *Northern Star* itself, a national organ, which at its height outsold all periodicals in England save *The Times* (Kemnitz 3). The press was critical to Chartism's success, part and parcel of its culture. The organizational network of the unstamped – publishers, booksellers, and agents who risked arrest to produce and distribute illegal papers – helped facilitate the rapid expansion of the new movement (Royle 13). As the struggle matured, the press ensured that local efforts would be identified as part of a common whole by encouraging the diverse groups within the movement – metropolitan artisans, northern mill workers, Welsh miners, Scottish operatives, textile outworkers, and dislocated agricultural laborers – to understand their experience in the light of one another's conditions and efforts (Chase, *Chartism* 17; Janowitz, *Lyric* 134).

Radical Fiction, or, Stories in Search of Their Protagonists

Some of the most dramatic experiments in early Victorian fiction can be found not in *Bentley's Miscellany*, *Household Words*, and the *Cornhill Magazine* but in such relatively neglected journals as the *Northern Liberator*, *Cleave's Gazette of Variety*, and *Notes to the People*. Chartist journals teemed with satire, historical fiction, adventure stories, didactic tales, *Bildungsroman*, allegory, romance, and poetry, as well as copious literary criticism. Straddling the demotic world of popular fiction and the respectable milieu of middle-class reforming novelists, radical authors invented syncretic forms that scrutinized the transformations of their industrializing society: picaresques interrupted with montage-like effects, Swiftian satires dense with scientific jargon, travel writing which detailed politicized and allegorical landscapes. As much as any manifesto, this literature reveals the breadth of Chartism, its attempt to imagine a social order on a more humane and egalitarian basis. Fiction and journalism addressed a series of topics beyond the movement's explicit program, including the role of women in politics and the economy; the significance of the colonial system for working-class Britons; and the relationship between education, individual ambition, and mutual improvement.

Although radical writing spurred a huge variety of literary forms, I pay special attention to innovations authors produced in two essential Victorian genres, melodrama and the *Bildungsroman*. In these modes, we see a startling shift from Victorian fiction's characteristic focus on indi-dual personality as writers attempted to create stories capable of narrating the suprapersonal causes of social change. Rob Breton aptly describes Chartist writing as "anti-fiction" for its critique and inversion of many of the conventions of the middle-class novel (1). The fact that social structures constrict and diminish the self in the radical canon, however, affiliates that canon with broad trends in Romantic and Victorian literature. From Scott's indecisive and passive heroes; through Dickens's nondescript pro-tagonists overwhelmed by a gallery of eccentrics; to Hardy's cast of victims pitched about by the forces of biology, economy, and religion, the tension between self-making and determination, subjectivity and circumstance, defines the nineteenth-century novel.

A critical tradition running from Lukács to Raymond Williams, George Levine, and Harry Shaw considers Victorian fiction in terms of such dichoto-mies. Alex Woloch's *The One vs. the Many* offers an innovative perspective on this same problematic. Woloch analyzes the relationship between minor characters and protagonists in Austen, Balzac, and Dickens. For Woloch, minor characters' restricted narrative function makes them, paradoxically, interpretively rich: minorness highlights the contradictory roles all fictional characters inhabit. Simultaneously made to represent a human personality and to function in a narratological scheme (i.e., as a helper or blocking mechanism), secondary characters wear a costume rife with contradiction. As Woloch explicates, the tension between their function as mimetic figures and as supernumeraries subordinated to the plot becomes explosively charged in mid-nineteenth-century fiction. The constrained roles and formulaic descriptions that define minor characters allow Dickens and Balzac to explore social stratification and the "asymmetrical contingency of social connections" (221).

Woloch's frame is useful for approaching the radical canon, which similarly uses the poetics of minorness to meditate on inequality and political exclusion. In Woloch's telling, Dickens's minor characters inscribe the hero's potential insignificance, reminding the reader that only capricious circumstance has saved him from obscure drudgery. Radical writing goes further, sketching a world in which all characters are minor, heroes and villains included. Seeking ways to narrate complex social processes and imagine forms of agency beyond individual actors, Chartist and anti-New Poor Law fiction shows persons thrown up against large abstract forces – hemmed in by the class structure, adrift on the tides of empire, defined by a nation that excludes the majority of its population from citizenship. This canon rejects traditional forms of closure centered on marriage and the discovery of a vocation, refusing to describe futurity in terms of the family and middle-class work. As Breton remarks, the repeated failure of individual protagonists in Chartist fiction underlines how political combination alone "can bring about the social changes needed to precipitate new narratives" (3).

This study explores how dissident authors adapted a variety of narrative forms, often in ways that readjust the attention given to primary characters. Chapter 1 considers William Cobbet's ironic use of gothic iconography in his *History of the Protestant Reformation*, which describes the dissolution of Catholic monasteries in the sixteenth century as the violent founding of modern property relations, in which elites seized vast resources held by the Church on behalf of the poor. Chapter 2 examines anti-New Poor Law short fiction and journalism to ask what happens to melodramatic convention when villainy is situated in the anonymous world of the market rather than with specific malefactors. Chapters 3 and 6 analyze the ways Chartist *Bildungsroman* question the premises of the middle-class novel of development by rendering their protagonists passive objects of social forces rather than self-authoring individuals. In Chapters 4 and 7, the focus shifts from the radical canon to its impact on middle-class social problem nove-lists, exploring the engagement of Elizabeth Gaskell and Charles Dickens with the writings and world view of Chartist and post-Chartist authors. Chapter 5 looks at domestic melodrama, investigating how Ernest Jones's manipulation of seduction plots isolates the structure of the paternalistic family, not aristocratic debauchees, as the greatest risk to women's well-being. In each of these cases, authors describe injustice rooted in fundamental patterns of social organization. In this way, radical fiction departs from the narrative of Old Corruption, a promi-nent current in radical thought, which blamed social ills on the depreda-tions of a grasping elite.[5]

Fiction in the radical press exhibits a complex relationship to literary convention. At times it copies the plot formulas, moralizing didacticism, and character archetypes of the newly ascendant mass-market periodicals. But more frequently it turns expected practice on its head.[6] Reworking popular and respectable genres, Chartist writers tease out the tensions and contradictions inherent within them. Ernest Jones's adventure stories, for example, share with theatrical melodrama a Manicheanistic moral outlook, a preponderance of *coups de théâtre*, and a penchant for scenes of physical suffering. At the same time, Jones's stories drastically reduce the role of the villain, a startling innovation given that character's typical centrality. Instead of presenting diabolic outsiders, Jones places his villains in quoti-dian contexts, revealing the kinds of institutional power upon which they depend. The fluency with which Jones keeps intact other melodramatic conventions while transforming Byronic supermen into the mere benefi-ciaries of the class system suggests that melodrama as a whole was more capable of analyzing systemic forces than conventional critical wisdom indicates. Similarly, anti-New Poor Law satire moves between promoting a "melodramatic" vision of social harm, in which malevolent individuals wreak widespread destruction, and a view which grapples with the circui-tous causality of a laissez-faire market, in which the authorship of injury can only with difficulty be ascribed to particular agents.

Radical authors were more conflicted about the conventions of the *Bildungsroman* and sought to unravel the uneasy synthesis of self-making and social integration that middle-class versions of the genre stitch together. "Merrie England – No More!" – a short story in Thomas Cooper's *Wise Saws and Modern Instances* (1845) – recounts the attempted departure of a young man from his impoverished village, but it does so from the surprising vantage point of his father and neighbors. Inverting the significance of this stock episode of the novel of development, Cooper

criticizes a narrative structure that equates self-realization with the slough-
ing off of childhood bonds. *Sunshine and Shadow* (1849–50) by Thomas
Martin Wheeler similarly rewrites narratives of individual self-making. It
utilizes the passive protagonist of picaresque in a story that is itinerant,
episodic, and fractured. The novel's unusual textual geography decenters
its genre's national commitments. Instead of tracing a youth's journey
from the provinces to the capital and dwelling on his experiences there,
Wheeler has his hero sojourn in the Caribbean and Europe. By demoting
London from destination to station along the way, *Sunshine and Shadow*
asks what it means to come of age in a nation that is an imperial power,
especially for a working-class hero who cannot identify with the empire's
prestige and receives little benefit from its promise of wealth.[7]

As the previous thumbnail sketches suggest, the radical canon was
syncretic. It existed on a borderline between respectable forms of middle-
class fiction and the sensational and prurient genres of melodrama and
penny bloods. Agnus Reach's description of Abel Heywood's Manchester
bookstore evocatively captures the "literary chaos" that formed the wider
context of radical writing: "Masses of penny novels and comic song and
recitation books are jumbled with sectarian pamphlets and democratic
essays . . . Double-columned translations from Sue, Dumas, Sand, Paul
Feval and Frederic Soutie jostle with dream-books, scriptural commen-
taries . . . and quantities of cheap music, Sacred Melodists and Little
Warblers" (38). Chartist authors such as Wheeler and Jones learned from
the formally capacious novels of Disraeli, Dickens, and Jerrold a journalistic sensibility, a highly rhetorical style of address, detailed focus on
domestic settings, and a belief that fiction could intervene in the broader
social and political world. At the same time, they adapted formulas from
the popular stage and cheap serial novels, the media with which the
movement press competed most directly for its audience. These genres in
turn had absorbed impetuses from the Gothic, and one can trace how
Gothic paranoia, disorientation, and unstable characterization reemerge in
the radical canon, especially the writing of Ernest Jones and G. W. M.
Reynolds. It is fitting that a literature born of the revolutionary decades at
the end of the eighteenth century bequeathed its sensibilities to fiction
arising from the political crises of the 1830s to 1850s. Yet when the Gothic
returned it did so with a difference: in early Victorian literature the world
of vice and violence is contemporary, not a phantasmagoric image of the
feudal past. By combining the obsessions, claustrophobia, and bewilder-
ment of the Gothic with quotidian renditions of work and home, Chartist
and anti-New Poor Law fiction anticipated the sensation subgenre of the

1860s. A crisis of realism became the talk of literary journalism when Collins, Braddon, and Wood overlaid "the opposing realms of romance and domesticity," but this crisis had its roots in the working-class literature of the preceding decades.[8]

Radical Print Culture

The inventiveness of radical writing was bound up with the format in which it appeared, usually as serial publications in newspapers and journals associated with protest movements. Journalistic accounts of the New Poor Law borrowed melodramatic devices from fiction and theater while social problem stories blended romance with a documentary style. Deeply journalistic, Chartist fiction described events that were recent and directly relevant to the reader (Breton 17–18). Its plots were fragmentary and friable, and the presentational context of the radical press further confused the boundary between fiction and the news. From week to week a novel was allotted variable space, much like news stories became less or more important over time. Fictional material was occasionally passed off as current events, the jest upon which the *Onion* is based today. According to the *Star*, Nicholas Nickleby won a seat in a reformed Parliament, and the cheeky *Northern Liberator* reported an experiment in which "Marcus," a fictional Malthusian from a notorious tract, gassed a newborn child before a congress of bishops, MPs, and philosophers (*NS* September 8, 1838; *Northern Liberator* March 2, 1839).

Beyond generic affiliations between fiction and journalism, literature received a particular meaning by appearing in the movement press. The Stamp Acts, which taxed periodicals containing news at the rate of 4d., fundamentally shaped working-class reading from the teens until 1855 when they were finally abolished. The "War of the Unstamped," the organized resistance to the "taxes on knowledge" from 1830 to 1836, in which publishers and vendors risked imprisonment to provide cheap periodicals, encouraged the communal consumption of newspapers, defined reading as inherently political, and created an imagined community of outlaw writers and readers, primarily among working-class people.[9] Fittingly, the *Poor Man's Guardian*'s motto – printed defiantly as a black stamp that replaced the Stamp Office's red one – proclaimed "Knowledge is Power." In this context, literature that seems only vaguely political became charged when included in illegal magazines. Even scientific or historical articles in the pedantic style of useful-knowledge serials meant something different in *McDouall's Chartist and Republican Journal* than in the *Penny Magazine*. After 1836, when the stamp tax was reduced to 1d. but the penalties for avoiding it made harsher, the radical press maintained the defiant ethos of the unstamped, even in papers that succumbed to the law. In its first number, the *Northern Star* believed it necessary to apologize for "that little red spot in the corner of my newspaper. That is the stamp; the Whig 'beauty' spot; your 'plague' spot" (December 16, 1837). Indeed, there was a significant continuity of personnel between the unstamped of the early 1830s and the radical press of the 1840s and beyond. George Julian Harney graduated from a newsboy for the *Poor Man's Guardian*, for which he served two short prison stints, to eventually edit the *Star* and later his own *Red Republican* and *Democratic Review* (W. E. Adams 219).

By the 1840s, working-class radical politics and the press were insolubly linked. Paul Pickering has wittily observed that "those at the forefront of the Chartist struggle for democratic reform did not have blood on their hands, they had ink, printers' ink" ("Mercenary" 190). Dozens of Chartist leaders, including Harney, Feargus O'Connor, Ernest Jones, Henry Vincent, Thomas Martin Wheeler, and William Lovett, were affiliated with papers as writers, editors, and publishers. Chartist periodicals covered a spectrum of genres ranging from educational journals such as the *Chartist Circular* to literary anthologies like the *Labourer* to news-driven weeklies such as the *Northern Liberator*. The *Star* in particular, which in its early days sold so many copies that it strained the Post Office's capacity along certain mail routes, played a vital role in making the movement coherent and national, affiliating local and disparate agitations with one another to create a sense of a single unified struggle (Chase, *Chartism* 17; Epstein, "Feargus" 51). Similarly, the *Star*'s "Chartist Intelligence" column chronicled hundreds of soirees, lectures, dances, reading group meetings, and dramatic and musical performances, defining the weekly events of local Chartist life as one culture. The *Star* became a central institution in its own right, celebrated (as was the press generally) by countless toasts, speeches, resolutions, banners, and poems.

The present volume explores the organization and rhetoric of radical papers to see how they interpreted social change while keeping in mind their various periodical genres. A journal's creation of meaning began with its title, which indicated its sense of its own significance. Titles were often sophisticated linguistic gestures which utilized allusions, metaphors, and puns.[10] Names of papers included in this study fall into three main categories. The first figured the press as a champion of the people, claiming an active, even combative role in social and political life. Examples of this type included the *Northern Liberator*, *The Champion and Weekly Herald*, the *National Vindicator*, and the *Poor Man's Guardian*. The title of the latter played on the notion that poor law guardians, officials who supervised the distribution of relief, were derelict in their duties. A second kind of title associated a paper with the views of one dominant personality. *Cobbett's Political Register*, which revolutionized publishing in 1816 when it circumvented the Stamp Act, founded this tradition in the radical press. Although this fashion had waned by the 1840s, G. W. M. Reynolds lent his name as a portable trademark to various highly successful ventures. Still, it was significant that the *Star* was not called something like *O'Connor's Instructor* and that neither Ernest Jones's nor George Julian Harney's several magazines ever bore their names – they were conceived as movement papers that would include a variety of viewpoints and transcend the perspective of one person. Even *McDouall's Chartist and Republican Journal* marked a shift in this regard by affiliating the editor's point of view with broader political currents.

A third group of titles rendered papers as so many sources of light, celebrating the educational and guiding function of the press. "[The press] may be denominated an INTELLECTUAL SUN," the *Western Vindicator* mused, "which diffuses light and heat – which fosters the germs of intellect, invigorates the judgment, and gives birth to talent" (September 28, 1839). The most important example of this genre was the *Northern Star*, poetically toasted at a political dinner in Ashton-under-Lyne as "the brightest luminary in the British hemisphere" (*NS* January 20, 1838) (Figure 1). The *Star* stood in a long line of Suns and Comets, but its name had a more specific connotation, for it was borrowed from the republican paper of the Irish revolution of 1798. It spawned several copies, such as the *Southern Star* and the *Evening Star* (a daily founded by O'Connor), both of which, however, failed to capitalize on the success of their namesake and quickly folded. When the title migrated to America as Frederick Douglass's *North Star* (established in 1847 following the abolitionist's two-year sojourn in England which brought him into contact with the Chartists), it obtained a more pointed resonance as the guide star to freedom at the end of the Underground Railroad. Thomas Cooper displayed his mischievous sense of humor in the luminous titles he gave the various magazines he published in Leicester in 1841 and 1842. After the *Midland Counties Illuminator* failed, he tried the halfpenny *Chartist Rushlight*, that is, an inexpensive type of candle favored by the poor, but it too folded within weeks (Gammage 404; Roberts, *Chartist* 71). With the *Extinguisher*, Cooper reversed course and emphasized the radical press's

Figure 1 The *Northern Star*, January 12, 1839. Here the *Star*'s masthead is at its most elaborated with a printing press giving off light. Note also the advertisement for "Cheap Books" in the upper left.

role as critic (snuffing out the false lights of other papers?), only to give up the joke with his last venture, *The Commonwealthsman.*

A significant amount of criticism still assumes that Victorian reading was a solitary affair, in which an archetypal middle-class consumer borrowed the latest triple-decker from Mudie's and enjoyed it in the privacy of his or her own home. Some critics of Victorian serialization present the effect of reading over time as affirming a cultural and political gradualism taken as characteristic of the age. Slowly developing narratives typify the celebration of steady reform and the rejection of radical change. Along similar lines, serialization is sometimes regarded as an embodiment of bourgeois values for the way it delays gratification and encourages patient, regular effort.[11] A study of the radical press and its literature implies an array of contexts that challenge these ideas. This canon was read at work, in coffee shops, at meetings, in discussion groups, and in prison, and in a variety of formats more jagged and fragmentary than in middle-class publications. A tradition from Cobbett downward encouraged the clubbing of funds to purchase and share periodicals. The dialect writer Ben Brierley recollects in his memoir how his father and "five others" joined together to afford a subscription to the *Northern Star* and how he would read it on Sunday mornings "aloud so that all could hear at the same time."[12] Social patterns of consumption were marked textually by an oratorical style designed to be read out loud and articles were frequently addressed to a plural "you" (Breton 28; Vernon 143–45; Yelland). In Birmingham in 1851, a rally celebrating a visit by the Hungarian revolutionary Kossuth commemorated the communal nature of the radical press. Following a procession of trade unions, printers worked a press set up on a movable stage, churning out copies of a poem by the Chartist Gerald Massey, which were given to the crowd (Finn 127).

The surprisingly intimate relationship between papers and their public was frequently remarked by middle-class reviewers of working-class periodicals, who noticed the letters-to-the-editor columns as a peculiar feature. Margaret Oliphant described "this odd reciprocity between writers and readers, this multitudinous movement on the part of the audience to originate as well as to receive their own amusement" (211). But what Oliphant saw in the *London Journal* and the *Family Herald* of the late 1850s was a pale reflection of the participatory aspects of Chartist newspapers, in which readers vociferously debated strategy; provided accounts of meetings, rallies, and lectures; submitted a huge quantity of verse and miscellaneous articles; and expected that their letters be included as a democratic right (Roberts, "Who Wrote" 56, 65). William Hill, the first editor of the *Star* remarked exasperatedly that "many persons complain of their Communications not being inserted. We should rather they would point out what could be omitted. If we were to print all communications we receive, we should, some weeks, require six or seven *Northern Stars*" (May 26, 1838).[13]

If the authorship of radical papers was in some sense communal, they nevertheless relied on a division of labor that separated professional scribblers from their audience. Thinking specifically of literature, this separation was more acute for fiction than poetry, for the latter could be composed in shorter amounts of time and while the author was occupied with other tasks. Nearly four hundred poets have been identified as contributors to the *Star* while fiction in all Chartist journals was likely the work of fewer authors (M. Sanders, "Jackass" 46). Nevertheless, the radical press attempted to foster closeness with its readers, a process aided by circumstances linking writers and audience. Not only did both groups share a sense of political purpose and a movement culture that touched many aspects of daily life, but broader social and economic circumstances also joined authors and readers. Writers discussed in the present study worked as a cabinet-maker, a joiner, a shoemaker, a cordwainer, a sailor, a woolcomber, and a teacher, as well as a doctor and a barrister, before becoming professional journalists, activists, and lecturers. The masthead for the *Charter* proclaimed its establishment "by the working classes" and George Julian Harney dedicated the *Democratic Review* "to the proletarians." Likewise, the weekly address in the *Star* to the "fustian jackets, unshorn chins, and blistered hands" promoted the journal as the property and advocate of the laboring population if in masculinist language that marked women's sometimes ambiguous relationship to the movement and frequent exclusion from its print culture.[14] Though education, cultural obtainments, and indeed literacy distinguished authors from much of the rank and file, the aspiration for learning and literature was widely shared. Nor does the presence of middle-class and gentlemanly "friends of the people" in Chartist ranks imply the kind of class-transcendent populism Patrick Joyce perceives in the movement.[15] Ernest Jones and Peter McDouall found in Chartism a path to downward mobility as polite society exacted heavy costs on its renegade members (Ashton and Pickering 149–53). Jones was imprisoned, investigated for censure by his professional society, and suffered severe financial difficulties, partially alleviated by a subscription on his behalf in the late 1850s.[16] Although Chartist leaders were celebrated in diverse ways, including portraits inserted into the *Star* and fetes honoring their visits, Jones himself repeatedly expressed skepticism of gentleman leaders of popular movements:

God deliver us from such assistance! Firstly, *No rich man means that which WE mean.* He cannot, in the very nature of things … Secondly, there is nothing more debases a movement, than looking up to rich men to make it live. (*NP* 659)

A final experience shared by many radical authors was that of prison. Whereas Dickens, Gaskell, and Carlyle each made touristic visits to one or more prisons at some point in their careers – Carlyle and Gaskell in fact touring Tothill Fields while Ernest Jones suffered its silent system – Thomas Cooper, William Lovett, John Collins, Henry Hetherington, Bronterre O'Brien, Feargus O'Connor, Peter McDouall, William Cobbett, Henry Vincent, George Julian Harney, William Aitken, Abel Heywood, and J. R. Stephens (to mention only authors considered in this book) were all imprisoned for inflammatory writing, seditious speech, or violations of the Stamp Act.[17] "Almost every man who rose to prominence in the Chartist ranks," recalled W. E. Adams, "came under the lash of authority" (213). More than one hundred editors or vendors were prosecuted per year in the War of the Unstamped, and hundreds of Chartists were imprisoned or transported. As much as polemics in print, state violence and physical repression were part of the contest to define the early Victorian public sphere (Haywood, *Revolution* 226). In a literal sense, radical writing was prison writing, and prison was often conceived as a center of intellectual activity and a badge of honor in movement culture (Legette 2, 7-8; Pickering, *Chartism* 148-51; Randall 180). Thus the *Western Vindicator*'s masthead proclaimed, "Edited and Conducted by Henry Vincent, Now Resident in Monmouth Gaol" (from May 8, 1839), Jones advertised poetry written "with the aid of blood and memory" in Tothill Fields (*Northern Star* July 27, 1850), and the free-thinker George Holyoake noted, "To have spent, without shrinking, some portion of life in prison in defence of public liberty, gives the same authority among the people as having graduated from university does among scholars" (118).

The experience of imprisonment marks radical literature in diverse ways: a reflective posture in the tradition of Bunyan; direct explorations of the power of the state; a sometimes paranoid sensibility that conceives society as panoptic; the ubiquitous use of metaphors of freedom and slavery; and an insistence on the consubstantiality of the private sphere and the public, political world (Figure 2). Putatively written from prison, a *Western Vindicator* article— signed by Vincent but actually composed by his partner Francis Hill— ironically employs Bunyan's trope of prophetic dreams, recording a nighttime vision modeled on the recent (and indeed seemingly dreamlike) events of the Newport rising: "Methought I was in the Welsh Hills, and that thousands of

Figure 2 "The English Town" by Ernest Jones. Drawn in 1849 while Jones was
imprisoned in Tothill Fields.

the sturdy Welsh were drawn into a battle array, well armed" (November 16,
1839; see also David Williams 83). Hill teasingly reminds Vincent's captors
that though behind bars he continues in the struggle: "I awoke, and
found 'twas all a dram [*sic*]. Of course I know nothing of the proceeding
without my prison; but in the event of an occurrence bearing any similitude to

my dream, my sentiments would be the same as those I have penned as being entertained in my visions" (November 16, 1839).

The Other Nation Reviews Its Condition

The literature column of the *Northern Star* amply illustrates the ambivalent and shifting attitude of the Chartists toward social reform fiction. This column, a prominent and important section of the paper, advanced the claim that the movement for democracy sought cultural as well as political citizenship. Although the editors excavated a long tradition of radical verse, culling Milton and Shakespeare for democratic passages and publishing these beside the poetry of Shelley, Byron, and Burns as well as Chartist authors, the journal's taste in fiction was decidedly contemporary. It regularly featured "A Bowl of Punch," which lifted jokes from the famous humor magazine. It filled out columns with Carlylean epigrams and Dickensian sketches. And it offered a series of reviews of social problem fiction by Jerrold, Gaskell, Dickens, Disraeli, and Frances Trollope. That fiction obtained a hearing at all represented a change from the previous generation of radical journals such as the *Black Dwarf* and Cobbett's *Political Register* (Murphy 67, 77–80). This shift marked not only the genre's increasing importance but also a sense that the reform tradition in Victorian literature signaled a "revolution in novel writing" (*NS* January 11, 1845).

While the *Star* engaged consistently with middle-class literary reformers, it did so haphazardly, with financial constraints and the crush of political developments affecting the attention devoted to literature. The Chartist paper never reviewed Gaskell's *Mary Barton*, which appeared in the fall of 1848 during a series of political trials which devastated the movement, although the paper did mention the novel in a short review of Gaskell's "admirable Christmas book" *The Moorland Cottage* two years later (December 28, 1850). And it is not clear that anyone associated with the paper ever read Carlyle's *Chartism*, the essay that coined the phrase the "Condition of England," though the *Star* approached it secondhand in an appraisal of an issue of the *British and Foreign Review*, which commented upon Carlyle's piece. Analyzing *Chartism* in this circuitous manner, the *Star* was decidedly tepid: "One thing is clear, that neither Mr. Carlyle, nor his reviewer, know what Chartism is. They deal somewhat largely in misrepresentations, but without that low abuse, and evidently willful perversion of facts, in which our opponents generally indulge" (November 6, 1841).

As in this case, the *Star's* encounter with contemporary letters often depended on review copies of magazines it received, most frequently *Tait's*

Edinburgh Journal, The Illuminated Magazine, and *Howitt's Journal*, reform-minded periodicals aimed at a lower-middle-class readership. The *Star* was enthusiastic about the new kind of periodical these magazines represented, expressing the hope that these "Encyclopedia[s] in miniature of all the great branches of literature" would disseminate a liberatory knowledge to a wide circle of readers (January 20, 1844). William Howitt's and Douglas Jerrold's ventures were the *Star*'s favorites. The author of the "Q Papers" in *Punch*, Jerrold represented the most radical side of the humor magazine in the early 1840s (Slater 121). The *Star* reviewed performances of his theatrical melodramas *Black Ey'd Susan* (written 1829) and *Rent Day* (1832), and *Black Ey'd Susan* was performed at a benefit at the Royal Marylebone Theatre to raise money for a Chartist hall (*NS* September 21, 1844; February 27, March 6, 1847). These plays anticipated many of the themes taken up by Condition of England fiction a decade later. When *Jerrold's Shilling Magazine* was launched at the end of 1844, the *Star* puffed it: "from beginning to end, page upon page, [it] proclaims the wrongs of the many, or vindicates their rights with an ability seldom excelled, and an earnestness never exceeded" (June 14, 1845). Knowing the shilling price was beyond the means of working-class consumers, the *Star* advised its readers to club together to purchase the journal or to demand that the coffee shops and libraries they patronized carry it: "Indeed, this is the *Magazine for the Millions*, and by them it should be universally read" (March 8, 1845; see also January 20, 1844). Given Jerrold's avowed intention to "make every essay ... breathe with a purpose," the *Star*'s enthusiasm was understandable (*Douglas Jerrold's* 1: iv). Even so, the Chartist organ was unabashedly millenarian in its praise: "Yet the grounds for hope – nay, certainty of future triumph, – [are] many and indisputable. Take only one: the new literature of the age, of which this magazine may be regarded as the type" (June 14, 1845). In the wake of the French Revolution of February 1848, the *Ashton Chronicle* (edited by the ex-Chartist J. R. Stephens) struck a similar note, asserting that contemporary literature was having transformative consequences: "Dickens and Douglas Jerrold are beginning to do in England what Victor Hugo, and Eugene Sue helped to complete, and consummate in France" (March 1848).

As one would expect, *Star* reviewers paid close attention to the politics of fiction, but literary craft was also important, especially from 1844 when the paper made a concerted effort to publish higher-quality poetry to advance an "argument from culture" about the worthiness of the working classes for the franchise (Sanders, *Poetry* 76–77). The previously mentioned notice of *The Moorland Cottage* anticipates contemporary Gaskell criticism in singling out the author's "penetration and discernment in the observation and depiction of mental phenomena" (December 28, 1850). Dickens was praised for his style, characters, and ability to awaken "the most varied emotions of which our nature is susceptible," as well as for his commitment as an "earnest and practical reformer" (March 13, 1852). The *Star* chuckled over the "positively Shandean . . . sophistries" of Betsy Trotwood in *David Copperfield* (December 21, 1850); reveled in the portrait of telescopic philanthropy in *Bleak House* (March 13, 1852); and lauded the advocacy for the poor in *A Christmas Carol*, a "toothsome taste" of which displaced Chartist verse in the 1844 Christmas number, a highlight of the paper's literary year (December 21, 1844). This "Shakespeare of our own age" was given pride of place, because he was transforming literature by focusing on the travails of ordinary people:

> Surely the reign of wrong is drawing to a close! Surely the day of suffering is coming to an end! When those to whom heaven hath given the gift of genius, no longer prostitute their powers to the service of falsehood and tyranny, but use them for the god-like purpose of vindicating the truth, and smiting oppression from the heights of power. (January 11, 1845)

Other Chartist papers also embraced Dickens, but journals such as the London *Charter* mainly reviewed or advertised down-market adaptations of his work, including Reynolds's *Pickwick Abroad*, Moncrieff's melo-drama *Nickleby and Smike*, and the twopenny broadsheet *Sam Weller's Scrap Sheet*.[18] The more culturally ambitious *Star*, on the other hand, focused primarily on Dickens's own writing.

During the *Star*'s fourteen-year run, only *Nicholas Nickleby* received negative comment among Dickens's novels, cold thanks for the paper's publication of sections of its opening parts. Sampling Dickens's serial in the fall of 1838 was a useful strategy to boost circulation, but after a few months the editors denigrated even the passages they passed along: "We are sorry to observe that Nicholas still declines. There is in this number considerably less of spirit – less vividness of conception, and less brilliancy of execution than even in the last" (August 18, 1838). A few weeks later: "Worse and worse. We should advise the author of this popular work to take a little rest, and try to recruit his intellectual energies" (September 8, 1838). And the final, decisive dismissal: "Nicholas lags again. There is a great deal of wiredrawing in this number. The only tolerable chapter is the one on pulling of noses" (December 15, 1838).

Carlyle was a more complicated case. Throughout the 1840s, he retained authority in working-class radical circles for his criticism of the market in *Sartor Resartus* and *Past and Present*, but his drift to the right was unmistakable. The *Star* repeatedly quoted his condemnations of laissez-faire as "one of the shabbiest gospels ever preached on earth" (September 28, 1844) and invoked his apocalyptic vision of social unrest as a warning to contemporary England: "Already we may see in the distance the realization of Thomas Carlyle's dread picture" (October 10, 1846).[19] But over time the paper came to regard him as "that sword-worshipper Thomas Carlyle – one-half a great man, and one-half a great humbug" (July 24, 1847) and to complain of his "barbarous jargon" (January 29, 1848) and his "weary ... bedlam-balderdash" (April 21, 1849). Even sympathetic quotation was highly selective. An excerpt from his "Corn Law Rhymes" omits a reference to the "uneducated working classes" (November 23, 1839) and one from *The French Revolution* renders a crowd of "gaunt figures" less weathered, more heroic (October 10, 1846). This process of subtle manipulation reached its climax when the *Star* published another extract from *The French Revolution* but appended biting commentary about the style of the now infamous author of the *Latter-Day Pamphlets*:

> We have scarcely altered Mr. Carlyle's words. A word indeed here and there, but not the sense. His expletives, some few of them at least, we now subjoin. "Bottomless Guilt" – "murky simmering" – "Madness, Horror and Murder" – "frantic Patriots" – "horny paws" – "unkempt heads" – "tiger yells" – "Night and Orcus" – "Phantasmagory of the Pit" – "howling seas" – "sabres-sharpening" – "sons of darkness" – "neither [*sic*] fire", etc., etc., etc. All of which had not much helped the story; but may now be applied by the judicious reader, wherever may seem most suitable. (October 11, 1851)

The *Star* isolates Carlyle's melodramatic language to advance a political critique. Comparing revolutionary bloodshed with the gradual violence of famine in Ireland, the paper asks why one merits sensational prose while the other gets little notice.

The playful confidence of the *Star*'s treatment of Carlyle serves as a salutary reminder of the limits of a text's ability to inculcate its values in the reader, especially as it circulates in contexts far from its original situation. The *Star* frequently appropriated problematic material, happily ignoring the portions of a work in tension with the Chartist program while trumpeting positions consistent with its agenda. *Mary Barton* could thus be recalled as a "powerful and truthful exposition of the evils inherent in the factory system," while the paper elided that it was also a story about political assassination, a parable for the need for Christian reconciliation between the classes, and an emigration narrative at odds with the *Star*'s position on that controversial topic (December 28, 1850). Similarly, the Scottish *Chartist Circular* quoted Harriet Martineau's praise of American institutions, although the radical press pilloried Martineau for her advocacy of orthodox political economy and retrenchment.[20] Most surprisingly, extracts of Frederick Marryat's anti-Jacobin naval fiction appeared in the *Charter*, even as it dissented from his "sly raps at republicans" (July 28, 1839). One imagines that if Marryat, Martineau, or Carlyle became aware of the Chartist press's borrowings, they would have reacted as Dickens did upon discovering his fiction in "vile, blackguard and detestable newspapers" in the United States: "Is it tolerable that besides being robbed and rifled, an author should be *forced* to appear in any form – in any vulgar dress – in any atrocious company – that he should have no choice of his audience – no controul over his distorted text?" (*Letters* 3:230).

Although the *Star*'s encomiums to the social problem literature of the 1840s highlights radical aspects of the latter's politics, the paper's editors remained aware of the divisions that separated middle-class literary reformers from a full embrace of Chartism. Nevertheless, the *Star* was more interested in finding common ground with popular authors than proclaiming its differences. Thus while consistently praising *Jerrold's Shilling Magazine*, George Julian Harney wrote a sarcastic letter to Marx and Engels complaining of Jerrold's liberal bias, his support for "Free Trade," and his dismissal of "*perfect equality*" as a "mischievous delusion" (Harney 247). And the *Star* continued to sample the offerings of "our facetious friend *Punch*" years after it lamented its abandonment of radical positions to become "little better than a mere illustrated copy of the [Anti-Corn Law] League, and just about as witty . . . as that delectable organ of the millocrats" (June 6, 1846).

No matter the *Star*'s practice of selective quotation, its criticism promoted reading as an active process demanding political and intellectual engagement, not a mode of passive consumption of completed and fixed products. Indeed, Chartist periodicals suggest how fragmentary Victorian reading could be as texts were excerpted, commented upon, and printed again in secondary and tertiary contexts. A notable example of this recirculation was the *Star*'s treatment of Disraeli's *Coningsby*, the paper's most prolonged assessment of contemporary fiction (November 30, 1844–March 15, 1845). Installments functioned as an annotated abridgement with selections ending at suspenseful points and the paper summarizing omitted events. But the space devoted to the novel also served as an extended book review with the *Star* interpolating commentary and framing its selection with criticism. In developing this hybrid format, the *Star* departed from the way, according to Nicholas Dames, middle-class literary journals used the prolonged extract. Rather than treating excerpts as "self-evident, requiring little or no work from the critic to demonstrate [their] significance," the *Star* interjected commentary into the middle of Disraeli's text, disrupting the experience of reading and modeling the kind

of scrutiny its readers should bring to literature (Dames 26). Even absent
commentary, the jarringly different context of *Coningsby* in the *Star* made
"publication legible as an independently signifying act" as in Meredith
Martin's formulation about American periodical culture (5).

The *Star* was drawn to Disraeli's political novel, historical survey, and
Bildungsroman for its diagnosis of the roots of the crises afflicting England
and its merciless dissection of a moribund conservatism as well as the
author's support for factory reform (November 30, 1844). But the recontex-
tualization of *Coningsby* in a working-class journal also inverted the voyeuristic views of the poor that Condition of England fiction retailed to the
middle-class public. Even as the *Star* pooh-poohed Disraeli's eulogies to
Eton, it offered its audience an excursion into the foibles of the other nation:

> Our readers can hardly fail to have been struck ... with the very elegant *slang*
> which, according to Mr. D'Israeli, prevails in the conversation of Etonians. We
> were aware that Eton had long been famous for the eloquence of its pupils, but
> ... not ... that ... *costermongering slang* formed so large an ingredient in the
> eloquence of Eton's boasted orators! "Lark" and "row," and many similar
> phrases, appear to be as natural in the mouths of these young patricians as in
> those of the humblest plebeians of St. Giles. (January 4, 1845)

The *Star*'s weekly excerpt became a contest over who possessed the most
compelling vision for social renewal, Disraeli or the *Star* itself. The paper
faulted *Coningsby* on many accounts, but foremost for its nostalgic paternalism. Hardly original, this critique of Young England had a particular
charge in the *Star*'s columns, because William Cobbett's *History of the
Protestant Reformation*, a foundational text for the anti-New Poor Law
movement, stood behind Disraeli's medievalism. Like Cobbett, Disraeli
traced contemporary crises to the "material and cultural displacements" of
the Reformation, which privatized quasi-public Church holdings (Ulrich
109). But the *Star* worked to reclaim Cobbett's legacy for a forward-
looking tradition: "The besetting sin of the 'New Generation' is, that
they will persist in looking backward instead of forward for measures of
public amelioration ... It is not to the vaunted 'wisdom of our ancestors'
we must look for political or social remedies" (December 14, 1844).

The *Star* also challenged Disraeli's realist methods, lampooning a
description of a manufacturing town "so *couleur de rose*, that we apprehend
both employers and employed will be astonished at his descriptions"
(February 22, 1845). The paper advised that the author might improve
his verisimilitude by seeking "a few useful facts" from the factory movement leader Lord Ashley, or by "[applying] himself to the Manchester

workers, [visiting] their homes, and [learning] from their lips, male and female, the workings of the system he so mistakenly lauds." The *Star* even encouraged its Bolton readers to undertake a fact-finding expedition to substantiate the novel's portrait of life in manufacturing towns. An invitation to seek "Mr. D'Israeli's Lancashire Eden" drove home in a humorous fashion the advantages the radical press – as a communal product in intimate dialogue with its readers – possessed over outside observers of working-class life (February 22, 1845).

Working-Class Writers, Middle-Class Readers

The *Star*'s suggestion that Disraeli turn to working-class informants points out how the dialogue between middle-class literary reformers and Chartist print culture could go in two directions. While Chartist journals frequently commented upon reform-minded fiction, the respectable world of letters was at least somewhat acquainted with a canon of radical literature and journalism. Elizabeth Gaskell's circle included several coreligionists who collaborated in Chartist organizations and were familiar with radical texts. Gaskell's Sunday School class at the Cross Street Unitarian Chapel in Manchester included children from Chartist families, and her husband taught Chartists themselves at the Manchester Mechanics' Institute. Dickens, whose *Household Words* offices shared the *Star*'s bohemian neighborhood, saw Thomas Cooper's poetry in manuscript; Charles Kingsley corresponded with this "laureate of labour"; and Jerrold, William Howitt, and W. J. Fox each sent congratulatory letters to a soiree honoring the Chartist writer (*NS* May 9, 1846; Shannon 83–91). Cooper himself wrote for *Jerrold's Shilling Magazine*, penning a cycle of reports on the "Condition of the People in England," which may have inspired Henry Mayhew's *Morning Chronicle* articles about working class life that became the encyclopedic *London Labour and the London Poor* (Slater 204).[21]

Reconstructing the social, institutional, and textual networks that connected middle-class writers to the world of working-class politics, this volume traces debts to the radical canon in the oeuvre of such figures as Gaskell, Dickens, Carlyle, Kingsley, Martineau, and Frances Trollope. In Chapter 1, I propose that Martineau's surprising ambivalence toward retrenchment in her poor law novellas stemmed from her necessary engagement with the radical ideology that would underwrite the anti-New Poor Law movement. In Chapter 4, I argue that Gaskell's portrait of working-class learning in *Mary Barton* drew on Chartist ideas about education. In Chapter 7, I suggest that Dickens's exposure to Chartist prison writing and controversies about republican internationalism shaped *A Tale of Two Cities*. This is not to say these authors uniformly sympathized with radicalism. On the contrary, each of these confluences was tentative and partial. But even texts antagonistic to radicalism were sometimes shaped by its writing. Harriet Martineau's poor law novellas, for example, lampoon Cobbettite claims of the right to poor relief, but they dispute on the terrain her ideological opponent established, taking up at length Cobbett's ideas about the poor laws as a social inheritance.

Movement publications, on the other hand, defined themselves in opposition to mainstream journalism, the "masked bravos of the press" in Harney's colorful phrase. Dubbing *The Times* "the crowning shame of England . . . consistent only in infamy," Harney lamented lacking the space his theme warranted: "volumes, instead of a couple of pages would be needed to do justice to *The Times*" (*Democratic Review* December 1850). Radical print culture, moreover, was distinguished from its middle-class counterpart by the politics of its publication history: Chartist journals emerged from a tradition of active resistance to the Stamp Acts, while Chartist journalists faced frequent prosecution for "seditious libel." Near the end of his life, the radical publisher Abel Heywood could recall how in the 1830s, "the bookseller was a fettered and chained being, who deviating ever so little from the narrow path marked out for him, found himself summoned before the magistrates" (qtd. in Maidment, "Manchester" 105). The fact of government surveillance and repression drastically qualifies Sally Ledger's assertion that "notwithstanding the caution with which [Dickens] approached the Chartist movement . . . [he] was writing in precisely the same cultural landscape and publishing environment . . . as the many hundreds of Chartists who took up the pen to further their cause" (*Dickens* 140). It goes without saying that Dickens, unlike Chartist writers and editors, need never have worried that the Home Office might peruse his journal for evidence for future prosecutions.[22]

Despite evident differences in politics and conditions of production, however, Chartist writing and mainstream reform-oriented literature influenced each other as their authors struggled over concepts held in common but with divergent meaning in differing contexts. Critics of radical literature have generally been more interested in the Thompsonian project of recovering and explicating a lost tradition than in coordinating this corpus with the more familiar ground of the middle-class social narrative.[23] While understandable, this focus has sometimes confirmed a view of the hostility of middle-class literary reformers to working-class social movements that underestimates the cultural importance of the latter. In fact, beyond influencing particular writers, the dissident press shaped mainstream print culture. As the most successful radical papers rivaled or exceeded the readership of *The Times*, they revealed to publishers a potentially vast audience, helping prompt the embrace of cheaper, serialized formats (Aled Jones, "Chartist" 1). The movement press influenced crucial middle-class publishing genres such as "useful knowledge" magazines (discussed in Chapter 4) and governmental Blue Books designed for a mass market (looked at in Chapter 1). Both ventures strove to displace radical papers as the most prominent source of news for working-class people but were themselves subjected to withering parody in working-class journals.

Social problem fiction itself often obscures its connections to the world of demotic writing. Carlyle's depiction of the democratic platform as "inarticulate cries as of a dumb creature in rage and pain" is echoed in many contemporary works, which take up an anti-mob tradition traceable to the French Revolution (Carlyle, *English* 199; Plotz 136–52). Carlyle's stereotyped view, however, was not the only image of working-class politics available. If *Alton Locke, Sybil,* and *Mary Barton* feature scenes of tumult and violence, they include as principal characters a working-class poet and radical bookseller, an Owenite newspaper editor, and working-class autodidacts who share sensibilities with their more militant brethren. Even Carlyle's *Chartism*, which claims to translate subaltern ravings into comprehensible language, is grounded in the world of radical print culture: it dwells at length on a sensational tract against the New Poor Law and orthodox political economy, from which it borrows key motifs and the rhetorical strategy of moving between melodrama and satire. *Past and Present* also includes unacknowledged debts to the radical canon, in this case, as in *Coningsby*, to William Cobbett's vision of the medieval Church as the habitat of humane relations and protection for the poor which the contemporary market has dissolved. Radical writers for their part were well aware of Carlyle's condescension, which they contested and returned. In Harney's *Democratic Review*, the Chartist feminist Helen McFarlane, who was the first English translator of the *Communist Manifesto*, mocks Carlyle's description of "Red Republicanism" as "mere *in*articulate bellowings": "This reminds me of the old saying – 'he that *hath ears*, let him hear what the Spirit saith to the churches.' Red Republicanism is just about one of the most articulate, plain-speaking voices, in the whole of Universal History" (April 1850).

Seven years after *Past and Present*, Carlyle offered a hostile portrait of Ernest Jones, "a philosophic or literary Chartist" reduced to inarticulacy by the silent system of Tothill Fields Prison, a condition Carlyle claimed to envy:

[The prisoner was] walking rapidly to and fro in his private court, a clean, high-walled place; the world and its cares quite excluded, for some months to come: master of his own time and spiritual resources to ... a really enviable extent ... I fancied I ... so left with paper and ink, and all taxes and botherations shut out from me, could have written such a Book as no reader will here ever get of me. ("Model" 53)[24]

A barrister and writer who threw his lot in with the working-class movement, Jones was an object of fascination for middle-class observers of Chartism. James Ward's "How I Became a Chartist" ventriloquizes the voice of a gentleman radical modeled on Jones. Stressing the literary context of the movement, the article describes its members as Frankenstein's monsters made out of texts:

The mind of a mechanic-chartist is a psychological curiosity – hard, unbendable, cramped, and crotchety ... There you will sometimes find the caustic wit of Voltaire, the coarse energy of Paine, the strong sense of Cobbett, and the ribald blasphemy of Meslier, hashed up in the most heterogeneous manner, and exhibiting itself in the most hideous and repulsive forms. (*Bentley's Miscellany* July 1848)

No matter the sympathies of these commentators, they each define working-class radicalism by its print culture. After visiting a lockout of 20,000 strikers in Preston in Northwest England, Dickens recorded in *Household Words* how he expected crowds of angry workers but instead discovered operatives reading placards. His report on the trip, which calls for mediation between the owners and strikers, becomes absorbed with all manner of writing: posters, poems, subscription lists, and a strike fund balance sheet headed with a quotation from Carlyle.[25] William Thackeray's "Half-a-crown's worth of Cheap Knowledge" goes so far as to puncture the cliché of the literary accomplishments of the other nation by satirizing fifteen cheap magazines: "[These papers are] the result of the remission of the stamp-laws ... and may be considered the 'March of Intellect,' which we have heard so much about: the proof of the 'intelligence of the working classes' ... To listen to Wakley, Vincent, or O'Connor, one would imagine that the aristocracy of the country were the most ignorant and ill-educated part of its population" (279).

Working-Class Radicalism and Condition of England Fiction

Beyond journalistic excursions into the literary world of "The Unknown Public," the title of a Wilkie Collins piece in *Household Words* on the same theme as Thackeray's essay, working-class protest sometimes exerted direct influence on middle-class literature. This section explores two examples of such influence, which bookend the Chartist decade and display strikingly different attitudes toward radicalism.

A putative autobiography of a disillusioned activist, Charles Kingsley's 1850 *Alton Locke*, explicitly rejects Chartism, naming it so much talk of "treason and slaughter."[26] By the novel's close, plot developments repeatedly distance the protagonist from his earlier commitments: the hero is imprisoned for fomenting a riot; he converts to Christianity, accepts the patronage of an upper-class mentor, and emigrates to Texas where he dies of fever. Even as a negative portrait of working-class politics, however, *Alton Locke* testifies to Chartism's cultural reach. Kingsley came to appreciate this side of the movement in his correspondence with Thomas Cooper. Stung by Cooper's attacks on his articles in the Christian socialist *Politics for the People*, Kingsley wrote the author of the much-admired epic *Purgatory of the Suicides* to ask for "insight into [the working class's] life and thoughts, as may enable me to consecrate my powers effectually to their service" (Kingsley, *Letters* 1:147; see also Klaver 143–44). The memoir Cooper sent Kingsley does not survive, but *Alton Locke* shares several aspects with Cooper's autobiographical short story "Dame Deborah Thrumpkinson and her Orphan Apprentice Joe." The education of both protagonists begins with the Bible and *Pilgrim's Progress*, broadens when they befriend working-class scholars, and leads eventually to their loss of faith. Both narratives, moreover, chronicle this fall through the perspective of the hero's grieving mother. Critics fault Kingsley for his protagonist's lack of definition, but this aspect might also have been learned from Chartist fiction, which, as discussed, often decenters the narrative from the putative hero (Gallagher, *Reformation* 89; Menke 100). Indeed, in "Dame Deborah," which is ostensibly a spiritual biography, the narrator turns from that genre's central rationale by repeatedly refusing to enter "the labyrinth of [the protagonist's] progressive train of thought" (Cooper, *Wise* 2:175).

Alton Locke makes clear how Kingsley's correspondence with Cooper modified his view of Chartism. His earlier writing, like that of other Christian socialists, stressed that the working classes required education before they could be trusted with the vote, lest they fall prey to demagogues offering bribes of money, "beer and gin" (Kingsley, *Letters* 1:118; Vanden Bossche 134). While *Alton Locke* still dehumanizes workers, making their degradation part of its indictment of the sweating system in the tailoring trade, the novel becomes deeply concerned with radical culture: "who ... do you think, have been the great preachers and practisers of temperance, thrift, charity, self-respect, and education. Who? – shriek not in your

Belgravian saloons – the Chartists; the communist Chartists: upon whom you and your venal press heap every kind of cowardly execration and ribald slander" (27). Chris Vanden Bossche remarks that a surprising aspect of the hero's trajectory is that Alton's frustrated desire for education, not the brutalizing conditions of his workplace, propels him toward Chartism (154). In fact, Alton's intellectual longings link him with the protagonists of fiction by Cooper and Thomas Martin Wheeler. Indeed, Kingsley's sensitive poet partially answers Wheeler's complaint in *Sunshine and Shadow* that "even the most liberal novelists" remain unable to "draw a democrat save in warpaint" (99). But if Kingsley shows Alton Locke without his "warpaint," it is only to fight the movement on cultural grounds: the hero becomes disillusioned when he discovers the movement press treats his writing in a dishonest and censorious fashion, revealing the false promise held out by Chartist culture.

A second novel that arose from an encounter with working-class politics was Frances Trollope's *Michael Armstrong* (1839). Along with *Jessie Phillips* (1843), *Michael Armstrong* helped establish the conventions and problematics that defined Condition of England fiction for the next two decades. Trollope was among the first novelists to focus on the industrial context of child labor and feature working-class ghettos as important settings (Heineman, *Frances* 67). She pioneered the use of strong female protagonists who break with their families and become the "repository of the social conscience," claiming a place for women in the public sphere as social reformers (Bodenheimer 26; Kestner 57). For Carolyn Betensky, Trollope initiated the plot of the fictional investigation of working-class social conditions, a storyline that came to dominate the genre (23–30). Looking at *Michael Armstrong* in light of the radical press further suggests Trollope's influence on social problem fiction, but in ways that challenge certain critical ideas. First, Trollope's encounters with radical working-class activists while researching the novel complicates the notion that this literature retails an outside and reified perspective on the life and politics of the poor. Second, Trollope self-consciously considers the constraints the novel form places on imagining the resolution of social problems, an emphasis that qualifies the critique that the genre's focus on individual protagonists undermines systemic analysis.

Initially published in shilling parts, both *Michael Armstrong* and *Jessie Phillips* attempted to reach a broad audience, which Trollope hoped would include members of the politicized working classes. Although she complained that no one seemed to care for *Michael Armstrong* "except the Chartists . . . a new kind of patron for me!" (qtd. in Neville-Sington 278), she had sought out exactly this market by advertising the novel in the *Northern Star*, as she would do again for *Jessie Phillips* (Heineman, "Emergence" 211; *NS* March 2, 1839, December 31, 1842). *Michael Armstrong* received positive notice in the radical press, including in the London weekly the *Charter*, which excerpted a section of the novel's conclusion (February 2, 1840). Other Chartist publications, suspicious of Trollope's attacks on democracy in *The Domestic Manners of the Americans*, focused on Trollope's method of research rather than the novel itself.[27] Prior to writing *Michael Armstrong*, Trollope had toured Manchester and the surrounding district for several weeks, visiting working-class homes, bookstores, and chapels with her grown son Thomas. Armed with letters of introduction from the parliamentary leader of the Ten Hours Movement Lord Ashley, she interviewed operatives as well as the factory reformer Richard Oastler, the union leader and radical bookseller John Doherty, and the Rev. Mr. G. S. Bull of Byerley, "the ten-hours parson" (Elliot 93). These activists appeared to her son "a rather strange assortment of persons . . . They were all, or nearly all of them, men a little raised above the position of the factory hands, to the righting of whose wrongs they devoted their lives" (T. Trollope 8, 10). Although Trollope's Manchester trip has been well documented, few scholars have grappled with what imprint her exposure to working-class politics left on her fiction, probably because by the time of the novel's volume publication Trollope wrote a preface harshly condemning Chartism's increasingly insurrectionary character and declaring she had abandoned a planned sequel in which Michael as an adult would join the factory movement. Despite Trollope's ultimate recoil, however, her encounters in Manchester informed *Michael Armstrong*'s rejection of paternalism and its depiction of the necessity of working-class agency. The novel offers a very different vision of mass politics than many contemporary accounts. When the protagonist attends a rally for factory reform, he is moved by the "peaceful tumult" of a crowd of 100,000 who "meet in peace and good order, to petition for legal relief from the oppression of a system" that has brought misery (442, 444).

Trollope's encounter with radical culture was notable both to the Chartist press and the middle-class literary establishment. The *Star* reported her tour with satisfaction: "We may differ from this lady on many points; but we cordially award to her the meed [*sic*] of our praise for the pains she is now taking thoroughly to understand the case of the poor wretch whom she has chosen as the hero of her next romance" (March 2, 1839). The respectable *Athenaeum*, on the other hand, likened Trollope to "the shallowest of physical force orators" who might as well have "been paid out of the

National Charter fund for writing the volume" (August 1839). The combination of the novel's polemical treatment of industrial issues and its (relatively) inexpensive format seemed particularly dangerous, for it threatened
to diffuse "firebrands" "among an ignorant and excited population to which
her shilling numbers are but too accessible ... We implore this lady to
remember that the most probable immediate effect of ... her pencillings will
be the burnings of factories, with sacred months [a Chartist term for a
contemplated general strike], and the plunder of property of all kinds." A
reviewer in the *Bolton Free Press* concluded that Trollope deserved "eighteen
months in Chester Gaol," the prison term the polemical ex-Methodist
preacher J. R. Stephens had recently received (qtd. in Neville-Sington
277–78). Ironically, during Trollope's stay in the Manchester region, she
had traveled to nearby Stalybridge to hear this famed Chartist orator preach
in a "miserable little chapel, filled to suffocation, and besieged by crowds
around the doors [about] the cruel and relentless march of the great
Juggernauth, Gold" (T. Trollope 12–13).

Written in support of the Ten Hours Movement, *Michael Armstrong* tells
the story of a factory boy adopted by a rich and powerful mill owner. Like
many Condition of England novels, it features a dual plot, offering an
account of both working-class suffering and a middle-class character's
encounter with that distress. In this way, the novel reflects on Trollope's
own investigations. Narrative focalization resides largely with the orphan
heiress Mary Brotherton and her circle. In the novel's first half, the reader
enters the working-class district only when a middle-class character acts as
guide. This mediation of working-class life through the eyes of a middle-class
heroine is typical of Condition of England fiction and frequently suggests an
objectifying process. Trollope, however, scrutinizes the power relationships
present in such a project (Priti Joshi, "*Michael*" 44). Before Mary crosses into
the poor neighborhood to better understand the lives of the mill workers
with whom she has become concerned, the reader encounters a series of
voyeuristic observers, including the mill owner and his overseer, whose
surveillance of the laborers problematizes Mary's undertaking.

As the heiress enters the disorienting world of the factory district, she
also navigates the willful ignorance of her own class. Although she speaks
with demoralized individuals, they possess knowledge the heroine lacks.
Wanting a basic vocabulary of industrial life, Mary is humiliated by her
inability to understand a girl's description of an injury caused by an
overseer's "billy roller" or club. The child's condescending attitude
makes clear her belief "that the young lady was more than commonly
dull of apprehension" (186). Mary's interviews reverse a set piece from

contemporary reports on the poor, which hold up working-class informants' cultural illiteracy to the reader's bemused frustration. Separation
from the other nation simultaneously prevents Mary's self-knowledge: the
novel tracks the heroine's difficult realization of her implication in what
she observes (Zlotnick 133). An inverted reflection of Jane Austen's protagonists, Mary's existential ground is uprooted not because the patriarchal
rules of inheritance threaten her share of the family's estate, but because her
claim to wealth derived from child labor is insoluble.

The barriers separating the classes are a central problematic of 1830s and
1840s social problem fiction. As the realist novel grappled with the difficulty of representing widening class division and faceless urban crowds, its
ambition to embody a national totality became more and more frayed. Like
many novels in the genre, *Michael Armstrong* dramatizes a face-to-face
encounter between classes kept apart by the chasm of inequality, but unlike
other variants it allows no final reconciliation between rich and poor, only
between members of the classes alienated from their origins. In this way, it
departs from its close contemporary *Oliver Twist*. The novels overlapped in
March and April 1839 when *Bentley's Miscellany* published the final two
installments of Dickens's work and Henry Colburn issued Trollope's first
two parts. As if playing on the novels' simultaneous appearance, Trollope
transforms Dickens's conclusion into the enabling problem of her story.
Like Oliver sheltered by the Maylies, Trollope's "factory boy" is plucked
from his damaged childhood when the mill owner Matthew Dowling takes
him in. Michael's rescue, however, comes too soon, and a devastating
portrait of paternalistic charity follows. The rescue itself parodies the
deus ex machina Dickens favors: Dowling chooses Michael at the urging
of a friend, who speciously imagines the boy has saved her from a rampa-
ging cow. After suffering humiliation in the Dowling household, where he
is made "a specimen . . . in a glass case," Michael wants only to return to his
brother and mother (39). Dowling refuses this request, realizing the propaganda value of taking "a dirty little dog of a piecer . . . into my own
house," a gesture made timely because a recent accident has killed a girl in
his mill (55). The girl's family name "Stephens" calls to mind the Chartist
preacher Trollope heard in Stalybridge, known as a tribune of the factory
children for his incendiary oratory on their behalf.

Studies of social problem fiction have frequently stressed the ways it
contains and limits protest, including caricatural portraits of working-class
activists, the deployment of anti-Jacobin stereotypes, and the displacement
of story lines about class conflict by other subject matter. Narratives like
North and South and *Hard Times* are taken as offering a systemic view of

entrenched social conditions but turning to individualistic solutions, including upward mobility, private charity, and even the embrace of the imagination.[28] James Adams summarizes this scholarship: "this quietistic stance would be echoed throughout the so-called 'industrial novel' – an emphatically middle-class genre" (98). Recently, Carolyn Betensky has advanced a sophisticated variation on this argument in describing how the sentimental education of middle-class protagonists learning to sympathize with the poor displaces attention toward the poor's material difficulties (1–13). More broadly, realism is sometimes faulted for naturalizing "a bourgeois reality that, in actuality, it helps to construct."[29] But one might remark how social problem novels themselves sometimes scrutinize the contradiction inherent in addressing social conditions while remaining focused on individual lives. *Oliver Twist*, for example, highlights the insufficiency of its happy end with a series of deaths Oliver's rescue fails to redress. The prostitute Nancy and orphan Little Dick stand in for the multitude from which Oliver is eventually separated. Spurning Rose Maylie's offer of support, Nancy says her refusal would be echoed by "hundreds of others as bad and wretched as myself" (337).

Nancy's and Little Dick's deaths are incongruous notes in *Oliver Twist*'s fantasy of social rebirth, but *Michael Armstrong* takes Dickens's ambivalent gesture further, becoming an extended meditation on the relationship between the desire for social change and the stricture of novelistic plotting. If, as in Bodenheimer's account, the protagonist's efforts to aid the factory child "develop in two simultaneous but mutually exclusive directions, one expressed in theoretical exposition, the other through the plot," this tension productively interrogates the possibilities and limits of the realist novel in the late 1830s.[30] In Trollope's narrative, even well-intentioned efforts to aid the poor go awry. The mill owner's daughter convinces Michael's mother to apprentice her son to complete his education, which dooms him to perilous work in a distant factory. When the heroine arrives to liberate Michael from the factory, she mistakenly learns he has died and departs with another child, his friend Fanny Fletcher.

When interventions do succeed, Trollope underscores how each escape leaves behind another parent, sibling, or comrade. First, Michael is taken into the Dowling house where he thinks of his sickly brother still working in Dowling's mill. Then, after Michael is apprenticed to the second factory, the heroine comforts his mother by promising to aid her elder son, whom she ultimately marries. The heiress's sympathy is to no avail for Mrs. Armstrong, however, for the mother's two children are "so twined and twisted together in her thoughts, that meditating upon her hopes for

Edward inevitably brought her terrors for Michael before her" (326). This elegantly chiasmatic structure culminates when Michael escapes Deep Valley, returns home, hears of his own death, which Mary has broadcast, and assumes his absent brother has perished instead. Michael's putative death shadows the novel's happy end in which Edward travels to Europe with Mary, becomes educated and marries the heiress.

The radical critique of paternalism inflects these multiplying plots of failed rescue. Just as Michael saves himself after Mary's failed mission to Deep Valley, a reforming clergyman informs the heroine that an organized working class is demanding legislative change, not philanthropy. The minister Bell makes explicit the political import of a narrative pattern in which any individual's escape highlights those left behind. He tells his protégé Mary, who is eager to use her wealth to ameliorate the conditions she observes, that even founding a charity school or benefit society would be ineffectual: "The oppression under which they groan is too overwhelming to be removed, or even lightened, by any agency less powerful than that of the law" (298).

When Michael returns to the mill where his working life began, he experiences a kind of survivor's guilt: "as he approached nearer, and perceived the dim shadowy figures slowly moving here and there, and thought upon the condition of each of them, he almost repented his selfish joy" (434). This ghostly chorus is an example of how as social problem fiction sets itself against the "abstract aggregations" of political economy (Poovey 133), aggregation's specter haunts it, marring the happy end vouchsafed to the few. Among middle-class reforming novels, *Michael Armstrong* most explicitly adopts a radical aesthetic, criticizing paternalistic and individualistic solutions to the structural issues of poverty and inequality. But the convoluted conclusions which exist throughout the genre – the emigration stories and flights into exile, the retreats to the countryside, the *deus ex machina* – might all be understood in light of the contradictory projects Trollope's novel pushes to their breaking point.

The literature and culture of early Victorian Britain look different if viewed from below. Fiction played a surprisingly prominent role in debates about poor relief, democratic reform, and the rights of émigrés. The only nineteenth-century mass movement named for a document, Chartism placed literature and journalism at the center of its struggle. The presentation of petitions in 1839, 1842, and 1848 advocating the adoption of the six points of the Charter became vast ceremonies in which texts weighing hundreds of pounds were carted to Parliament to advance the claim of democratic rights. The millions of signatures the petitions contained asserted mass literacy as an undeniable political fact (Brantlinger, *Reading* 93). These demonstrations were the culmination of decades-long popular movements that were cultural as well as political. Fiction affiliated with working-class radicalism adapted the social problem narrative of reforming authors and engaged popular genres in an attempt to forge experimental forms adequate to a market economy and a global, imperial society. The challenging vision of the radical press shaped Victorian culture in turn, an influence evident in the fiction and essays of such authors as Gaskell, Dickens, Disraeli, Trollope, Martineau, and Carlyle. Even when hostile to the ends sought by working-class social movements, these writers learned from the radical canon they sought to refute. The following chapter takes up an early example of the impact of social movements on middle-class fiction by beginning a decade before the birth of Chartism with the 1820s and early 1830s debate over the poor laws.

PART I

Social Citizenship in the Poor Law Debates

Social Inheritance in the New Poor Law Debate: William Cobbett, Harriet Martineau, and the Royal Commission of Inquiry

The Poor Law Amendment Act of 1834 was a watershed in British social and economic history as much for the ideological vision it sanctioned as for the policy changes it brought about. What came to be called the New Poor Law supplanted a system of relief that had existed since the beginning of the seventeenth century in England and Wales. Under the Old Poor Law, a mosaic of policies had grown up in more than 15,000 parishes with local (secular) officials adopting a huge variety of measures, including pensions for the aged, work or payment for the unemployed, temporary assistance to meet health and other emergencies, in-kind contributions of clothing, food and fuel, and stipends for the foster care of orphans (Englander 2). By the late eighteenth century, many parishes had embraced the allowance system, supplementing wages against the high cost of food. In sum, although the treatment of the poor was often harsh and punitive, the Old Poor Law afforded "assistance as a right to the fraction of the labour force unable to make a livelihood – from disability, unemployment, family burden or insufficient wages" (Vinokur 172). The New Poor Law promised to sweep aside these arrangements, replacing them with a centralized bureaucracy and a series of impersonal tests that would determine who could receive relief. A program of negative social engineering that attempted to decrease poverty by rationalizing and restricting public charity, the law sought to render welfare provision more compatible with a free market in labor by ensuring that support would be given only on terms that made it less attractive than paid work (Poovey 11; Poynter 305). Humiliating barriers to receiving aid – such as performing menial labor or entering a workhouse and agreeing to be segregated from one's family – stigmatized relief and separated paupers from the respectable community. Put bluntly, the law sought to create a relief system that few would want to use.[1]

The New Poor Law's attempt to weaken the poor's claim on the community met widespread opposition from both the laboring poor and sections of the middle and upper classes. The law was widely perceived as an attack on working-class marriage, an unjust dictation from an over-reaching central authority, and a policy ill suited to the problems of industrial areas such as cyclical unemployment. In crucial ways, critics of the law slowed and shaped its implementation. In the late 1830s when the government tried to institute its policy in the north of England, it faced a mass movement armed with an array of tactics, including petitions; rallies; an electoral strategy that attempted to place opponents of the law in charge of its local administration; boycotts; and direct action, such as the disruption of meetings of the poor law bureaucracy and the destruction of workhouses. This resistance forced the Poor Law Commission to make a series of concessions to local administrators, so that outdoor relief continued to exist in many parts of the country. Despite reformers' grand vision and the successful implementation of certain kinds of retrenchment – including cuts in the amount of support, work requirements for the receipt of aid, the abolition of parish wage supplements, and restrictions on relief to able-bodied men – the New Poor Law remained for decades a patchwork of policies subject to renegotiation between Poor Law commissioners, local officials, and the poor they served.[2]

No less fierce than the contest over the implementation of the law was the debate over the values of economic individualism it promoted. Understanding that stiff opposition would greet changes to an institution upon which nearly a million people relied, the government attempted to shape public opinion with an elaborate propaganda campaign in the months before the law's passage (Webb, *Working-Class* 125–36). The Royal Commission of Inquiry of 1832–34 was central to this effort. With great fanfare, eight commissioners and twenty-six assistants examined the efficacy of current relief provisions by interviewing magistrates, overseers, clergymen, and employers from across the country, a cross section meant to stage and define the national community.[3] Relatively inexpensive serial editions of the commission's reports broadcast the failures of the Old Poor Law. Safely removed from parliamentary politics and therefore free to endorse unpopular changes, the commission engaged in "an effort at mass education, propagating the principles of political economy for the benefit of the entire nation" (Frankel, *States* 40; see also Poynter 317). This public relations campaign was a significant development in its own right, helping inaugurate a new mode of governance Oz Frankel has termed "print statism," which describes the government's attempt to influence public opinion through "a massive circulation of printed texts" (*States* 39, see also 4–5). Narrative fiction, too, occupied an important place in the government's efforts. Lord Brougham, a chief parliamentary advocate of poor law reform, tasked the young novelist Harriet Martineau with creating poor law stories modeled on her highly successful *Illustrations of Political Economy*. Brougham's Society for the Diffusion of Useful Knowledge published the novellas that resulted.[4]

One of the earliest examples of social problem fiction, Martineau's *Poor Laws and Paupers, Illustrated* draws heavily on the Royal Commission's report, both for concrete proposals and anecdotal evidence.[5] Translating Blue Books to didactic fiction, Martineau forcefully advocates the central values of the New Poor Law: the need for the abolition of outdoor relief, the principle of less eligibility, and the formation of a central bureaucracy to enact these changes (Huzel 66). Martineau's fiction even adopts the schizophrenic tone of Royal Commission reports, which alternate between confidence in the commission's policy prescriptions and despair at the enormity of the crisis. Because of Martineau's evident reliance on government source material, critics have seen her as fundamentally separated from the lower-class population she depicts. In this regard, her work anticipates the objectifying tendency that for many critics defines social problem fiction from the 1840s (Guy 29; Keating 47; Sheila Smith 139–45). Blue Books themselves often retail the idea of the "two nations," a common conceit in social problem fiction about the barriers separating the cultural worlds of the working and middle classes. Thus in an 1842 report on sanitary conditions, Edwin Chadwick writes that details of the lives of the "laboring population ... have been received with surprise by persons of the wealthier classes living in the immediate vicinity, to whom the facts were as strange as if they related [to] ... the natives of an unknown country" (Chadwick, *Sanitary* 397; see also Frankel, *States* 158).

Seeing Martineau's work against the backdrop of broad popular resistance to the New Poor Law affords a somewhat different view. While utilizing the still inchoate rhetoric of the "two nations," Martineau's stories simultaneously reflect the importance of radical print culture and working-class political organization. Martineau demonstrates an acute awareness of the threat radical theories of social obligation pose to the project of liberal reform. In particular, her novellas parody the ideas of the great radical journalist and publisher William Cobbett, whose *History of the Protestant Reformation* (1824–26) set the terms of the poor law debate of the 1830s. Martineau's familiarity and active engagement with Cobbettite theories, though unremittingly hostile, speaks as much to a dynamic interplay between the worlds of middle-class reform and working-class radicalism as to their separation.

William Cobbett's *History of the Protestant Reformation* offers a nearly mythopoetic basis for relief as a guaranteed social legacy. A gothic tale centered on the dissolution of the Catholic monasteries, *History* figures the

Church's once vast holdings as a charitable trust maintained for the people and describes the Poor Laws as recompense for the loss of that common property. No less central to the British constitution than Magna Carta, the Poor Laws represent for Cobbett a foundational part of the social contract. Cobbett's ideas were echoed throughout the protracted contest over changes to poor relief, a debate that took up questions of how social bonds should be imagined and what was the relationship between private property, the community, and the state (Graff 63). Following Cobbett, opponents of the New Poor Law asserted a right to relief founded on historical precedent, biblical injunction, and the labor theory of value, warning that the abrogation of social provisions for the poor would displace civic and Christian virtues, destroy families, and in effect cancel the social contract (Collings 225–26; Edsall 177; Knott 99). The factory reformer Richard Oastler prognosticated the dire effects of implementing the law: "You will untie the knot which binds society together. You will blot out the *parchment title* to Property – you will throw back the family of man to its first elements, *and all things will again belong to all men*" (*Northern Star* January 20, 1838). Critics of retrenchment cast the rights of the poor as a social legacy, more sacred than the individual's right to property. Stories of real and figurative inheritance animated literary polemics for and against reform. The trope of inheritance translated a spatial relationship (between members of a parish or nation) into a temporal one (between tradition and futurity).

Martineau and her fellow supporters of the New Poor Law were forced to rebut Cobbett's narrative and its frequent adaptations. Grappling with this history, however, created tensions and ambivalences in Martineau's stories as in the governmental reports upon which they were based. The workhouse and work tests the Royal Commission advocated were designed as market mechanisms, in which the impersonal device of self-interest would distinguish between true poverty and the fraudulent claims of the improvident, a task no parish bureaucracy could accomplish. Parish overseers would no longer need to judge the veracity or weigh the gravity of claims put forward by the indigent, who would be free to enter or leave the workhouse or work project at any point (Goodlad, *Victorian* 53–60). Decreasing and stigmatizing relief would help transform a demoralized population into rational, self-regulating individuals (Hadley, *Melodramatic* 95; Poovey 107). The presence of a powerful alternative account of social connectedness, however, meant that poor law reformers had to dramatize the proposed law in terms of not only economic individualism but also its anticipated effect on community well-being. For liberal reformers,

Cobbett's fantasy of a generalized connection extending over centuries frayed the actual basis of social bonds. A belief in the social right to support only encouraged the poor to shirk familial responsibilities. By refashioning Cobbett's metaphoric inheritance plot into diminished and parodic versions of paupers struggling over real property, poor law reformers attempted to exorcise an account of social obligation and indebtedness to imagine the market a space in which economic individualism, left untrammeled by the claims of the community, could lead to prosperity and, paradoxically, to social cohesion.

Poor Laws and Property Rights in William Cobbett's *History of the Protestant Reformation* and *Legacy to Labourers*

William Cobbett's *A History of the Protestant Reformation* (1824–26) and his 1835 pamphlet *Legacy to Labourers* provided the anti-New Poor Law movement with its lingua franca. In vividly vernacular language, Cobbett's texts armed opponents of retrenchment with historical and philosophical justifications for the right to relief. The nature of Cobbett's ideological vision, however, has been a matter of some controversy. Many historians – including Patricia Hollis, Gertrude Himmelfarb, and E. P. Thompson – have interpreted Cobbett's work in terms of radicalism's focus on "Old Corruption," a framework prevalent in the 1810s and 1820s (but persisting to mid-century and beyond).[6] The language of Old Corruption blamed a venal, decadent government for the ills afflicting the nation and the poor, identifying such issues as sinecures, the national debt, paper money, and high taxes as the principal causes of immiserization. In this section, I argue that Cobbett's writing on the poor laws actually shared affinities with a new orientation that emerged in working-class radicalism in the 1830s. What Gertrude Himmelfarb has termed the "new radicalism" shifted focus from questions of bad government to issues surrounding property and class. It identified inequality, the power of capitalists, and the ideological sway of orthodox political economy as the core causes of poverty (Huzel 189). Although certain tendencies within radical politics distanced them from Cobbett's celebration of an earlier England, his writing on the Poor Laws provided radicals of all stripes with a powerful narrative about the origins of stark inequality and the disempowerment of the poor, a narrative that anticipated emphases of the 1830s and remained relevant throughout the Chartist decade.

Cobbett was clearly one of the most prominent proponents of the "old analysis"; he fulminated against sinecures, placemen (i.e., governmental appointments made to reward political loyalty), the debt, and paper money across thousands of pages of print. As E. P. Thompson puts it, he personalized politics, scapegoating the "parasitism of certain vested interests" (a world view that also underwrote the anti-Semitism that appears in Cobbett's work):

> He could not allow a critique which centred on ownership; therefore he expounded (with much repetition) a demonology, in which the people's evils were caused by taxation, the National Debt, and the paper-money system, and by the hordes of parasites – fundholders, placemen, brokers, and tax-collectors – who had battened upon these three.[7]

Cobbett's centrality in the older style of radicalism, however, has sometimes obscured his partial embrace of the new analysis in the last decade of his life.[8] His celebration of the pre-Reformation Church in *A History of the Protestant Reformation* might seem a surprising place to locate a burgeoning interest in issues of property, inequality, and the market. *History*, however, draws attention to exactly those issues. Setting the world of the medieval Church against the nineteenth-century embrace of free market principles, it variously describes Catholic institutions as a kind of welfare state, a reservoir of communitarian values, and a lost utopic sphere that removed a substantial portion of the nation's wealth from the destructive forces of a market economy. The narrative of the dissolution of the monasteries, moreover, provided opponents of the New Poor Law with a powerful critique of property rights, which Cobbett claimed had their origin in the violent expropriation of the public realm of the Church. In *Legacy to Labourers*, Cobbett translated his historical narrative into a theory of intrinsic rights, which also contested the sanctity of private property. Showing how the individual's right to property depends upon a set of social obligations, Cobbett paradoxically argues that private property guarantees the poor social citizenship.

To understand the remarkable reach of Cobbett's writing on the Poor Laws, one must appreciate his centrality in both radical politics and the history of journalism. Cobbett is best remembered for his weekly magazine, the *Political Register*, which appeared for more than three decades from 1802 to the beginning of 1836. It included bylines from Newgate prison, where Cobbett was confined from 1810 to 1812 for articles critical of corporal punishment in the army, and from the United States, where he lived in exile from 1817 to 1819, fearing imprisonment during the repression of radicalism in the postwar years. Cobbett began his career as a fierce anti-democrat, but in 1805 he threw his lot in with the radicals with a series of essays in the *Register* about the misuse of government funds.[9] For the next three decades, he used the columns of the *Register* to excoriate sinecures, predatory taxes, military spending, and the national debt while championing Catholic emancipation; the expansion of suffrage; the maintenance of generous poor relief; and the end of Irish coercion, a program that represented Cobbett's "weekly warfare in the services of the poor" to the *English Chartist Circular* (1:8). It would be hard to overestimate the importance of Cobbett's writing to radical culture (E. P. Thompson, *Making* 746). In *Passages in the Life of a Radical*, Samuel Bamford credited Cobbett with his generation's political education: "At this time the writings of William Cobbett suddenly became of great authority; they were read on nearly every cottage hearth in the manufacturing districts of South Lancashire, in those of Leicester, Derby, and Nottingham; also in many of the Scottish manufacturing towns" (13). The Chartist William Lovett could still remark in 1841 that Cobbett's works circulated "through the length and breadth of the land" (*English Chartist Circular* 1:8).

Cobbett played an equally noteworthy role in the annals of British publishing. His slashing and ironic articles virtually created editorial journalism, and he is credited with introducing to the British press the soon-to-be-popular device of the editorial leader (Altick 324; Dyck, "Cobbett"). The *Political Register* earned Cobbett the epithet "a kind of fourth estate in the politics of the country": Hazlitt's famous phrase was coined not to describe the press generally but the impact of one individual. In 1816, Cobbett transformed the periodical market by re-issuing articles from his shilling-halfpenny magazine in a twopenny-format designed to circumvent the stamp tax (Altick 325; Hollis, *Pauper* 95). Both the low price and Cobbett's vernacular style made the paper accessible to the laboring poor, creating an economy of scale previously unimaginable for the periodical press. The first inexpensive issue sold 200,000 copies over the course of a year, and issues averaged 40,000–70,000 copies sold (Hollis, *Pauper* 96). By comparison, the total circulation of all Sunday newspapers in 1823 was 100,000 (Nattrass 3). In 1819, the government passed the Newspaper Stamp Duties Act in large part to force Cobbett to cease publishing his cheap edition. But a generation of radical journalists had already learned the potential of cheap print from Cobbett's experiment and risked imprisonment by illegally publishing unstamped papers. Cobbett himself never did so. However, in 1819 the *Political Register* still easily outsold *The Times*, even with the 4d stamp that tripled its price (Huzel 109). Its popularity remained such that W. T. Moncrieff waggishly remarked during the upsurge of political agitation that marked the early 1830s that the poor would "rather go without a fire / than Cobbett's Register" ("March").

Among Cobbett's many popular works, *A History of the Protestant Reformation* was likely the best selling and quite possibly the most influential. According to Cobbett's biographer George Spater, the sixteen parts in which *History* appeared had a combined sale of 700,000 in England, excluding partial reprints and pirated versions, and probably more than 100,000 in the United States (Spater 2:445; see also Cole, *Life* 289; Nattrass 1–3, 157). Editions also appeared in Ireland, Australia, Italy, Spain, Portugal, Germany, Holland, Romania, Venezuela, and France, including three translations in Paris alone. Cobbett himself boasted (with characteristic puffery) that sales of *History* exceeded those of any other book in the world, save the Bible.

Drawing heavily on the Catholic priest John Lignard's *History of England* (1819–30), Cobbett's history entered the fracas around Catholic Emancipation, "the most violently agitated political question of the 1820s," by calling for the full extension of civil rights to Catholics (D. Culler 155). Utilizing a characteristic genre of early nineteenth-century religious debate, Cobbett attempts to counter the "*din, din, din*" of anti-Catholic propaganda (Cobbett, *History* 1:24).[10] In doing so, his work created a small but crucial layer of popular support for emancipation and became an important factor in the passage of the Catholic Relief Act of 1829, which allowed Catholics to vote and sit in Parliament (Cole, *Life* 289; D. Culler 156). Critics have remarked *History*'s wide-ranging influence on Victorian letters, particularly the way its medievalism shaped such diverse texts as Carlyle's *Past and Present*, Disraeli's *Sybil*, Ruskin's *For Clavigera*, Trollope's Barsetshire series, and Morris's *Socialism: Its Growth and Outcome*.[11] Scholars have mostly overlooked, however, the work's significance on the literature of the poor law debate. Yet *History* owed its popularity not to its advocacy of Catholic rights, which remained divisive, but to its treatment of inequality, the institution of property, and the rights of the poor to welfare provision.

On one level, Cobbett's arguments in *History* echo the framework of Old Corruption, ascribing the problems of Britain to the depredations of a sinister elite. Cobbett's account of the Reformation recasts a crucial episode of national history as a series of lurid crimes committed by a depraved ruling class – "the plunderings, persecutings and murderings of the 'Reformation' people" – against a helpless clergy and oppressed population (1:192). In Cobbett's telling, Catholic institutions performed a wide variety of social labor. The Church "amply provided for all the wants of the poor and distressed. It received back, in many instances, what the miser and the extortioner had taken unfairly, and applied it to works of beneficence" (1:206). Art also flourished as the Church's architecture "set the generous example of providing for the pleasure, the honour, the wealth and greatness of generations upon generations yet unborn" (1:155). In light of these charitable functions, the seizure of monasteries, churches, and hospitals removed crucial support for the needy. It was "robbing the people under pretence of reforming their religion" (1:166). The effects of this expropriation, moreover, continued to be felt in the nineteenth century. Leaving laboring people exposed to economic insecurity without the Church's support, the Reformation impoverished subsequent generations. Although Cobbett's narrative stays rooted in the sixteenth century, the reader glimpses aspects of the modern dilemma in its melodramatic version of events. The monks displaced by the Reformation, "torn from their dwellings, and turned out into the wide world to beg or starve" stand in for the contemporary poor; the repression and hardship they suffer anticipate the vulnerability of laborers in a world of unfettered economic competition (1:131).

Yet even in its reliance on melodramatic themes, *History* departs from an earlier style of radicalism. The text draws much of its rhetorical power from the way it transvalues conceits from the Gothic, playing on the latter genre's conflicted attraction to the medieval period. Like Gothic fiction, Cobbett utilizes hyperbolic language and sensational situations while presenting a world full of vice and violence (Botting 2). But *History* transforms the topoi of the gothic novel, making cloisters and churches places of protection, not confinement. Monks, priests, and nuns, the genre's preferred villains, become innocent victims (Simmons 163–64). The Catholic other is celebrated as part and parcel of the English constitution, and British liberty is traced to the Church of Rome: "If, however, we still insist, that the Pope's supremacy . . . produced ignorance, superstition and slavery . . . let us sweep away the three courts, the twelve judges, the circuits, and the jury-boxes; let us demolish all that we inherit from those whose religion we so unrelentingly persecute" (1:93).[12] Whereas Gothic fiction presents the frightening "survival of archaic forms of despotism and . . . superstition," Cobbett shows the cost of modernity supplanting an older order (Baldick xix). *History's* landscape, as alien as any Gothic nightmare, transforms the genre's "angry and potent ruins" (Punter 4) into once beautiful structures degraded and dispersed into a fallen world:

> Go to the site of some once-opulent Convent. Look at the cloister, now become, in the hands of a rack-renter, the receptacle for dung, fodder and

fagotwood: see the hall, where, for ages, the widow, the orphan, the aged
and the stranger, found a table ready spread; see a bit of its walls now helping
to make a cattle-shed, the rest having been hauled away to build a workhouse: recognize, in the side of a barn, a part of the once magnificent
Chapel. (1:155)

Cobbett's double vision is reminiscent of the politicized landscape of *Rural
Rides*, in which the narrator's consciousness jolts between pastoral reflections and rage at corrupt political institutions, which intrude into the
remote countryside and the narrative texture (Cobbett, *Rural* 35, 58;
Woodcock 7).

Cobbett's treatment of the historical past in *History* appears on the
surface similar to the themes of Old Corruption, but probed more deeply
it suggests a different approach. Critics have often characterized *History* as a
celebration of paternalism, considering its implicit alternative a return to a
world of generous elites. Cobbett's evocation of the medieval past has been
called "an agrarian Utopia under the dual guidance of a benevolent church
and a benevolent gentry," "a prelapsarian world of interclass harmony,"
and "an essentially reactionary longing for an agrarian Utopia based on
paternalism and cottage industry."[13] *History*'s paternalism, however, is of a
peculiar stripe. If Cobbett describes a socially organic society, it is one from
which the political and economic rulers are essentially excluded. Unlike
Carlyle's *Past and Present*, which celebrates tenants' love for their landlords
and rulers, Cobbett argues that the Church acted to shield the poor from
these very elites, and that a negative result of the Reformation was to force
the impoverished to rely on the capricious charity of the rich instead of
guaranteed aid from the Church (Carlyle, *Past* 54–56; Cobbett, *History*
1:52, 1:206). In this light, the Church seems less the keystone of an
integrated feudal order than an autonomous zone independent from the
pressures of a capitalist economy. Cobbett stresses how monasteries bought
and sold locally, helping retard the expansion of a far-flung market. Less
concerned with profit than individual landlords, less likely to evict tenants
or pressure them to increase the productivity of their lands, the Church
sheltered farmers from the fluctuations of the market: "The monastery was
a proprietor that never died . . . its lands and houses never changed owners;
its tenants were liable to none of many uncertainties that other tenants
were; its oaks had never to tremble at the axe of the squandering heir"
(1:152). Far from supporting the elite, the Church was important precisely
because it offered protection from the rich's depredations.

The values of the Church which Cobbett sets at odds against contemporary economic relationships represent a breakthrough in Cobbett's

thought, moving significantly beyond the "old analysis" of corrupt govern-ment (1:453–54). *History* focuses on the Reformation's social and political consequences: increasing inequality and the concentration of property, emphases that anticipate prominent themes in 1830s radicalism.[14] Cobbett discovers an economic basis for the state's oppressive power by showing how a class of yeoman who were economically and politically independent flourished under monastic landlords. The Reformation destroyed this class by unleashing capitalist dynamics onto agriculture, dividing farmers into "rack-renters and absolute dependants, as we see them to this day" (1:151). Characteristic motifs of Old Corruption reemerge by the end of *History*. Cobbett suggests that the Reformation precipitated a series of wars that created the national debt and cripplingly high taxes, which in turn pauperized the population. His overall focus, however, remains on the penetration of market dynamics into a social and economic realm that previously nurtured communitarian values.

History is an important example of a genre that emerged in the 1820s in which the modern world compares unfavorably with the medieval age (D. Culler 152, Chandler 75). Cobbett's medievalism set the terms for Carlyle's *Past and Present* and Disraeli's *Sybil*, works that made this new genre central in the Condition of England debate of the 1840s. Like these later examples, *History* invokes a forgotten past as a means of defamiliarizing contemporary relations. In particular, Cobbett anticipates the Carlylean theme of social estrangement brought about by the "Mammon-Gospel" (Carlyle, *Past* 148–49). Parallel to Carlyle's account of the cash nexus loosening social bonds and transforming "society" into "mutual hostility," Cobbett suggests the Reformation fostered a competitive ethos, "that everlasting wrangling and spite, which now stare us in the face and stun our ears at every turn, and which the 'Reformation' has given us in exchange for the ease and happiness and harmony of Christian charity" (Carlyle, *Past* 148–49; Cobbett, *History* 1:4). Luther's rejection of the idea that good works are necessary to salvation finds its endpoint in the "schemes of Parson Malthus," who denies that charity is a Christian duty and suggests it aggravates the problems it means to solve (Cobbett, *History* 1:6).

Like the ubiquitous language of the Norman Yoke, which describes the origin of political power in ancient acts of violence, Cobbett constructs a foundational scene in which modern property rights derive, literally, from one grand instance of theft.[15] The violation of the Church's economic and moral domain thus has immense consequences. As contemporary property relations are founded on the violent dissolution of the Church's utopian sphere, the very legitimacy of private property stands open to question. The account of a king plundering the monasteries narrativizes the workings of an exploitative system, offering a literal vision of massive property taken from the people: "[A law authorizing the seizure of Church property] was the first of that series of deeds of rapine, by which this formerly well-fed and well-clothed people have, in the end, been reduced to rags and to a worse than jail-allowance of food" (1:166). Cobbett's descriptions call to mind the violence of the Norman conquest, reminding readers that their rulers descend from alien occupiers: "The whole country was, thus, disfigured; it had the appearance of a land recently invaded by the most brutal barbarians: and this appearance, if we look well into it, it has even to this day" (1:182). The second volume of *History* provides a county-by-county table of the churches, abbeys, hospitals, cathedrals, and colleges seized during the sixteenth century; their recipients; and their contemporary value. Purporting to show that one-third of the wealth of the entire British economy was owned by the Church, the catalog, which runs to more than 400 pages, acts as title to a lost social legacy, a counter-deed to individual property rights.

Intervening in debates about the Poor Laws, *History* answered increasingly clamorous calls to abolish relief, which led to abolitionist legislation in the early 1820s (Poynter 295–300). Cobbett suggests that the Elizabethan Poor Laws were a response to the economic insecurity and social strife that followed the destruction of the monasteries. When punitive measures failed to restore order, Elizabeth made "some general and permanent and solid provision for the poor" in order to purchase social peace (1:333). If the Reformation "despoiled the working classes of their patrimony; it tore from them that which nature and reason had assigned them" (1:127); the Poor Laws, despite the cynical motives of the Protestant state, acted as partial compensation, roughly approximating a destroyed social inheritance:

> We are always to bear in mind that the money, or food, or clothing, proceeding from the poor-rates, is the poor's property. It is not alms; it is what they have a right to by the law of nature, by the law of God, and by the common law of the land; aye, that same law, which, and which alone, gives a man a right to the enjoyment of his field or garden, also gives the poor and necessitous a right to be relieved out of the fruits of the earth. (2:19; see also 1:334)

The abolition of the poor laws, envisioned by Malthus and others, would return society to a state of nature in which the poor "when they want food" would be compelled "to take it where they can find it" (2:20). Turning Malthus on his head, Cobbett argues that rather than dooming the poor to inevitable scarcity, natural law guarantees a "right to subsistence," which if necessary can be asserted with recourse to violence (Huzel 135).

By 1835, Cobbett's case for guaranteed poor relief had become urgent in light of the passage of the New Poor Law, which undercut the poor's right to support by decreasing and stigmatizing welfare provision. Like *History, Legacy to Labourers* became a foundational text of the anti-New Poor Law movement. Countering reformers' characterization of generous provision to the poor as a violation of individual property rights, *Legacy* provides legal and philosophical justifications for the state to redistribute wealth. Despite its title, *Legacy* alludes only fleetingly to the sixteenth-century seizure of Church property, but *History*'s framework reappears in Cobbett's conception of how society retains an interest in private property. Since property rights are created by and exist within society, the community, Cobbett asserts, exercises a claim upon the wealth possessed by individuals. While *History* attempts to show that the Catholic Church held its immense resources on behalf of the whole community, *Legacy* goes one step further. It argues that all private property includes within it the rights of society, and particularly of the poor, and that the poor laws, which redistribute a portion of the rich's wealth, are the best expression of those claims.

Legacy takes as its starting point the poor law reformers' assertion that ever-increasing rates will "soon swallow up the estates of the lords and gentlemen" (8). Property rights, Cobbett argues, have never been absolute in Britain. Rather, all property is conditional, held in trust for the king: "men lawfully possess only the USE of land and of things attached to the land" (Cobbett, *Legacy* 73; see also Collings 247). The king's title to property, moreover, derives not from divine right but from an act of Parliament, an origin that establishes the community's stake in private property. Restrictions that prevent property owners from harming the public good further indicate the public's precedence over individual possessors. One has no right to sell the beach to the king of France, to burn down a house in a populated area, to pollute the city with smoke or "nauseous smells," to disturb neighbors with excessive noise, or, most pertinently, to drive the poor laborer from "the country where he was born" (82). Reversing the idea that taxes in the form of high poor rates effectively steal property from the rich, Cobbett justifies the poor's claims upon wealth by establishing its social nature. Although Cobbett likens poor relief to the rich's interest in their property, he redefines what property rights mean in the first place. The poor's right to relief and the rich's right to security are both positive claims they make on the community, not negative limits on what the community might demand. As Raymond Williams puts it, by arguing for the right to subsistence for all, Cobbett "arrives at a subversive dissolution of the property rights in the existing state" (*Cobbett* 32).

Cobbett stakes his claim that the poor have a right to relief on three interlocking sources: constitutional precedent, biblical injunction, and natural law. That these arguments shade into one another demonstrates how universalist theories of rights often coexist with historical justifications in the same body of thought (D. Culler 105; Epstein, *Radical* 21). Cobbett's arguments from scripture, for example, advance both a traditional and a universal claim. The biblical commandment to tithe establishes not only a moral imperative to individual charity but also a social guarantee for the care of the poor, affiliating God's law with the constitutional inheritance of the freeborn Englishman (116). On the other hand, a Pauline epistle affirms the natural rights of the poor by anticipating the labor theory of value:

> Without the labourer, the land is nothing worth. Without his labour there can be no tillage, no inclosure of fields, no tending of flocks ... A nation may exist without landlords; but, without labourers, not only its political, but its physical, existence is impossible; and therefore it is that the Apostle says, that "The husbandmen that laboureth must be the *first* partaker of the fruits." (138–39)

As we have seen, Cobbett's *History* countered Malthus by asserting that the "law of nature" alongside the "common law of the land" establishes a right to subsistence (2:19). Still, *Legacy* marks an important shift. No longer stressing the Reformation as an originary loss, Cobbett's arguments converge with those of other 1830s critics of retrenchment, who substituted ongoing forms of expropriation, such as taxes, profits, and rents, for a specific historical explanation.

Both *History* and *Legacy* profoundly influenced the ideology of the anti-New Poor Law movement, and Cobbettite ideas appeared in editorials, speeches, and sermons. From the MP Poulett Scrope's use of Cobbettite history to allusions to Cobbett's narrative in the popular anti-New Poor Law movement, the idea of a historic right to the land as a guarantee of poor relief became virtually ubiquitous.[16] At a gigantic demonstration in the West Riding in May 1837, the most popular banner was "The poor have a claim of the soil, and verily they shall be fed" (Knott 114–15). In the year of the New Poor Law's passage, the *True Sun* asserted, "The Poor Laws are the real *Magna Charta* of the labouring classes. The Poor Laws secure to the labouring classes a conditional mortgage over all the land of England" (May 8, 1834). Cobbett's framework remained important throughout the Chartist period, an indication of how ideas of social citizenship were integral to the Chartist's vision of democratic reform. The *Western Vindicator* promulgated Cobbett's theory of the Reformation, the *Northern Liberator* advertised "The Cobbett Library"; and both papers published excerpts of *Legacy to Labourers*, of which Thomas Cooper purchased fifteen copies for the night school of the "Shakesperean Chartists" of Leicester.[17] William Lovett remarked that the latter pamphlet "forms the charter and title-deed to [the poor's] legitimate rights" (*English Chartist Circular* 1:8; see also Chase, "Cobbett" 123).

At the same time, radical journals extended Cobbett's analysis in new directions, broadening it to other aspects of society touching the institution of private property. The *Poor Man's Guardian*, the most important paper in the "war of the unstamped," adapted Cobbett's idea that the usurpation of land was the basis of elite political power. If the New Poor Law violated the social contract by restricting relief, the *Guardian* suggested, then so did poverty itself.[18] Ultimately, *The Poor Man's Guardian* synthesized Paine's theory of government with Cobbett's model of private property and the public good, arguing that an individual can build on the land only with the agreement of all – and that this agreement must be ratified by each succeeding generation through democratic government (February 21, 1835).

Chartist candidates in the 1847 parliamentary election called for the restoration of Church property to the poor, and the 1851 Chartist program advocated home colonization as a means to restore the commons as well as Church property to the people (Chase, *Chartism* 284, 339). Finally, the Chartist land plan, in the words of the novelist Thomas Martin Wheeler, held "firmly to the opinion that the land was national property" (176). If these proposals made demands well beyond what appears in Cobbett's writing, it is important to recognize how Cobbett's texts encouraged such conclusions.[19] The failure of society to treat the poor with justice threw open fundamental questions about the arrangement of property:

> Well, then, what is the conclusion to which we come at last? Why, that the labourers have a right to subsistence out of the land, in all cases of inability to labour; and that, if the holders of the land will not give them subsistence, in exchange for their labour, they have a right to the land itself. (*Legacy* 140)

Inverting poor law reformers' image of paupers destroying landowners' estates, Cobbett suggests that the New Poor Law itself acts as a menace to those possessions. By undermining traditional rights, the act loosens "all the ligaments of property" and threatens to precipitate a catastrophic contest between rich and poor (124).

With the passage of the New Poor Law, Cobbett abandoned whatever lingering belief he might have held that the English elite would protect the poor (Dyck, *Cobbett and Rural* 208–9; Huzel 142). He began instead to train his sights on political economy and the propagandists for the New Poor Law. In an article about Martineau's support for this legislation, Cobbett concludes, "Then [Martineau's writings] became serious things: then they became a line of demarcation: then they cried 'war to the cottage:' then, at any rate, they decided me, never again, with tongue or pen, to utter one word more than law compelled me to utter, in support of the aristocracy or the [Anglican] Church" (*Poor Man's Guardian* January 10, 1835). But Martineau was equally aware of the kinds of arguments that Cobbett put forward and sought to counter them in her literary work. I turn next to Martineau's "serious things," which Cobbett might well have found unsettling for the ways they engaged his ideas and their diffusion in the anti-New Poor Law movement.

Illustrating Pauperism: The Writings of Harriet Martineau, the Royal Commission of Inquiry, and the Poor Law Commission

Harriet Martineau's *Poor Laws and Paupers Illustrated* stands as a rare instance of a fictional work commissioned by a parliamentary leader.[20] Lord Brougham, a forceful advocate for the Poor Law Amendment Act and leading light of the Society for the Diffusion of Useful Knowledge, proposed the series to Martineau and sent her manuscript versions of the findings of the Royal Commission, from which she drew narrative vignettes and ideas for policy prescriptions. Like the Royal Commission's published reports, Martineau's stories stigmatize dependent poverty while celebrating the liberal ideals of retrenchment, individual responsibility, and rational administration, all supported by a panoptic effort at social research. Nevertheless, despite its quasi-official status, Martineau's poor law fiction is unexpectedly divided about its own project, unsure of the ultimate consequences of reform.

Recent critics have drawn attention to the surprisingly conflicted politics of Martineau's more famous series of didactic stories, *Illustrations of Political Economy* (1832–34). Mike Sanders remarks that although Martineau's narrators expound a "theoretical commitment to the harmony of interests" between classes, her plots "positively revel in class conflict" ("From 'Political'" 193). Eleanor Courtemanche parses Martineau's multisided depiction of industrial conflict in *A Manchester Strike* – which alternately views a walkout as justified and unavoidable and as naïve and doomed to fail. Linda Peterson demonstrates how Martineau adapts the formal techniques and physical format of evangelical "little books" to advocate an agenda of political reform, the expansion of educational opportunities, and equality for women alongside the tenets of political economy (2, 6–8). In sum, although Martineau's didactic tales seem to endorse the "social morality" of an emergent "bourgeois industrial order," at the same time they expose a catalog of contemporary abuses and criticize the entrenched power of industrialists, financiers, slaveholders, and others (Webb, *Martineau* 118).

One way to account for the divided nature of Martineau's fiction is to recognize the degree to which she was forced to contend with working-class radicalism, which presented alternative explanations and solutions to the social problems she addressed. Rather than writing from a position of undisputed ideological dominance, a dialog with radicalism shaped Martineau's series. In the poor law novellas, Martineau explores whether reform can be successful given anticipated resistance to the proposed changes. Surprisingly, two of her four stories chronicle the defeat of reformers, reflecting the limits of the principles of political economy to transform the social and political world. At the same time, her story lines reformulate the Cobbettite narrative of inheritance and dispossession as her characters expound or refute justifications for relief. Nervous about the prospect for reform in an environment saturated with the belief in the right to social citizenship, her stories show how the poor laws substitute a fantasized connection to a social family for responsibilities uniting real ones.

The publications of the Royal Commission (and later of the Poor Law Commission) were also framed with radical opposition in mind. In fact, these reports were connected with efforts to supplant the radical press as a primary source of news for working-class people. Seeking a format likely to arouse the public's interest, the Royal Commission of Inquiry turned to serial publication (Frankel, *States* 9). Extracts of the Royal Commission's findings on the poor laws appeared in 1833 in a relatively inexpensive edition which sold 15,000 copies, perhaps more than all "other state papers put together," according to the Poor Law Commission's first secretary Edwin Chadwick (Chadwick, "First Annual" 505). The government sold 10,000 copies of the final report and distributed a like number for free to parish poor law officers (Himmelfarb 155). This unprecedented public relations campaign continued after the passage of the New Poor Law. Chadwick composed and Charles Knight published annual reports in a format designed for a wide audience. To increase popular appeal, Blue

Books combined scientific rhetoric with anecdotes laced with humor, irony, and dramatic conflict. The effort to adapt novelistic techniques to bureaucratic writing was appreciated by an anonymous reviewer of the reports of the commission on the employment of children, who marveled that "three ponderous folios" disclose "in our own land, and within our own ken – modes of existence ... as strange and as new as the wildest dream of fiction" (*Quarterly Review* June 1842).

Knight's involvement with the Poor Law Commission illustrates the close connection between print statism and Whig efforts to reform working-class reading. Knight's *Penny Magazine* was explicitly designed as a politically safe alternative to the "contraband newspapers" of the radical press (Knight 2:180). The radical press responded in turn to the onslaught of governmental print. Cobbett vociferously criticized the Royal Commission's findings in both *Legacy to Labourers* and the *Political Register* (Frankel, *States* 44; Huzel 139). *Legacy* argues that although the Royal Commission only surveyed the elite and their subordinates as "persons likely to suit their purpose," even evidence drawn from "lords, baronets, squires, parsons, overseers, and great farmers" does not support the recommendations of the Commission, a criticism modern historians affirm (Cobbett, *Legacy* 17–18; Huzel 139).

Martineau came to regret her involvement in the bitter partisan conflict surrounding poor law reform. *Illustrations of Political Economy*, which began in 1832 and eventually overlapped with *Poor Laws and Paupers Illustrated*, reached tens of thousands of readers drawn from all segments of British society, including, apparently, the future queen, making the new author the "most widely read" popularizer of ideas of political economy.[21] *Poor Laws and Paupers Illustrated*, on the other hand, was a professional disaster. The series lost a tidy £380 and Martineau would complain that her connection to Lord Brougham and the Society for the Diffusion of Useful Knowledge was "so much mere detriment to my usefulness and my influence" (*Autobiography* 177). Brougham's treatment surely heightened Martineau's resentment. Although the lord chancellor had commissioned the four novellas and agreed to supplement the £75 fee the publisher Charles Fox paid for each, he dropped out of contact when payment came due, and Martineau received £300 instead of the promised £400, illustrating Whig economy in an unexpected fashion (Martineau, *Autobiography* 177).

The series' losses testify to the marked unpopularity of poor law reform with the novellas' intended working-class audience. For its part, the radical press was merciless to the series and its author. Cobbett gave the "poor gossiping creature" the dubious honor of christening the New Poor Law "the Mother Martineau Bill," an ironic swipe at her unmarried status (*Poor Man's Guardian* January 10, 1835).[22] The breakaway Methodist J. R. Stephens and the militant Newcastle paper the *Northern Liberator* affiliated Martineau's writing with the notorious Marcus pamphlet, an anonymous satire calling for euthanizing the children of the poor (a text treated in the next chapter). Stephens's apocalyptic rhetoric thundered in the *Northern Star*: "those iniquitous and damnable laws that have been purposely framed to carry into effect the objects of the bloody trio – Marcus, Malthus and Martineau" (May 11, 1839). The frontispiece of an unnamed London tract described by the *Poor Man's Guardian* equated Martineau's writing with the oppressive legislation. According to the *Guardian*, the tract showed a blindfolded John Bull clinging to the Bible and Bill of Rights as poor law commissioners and the Whig leader Althorp pilfered his pockets. The latter "[tramples] underfoot the Poor Laws of Elizabeth, while the Gibbeting Bill, and the Glasgow Lottery Bill, are seen in his pocket, together with a letter addressed to Miss Martineau" (September 27, 1834). Finally, a satirical story in the *Northern Liberator* features Brougham's ghost encouraging Martineau to jilt a fictional fiancé on Malthusian grounds. A possible precedent for Dickens's specters in *A Christmas Carol* (1843) and *The Chimes* (1844), which similarly take up Malthusian themes and satirize Brougham, the *Liberator*'s story has the shade give his favorite author "a tract on 'Prudential and Moral Restraint,' by the Useful Knowledge Society, which smelled most awfully of brimstone" (*Northern Liberator* January 11, 1840; see also Glancy, "Introduction" xiv).

These attacks paid Martineau the backhanded compliment of crediting her with extraordinary influence, making the young writer the symbol of government policy. Martineau assumed an important role in radical demonology, not only because the popularity of *Illustrations of Political Economy* made her an influential target but also because she was an astute critic of the ideological tendencies of working-class radicalism. Her stories offer a prescient geography of the resistance to poor law reform, mapping the variety of techniques available to the popular movement. In Martineau's rural counties, the radicals rely on surreptitious violence against property, the rick burnings and "Swing" riots Hobsbawm and Rudé describe. In urban settings, the paupers adopt strategies designed to influence the election of parish officers – packing meetings, harassing reformers, and threatening to boycott the businesses of ratepayers who support punitive overseers. At the same time, Martineau's stories engage radicalism in a war of ideas, satirizing, refuting, and co-opting justifications for relief.

Martineau's narratives pick up central motifs from the writings of the Royal Commission, which argue for the need to find an institutional basis for poor relief that would insulate its agents from community pressure. These reports detail corrupt "jobbing" (whereby connected tradesmen gouge prices) as well as the difficulties faced by well-intentioned officers subject to influence from their clients, employees, and poorer relatives (*Extracts* 164, 204, 210). Both supporters and critics of the New Poor Law recognized that the attempt to make relief more centralized would not only create more efficient economies of scale but would also remove social welfare policy from local networks of pressure and obligation.[23] Richard Oastler remarked that centralization meant that decisions about relief would depend upon "a 'Commission' of Strangers, whom the poor can never find, and who will never care two straws whether the poor die in their beds, in the hedge bottom, or on the gallows" (*Poor Man's Guardian* July 20, 1834). On the other hand, the Royal Commission's *Extracts* recount abortive attempts at reform under the Old Poor Law, describing how local pressure, including incendiarism and machine breaking, shackled local magistrates' hands: "The apprehension of this dreadful and easily perpetrated mischief has very generally affected the minds of the rural parish officers of the county, making the power of the paupers over the funds provided for their relief almost absolute, as regards any discretion on the part of the overseer" (*Extracts* 138). Nassau Senior, political economist, Oxford professor, and member of the Royal Commission, put it succinctly: "The enforcement of improvements must devolve upon those who had no stacks to be fired" (qtd. in Brundage 50).

Like the reports of the Royal Commission, Martineau's novellas consider the texture of pressures and loyalties that surround the poor laws, illustrating the complex web of debts and responsibilities transacted through relief. At the same time, her representations of reform offer a fantasy of relief freed from the relationships she evokes. Her stories never advocate a central administrative body, one of the few suggestions of the Royal Commission they fail to voice. Instead, the stories dramatize this recommendation by creating characters independent from the world they wish to reform. In certain respects, the social geography of Martineau's novellas anticipates social problem fiction of the 1840s, but in other ways it differs markedly. The stories involve two sets of characters, a cast that forms an analog to middle-class respondents to the Royal Commission of Inquiry and to the population upon which it reported. Paupers and laborers and reformers, employers, and the poor law bureaucracy constitute separate but interconnected universes. Martineau wants to show how the fates of the classes are intertwined, but her groups rarely interact, their stories unfolding on parallel tracks. In fact, only the Poor Laws and the related institutions of employment and private charity mediate the working-class and middle-class plot lines. There are no interclass friendships or romances; no religious or civic rituals unite the worlds; contingencies of crime or sickness do not bring the characters together; no inheritance plots reveal hidden family ties.

Stylistic features also distinguish the groups. With documentary precision, Martineau attends to the daily lives of her working-class figures. Extended descriptions of work and meticulous sketches of household management stand as a significant development in the art of realism, helping establish what Valerie Sanders calls a new domain "for the novel to claim as its legitimate territory" (195; Logan 42). But this detail is missing from Martineau's representation of middle-class characters, about whose professional and private lives the reader learns almost nothing. The introduction of the protagonist of *Cousin Marshall* (a poor law story published as part of *Illustrations of Political Economy*) is typical. After identifying the reform-minded Mr. Burke as a "surgeon" returning to town from a late-night visit to a rural patient, the narrator's gaze turns outward as Burke notices vagrants "who still loitered in the streets, and occasionally disturbed the repose of those who slept" (218–19). Throughout *Poor Laws and Paupers Illustrated*, the middle-class characters lack defining habits and emotional quirks and speak a monotone language. But it is too simple to call them flat. Though drained of personality, they are surprisingly dynamic, because the positions they advocate differentiate them. They change and develop, have conflicts and crises, but all in the realm of ideas.

The dichotomy between limited characterization that makes middle-class figures ideological mouthpieces and the finely textured realism with which Martineau describes the lives of the poor sheds light on a central problem the novellas pose: who can effectively reform relief given an entrenched opposition to change – one that exists among both the poor and the middle classes? *The Hamlets*, the second novella of the series, explores the difficulty parishes face finding administrators willing to take up the challenge of enforcing rational poor relief. It begins with images of a pauperized village, focusing on the fisherman Monks, who relies on the parish to pay his rent. The novella makes clear, however, that the administrators of the poor laws share blame for the problems afflicting the parish, because they supplement wages and grant relief indiscriminately. Confronting the crisis, ratepayers discuss the need to replace the current overseer, a shop owner dependent on the custom of laborers, who pressure him to grant unjust claims. The new overseer Barry is new to the district and has an independent fortune from an unspecified source. Like the professional bureaucrats the New Poor Law would establish above local officials, Barry's lack of connection to the parish (and to Martineau's story world) allows him to reform relief practices.

The reform-minded characters in *Cousin Marshall* similarly embody the technocratic ideals of reform. Martineau completed *Cousin Marshall* shortly before beginning *Poor Laws and Paupers Illustrated*, and the novella differs from the second series in that it advocates abolition of the poor laws along Malthusian lines instead of seeking their overhaul via retrenchment, the workhouse test, and other reforms. Like many abolitionists, Martineau shifted positions in light of the recommendations of the Royal Commission. *Cousin Marshall* tells the story of the orphaned Bridgeman children, who depend on public relief and the generosity of relatives. It illustrates how familial aid encourages self-sufficiency whereas official charity leads to indolence and sexual profligacy. The children's trajectory intersects with the efforts of the Burkes to improve the parish. Mr. Burke lobbies local gentry to phase out private charity and reform the poor laws while his sister Louisa teaches at a pauper school trying to instill diligence and thrift in her charges. Consistent with the scant characterization the Burkes receive, their actions are mostly negative: in a series of educational vignettes, they convince others not to interfere in the lives of the poor.

Yet the Burkes' attempts to transform their fictional parish ultimately suggest Martineau's sense of how besieged reform efforts would be. In earlier didactic fiction, such as Hannah More's, educational scenes tend to confirm the narrator's perspective. In Martineau's stories, the matter is not so simple. Reformers are taunted by those they would educate; conversations break down; examples of miseducation shadow the middle-class characters' efforts as paupers persuade peers that relief is a traditional right. The story tracks the *Bildung* of the apprentice beggar Hunt by the veteran Childe, who demonstrates for his pupil how to obtain relief by faking a disability (257). Hunt's advice to Childe rhymes with Louisa Burke's appeal to laborer's self-interest, but where Louisa's visits cannot counteract the negative influence of the workhouse environment, Hunt successfully inculcates antisocial values into his pupil (235).

Although Martineau borrows from Malthus in many respects, she shifts his justification for social austerity from a naturalistic theory of population to a cultural explanation.[24] For Malthus, the poor laws were problematic because they suggested a nonexistent abundance of social resources and thus disastrously increased the birth rate. For Martineau, the poor laws were primarily an ideological question; the stories show pauperism spreading through the contagion of belief. For this reason, throughout the novellas Martineau responds to political arguments in favor of relief, giving voice to alternative views in order to refute them. Burke explains to his sister that guaranteed support is founded on a flawed analogy likening society to a family (245). In this theory, society's poorest members exert the same claim upon the community as children do their parents. However, the metaphor ignores that parents choose to have children whereas society cannot decide who will be born into it. Without the ability to limit the population, the promise of relief is meaningless, because scarce natural resources will circumscribe any effort to lessen the severity of poverty (247). Burke's family/society analogy diminishes radicalism's theories about social obligations to a simple paternalism radical publications rejected, a question discussed in the following chapter. At other moments, however, Martineau's fiction grapples more precisely with tendencies within working-class politics. *The Parish* describes the manipulation of the language of deference such that respectful formulations disguise a satiric edge and an expanding sense of entitlement (116; see also *Land's End* 70–72). *The Town* satirizes radicalism's use of biblical precedent to justify charity: a pauper defends her appetite for meat and beer by reminding the overseer that "man cannot live by bread alone" (22). And *The Land's End* turns radical Christianity against the Old Poor Law when the protagonist, a down-on-his-luck Methodist miner, describes how high rates under the old system violate God's law "that there shall be no oppression of the hired servant that is poor and needy" by driving impoverished but self-sufficient rate-payers into pauperism (91).

Most importantly, several stories take up the Cobbettite idea of the poor laws as a social inheritance. In *Cousin Marshall*, Miss Burke asks her brother how such a destructive institution arose in the first place. In answer, he reiterates crucial aspects of Cobbett's *History*, explaining that Queen Elizabeth established the laws as recompense to the poor for the loss of Catholic charity caused by the dissolution of the monasteries (247).[25] Several episodes also satirize Cobbett's notions. In one, the beggar Childe describes the retirement he anticipates at "Childe's hospital" in London, a foundation established by a benefactor with his same last name, a name made rare by the "e" at its end (254). A single, silent letter guarantees the grifter a life of ease, his capricious inheritance burlesquing the assertion that the Elizabethan poor laws act as a universal legacy.

Childe is juvenile in terms of his dependence, not his innocence, but the story also depicts orphaned children as archetypes of individuals who suffer economic exposure and must rely on community support for survival. Their stories mock Cobbett's claim that the poor laws are a social legacy by showing that public welfare provision encourages adult relatives to ignore their responsibilities toward helpless dependents. Founded on an idealized vision of society as a family, poor relief undermines real families by injecting into them a calculus of self-interest. The novella contrasts the generous treatment the orphans receive from the eponymous heroine, who disdains charity, with the crass calculations of their other surviving relative. Having defrauded the parish for years, the children's aunt Mrs. Bell exemplifies the negative consequences of poor relief. She advocates sending the children to the workhouse, which she sees as their right and a convenient means for shirking her own responsibilities (224). *The Parish* instantiates a similar argument. A reforming overseer describes how a laborer has abandoned his children to the workhouse and how they in turn will not support their father in his old age (16–17). For Martineau, the Old Poor Law's promise of social obligation encourages families to neglect their actual responsibilities; the New Poor Law, then, will revive family life by reaffirming the duties kin owe one another.

In *Cousin Marshall*, liberal critics of the Old Poor Law articulate the hypothetical case its supporters would make. In *Poor Laws and Paupers Illustrated*, radicals stake their own claims. In *The Parish*, the apothecary Jay defends poor relief as a modern version of the poor's traditional right to the land: "You do not deny, sir, I presume, that man possesses the earth. From this it follows that all men possess by natural right all the land and all the fruits of it, through the whole extended universe" (90–91). In Jay's theory, landlords "mistake their title, and are only tenants," an idea implicit in Cobbett's *History* and made explicit a few years later in *Legacy to Labourers* (91). Jay's glib syllogism is typical of Martineau's ironic treatment of radicalism; in the very scene, Jay is thrown from his horse and lands in the mud, taking literal possession of a soggy patch of his birthright.

As if anticipating the blistering attacks with which Cobbett greeted the Royal Commission's reports, the report's *Extracts* also satirized Cobbettite history and its diffusion among the impoverished. By vividly describing the grasping demands of individual paupers for a pittance of support, Edwin Chadwick deflates the high-minded assertion that the poor laws are part of the patrimony of all "free-born Englishmen":

> John Brenn is a mechanic, I believe a weaver, at present residence in London, and had 3s. a week sent to him, – on what ground except as a

patrimonial claim, on what evidence except his own statement that he wanted it, and must return to the parish if it were not sent to him, I was unable to ascertain. (*Extracts* 219)

The inclusion of a genealogy of the Brenn family, which begins with John's parents, "Pater" and "Mater" Brenn, and encompasses his siblings and dozens of nieces and nephews, all of whom live on the poor rates, grotesquely literalizes the idea of relief as a legacy guaranteed to all. James Kay, whom the government eventually charged with founding a system of normal schools to train teachers for union workhouses, accepted Cobbett's association between the poor laws and Catholic charity but reversed its significance. In an influential 1832 essay on education, he writes, "the poor-laws, as at present administered, retain all the evils of the gross and indiscriminate bounty of ancient monasteries" (Kay-Shuttleworth, "Moral" 51). As in Martineau, the fantasy of society as a family destroys intergenerational bonds because "oppressed children" come to resent idle parents and abandon them in old age to the "scanty maintenance derived from parochial relief" (58).

Although both Blue Books and Martineau's fiction characterize radical justifications of the poor laws as destructive and absurd, they recognize their potency. The Royal Commission records a shifting norm as more and more of the laboring poor come to believe that no stigma should attach to receiving aid. The report cites examples of self-sufficient families pressured into pauperism so their independence will not undermine the claims to respectability of those who benefit from public charity (*Extracts* 213–14). Reformers also criticized the practice of supplementing low wages because of that practice's ideological implications. By effectively ensuring a minimum wage known as the parish rate, the allowance system confused the master-employee relationship with that between parish and pauper. C. H. Cameron, an assistant to the Royal Commission, argues that "the notion of wages as a contract beneficial to both parties seems to be nearly obliterated from the minds of the people of West Wycombe," a dynamic Martineau repeatedly dramatizes in *The Land's End* (*Extracts* 82). Work has taken on the negative aspects of relief: because workers know a wage floor is guaranteed and that they will receive relief if unemployed, they view employment as a secure and traditional right.

Although *The Hamlets* and *The Land's End* conclude with positive change in sight, the other stories in *Poor Laws and Paupers Illustrated* are more pessimistic than even *Cousin Marshall*. While aiming to encourage reform, they stage its difficulty in the face of the entrenched belief in the right to relief. Where *Cousin Marshall* evokes the danger of property being swallowed up by the pauper hoard, in *The Parish* calamity has already arrived. Throughout the novella, middle-class characters describe incendiary fires approaching ever closer to their district. When the farm of the employer Goldby is burnt to the ground, his own employees and other villagers look on indifferently (152–53). The story concludes with Dr. Warrener, the reforming local minister, sermonizing about changes in the administration of the poor laws necessary to avert future disasters (158). But it is too late for the story's characters: Goldby leaves the district and several of his employees are driven onto relief.

The Parish documents the desperate need for reform and concludes with the ratepayers poised to take belated action. *The Town*, on the other hand, depicts an attempt at change bedeviled by difficulties. The story opens with the election of two overseers. The first has venal motivations for seeking office, including a desire to provide for poor cousins out of the public purse. The cooper Guthrie, on the other hand, is committed to reform. Notably, though, Guthrie departs from Martineau's middle-class characters, and the attributes that make him a rounded figure limit his effectiveness as a parish officer. He knows collecting debts from recalcitrant ratepayers will offend the parents of his daughter's friends and cost his business customers (84–85). Similarly, his investigation of fraudulent claims is hampered when one unmarried mother falsely asserts that he is the father of her child. By the story's end, the reform movement collapses; the parish reverts to an open-vestry structure (in which the Board of Guardians is composed of volunteers rather than elected members) and fraud becomes rampant again. Guthrie's failure suggests the need for a professional class of poor law administrators supervised by a distant bureaucracy – his connections to people in the parish make it difficult for him to implement positive change. This advocacy, however, remains implicit. The reader observes that pressures brought to bear on reformers make any progress difficult. Family loyalties, career ambitions, friendships, rivalries, and romances, all mean that questions of public policy do not occur in a vacuum.

The problems confronting Guthrie as he attempts to enact a theoretically sound program onto the living texture of a community resemble the challenges Martineau faced as a popularizer of economic theories, who had to render the abstract propositions of political economy in fictional narratives.[26] Through a process of stylistic abstraction and theoretical rigor, Ricardian political economy sought to isolate economic laws from moral, ethical, and political issues, but the techniques that allowed economists to constitute their discipline as an objective science limited the accessibility and popularity of their writings. By translating formal treatises into narrative form, writers such as Martineau and J. R. McCulloch made the basic principles of political economy accessible to a wide audience. The illustration of economics in fiction, however, changed the content of the theories Martineau utilized, and the effort to synthesize "such divergent modes of discourse" involved profound difficulties (Klaver 58). The moral and political frameworks from which political economists strove to separate their discipline reemerge in Martineau's stories, which sometimes offer a perspective critical of the harsher aspects of economic laws. While some critics have pointed out the ways Martineau straitjackets complex problems into reductive frameworks, her plots sometimes pull the reader's sympathy in ways that do not easily align with the core of her didactic message. *Cousin Marshall*, for instance, tracks the fate of four orphan children left homeless after a fire, and the narrator makes clear that they are blameless for their poverty, even as the story polemicizes against the ability of the poor laws or charitable institutions to help them. Cousin Marshall herself, who generously shelters two children while denouncing the system of public relief, ends the novel ostracized by her neighbors for her condemnation of charity, a conviction she holds to so firmly that she will not even allow her son to allay her penury in old age. Isolated and impoverished, Martineau's heroine becomes an ironically frightening vision of "homo economicus."

The Hamlets likewise confuses its explicit message with troubling undercurrents. The story demonstrates the virtue of hard work as a solution to dependent poverty by chronicling how the fisherman Monks becomes a dedicated wage earner after being denied outdoor relief and how his foster children Harriet and Ben become self-sufficient through entrepreneurial schemes. Monks's original justifications for idleness, however, disturb the novel's advocacy of individual effort as a universal solution to poverty. As the story opens, Monks tells his wife that he cannot go to sea because a storm threatens. His wife's skepticism reveals his excuse as a screen for desultory habits. Eventually, having learned the value of diligence, Monks fishes every night regardless of weather. The novella reaches its climax when Monks and his adopted son are caught on the water during a violent storm. The reader waits with Harriet and her terrified surrogate mother for Monks's and Ben's return. They arrive home safely, but a neighbor's death by drowning leaves a widow and five orphans without the means of support. Although the story chronicles the successes of poor law reform in fostering virtuous individuals, it includes this note of dissonance:

lacking community support laborers expose themselves to potentially deadly work, which paradoxically threatens the self-sufficiency of their families.

The reliance on narrative anecdote in the reports of the Royal Commission and the Poor Law Commission creates some of the same tensions that entangle Martineau's fiction. The New Poor Law was premised on the notion that questions in the economic realm should be independent from politics, morality, and religion. Poor law reformers hoped to substitute the self-acting mechanisms of less eligibility and the workhouse test for an evaluation of the moral fitness of paupers. But Martineau's, the Royal Commission's, and the Poor Law Commission's advocacy for reform continually reverted to moral categories to justify what was supposed to be a morally neutral policy. They cataloged, for instance, the ways the Old Poor Law encouraged fraud and vice and argued that reform would cure those same ills. Radical critics highlighted this residual paternalism, pointing out the difficultly of justifying retrenchment and punitive deterrence as species of charity.

A final paradox concerned the mechanisms of social verification the New Poor Law pioneered – the workhouse test (said to require no knowledge of the poor) and comprehensive investigatory research (which by definition strove for the opposite) (Frankel, *States* 171–72). The tension between these methods is on view in the Royal Commission's treatment of fraud, a problem addressed, like many issues, through illustrative anecdotes that buttress the commission's proposals. After delineating six types of fraud, Chadwick includes several accounts of officials discovering hoaxes. In one, a washerwoman informs a parish officer that a shoemaker on relief lives affluently. When an overseer tells the officer that they must continue giving the man relief because the shoemaker has signed a statement affirming his need, the officer investigates the claim. After learning the shoemaker has concealed some of his wages, the official confronts the cheat, who never asks for aid again (*Extracts* 211–12). Since in such episodes officers uncover fraudulent claims haphazardly, the stories promote the necessity of the workhouse test, which moots the need to evaluate paupers' assertions: anyone with actual need will avail him- or herself to relief inside the workhouse, while anyone who demands relief but refuses to go to the workhouse will demonstrate a lack of legitimate need. Chadwick implies that fraud is so difficult to police that no poor law bureaucracy could monitor paupers' claims. Stories of imposture, however, have a second effect. They prove that many poor people do not really need assistance and therefore that a policy of retrenchment is justified. Chadwick wants to argue that paupers' stories cannot be verified and should be irrelevant in evaluating claims of relief, but he repeatedly chooses anecdotes that *negatively* verify paupers' claims. Harriet Martineau's novellas repeat this paradox. Her advocates for reform stress the impossibility of knowing the real lives of the poor to justify self-acting measures such as the workhouse test, but the omniscient narrator reveals (and poor law officers eventually discover) paupers living high on the hog. Thus narratives about the lives of the poor came to play a central role in propaganda for a policy premised on the idea that learning the story of an individual's life should be irrelevant to whether or not he or she received relief.

Martineau's inability to present poor law reform in an unambiguously positive light is a final indication of her engagement with the world of working-class radicalism. In *The Town*, reform collapses as entrenched problems return and take hold of the parish. Yet the reader cannot entirely regret the reformers' failure, for the breakdown of their efforts appears as a stroke of good luck for John Waters, a kind-hearted shoemaker, whose difficulties the narrative sympathetically traces. Waters loses his job when a reformer refuses to pay his master the inflated prices the latter receives for supplying the workhouse with shoes. He complains bitterly about his master's jobbing – "The natural wages of my employment have been deranged by [his] plotting" – and he suffers greatly as a result of his unemployment, even attempting suicide (*Town* 128). A victim of the Old Poor Law but also of reform, Waters benefits when the parish reverts to its former ways, because he receives back his former job, inflated wages and all.

Martineau's vision of the collapse of poor law reform in her unnamed town proved partially prophetic. It was in the northern cities and industrial centers where a militant and well-organized resistance slowed and altered the implementation of the New Poor Law, helping shape relief policy for decades to come while asserting a claim to social citizenship that would remain a constituent element of working-class radicalism and inform the Chartist movement's demand for working-class political power. Just as Martineau grappled with the arguments of opponents of the New Poor Law, so too did the Poor Law Commission have to confront intense political and intellectual resistance from working-class radicals, who insisted on injecting questions of morality and politics into the fantasized space of an idealized market economy. The following chapter takes up that movement's critique of the New Poor Law's uneasy synthesis of punitive paternalism and free market liberalism.

CHAPTER 2

Books of (Social) Murder: Melodrama
and the Slow Violence of the Market in Anti-New
Poor Law Satire, Fiction, and Journalism

In the fall and winter of 1838–1839, readers of radical working-class newspapers encountered frequent mention of a strange, pseudonymous document referred to as the "Marcus pamphlet." The so-called Marcus – whose identity was never discovered – advocated a novel solution to the much-debated problems of overpopulation and entrenched indigence: namely the gassing to death of all infants born into working-class households with more than two children. Playing upon popular anxiety about the disruption of long-standing forms of poor relief in an era of destabilizing economic transformation, the tract would become one of literary history's most successful pranks.

At first largely ignored, the pamphlet obtained notoriety when the popular ex-Methodist preacher and Chartist firebrand Joseph Rayner Stephens accused members of the Poor Law Commission of authoring and distributing it themselves in fulfillment of their plans to "de-pauperize" the country. The publicity the radical press gave Stephens's assertion – reiterated weekly in outdoor sermons that were printed in the *Northern Star* – sparked an improbable brouhaha in which the Poor Law Commission was forced to declare publicly that its antipoverty program did not hinge on infant murder. But the government's embarrassed disavowal only heightened the public's interest, which publishers met by printing various cheap versions, including the *Northern Star*'s "People's Edition" and the radical pornographer William Dugdale's *The Book of Murder*, which appended a refutation of Malthusianism to Marcus's essay (*NS* February 23, 1839; *Northern Liberator* March 2, 1839; McDonagh 106). The Newcastle *Northern Liberator* surveyed with satisfaction the uproar it helped create: "We see that our exposure of this shocking publication has done its work, and that the country rings with execrations of it and of its authors" (January 12, 1839).

A culmination of the propaganda war over the principles of poor relief and an opening salvo of the Chartist bid to win political power, the Marcus pamphlet illustrates the shifting, self-conscious, highly ironized way the working-class radical press used melodrama to criticize the New Poor Law, political economy, and the emergent regime of print statism. Taking literally the Malthusian principle that the poor have no right to subsistence, Marcus reflects on the nature of social responsibility and the market. He inverts the Smithian conceit that individuals seeking their own self-interest create prosperity and social harmony, describing instead the penetration of market principles into social welfare policy as literally and directly responsible for crime. Half exposé of a bloody conspiracy, half fanciful demonstration of the logic embodied in government policy – the pamphlet renders the market a dystopic space, a world in which mad philosophers sacrifice the poor to eliminate poverty and a central bureaucracy claims vast power to enforce a program of neglect.

Like Cobbett's *History of the Protestant Reformation*, Marcus condenses social processes into a simplified narrative of actual crime, "a *bona-fide* grave, earnest, scientific proposal," in the words of the *Northern Liberator*, "to murder every third infant (with a few exceptions) by 'painless extinction,' by means of (carbonic acid) 'gas'" (January 12, 1839). But the "demon author" and his coconspirators in the radical press, who played along with the satire by full-throatedly denouncing it, disclose a dialectic in melodramatic discourse between a vision of villainy perpetrated by isolated individuals and a view of harm arising from flawed social organization. The conspiracy theory promoted by the pamphlet presents at once a fantasy of abuse by an aristocratic clique and an enabling alienation in which new economic realities and state institutions are rendered frighteningly strange. This chapter suggests that the oscillation between these poles was typical of anti-New Poor Law journalism and fiction. Writing critical of the law was often melodramatic, relying on the extreme situations, heightened emotional states, and moral Manichaeism of popular theater to characterize the architects of retrenchment as willfully criminal. But other narratives turned from melodramatic convention to pioneer stylistic techniques that captured the anonymous and fractured nature of the market, creating stories with no villain except the competitive system itself.

Both these strategies responded to the representational challenge of describing what Rob Nixon – writing in a different context – has termed "slow violence." For Nixon, contemporary environmental degradation and its human consequences typify "a violence that occurs gradually and out of sight, a violence of delayed destruction that is dispersed across time and space, an attritional violence that is typically not viewed as violence at all" (2). Confronting the displacements, chronic insecurity, and long-term physiological and psychological consequences of social welfare retrenchment, writers crafted narratives that distilled and intensified ongoing processes into dramatic episodes of crisis – as in melodrama. At the same time, they sought to illustrate the occluded and disconnected nature of relationships in capitalist society, exploring the difficulty of assigning blame in a world in which various connections had given way to what Carlyle termed the "cash nexus." The radical journalist Bronterre O'Brien responds to this conundrum in an essay answering Robert Owen's criticism of attacks on the capitalist class:

> As regards [the capitalist's] relation to the producer … he is as perfect a plunderer as the highwayman or pickpocket, the only difference being that he robs in a safe "respectable" way, *according* to law, while the other unfortunate must rob *in spite* of the law, because he has got no money "capital" … We do not accuse the monied capitalist of intentional robbery … These spoliations they commit, not from sinister design, but from accidental position in society; or rather the spoliations are committed *for* them by the silent operation of causes over which they have no control under the existing arrangements of society. (*Poor Man's Guardian*, March 21 1835)

Radical writing on the New Poor Law confronts similar paradoxes. Though it depicts the rich and poor law officials as versions of "highwaymen," it frequently acknowledges they act from their "accidental position in society" rather than "sinister design." Short fiction, media criticism, journalistic accounts of infanticides among the poor, and the Marcus pamphlet itself, all seek ways to narrate violence in a social system where causal relationships are no longer simple, direct, or transparent.

Media Criticism and Melodrama in the *Champion and Weekly Herald* and Anti-New Poor Law Short Fiction

The Marcus pamphlet comments on both Malthusian political economy and the emerging world of print statism. Just as Swift's *Modest Proposal* dons the guise of an economic essay to counter that genre's increasing importance in eighteenth-century Ireland (Moore 169), Marcus parodies the utilitarian language of the Poor Law Commission. By exposing how bureaucratic formulations mask proposals with drastic consequences, Marcus criticizes the way Malthus and his followers shift political questions to the supposedly neutral ground of demographics and economics (Poovey 9). The opaqueness of Marcus's language, as well as the insistence that the text is intended "for Private Circulation," reverses the rationale of official reports, which sought to gain support for policy initiatives by rendering "the process of governing visible for public observation" (Marcus 4;

Frankel, "Blue" 316). This parody of the language of reform makes the pamphlet a kind of media criticism, a key aspect of the radical press in the 1830s.[1] While oppositional movements scoured Blue Books for material that supported their positions, their journals also scrutinized unsympathetic governmental reports and lambasted the publicity the mainstream press gave these (Poovey 57).[2]

In particular, the unprecedented media campaign supporting the New Poor Law prompted a vigorous counterattack in the radical press, which defined governmental publications as much a symbol of the law as the hated workhouse: "The Commissioners, who were let loose on the country in 1833, and on whose Report the Act was founded, spread the falsehood and the nonsense over thousands of pages of print" (*CWH* May 27, 1837). Thomas Doubleday's allegorical novel *Political Pilgrim's Progress* (1839) similarly depicts print as an intrinsic part of the corrupt order, expressing awareness of the threat print statism and allied endeavors posed to the radical press as alternative sources of cheap reading material.[3] Radical, the update of Bunyan's Christian, confronts Dr. Foolscap and Mr. Quarto in the scientific quarter of Vanity Fair where "were seen ... thousands of sheets [of newspapers] flying in the air, like flakes of snow, and eagerly seized on by the people round about. These immense establishments were generally the property of political partizans; but nothing could be a more heinous offence than to call in question their complete and perfect independence" (44–45). Radical journalism similarly sought to demystify the "scientific" discourse of political economy and the Poor Law Commission, revealing its political commitments through satire.

Among radical publications, the *Champion and Weekly Herald* most consistently drew attention to governmental reports to demonstrate how they were partisan rather than broad based and objective. Established in London in the fall of 1836, the year of William Cobbett's death, the *Champion*, a weekly costing 4d., sought to preserve the legacy of the great popular radical. John Fielden, Cobbett's friend and fellow MP for Oldham, provided financial backing; Richard Cobbett, one of William's sons, managed the paper; and another, James Paul Cobbett, joined John Morgan as editor. The journal's circulation peaked between eight and nine thousand in December 1836. But this number fell short of the financial break-even point; until the paper folded in 1840, it cost Fielden substantial losses, sometimes up to £20 per week when its sales sagged to only three thousand per issue after 1838 (Weaver 158–59). The *Champion* emulated the style the elder Cobbett pioneered, reprising his idiomatic language, familiar addresses to the reader, and aggrieved posture. Its relentless focus on the poor laws also followed in Cobbett's footsteps. Across multiple articles in a single issue, it recorded abuse and misery in workhouses and hailed protests against the implementation of reform. The paper directed its greatest ire, however, toward the advocacy of retrenchment in official reports and sympathetic newspaper articles.

The *Champion*'s criticism stands as an example of how governmental documents did not simply dominate a discursive field but were themselves subject to withering critique. Upon publication of the Poor Law Commission's annual report of 1837, the paper argued the law embodied partisan interest, not a neutral technocratic agenda. The newspaper attacked the commission's empirical rigor by calling out its methodology, which relied on only the perspective of middle-class bureaucrats and employers (May 27, 1837).[4] Beyond particular criticism, the paper trained its readers to regard governmental documents skeptically, often worrying a single sentence to make its case. A banal line from a governmental circular – "the Commissioners entertain a confident hope that you will enter upon your office with a *firm assurance of the ultimate efficacy of the system which you are about to administer*" – demonstrated how the commissioners were ideologues and theorists: "What do the words *mean*? ... What do the words *mean*? Why that, before they have had experience, they are to be assured of the result" (May 13, 1837). Finally, the writers of the *Champion* repeatedly expressed frustration that their interlocutors hid behind philosophic cant and refused to articulate their true intentions in a fittingly melodramatic fashion:

> The worst ... of this last cruel attempt of the faction to impoverish and cow down the nation is, that they have gone forth in the war of starvation and degradation ... like Whigs, true to the ways of the old, treacherous, country-killing faction, with tongues that stunned us all the while with *liberality, liberality, liberality!* (November 25, 1837)

The Champion also ransacked middle-class newspapers to find stories that illustrated suffering caused by the New Poor Law. It treated such articles in different fashions depending on their politics. *The Times* and other papers hostile to retrenchment provided stories that drew supportive comments.[5] *The Champion* wrenched other items out of context, making connections between the poor laws and a variety of issues that mainstream publications kept wide apart. A gossip column from the *Globe* quoted in Richard Oastler's oratory yielded a description of the elegant dress the wife of Poor Law Commissioner Frankland Lewis wore to a ball: "He would beg of them to remember that the lady's dress was all of British manufacture – all made by the poor slaves that are to be clothed in grogram!" (May 20, 1837). The *Champion* delighted in applying the language of pauperism to anyone receiving a government salary, from lowly clerks to the monarch. It reported the awards of "Orders of Merits" for the two authors Lady Sidney Morgan and Mary Russell Mitford, under the title "SPLENDID PAUPERS – OUTDOOR RELIEF." Aping the language of poor law reform, the *Champion* argued that such "outdoor relief upon a grand scale" must demoralize the country – only in this case by encouraging a specific species of idleness, the reading of novels (July 8, 1837). As these examples illustrate, ironic juxtaposition constituted a crucial ingredient in radical satire. As the *National Vindicator* put it in an article that announced a royal birth as the "Birth of a Burden!": "The 'Court' and the 'Workhouse' will be our prominent features: we believe that they came into the world *together*, and can form a shrewd guess that *thus* they will make their departure" (November 20, 1841).

Similar to its treatment of governmental reports, the *Champion* excerpted stories from other papers to educate its readers about the ideological biases of its opponents, calling out "the fiction of impartiality" that was a crucial posture of early Victorian journalism (Vernon 46). The inquest following a poor laborer's suicide seems straightforward in the *Morning Chronicle*'s account:

> It appeared from the evidence that the deceased, who was a labourer, and had a wife and family, was in the receipt of 2s. 6d. from the union. He was a man of very desponding disposition. It being reported that he was getting a livelihood by his own exertions, assisted by his wife, the board of guardians of the Hambledon union took off his allowance; after which, however, his earnings increased. During the last few days he was observed to be particularly melancholy. (562)

But the *Champion* rails at the report:

> This is what is called a *cock-and-a-bull story*, of the *Chronicle*. Observe the statement so carefully made, that Kemp's *"earnings had increased"* after his being cut off from parish aid, and believe, if you *can*, it appeared from the evidence that the deceased, who was a labourer, and had a wife and family, was in the receipt of 2s. 6d. from the union. He was a man of very desponding disposition ... To be sure, he was: had always shown a disposition to kill himself, eh? But why did he put it off till he was made "an independent labourer"? ... He was a *nervous* man, perhaps; ... how came his nerves to carry him on safely through the distresses which brought him to parish relief, and quit him the moment he became an "independent labourer," living on an increase of wages? Oh! These lies; these poor-law lies,

are atrocious! We do not hesitate to record this as another item in our already frightful catalogue of *Poor-Law murders*. (September 9, 1837)

Here, the strategy of satirical juxtaposition remains, but the contrast is linguistic. Colloquial expressions, italicized phrases, exclamations, hyperbole, and rhetorical questions proliferate, invading and subverting the *Chronicle*'s temperate prose until the news item itself, another example of "poor-law lies," becomes implicated in the man's death.[6] And, at the last, the *Champion* suggests a kind of discourse more appropriate to the suicide: the language of melodrama.

Elaine Hadley offers a formidable analysis of the rhetoric and ideology of the opposition to the New Poor Law (*Melodramatic* 1–12, 77–132). Hadley argues that critics of the law across the political spectrum – from *The Times* to Charles Dickens to the unstamped press – operated in a "melodramatic mode," framing a social crisis in terms of plots about the alienation and reunification of literal families. Hadley shows how aspects of melodrama – the representation of extreme emotion, resolutions that hinge on providence, and the personification of moral absolutes – structure a wide variety of sources critical of the New Poor Law. Hadley's concept of melodrama as a "mode," a habit of expression, and "structure of feeling" that extends beyond literary genres, is particularly useful for considering a discursive field in which speeches, journalism, and pamphlets both borrowed from and influenced the conventions of fiction.

It is important to recognize, however, that melodrama was only one rhetorical choice available to opponents of the New Poor Law, and this mode existed side-by-side with other styles of argument. Radical journals frequently adopted a self-consciously learned and objective posture. Stories about the desperate actions of the neglected poor appeared next to editorials based on biblical exegesis, sociological analyses, and detailed historical reconstructions. The *Champion* defended the aid-in-wages of the Speenhamland system by investigating its origins in the depression of 1795 (May 27, 1837). The *Poor Man's Guardian* encouraged debate between readers, publishing a long exchange between "Vindex," "Political Corrector," and "Justitias" over population growth and the efficacy of emigration schemes (October 26, 1833 to April 26, 1834). Peter McDouall's "Lectures on the Factory System," which includes long sections on pauper labor, presents itself as a mock parliamentary investigation. Calling the reader "to enter into an extensive and interesting inquiry," the Chartist doctor advises the public to "listen, then, calmly, judge honestly, decide impartially," though his style modulates rapidly between the reasoned and the melodramatic (*McDouall's* April 3, 1841).

The radical press also expressed ambivalence toward sensationalist content. "A Simple Story," which appeared in *The English Chartist Circular* in 1840, recounts an act of charity in which artisans share their lunches and give a few shillings to a young fellow worker whose parents and siblings are starving.[7] The tale memorializes day-to-day activities to correct the association that Newgate fiction and court reporting makes between working people and crime. In reprinting an article from *The Times* about a mother's murder of her children and failed suicide attempt, the *Champion* condemns the distribution of such content but anticipates a positive effect from the present case:

> We feel the strongest possible dislike to publishing accounts of this nature, when they contain no political information, knowing well, that, generally, the perusal of them by the public can tend, to say the least of it, to no good. The present, however, differs widely from most cases of the kind: it is the most horrifying evidence of the dreadful state of misery to which the people are reduced that we have ever heard of. – The minister or member of Parliament, who can witness scenes like this . . . and then seek his rest without having done his very utmost to destroy the system of government under which such things can take place, must be a perfect monster! (June 10, 1837)

Rob Nixon has described how the corollary to media sensationalism is the erasure of slowly unfolding catastrophes, such as the lingering environmental and health consequences of industrial accidents even on the scale of the Union Carbide disaster in Bhopal (16). In the preceding passage, the *Champion* gestures toward an analogous insight, one that seems to have informed the editorial policy of certain radical papers in the 1830s and 1840s. Such publications as the *Poor Man's Guardian*, *Northern Star*, and *Northern Liberator* gave relatively scant attention to the crimes, shipwrecks, and other sensational topics that crowded other newspapers, but they commented extensively on shocking events when these reflected ongoing social injustice.[8] Shunned in certain contexts, scandalous content was fair game in terms of the New Poor Law. Indeed, three lurid plots comprise a significant portion of journalism about the law's effects: suicides by older male workers who have lost their means of support, scenes of women giving birth in public after being denied entry to a poor house or hospital, and most prominently accounts of infanticide.

Nevertheless, the characterization of writing about the poor laws as melodramatic needs careful specification. A pair of un-attributed short stories that appeared in 1838 in the radical miscellany *Cleave's Gazette of Variety* illustrates the complexity of the issue.[9] In "The Widow and the Fatherless," all characters save one are unnamed. This device emphasizes

the unexceptionality of the events of the story, signaling how the text
eschews sensationalism to describe common economic catastrophes. The
effect is especially striking for the protagonist, because so much of the story
attempts to verify her narrative or establish her social identity. The title,
derived from a biblical quotation popular with the anti–Poor Law movement, "oppress not the widow, or the fatherless, the stranger, or the poor"
(Zechariah 7:10) defines the woman in terms of her family relationships, a
tendency shared by the radical press and the poor law bureaucracy.[10]

The woman's sometimes successful and sometimes frustrated efforts to
iterate her life history constitute the central motif of the tale. It begins *in
medias res* with the woman telling her difficulties to a magistrate before
whom she appears after being arrested for begging. The narrative then
proceeds as a flashback that parallels the story the woman has just completed, and it goes on to stage the woman communicating her circumstances several more times: to a sympathetic stranger who gives her a
shilling and later more substantial help; to a policeman who turns "a
deaf ear"; to the servant of the workhouse overseer, who relates the
woman's story to her master; and to the Board of Guardians, which allows
her entry into the workhouse on condition she send her children to the
parish of their father. This sequence of narratees gives the reader several
possible points of identification for how one might respond to the woman's
story, and the tale models the ideal reaction in the generous actions of the
stranger and the magistrate, who together rescue the woman from the
workhouse and secure her employment.

Portraits of Fagin, the Artful Dodger, and Charley Bates appear above the
text in *Cleave's Gazette*, but Dickens's thieves are a false lead, for the story
will neither chronicle the London underworld nor rely on melodramatic
villains (Haywood, *Literature* 7). Notably, staccato, matter-of-fact reportage
records the anonymous heroine's travails after the death of her green-grocer
husband: "Customers rapidly fell off – new and well-filled shops in the same
line opened – tax-gatherers and creditors for petty sums became clamorous –
the landlord distrained – and the unhappy woman was driven from her once
happy home" (34). Evictions were a stock situation in stage melodrama of
the 1830s, most famously in Douglass Jerrold's *Rent Day*, which ran for
twenty years after its 1832 debut. Concluding acts with tableau vivants based
on David Wilkie's paintings, *Rent Day* freezes the action at moments of
crisis. Unlike its stage equivalents, however, "The Widow and the
Fatherless" does not emphasize the extremity of the woman's situation.
Instead, it details how the impersonal workings of the market economy
lead to the woman's difficulties, exploring a state that Lauren Berlant has

usefully described as "crisis ordinariness" (101). Berlant argues that social problems such as obesity or drug addiction should be characterized as endemics rather than epidemics, because they transpire not as sudden events but within "a zone of temporality marked by ongoingness, getting by, and living on, where structural inequalities are dispersed and the pacing of experience uneven" (99). Berlant's insight can help recuperate what treatments of radical fiction focused on melodrama sometimes overshadow: the extent to which this fiction allies the sensational and the commonplace, showing crises as "an amplification of something in the works," rather than a sudden, traumatic break (Berlant 10).

Radical social problem fiction frequently suggests systemic and impersonal causes for the hero's difficulties. Eschewing melodramatic villains, several stories in the *Chartist Circular* affiliate negative climaxes with the open-ended conditions of sickness, hunger, and poverty.[11] In "The Widow and the Fatherless," the protagonist's situation worsens when she sells possessions to pay for a move to the country, having accepted an offer from her husband's former assistant to work as his housekeeper. The assistant reneges on his promise and fires the woman after a few weeks, but even this betrayal is passed over quickly: "In vain did she remind him of the promise he had made to her previous to her quitting town, and the expense she had been put to. He coldly expressed his regret, declaring he had but recently determined upon marriage; then handing her a small balance due to her, he retired" (34). The story likewise frustrates what should count as its central confrontation – the woman seeking relief from the parish overseer, who refuses to see her but permits the workhouse servant to relay her claims.

Ultimately, the intervention of the magistrate and the generosity of the stranger save the anonymous woman from the degradations of the workhouse. In some regards, the capriciousness of this ending undercuts the story's social criticism. However, as Rob Breton has shown, the *dei ex machina* that occur occasionally in radical fiction can be understood not as simple wish fulfillment but as a challenge to the middle-class ideals of self-reliance and perseverance. A "contrived and far-fetched ... outcome" undermines the notion that diligent application brings economic security (Breton 138). Furthermore, while the story's resolution seems only to invert the anonymous operations of the market that caused the heroine's downfall, the magistrate's involvement serves to promote a return to aspects of the Old Poor Law, under which local justices of the peace had more power. The New Poor Law was designed to prevent "Poor Man's JPs" from intervening in the working of relief by establishing unions of several parishes, which were required to act in compliance with the regulations of the centralized Poor Law Commission. In this way, the story seeks both to rejuvenate aspects of the old system of relief and to demonstrate the inadequacies of paternalism in the new political economy of the 1830s, in which anonymous economic forces, not villainous malefactors, are to blame for the suffering of the vulnerable.

"Will Harper: A Poor Law Tale" (also published anonymously in *Cleave's Gazette* in 1838) more explicitly nominates a figure of the old paternalistic social order as a *deus ex machina*, but at the same time the story indicates the limits of this kind of happy ending, its irrelevance given the changed and broken social world.[12] Harper, an agricultural laborer, is the "boast of his village" for his friendliness, charity, and athleticism: "the excellent vicar was proud of one whom he regarded as a most worthy member of his flock, and the squire, whenever he met him, would stop and chat with as much familiarity as though he had been an equal" (26). After losing his job, the protagonist applies for relief at the workhouse, but the overseer Mr. Wasp insults him for idleness. Harper leaves after promising Wasp that "a day will come, and that too, ere long, when you shall be made to feel that poverty may have its hour of triumph over the heartless oppressor" (30). The squire sees Harper on the way home to his wife, gives him money to meet his immediate needs, promises to intervene in the case, and tells him to visit his estate the next day to learn the results of his efforts. But before Harper arrives home, he meets a fellow laborer turned "desperate poacher," who wiles him into a night of debauchery. The following day Harper is so ashamed that he does not make his visit to the squire, and the poacher convinces him to join his crew by mocking him for "looking to others for support, when he had it in his power to assist himself" (30). Eventually, Harper is arrested for attacking Wasp with a knife, the promised revenge acting only as the last step in the hero's ruin.

The failure of the squire's charity is overlaid with multiple ironies. First, the poacher, like Fagin in *Oliver Twist*, parrots the language of political economy: the imperative to "assist oneself" implies a world of individualistic competition and lawlessness. Second, squandering the squire's gift while a wife and children starve at home represents the kind of demoralization that poor law reformers saw as the result of the profligacy of the old law. Only the cause here is more complex. Charity is no longer part of the reciprocal obligations of the social classes but has been stigmatized by Wasp's insults, which causes Harper to abandon his deferential attitude. Next, Harper refuses the relief Wasp offers in order to maintain the integrity of his family – they would be separated in the workhouse – but his life as a criminal destroys the bonds between the couple. Finally, by poaching on the squire's land the hero commits a crime against his possible benefactor. "Will Harper" thus marks the passing of a fantasized world of social cohesion that it will not attempt to reconstruct. Charity and paternalism, it suggests, are no longer ways to bind the fragmented social universe back together.

Elaine Hadley argues that the anti–Poor Law movement (and the melodramatic mode more generally) idealized and hearkened back to the status hierarchies of a lost patriarchal world (*Melodramatic* 100–1). For her, the melodramatic mode viewed society as a family; anti-New Poor Law narratives sought to regenerate paternalist attitudes between portions of the family that had become estranged (111).[13] Oliver Twist, a pauper child reintegrated into the pastoral idyll of lost relations, stands as an exemplary case. But the failure of the squire to save Will Harper demonstrates how the attitude of radicals toward the fantasy of a golden age in which elites fulfilled their duties to the poor was conflicted.[14] Radical journals typically deployed the language of paternalism not to describe vertical acts of charity but mutual support among the poor themselves.[15] Before Will Harper's ill fortune, the protagonist "had at all times a hand ready to relieve the necessities of those upon whom Fortune frowned" (26). Peter McDouall, in *McDouall's Chartist and Republican Journal*, similarly depicts the handloom weaver of the preceding generation (now pushed to the wall by the factory system) as if he were a feudal lord: "His voice was heard for the oppressed, his aid was given to the weak, and his generous home received the defenceless poor" (April 10, 1841). The Chartist novelist Thomas Martin Wheeler reminds his readers "that it is not at our west-end palaces, nor at our merchant's counters, or from our shopkeeper's tills, that [the severely distressed] will receive the dole of charity, but at the residences of those who are but one remove from themselves," a situation the story "Mary Lyle" in the *Chartist Circular* also instantiates (Wheeler 89–90; *Chartist Circular* April 11, 1840). Dickens's Christmas story "The Chimes," an infanticide narrative the *Northern Star* significantly excerpted, contrasts the support the poor provide one another and the lack of paternalism from the upper classes ("Chimes" 134; *NS* December 21, 1844). The very title of the *Poor Man's Guardian* claims the paternal role that the journal contends actual poor law guardians have abandoned. And the *Champion* makes hay with the irony that local boards of guardians relied on protection from outside police officers:

> How long is this to go on? Picked men, armed with cutlasses, and sent to afford protection to a poor-law Commissioner! But the worst part of it . . . is,

that these "very muscular" protectors are brought all the way from London . . . for the protection, not merely of a Roving Commissioner, but to guard, also, the persons of those *neighbours* of poor people, those *local guardians* of the humble in distress, who ought to find, and who, in a less unnatural state of things, would find, sufficient protectors, if they needed any, in those very poor people whose interests they are appointed to guard! (November 25, 1837)

However radicals used the enabling fiction of the past to criticize contemporary society, they described the passage of the New Poor Law as a decisive break: even those who spoke of a lost time of unity, recognized in the law the dissolution of the older world. The Radical ex-Methodist minister J. R. Stephens demonstrated the extent of this rupture when he proclaimed:

I will lay aside the black coat for the red, and with the bible in one hand – and a sword in the other – so help me the God that made me – I will fight to the death sooner than that law shall be brought into operation on me . . . So help me God, I and the worthier men with whom I act will shake England to the center sooner than see this treason established as the law of England. Perish trade and manufacture – perish arts, literature and science – perish palace, throne and altar – if they can only stand upon the dissolution of the marriage tie. (Stephens 16)

It was this acute sense of social alienation that rendered an obscure satire advocating child-murder a subject of intense public controversy.

Anti-New Poor Law Journalism, Slow Violence, and the Marcus Controversy

Far more people became aware of the Marcus pamphlet than ever read the text, for the leaflet received considerable publicity in *The Times* and the *Northern Star*, the two most widely distributed newspapers in Britain in 1838–39, as well as in many smaller papers from across the class spectrum, including the important literary journal *Blackwood's Edinburgh Magazine*. Joseph Rayner Stephens was a key figure in the controversy around the pamphlet. His denunciations of its murderous program before audiences of thousands and especially his controversial assertion of its authorship by the Poor Law Commission kept the tract before the public for several months. The son a Methodist minister, Stephens as a teenage boy witnessed the massacre at Peterloo. After taking the cloth at age twenty, he spent time in Sweden as a missionary. In 1834, his vocal support for Church disestablishment led to his expulsion from Methodism, but he soon found a congregation of fellow ex-Methodists in an independent chapel in

Ashton-under-Lyne, a mill town near Manchester (Knott 96). His fiery sermons, which mixed Christian eschatology with the need for factory reform and the repeal of the New Poor Law, won him a large working-class following and national prominence.[16]

The tension between systemic critique and melodramatic conspiracy played out not only in the Marcus Pamphlet's text but also in its reception history as well.[17] Papers such as the *Liberator* and the *Star* participated in the prank by taking the pamphlet in earnest while also treating it meta-phorically as a reflection of the ideology underwriting the New Poor Law (McDonagh 100). This dual posture was present even in Stephens's allega-tion that the Poor Law Commission wrote and distributed the work. Following Edwin Chadwick's denial of Stephens's charge on behalf of the commission, the preacher insinuated that an assistant commissioner, some other member of the government, or their literary supporter Harriet Martineau could be the author instead. This assertion precipitated a remarkable exchange in *The Times* in which Assistant Commissioner Power insisted that neither he nor his branch of government intended to have the children of the country murdered, offering to resign if the allegation proved true:

> It has been suggested to me, that the imputation which has been so indig-nantly repelled by the Poor Law Commissioners may attach to the persons of the Assistant Commissioners unless also disavowed by them. I beg therefore to state ... that I had no previous knowledge of the existence of the publication which appears to have been referred to by Mr. Stephens, and that I have not assisted in, or countenanced, the circulation of that, or any other, work containing doctrines or opinions in the slightest degree resembling those described by him. Allow me to express my conviction, and upon this fact I willingly stake the retention of the office I hold, that none of my colleagues, the Assistant Commissioners, have taken any part in suggesting or recom-mending the dreadful practices which Mr. Stephens states are about to be adopted for the purpose for checking the population of the country.[18]

Stephens's response was telling. On the one hand, it derides Power's skittish use of euphemism; on the other, it points out his denial is over-literal and fails to perceive the connections between the pamphlet and ongoing reforms:

> That the Poor Law Commissioners should manifest this more than maiden modesty at the casual connexion of the work in question with their names, refusing, even for a moment, to wear the inappropriate honours of this moral wreath, placed by a too officious hand upon their blushing brow – that they should betray a sensitiveness so extreme – an earnestness so solemn – and

indignation so intense, at the bare idea of any association of such sentiments with the principles they profess officially to entertain, and consider themselves bound, in justice to the poor, to "carry out," and that they should be horrified at the premature disclosure to the people of this yet Christian country, of the practical, business-like, matter-of-fact results of the humane system of their idol, Malthus, when brought into full operation, will be a matter of wonder to no one who has followed them in that career of benevolence and mercy which has inspired the perishing thousands of our land with gratitude, and brought the blessings of the widow and the fatherless upon their honoured heads. (*NS* January 19, 1839)

Stephens's letter balances carefully between a renewal of his original charge, insinuating that Power is upset only at the "premature disclosure" of his program, and a shift from a literal accusation that renders the book a crystallization of the values behind the government's policy. Continuing to collapse fact and poetic truth, Stephens repeatedly suggested that the absence of a prosecution of the pamphlet's author signaled the government's support for the writer's principles, a contention made resonant given Stephens's own impending trial and eventual imprisonment for seditious libel as part of the suppression of the Chartist movement in the winter of 1838–39.[19]

Stephens's ambivalent stance was taken up by the radical press, which exploited the pamphlet to attack both the New Poor Law and issues further afield. Henry Vincent's *Western Vindicator* borrowed Marcus's trope of mass poisoning to assert that alcohol was being used to "CARRY OFF THE SURPLUS POPULATION" (January 29, 1839). Three years later, the *National Vindicator* (also edited by Vincent) declared that a "New Marcus" was trying to thin the ranks of the working classes through an emigration scheme. Though government-assisted emigration amounted in the *Vindicator*'s eyes to penal transportation by a different name, the plan was "a decided advance" over the "scientific" proposal of "killing off the young 'uns as fast as they were born," a policy the government found had to be "postponed till the coming of a more enlightened day" (November 27, 1841). The *Northern Liberator*, on the other hand, used the pamphlet to bludgeon Malthus and the Poor Law Commission (December 22, 1838; January 12, 1839; January 26, 1839). The *Liberator* asked "who will take" seriously the commission's denial of having authored the pamphlet, because "they are quite capable of doing this deed, and even worse. It is their daily and hourly occupation to inflict cruelty and oppression upon the helpless and innocent ... WE KNOW THE MEN and we assert it is impossible to libel THEM" (January 18, 1839). At the same time, the

Liberator regarded the tract as tongue-in-cheek, treating it one week an object of horror, the next as hilarious fun. Its macabre humor reached Colbertian heights when it breathlessly reported attending a "Marcusian Lecture" in which the sage appeared before a dignified assembly, including Martineau and Brougham, to demonstrate the painless but fatal effects of carbonic acid on an infant "kindly furnished through the zeal of one of the members of the Society for Promoting the Happiness of the Offspring of the Poor" (March 2, 1839). (See Figure 3.)

If Stephens's and the *Liberator*'s assertions appear the stuff of outlandish cranks, anti-New Poor Law journalism anticipated Marcus's thrust by frequently asserting that the relief provisions established by the government precipitated violence in society. William Cobbett and Richard Oastler predicted an increase in crime resulting from the changed policy, not only because economic insecurity would create more temptation to steal but also because denying the poor their right to relief would undermine property as an institution. More striking in the context of Marcus, the theme of child murder frequently surfaced in the radical and middle-class press. Newspapers were full of graphic accounts of the deaths of infants and their older siblings at their parents' hands (Goc 47–90; McDonagh 97–99). The *Staffordshire Advertiser* even reported an example of a copycat killing whereby a mother murdered her three youngest children after receiving a "great impression" from the accounts of a Nottingham man who strangled his four offspring.[20]

These reports render the parent murderer (usually but not always the mother) surprisingly sympathetic by detailing her difficult material circumstances, her fears for the future, and her devotion to her children (*CWH* June 10, 1837). Evocations of the persistence of maternal affection after the completion of the crime paint portraits of women driven to despair, innocent Medeas who protect their children, if perversely, from the threat of starvation and the workhouse regime (*CWH* June 10, 1837). The gender politics of such stories were more conflicted than those of other polemics against the New Poor Law, which often imagined a masculine movement rescuing distressed femininity. Thus, as we have seen, Stephens promised to "shake England to the center" with "the worthier men with whom I act" to stop the New Poor Law's assault on working-class families (16). In infanticide narratives, on the other hand, female victimhood crosses into nihilistic agency. Dickens draws heavily on such accounts in "The Chimes," which similarly brackets judgment against parent murderers by seeking to understand the circumstances surrounding their actions (McDonagh 116–22). The story's working-class hero Toby

MARCUS UNVEILED.

MARCUS' EXPERIMENT ON THE SLEEPING INFANT.

We may, without arrogance, congratulate ourselves on being selected to convey to the world the first account of the brilliant dawn of a new era in science. That we were so selected we are slow to attribute to any peculiar merits of our own.

Of a love of truth, and, of course, we suppose of modern philosophy, we may fondly boast. To courage and zeal, unconquerable in making that truth known to an ungrateful world, we can lay equal claim. But to our talent for seizing upon the most valuable and striking points of a lengthened, and erudite, and, at times, empassioned philosophical discourse, we are probably indebted for this honour. We now proudly apply ourselves to our unique task, and shall do our best to give our readers a sketch at once vivid, graphic, and picturesque, of one of the most thrilling, astonishing, and enchaining scenes that has occurred in the history of science and of philosophy since the volcanic catastrophe of Pliny, the elder, in the eruption of Mount Vesuvius.

On Thursday, the 7th of February, a day destined to be immortal in the annals of modern philosophy, that celebrated room where the sage Mal-

sandy colour; the eyes a dull leaden blue, inclining to grey; and the neck short. Marcus is pitted with the small pox; and appears to be of the age of fifty. He was plainly dressed in black silk stockings, and inexpressibles;—a flowing white waistcoat, and dark green coat with gilt buttons. Under his neckcloth he displayed a somewhat old fashioned worked shirt, the deep laced wristbands of which were pulled down to his knuckles. His whole look reminded one of an accoucheur of forty years ago; and one eye was remarkable for a slight squint, from which the other was free.

Having laid an old fashioned snuff box on the table before him, he commenced his address by remarking, that the celebrated man who had been his predecessor in that room, had unquestionably laid the foundation stone of the true science of population; but he had not raised such a superstructure as such a foundation merited. Malthus had, undoubtedly, not carried out, to their full extent, the consequences of his own reasoning. He had established his premises; but shrunk from the conclusions; to use the words of the poet—

"Scared by the sound himself had made."

He, Marcus, was there with nerve, to do what that

Figure 3 "A Marcusian lecture." Illustration from the *Northern Liberator*, March 2, 1839.

Veck becomes forlorn after reading a newspaper article about "a woman who had laid her desperate hands not only on her own life but on that of her young child" (Dickens, "Chimes" 136). He turns from suicide, however, when he recognizes that only extremity could drive women to such action: "O, have mercy on me in this hour, if, in my love for her, so young and good, I slandered Nature in the breasts of mothers rendered desperate!" (178).

As part of an extended campaign against the Bastardy Clause of the New Poor Law, which made it more difficult for impoverished mothers to gain financial support from their children's fathers, a September 1839 editorial in *The Times* argues that the law not only has increased the number of infanticides but decreased convictions because juries have become unwilling to condemn desperate women (September 7, 1839). Radical newspapers likewise highlighted the inadequacy of the response of the government's legal apparatus to the outbreak of child murders, but their emphasis differed. They lamented that though inquests might censure the law for contributing to the death of a child, they were incapable of bringing formal charges against the broader political and economic system.[21] As radical accounts of infanticide attempt to understand and mitigate the actions of the parent, they assign responsibility more generally, holding the architects of the New Poor Law accountable for a species of social murder in language that echoes platform oratory calling for Lord Brougham – the act's sponsor in Lords – and other members of the government to be arraigned in the place of parent murderers. At a public dinner in Manchester, John Fielden declared, "I hope to live to see the day when the authors of the New Poor Law will meet with that condign punishment which they deserve."[22] In these narratives, private individuals, not the state, commit acts of violence against themselves and their own, but their actions reveal the inner logic of the government's policy (*Northern Liberator* April 6, August 24, 1839; McDonagh 98). The violence implicit in the law spills into the rest of society even while commissions, boards of guardians, and advocates of retrenchment hide behind bureaucratic cant. Just as the Marcus pamphlet turns the architects of state policy into murderous fiends, the links drawn between crime and the New Poor Law characterize the government's neglect of the poor as an active, positive relationship, translating the denial of the right to support into vigorous, malevolent action.

The perceived relationship between the New Poor Law and increased acts of violence against children built on a long anti-Malthusian tradition in the radical press. Malthus had left himself vulnerable to the charge that he encouraged infanticide (which he explicitly decried), because, starting with the second edition of *An Essay on the Principle of Population* (1803), he advocated the gradual abolition of the poor laws under a plan that would deny support to those born one year after its adoption. Singling out infants as the first casualties of retrenchment struck critics as callous, a concern in no way allayed by Malthus's tone: "With regard to illegitimate children . . . they should on no account whatever be allowed to have any claim to parish assistance . . . The infant is, comparatively speaking, of no value to the society, as others will immediately supply its place" (Malthus 263–64; see also Huzel 26–27; Poynter 157). Given this provocation, it was no large step to claim that Malthus plotted the death of children. In the teens, Cobbett suggested that Malthusians might go beyond their advocacy of moral restraint and begin serving the poor as food or adopting "the measure of Pharaoh, who ordered the midwives to kill all the male children of the Israelites" (*Political Register* November 2, 1816). Wooler's *Black Dwarf* and the *Pioneer* echoed these claims in the 1820s and 1830s, and Cobbett kept up his drumbeat, notably in the 1831 dramatic comedy *Surplus Population*, in which the Malthusian Squire Thimble declares, "Nothing can save the country but plague, pestilence, famine, and sudden death. Government ought to import a ship-load of arsenic" (Cobbett, *Surplus* 270; see also Huzel 171, 178).

In one sense, the repeated assertion of social ills caused by the New Poor Law simply extended this earlier language. At the same time, by engaging with the difficulty of representing harm brought about by indirect and out-of-sight factors, anti-New Poor Law journalism did more than paint the commission as a force seeking to harm the poor. Here, again, Nixon's theory of "slow violence" can illuminate the ways the radical press grappled with questions of causality. Reporting a funeral oration by Henry Vincent, the *National Vindicator* broadens the focus from the government to unseen social causes, asking "How many are murdered by Society of whose deaths we never hear! . . . Society, so far from protecting the weak, aids the government in effecting their murder . . . In England the weak are murdered by toil, taxes, cold and hunger!" (January 22, 1842). In the characteristically titled "Murder of the Poor," the *Northern Liberator* likewise develops a vision of distended social violence to call into question official inquiries that downplay food scarcity as a cause of death. The journal quotes a highly melodramatic address from "the Northern Political Union to the Middle Classes": "Blood is on the land; it falls without a record – hecatombs are yearly sacrificed to famine and a broken heart; the old – the helpless – the unresisting, die, and no man writes their epitaph" (October 5, 1839). The *Liberator*, however, complicates the address's discourse by juxtaposing it with a work identified as *Howard on the Morbid Effects of Deficiency of Food*, which argues that "inadequate nutrition" exacerbates underlying health issues in ways routinely overlooked by governmental inquiries:

> If structural disease of any important organ is found, it is too generally assumed . . . that death has arisen from natural causes. Yet no conclusion can be more fallacious, for persons affected with organic diseases are certainly not less susceptible of the effects of deficiency of food than healthy individuals, and not less likely to perish in consequence. (October 5, 1839)

Synthesizing the political union's idiom of the murder of the innocent with a theory of increased morbidity resulting from malnutrition, this article demonstrates how melodramatic discourse could be stretched to encompass structural issues, chronic conditions, and attritional violence.

The concerns of the Marcus pamphlet found echoes in middle-class social problem fiction as well, another indication of the cultural importance of the radical press. Researching the factory novel *Michael Armstrong*, Frances Trollope accompanied her son Thomas to Stalybridge "to hear the preaching of Stephens, the man who has become the subject of so much newspaper celebrity" (T. Trollope 2:12). Stephens's "newspaper celebrity" apparently left a deep imprint on Trollope; her 1843 novel *Jessie Phillips* tells the story of a poor woman falsely accused of infanticide, whose exoneration calls to mind the radical press's framing of such narratives. Dickens's *Oliver Twist* likewise grapples with the relationship between individual guilt, institutional responsibility, and social blame in ways that resemble accounts in the radical press. Good-intentioned but ineffectual juries appear twice in the novel and count among the few references Dickens makes to the protest movement from which he borrows several motifs.[23] The narrator reports how juries at inquests for children who die on baby-farms (like the one where Oliver is first raised) sometimes "take it into their heads to ask troublesome questions, or the parishioners would rebelliously affix their signatures to a remonstrance: but these impertinences were speedily checked by the evidence of the surgeon, and the testimony of the beadle" (49). Along similar lines, the beadle Bumble complains to Oliver's master that "juries is ineddicated, vulgar, groveling wretches" and fantasizes about breaking their spirit if they ever enter his workhouse (70–71). Bumble is upset because a jury has implicated negligent parish officers in the death by exposure of a "reduced tradesman." Although these episodes are only temporary annoyances to the poor law bureaucracy, Dickens's depiction of the inability of the legal system to hold the keepers of pauper children responsible for the harm they inflict adds a note of ambivalence to the novel's resolution, in which the fence Fagin is condemned for his part in the murder of the prostitute Nancy by another branch of the same courts.

The chapters with Little Dick's death and Fagin's trial appeared in *Bentley's Miscellany* in early 1839, at the height of the controversy surrounding the Marcus pamphlet. Both the sensational essay and Dickens's novel parody the vocabulary of political economy and imagine violence against children as a way to reflect on the nature of social responsibility, the market, and the New Poor Law (Bodenheimer 121). In *Oliver Twist*, Fagin's trial replaces an inquest for Little Dick, whom the reader learns has starved to death in the workhouse at the moment Oliver and his restored family return to rescue him. The narrator passes over Little Dick's death in a single sentence, and the next paragraph (beginning a new chapter) turns from the workhouse setting to evoke the courtroom where Fagin will meet his fate:

> The court was paved, from floor to roof, with human faces. Inquisitive and eager eyes peered from every inch of space. From the rail before the dock, away into the sharpest angle of the smallest corner in the galleries, all looks were fixed upon one man – the Jew. Before him and behind: above, below, on the right and on the left: he seemed to stand surrounded by a firmament, all bright with gleaming eyes. (456)

As several critics note, Fagin's gang functions not as an alternative to the workhouse regime but its extension (D. A. Miller 4–10; Goodlad, *Victorian* 60–68). Speaking the idiom of the poor law reformers, Fagin praises the virtues of industriousness and punishes members of his group for their "misery of idle and lazy habits" (112). Fagin's caricatured anti-Semitic attributes, alongside the narrator's focus on how he profits by recruiting to his gang children and youth who come to London from the provinces, make clear he is an overdetermined figure, meant to embody destructive aspects of a free labor market (Bodenheimer 127). But during Fagin's trial and confinement, the sympathy of the narrator shifts markedly. Even the anti-Semitic stereotypes largely fall away, and Fagin appears a vulnerable individual. The opening scene in the courtroom, partially focalized through Fagin, enlists the paranoia the reader feels on behalf of Oliver – the boy's fear that he will be seen by and returned to Fagin's gang – and transfers that anxiety to the novel's villain.

The end of the novel thus has two movements in tension with each other. On the one hand, Fagin's destruction, which allows Oliver to be integrated into the Maylies' and Brownlows' pastoral, signals that injustice in the broader social realm has been righted. But if the execution sends to the grave the forces that menaced the hero, the reader is left with an image of a distracted and powerless man facing his public death. By highlighting the gap between what Fagin represents and the broken individual who will have to pay, Dickens calls attention to the insufficiency of his last gesture, a worry that the death of his scapegoat, like the earlier inquests, fails to redress the social murder of Little Dick.[24] It should be noted, however, that the fact of Oliver's happy end, and especially the paternalism that under-writes it, crucially distinguishes Dickens's novel from much anti-New Poor Law and Chartist fiction, which refuses to instantiate fictive solutions for individual characters while the underlying social and economic conditions remain unchanged (Breton 24–26).

Books of Social Murder: Malthus and Marcus

From the rash of infanticide stories in the radical press, there is little distance to travel to William Dugdale's edition of the Marcus pamphlet, *The Book of Murder*. Dugdale subtitles his version "A Vade-Mecum [i.e., reference manual] for the Commissioners and Guardians of the New Poor Law" and identifies Marcus as "One of the Three," an open allusion to the Poor Law commissioners, often styled the three tyrants of Somerset House. In the pamphlet, the infuriating indirection of bureaucratic discourse is transformed into direct confrontation, for the parody purports to show poor law reformers at last speaking forthrightly about their criminal intent, demonstrating in the editor's words that "murder hath a tongue, and doth speak with most miraculous organ!" (5). If advocates of retrenchment disguise drastic policies behind respectable rhetoric, Marcus literalizes the popular perception that the Poor Law Amendment Act challenges the poor's right to exist by overturning centuries-old relief practices (Englander 43). But the Marcus pamphlet is not only about melodramatic conspiracy, the murderous designs of a diabolic cadre bent on destroying the virtuous poor. Its stylistic techniques – turgid prose full of theoretical jargon, poker-faced irony, and elaborate descriptions of technical minutia – also suggest efforts of opponents of the New Poor Law to criticize the abstract world of the market and utilitarian philosophy, in which material harm can arise through no individual intent.

Marcus's parody is directed first and foremost against Malthus's theories of overpopulation, a cornerstone for nineteenth-century political economy and social theory and especially the poor law debate.[25] The satire attacks not only Malthus's idea that natural checks subvert efforts to improve the condition of the poor but his discursive procedures as well. Beyond particular arguments, the importance of Malthus's *Essay* stemmed from the way it shifted the ground on which social policy questions were contested. As David Collings describes, Malthus's claim "to possess a pre-political truth about the social body that can resolve political debate" became an important posture in subsequent writing about economics and policy (178). By under-lining how Malthus falsely characterizes "the consequences of human ignor-ance as the act of God," the pamphlet's introduction, like much writing in the radical press, shifts back the ground of argument, contending that Malthus's deterministic theories give ideological support to laws and institu-tions that make inevitable the kind of crises his system predicts (8).

Carlyle's gloss of the pamphlet in his 1839 essay *Chartism* highlights the way Marcus burlesques the language of expert outsider or social engineer, but Carlyle misreads the tract, mistaking satire for serious recommendation:

> Marcus is not a demon author at all: he is a benefactor of the species in his own kind; has looked intensely on the world's woes, from a Benthamee-Malthusian watchtower, under a Heaven dead as iron . . . [He is] the saddest scientific mortal we have ever in this world fallen in with; sadder even than poetic Dante. (*English* 237)

Although Carlyle remains deaf to Marcus's irony, he provides suggestive hints about the pamphlet's style. He complains how Marcus proceeds "with much longwindedness, in a drawling, snuffling, circuitous, extre-mely dull, yet at bottom handfast and positive manner." Carlyle overlooks, however, that it is Marcus's dry tone, oblique formulations, and alternately baroque and schoolmasterly style that most effectively parody the amoral prescriptions of political economy. Furthermore, although Carlyle takes Marcus for "grim earnest," he borrows the heart of the tract's satire, twice suggesting that "arsenic" would serve as a "milder" method of doing away with the poor than the system of laissez-faire, which starves them slowly (*English* 175, 236–37). Published four years later, *Past and Present* also owes a debt to Marcus. It turns to the motif of infanticide and uses melodra-matic language to describe violence the causes of which remain obscure: "And we here, in modern England, exuberant with supply of all kinds, besieged by nothing if it be not by invisible Enchantments, are we reaching that? – How come these things?" (8).

The Book of Murder calls to mind Jonathon Swift's *Modest Proposal*, an essay which must have seemed ready-made for critics of the New Poor Law. The differences between the satires, however, also illuminate Marcus's strategies. In Swift's essay, the speaker's voice fluctuates between righteous indignation (when diagnosing Ireland's problems) and sunny, good-natured optimism (presenting his infanticidal plan). These tonal shifts task the reader with trying to understand the essay's genuine stance while providing a means of doing so (W. Booth 113–14, 117). Marcus's more arid irony affords no such luxury, as his tone remains consistently that of an abstruse, put-upon, but still hopeful academician. To adapt Wayne Booth's characterization of the voice of Swift's speaker as "a kind of mad reasonableness," Marcus seems possessed by mad pedantry (109). While Swift builds "a carefully reasoned and consecutive argument," Marcus's case remains elliptical and digressive (Griffin 104). Even to realize what the essay advocates, the reader must penetrate layers of cryptic jargon: "subjecting nature to discretion . . . facilitated by artful gradations physical and oral" is one reference to infanticide early in the tract (14). Yet for these departures, Marcus, like Swift, attacks a set of beliefs by undermining a discursive mode from within. Marcus inscribes popular grievances in the texture of officialdom's language, revealing how learned essays participate in a system of displaced violence even as they shift political questions to the supposedly neutral ground of demographics and economics. The pamphlet, to borrow Sambudha Sen's telling formulation about Cobbett's satire, destabilizes "the very discursive protocols on which official pronouncements based their legitimacy" (24). In this regard, the tract scripts in advance the controversy around its authorship. Attributing the pamphlet to the Poor Law Commission or its allies, the *Northern Liberator* declared, "Amongst THE GANG, then, the authorship rests. We are well read in 'styles;' and we say that 'Marcus,' whoever he be, has read Jeremy Bentham's works much; and that the style is tinged with that of the Malthusian sage" (January 12, 1839).

Marcus begins by acknowledging Malthus as his forbear and outlining the Malthusian maxim that overpopulation is the main evil confronting society: "every superfluous portion of population is not merely doomed itself to degradation and suffering, but is an agent force, constantly pulling down and deteriorating the order of society to which it immediately belongs, and ultimately, the whole social body" (11). Marcus's rapid syllogisms suggest the fatality of Malthus's system. Once Marcus's assumptions are accepted – and the author passes over them quickly because he takes for granted that they will be – extraordinary conclusions follow. Abstract categories are disaggregated from ethical and social values. Natural disasters, famines, and epidemics are referred to as "casual clearances" and their victims as "superfluous." Malthus's scandalous assertion, which, in Catherine Gallagher's account, links healthy individual bodies with a diseased body politic, is inverted in turn, so that lifeless individuals come to signify and create social well-being (*Body* 36). Infanticide serves as the logical end point of the Malthusian framework, which views the poor as inevitably pitted against one another and considers reproduction a precursor to famine (Collings 167; Himmelfarb 129; Vinokur 171). Yet no matter how extreme his vision, Marcus's logic is always tangential. In a dead-pan style, he gives scrupulous attention to trivial details of his plan: "I pretend not here so much to name all the difficulties ... of the practical operation of the Remedy; of the executive and sanctioning formalities. I will advert only to three of them, and that in a cursory manner" (30). So begins chapter five, titled "Difficulties," but what follows is a rarefied discussion of how population can be maintained at equilibrium given the effect of such variables as the early death of prospective parents. A Benthamite philosopher working out intellectual niceties, Marcus barely acknowledges the possibility of ethical objections. This refusal to articulate a moral framework, instead subordinating morality and politics to an economic analysis that claims objectivity, characterizes the threat of the New Poor Law as much as direct malevolence.

The sense of the absurdity of the rhetoric of officialdom finds its fullest expression in the final pages of the Marcus pamphlet. Like *A Modest Proposal*, which only countenances counterarguments in the essay's closing paragraphs, Marcus takes up anticipated criticism in the last section of the tract. Technocratic justifications of violence with recourse to property rights call to mind Malthus's most notorious passages in which he asserts that "at nature's mighty feast there is no vacant cover" for those "born into a world already possessed" (Malthus 249). Whereas Malthus grasps for the "poetry of deidealization," Marcus prefers the blandly legalistic (Collings 170). Though homicide is a crime because it violates "the right of property in life inherent in the living person himself," an infant's property rights are only imaginary because he has not actually possessed life and will not regret its loss (37–38). Again and again, Marcus brings discordant sets of discourses into uneasy contact, forcing frivolous arguments from biology to solve ethical problems, thereby spoofing Malthus's claims that natural laws trump the values of the social world. Highlighting the physiological pleasures of pregnancy, Marcus rejects the idea that the pains a mother suffers give her a claim on the child (40). The macabre solicitude Marcus shows pregnant women while gleefully advocating the sacrifice of their children contrasts with the Poor Law Commission's hysteria toward the corrupting influence of indigent mothers. The pamphlet concludes with an extended description of how infants suffocated by gas will not feel pain, because they will perceive the absence of air as the failure to excite and develop their capacity to breathe, not as actual deprivation (43).

Radical critics of the New Poor Law took for granted the connection between Malthus's theories and the government's embrace of austerity. The Bastardy Clause and the attack on outdoor relief seemed to embody Malthus's denial of the universal right to life. As Cobbett puts it in *Legacy to Labourers*, Lord Brougham "applauds all the sentiments of Malthus" (130). To the same end, the *Northern Liberator* conflates Malthus's ideas with current developments, quoting the hated author to tar the new regime: "'[the laborer] should be taught that *the laws of nature had doomed him and his family* TO STARVE; that HE *had no claim on society* for the *smallest portion of food* . . . The principle here laid down is that on which the New Poor Law is grounded" (October 19, 1839). Contemporary historians, however, have complicated this simple equation, showing the ways that the Poor Law Commission diverged from Malthus's theories.[26] Malthus hoped to abolish the relief system rather than reform it; his underlying framework also differed from that of the framers of the New Poor Law. The latter partially rejected the idea that a crisis of overpopulation and limited resources menaced the country. Although advocates of retrenchment continually pointed to the "congestion" of pauperism and worried that the nation would soon be overwhelmed by expanding poor rates, they thought surplus population illusory, an artificial creation of flawed institutions that would dissipate once charity and parish relief became "less eligible" than earning a livelihood as an independent laborer (Chadwick 498). The commissioners filled their reports with examples of paupers being "absorbed" into the working population. They frequently compared reformed and unreformed parishes with similar economic and demographic situations to show how normal economic activity, in the absence of interference from the state, could support the laboring population. In this way, the New Poor Law embodied an underlying optimism about the possibilities of an unfettered labor market at odds with Malthus's vision of necessary, periodic disequilibriums between population and resources. In Malthus's writings, even the mechanisms of the market, such as wages rising in response to a shortage of laborers, would create overpopulation and lead to future crises. The Poor Law Commission adopted a more sanguine view, arguing that a market no longer distorted by overgenerous public charity would ameliorate extreme poverty without creating the surplus population characteristic of the Old Poor Law.

In other ways, however, advocates for reform remained within Malthus's framework. They played on Malthusian fears even as they promised to resolve the perceived crisis of overpopulation. Reform propaganda fantasized about the fertility of the poor and obsessively counted the calories paupers consumed. Blue Books propagated salacious accounts of sexual escapades in workhouses and warned of an increase in the number of bastard children (*Extracts* 98, 115; Huzel 43–44). The policy of granting aid in wages, or supplementing a laborer's pay to meet a standard rate set by the parish, was denounced for creating incentives for poor people to marry improvidently (*Extracts* 236–39). One anecdote records a newlywed couple traveling from chapel to poor law board to demand a bed to sleep in on their wedding night (*Extracts* 236). These examples reflected the fear that poor relief compounded a population crisis. To the commissioners, relief created surplus populations not only by encouraging biological reproduction but also by sanctioning attitudes opposed to independent labor, thus spreading the values of pauperism. The commission's reports paid as much attention to shifting community norms as to the rates of children born out of wedlock. Whether surplus population was seen as an economic, cultural, or political question, however, the commission reached similar conclusions as Malthus: efforts to ameliorate the condition of the poor through relief were doomed to fail, because they increased the consumers of the nation's resources without a corresponding increase in the production of wealth. Himmelfarb's rich suggestion that the New Poor Law embodied a Smithian optimism about the market is therefore only partially correct (Himmelfarb 175). Writings in support of the New Poor Law (like those of many supporters of free markets ever since) simultaneously evoke Adam's Smith's providential order and Malthus's lowering catastrophe. In reformers' accounts, government-sponsored charity under the Old Poor Law ensured that paupers would increase until they swallowed the productive resources of the country. But restricting state intervention would activate the workings of rational self-interest and the market would become a realm of social cohesion and individual possibility.

In a way few contemporaries did, the Marcus pamphlet recognized this ambivalent use of Malthus's thought by the Poor Law Commission, pointing up the tension between the commission's claims to act with benevolence to help the laboring classes and its underlying reliance on a fatalistic theory that proclaimed the necessity of stark inequality and the fruitlessness of any ameliorative solution. Between the first and second parts of the pamphlet, Marcus's orientation toward Malthus abruptly changes. Whereas the first section honors Malthus as a precursor, the second lambastes the philosopher's determinism, arguing that a simple plan would solve problems Malthus deemed intractable: "'Accept this misery!' So says to man the first author upon Population: 'accept this capitulation with your destiny'" (36). Malthus himself had tried to soften his system's pessimism by the second edition of his essay, which conceded "moral restraint" might act as a "preventive check" to population. Abstinence from sex offered a virtuous alternative to the immoral preventive checks upon which the first essay focused (contraception, homosexuality, and abortion) as well as to the misery and vice entailed in the positive checks of disease, violence, and starvation (Collings 118; Huzel 18; Winch 37). In the Marcus pamphlet, infanticide – perfectly poised between Malthus's categories of "preventive" and "positive" – replaces the "moral restraint" in which Malthus ultimately placed little confidence.[27] Like the poor law reformers, Marcus proclaims that his system will transcend the cyclical crises of overpopulation and famine: by limiting the size of families, humankind will enter a new realm of freedom. If Malthus undermines Godwin's and Condorcet's utopianism as well as Smith's belief in progress based on the harmony of the interests, Marcus restores both: "if once the thing be rendered possible, the beauty of order and happiness will sufficiently ensure the assent and co-operation of all men. The kindlier feelings, we might say, exist in every breast" (19).

In the final section of the pamphlet, Marcus compares his system to what he deems only partial solutions to the problem of poverty, such as saving banks, which temporarily raise the wealth of workers but ultimately lead to overpopulation (42). This example presents one final difficulty, because it suggests Marcus's plan itself might eventually falter by increasing the nation's prosperity and hence its population. Following Malthus's logic that any improvement sets the pendulum swinging toward higher rates of reproduction, Marcus worries that even a program of infant murder will precipitate overpopulation. As a remedy, Marcus proposes using the increased national wealth his plan will secure to create a memorial where the mothers of infants killed in the name of the public good can go to contemplate their lost children, whose deaths have so augmented the health of society. His fanciful description of the park is worth quoting at length:

> Nevertheless it will be possible to distribute comfort and prosperity in ways that shall not, directly or remotely, tend to the multiplying of men; – nay, more, it will be possible to make of it a premium for those who shall have observed the great rules for limiting numbers, a reward conveying at once moral approbation and material increase of enjoyment ... Let there be a burial ground – call it rather a repository, for the privileged remains of these infants unadmitted into life. Let it have nothing funereal about it, but all that is cheerful and agreeable ... Imagine then a colonnade, closed and gently warmed in winter, fresh in summer, verdant always, yet not expensive in exotics; not too distant for the daily disport of all classes, yet silencing

vulgarity by an amiable and religious formality. Let this be the infants'
paradise; every parturient female will be considered enlarging or embellish-
ing it. This field of fancy will amuse her confinement, and will please by the
reflection that her labour will have been not in vain, and that even posterity
are to be the better for it. (42)

A parody of the Smithian harmony of the interests, subtle commentary on
poor law reform's uneasy yoking of Malthus and more progressive theories,
and an outrageous rehabilitation of the violated ideals of sentimental mother-
hood, the park is meant as the perfect space of political economy: an abstract
utopia where no needs are met. Confronting the hostile, atomized world the
New Poor Law represented and the political exclusion that had brought that
world about was the task set by Chartist fiction. The following two chapters
take up how that fiction and the culture it grew out of imagined alternatives to
middle-class plots of self-making and upward mobility.

PART II

Chartist Fiction and Culture

CHAPTER 3

A Life in Fragments: Thomas Cooper's Chartist Bildungsroman

The improbable course of Thomas Cooper's (1805–92) career – from shoemaker and autodidact to schoolteacher to Methodist circuit rider to Chartist activist to prison poet and finally to lecturer and editor – encapsulates the tensions and contradictions of Victorian self-help and provides a lens into the impetus and contours of the cultural politics of the Chartist movement. Fiercely devoted to projects of self-education, Cooper as an apprentice craftsman in Lincolnshire memorized *Hamlet* and significant portions of *Paradise Lost* and taught himself Latin, French, and some Hebrew. These accomplishments, along with the publication of *The Purgatory of the Suicides*, the epic poem for which he was best known, made Cooper a "laureate of labour" within Chartism and a minor celebrity in the world of middle-class literary reformers. The Christian socialist novelist Charles Kingsley discerned in his commitment to "the pursuit of knowledge under difficulties" an alternative to political militancy and loosely based *Alton Locke*, the story of a disillusioned Chartist hero's spiritual redemption, on Cooper's life. Samuel Smiles rendered Cooper an avatar of a universally available national culture, arguing that his literary achievements placed him in "the same class as Burns, Ebenezer Elliot, Fox, the Norwich weaver-boy, to say nothing of the Arkwrights, Smeatons . . . and the like, all rising out of the labour-class into the class of thinkers and builders-up of English greatness" (244).

But Cooper's tenure in the early 1840s as the self-styled "general" of the "Shakesperean Chartists" of Leicester – at the climax of his Chartist activity – also discloses how mutual improvement could be imbued with a utopian ethos and radical aims.[1] Cooper orchestrated an impressive array of cultural activities for Leicester's depressed stockingers, and these endeavors contributed to Chartism's phenomenal growth in the town, because they tapped a persistent desire for literacy, education, and art – the exclusion from which was felt alongside political and economic grievances. A musical society sang hymns composed by area poets (gathered in the *Shakesperean Chartist Hymn*

Book); a weekly teetotal meeting pledged abstinence until the victory of the Charter; a discussion group read and debated political theory; theatrical performances included a production of *Hamlet* that cast Cooper in the title role, a martyr in the struggle against the usurpation of just authority; and frequent lectures drifted from political themes to literature, the history of England, geology, and phrenology.[2] The connection between education and political struggle was perhaps most clearly indicated by a weekly Sunday school (open to men, women, and children), which named class sections for history's great radicals, from Luther and Milton to William Cobbett and Feargus O'Connor, a typological gesture suggesting that study would nurture the next generation of movement leaders.

In 1843, Cooper was sentenced to two-years' imprisonment in Staffordshire Gaol for polemical speeches made during the "Plug Plot" riots of the previous year, a national strike wave that involved nearly 500,000 workers, had diverse connections to the Chartist movement, and substantially became a political strike for working-class enfranchisement (Jenkins 161–90). In prison, Cooper completed two major works: *The Purgatory of the Suicides* and a two-volume collection of short stories, *Wise Saws and Modern Instances*, both of which Jeremiah How published in 1845 upon Cooper's release.[3] Taken together, these works explore the contradictory nature of education in a politicized context, alternately considering it as a vehicle for individual mobility and a necessary tool for social change. They reflect the irony that Cooper's own tenacious commitment to self-help led inexorably to a radical confrontation with the British state, to defeat, and to imprisonment.

Of Cooper's prison compositions, *The Purgatory of the Suicides* has received more attention from scholars and critics than the short stories, a trend established in Cooper's own time by Samuel Smiles writing in *Howitt's Journal*, as well as reviews in other papers, including the *Northern Star*. In the past decade, chapter-length studies have analyzed Cooper's manipulation of epic form (Kuduk; Kuduk Weiner 66–96) and the role Cooper played as "Labour's Laureate" in shifting Chartist aesthetics from a demotic, oral tradition to a more ornate literary style (Janowitz, *Lyric* 159–94).[4] As Kuduk Weiner persuasively demonstrates, *The Purgatory of the Suicides* recasts the conventions of epic to make Chartism a culminating episode in the history of the nation (Kuduk 166). The poem alternates between a series of visions in which the ghosts of Greek, Roman, and Christian figures debate the progress of democracy and other philosophic questions and exordia at the beginning of each of the work's ten books, which return to the setting of Cooper's cell for more immediate reflections. Although certain critics have faulted the poem's erudition as self-conscious and heavily worn and its Spenserian stanza structure as overwrought, Cooper's classicism highlights the disjunction between an all-encompassing imaginative vision and the impossibility of liberty in contemporary England. The poem's attempt to lay claim to a classical cultural heritage is also consistent with the faith it articulates in the emancipatory power of learning. The final book forecasts that an enlightened people will one day emerge as their own liberators:

> The sinewy artizan, the weaver lean,
> The shrunken stockinger, the miner swarth,
> Read, think, and feel; and in their eyes the sheen
> Of burning thought betokens thy young birth
> Within their souls, blithe Liberty! (X: 16)

The quotidian activity of the autodidact – his homely sacrifice studying late into the night, his reflection at "frame or loom" – becomes in the poem part of a millennial contest between despotism and freedom, a precipitant and augury of the collective transformation Chartism promises.

Cooper's prose work is the formal and thematic negation of his epic. Eschewing the latter's ornate style, *Simple Stories of the Midlands and Elsewhere*, Cooper's preferred title for the collection – which was rejected by the publisher – describes an untransformed world in which the individual is stranded outside history, able to perceive, but not to shape, the conditions that define his life. If scenes of education feature in Cooper's short fiction, any solution learning offers appears provisional and incomplete. The final stories in the second volume began as chapters in a discarded autobiographical novel, which Cooper attempted before joining the Chartist movement. Poverty frustrated the effort, a circumstance to which "London 'Venture; or the Old Story Over Again" alludes. However, biographical details surface throughout the series, and Cooper's stories manipulate the expectations of their earlier form. Repeated accounts of childhood reading, of migration by young adults from the countryside to the city, and of struggles in the metropolis fill the work. *Wise Saws and Modern Instances*, in other words, utilizes constituent plot elements of the *Bildungsroman*. But the segmentation implicit in a series of loosely linked narratives profoundly troubles the conventions of that genre. Certain stories elaborate the interior lives of their characters; others obscure even the protagonist's thoughts and emotions, focusing instead on material circumstances and narrative event. These divisions create unsettling effects, suggesting that an individual's activities and choices in one portion of his life cycle might be connected only tenuously to his ultimate trajectory. From this perspective, *Wise Saws and Modern Instances* revises middle-class narratives of education and self-formation, which, in Franco Moretti's account of the "classical *Bildungsroman*," define a life as meaningful via a double movement in which the protagonist recognizes "the internal connections of individual temporality" while coming to understand his or her experience in an "ever wider or thicker network of external relationships" (*Way* 18). Cooper's stories, on the other hand, highlight disjunctions and fractures in the process of development while describing moments of alienation that do not form part of a progression toward integration. This chapter selects four stories from Cooper's collection that taken together might comprehend a life, but in which childhood learning, adolescent apprenticeship, adult labor, and the experiences of old age seem fragments of an existence that cannot cohere into a single narrative.

The technical inventiveness of the stories in *Wise Saws and Modern Instances* makes the collection a significant, if underappreciated, landmark in Victorian literary history. By refashioning the *Bildungsroman* as a set of discrete tales, Cooper effectively splinters narrative perspective and embraces a dialogic structure. But *Wise Saws* offers more than an experiment in form. The collection gives expression to a working-class revision of the classical *Bildungsroman* narrative, in which the passage to adulthood is defined in terms of independence and self-sufficiency obtained through career success and marriage to an appropriate love object. In Cooper's vision, individuation is not self-realization, but loss. Freedom is negative, the separation from a community, rather than a vista of possibility. And economic activity is no longer typified as the discovery of a vocation which expresses an inner subjectivity but appears rather as an anonymous struggle against blind market forces. The poignancy and power of the collection derive from a lingering sadness about the unavailability of the promise of autonomy, the frustration of the hope that an individual can transform his own life and the world through faithful study and diligent application. But alongside this sense of regret about the limits of individual agency appears a forceful critique of those aspirations in the first place, a critique grounded in Cooper's political radicalism and his participation in the mass politics of the Chartist movement.

Rewriting Spiritual Memoir

The second-to-last piece in the collection is a spiritual biography of a child raised by a female cordwainer, or shoemaker, in rural Lincolnshire. The title of the story, "Dame Deborah Thrumpkinson, and her Orphan

Apprentice Joe," signals how the narrative will turn away from the idea of self-making, for pride of place is given not to the protagonist, but to his adoptive parent, who closely resembles Cooper's own mother as depicted in his 1872 autobiography. Deborah is a charismatic woman, who smokes, supports herself as a master artisan in charge of her deceased husband's business, and exhibits a strong practical intelligence. In the story's first scene, focalized from the widow's perspective, a menacing chimney sweep encourages Joe's mother to apprentice her son to him, an invocation of the atomistic world of *Oliver Twist*, in which the sweep Gamfield tries to profit from child labor. The muscular intervention of Deborah (who threatens to shake the liver from the man's body) rescues the child and suggests that in Cooper's setting self-interest has not entirely displaced communitarian values. When the boy's mother dies, Deborah takes him in, becoming his "godmother and protectress" (2:159). Cooper thus reinterprets the motif of the orphan, the quintessential Victorian figure for the dissolution of traditional social ties. In Bruce Robbins's account, orphanhood mitigates ambivalence about the success of an upwardly mobile protagonist by "removing the tenderness or early attachment that would guarantee a later conflict of loyalties ... We can think of orphanhood as the disguised vestige of an earlier murder. For it shoves out of sight in the past a murderous rejection that was a logical necessity in order for upward mobility to happen" (*Upward* 57–58). By emphasizing the protagonist's status as a beloved foster child, Cooper keeps his debts in full view; the story of Joe's development will be one of relationships, not self-invention.

Detailed accounts of reading structure the narrative, tracing Joe's intellectual and spiritual trajectory from orthodox Christianity to Methodism to free thought. These scenes afford Cooper the opportunity to scrutinize various kinds of writing, and they embed Joe's education in material circumstances and community practices, underlining how reading is at root a social, not solitary, activity. In this way, the story departs from middle-class biographical sketches of working-class learning such as George Craik's famous volume, which emphasizes the exceptional achievements of solitary individuals. Deborah commences the protagonist's scholastic career by teaching him to read: "No benefit she conferred upon him in after-life was more thankfully remembered by him than this, her humane and patient initiation of his infantile understanding into the mystery of the alphabet ... Here her labour ended, for her science extended little further" (2:159–60). Next, the village tailor and radical introduces the boy to *Robinson Crusoe* and *The Pilgrim's Progress*, seminal texts of working-class reading.[5] When the village parson warns Deborah that her charge is reading "secular" writing, Joe learns a lesson about the political nature of literature. Chafing at the subsequent restrictions his mother places on his study, the hero converts to Methodism under the influence of a revival preacher, who interprets and applies the boy's first primer, Holy Scripture (2:165). Finally, literature effects the last conversion of the story, Joe's loss of faith.

If "Dame Deborah" situates development in familial and local networks, Joe's education ultimately threatens these early ties. The story's climax transpires when as a teenager the hero visits the market town of Gainsborough and discovers two texts in a bookstall. As the adolescent thumbs a treatise by an unnamed French philosopher, an event at the market seems to endorse the author's religious skepticism, providing a "running commentary on what [Joe] had hastily read" (2:180). A hawker attracts a crowd by describing a pious tract, in which a jilted young woman returns from the dead to warn her rakish lover of his imminent demise. Though the peddler swears the story occurred in Cornwall within the past month, Joe has just put down a dusty volume that included the same tale. The gullibility of the crowd in accepting the recycled narrative sets Joe on the path toward freethinking, the supernatural story acting as a proxy for religious orthodoxy.

Yet Cooper makes clear that Joe's rejection of his mother's religion is not a simple act of self-making, emphasizing instead the way contingent events influence the protagonist's destiny. The narrator describes the French treatise as

> a medicine, – seemingly hazardous, – but yet, signally well adapted for his disordered mental condition, [which was] opportunely disclosed from the womb of Circumstance, – the great productive source of new thinkings, new resolves, and new courses of action, which, in mockery of ourselves, we so often attribute to our own "will" and "intelligence." (2:172)

If hazard mocks the idea of Joe as the significant agent in his own life, the narrator is reluctant to specify what larger forces shape his story:

> At successive periods of his after-history, Joe attributed this occurrence to the operation of the inevitable laws of necessity, to accident, to permissive Providence: but, without entering into the labyrinth of his progressive trains of thought, or solving the question of the validity of any of his conclusions, – suffice it to say, that the purchase of that book produced a sequel of the most intense interest to the young and undirected inquirer. (2:175)

Christian's mystical journey sits over Cooper's text, suggesting a model for the child's spiritual maturation. "The 'Pilgrim,'" Joe is assured by his tutor

Toby Lackpenny, has "a hidden and all-important meaning, which he must endeavor to discover, and apply to his own spiritual state as he went along" (2:161). But "Dame Deborah" traces Joe's disappointing realization that his actions lack universal meaning, and the refusal to ascribe allegorical significance to the events at the market turns from the example set by Bunyan. As a new Methodist, the protagonist oscillates between paroxysms of doubt and ecstatic faith, but ultimately he fails to understand his life as a battleground where opposed cosmic forces meet, to interpolate himself into Christian's world.

In addition to lacking transcendent meaning, Joe's spiritual biography is destabilized by multiple conversions. Andrew Tate describe how Victorian conversion narratives are predicated on a radical discontinuity of self such that newfound belief allows a "biographical reshaping" in which an individual abandons "the limits of the past . . . to enter a new, more authentic state of selfhood" (15). In Cooper's story, however, the situation is more complicated. Instead of encountering a single transformation that justifies the tale and provides a retroactive interpretive frame, the reader witnesses a series of changes: Joe's discovery of the Bible; his conversion to Methodism; his incipient atheism; and his eventual disillusionment with free thought, as his "self-gratulation [at] thinking diversely from the mass of his fellows" mellows into melancholy loneliness (2:187). In the second passage quoted in the preceding paragraph, the narrator becomes briefly impatient with his own interpretive project and refuses to enter "the labyrinth of [Joe's] progressive trains of thought." This diffident posture toward the hero's development anticipates the story's finale, in which the hero as a young man reflecting on his travels seems to weary of the question of belief:

> And what an altered man was Joe! A residence in the manufacturing districts had unveiled to him a world of misery – contention – competition – avarice – oppression – and suffering – and famine – that he had never supposed to exist! As for his religious opinions they changed, and changed again, – amidst varnished, high-sounding professors of sanctity . . . – and starving thousands, who in the pangs of despair charged God with the authorship of their wretchedness. (2:202–3)

The wrenching sadness of this ending lies in part in its inability to quit the themes of the preceding story. Even as the narrator comes to regard the subjective crises which structure the biography an insufficient frame to the broad, external "world of misery," social suffering continues to be described only by the reflection it casts in Joe's conscience.

Nineteenth-century working-class autobiography frequently secularized
the tradition of spiritual memoir inherited from the Civil War period,
maintaining the improving ethos of religious literature but transferring
the belief in the moral significance of an unprivileged life to worldly
subject matter (Vincent 14–18). "Dame Deborah" on the other hand,
leaves intact the spiritual content of its inherited genre but turns against
its hereditary form, suggesting that neither religious belief nor a generalized meditative sensibility will be sufficient to make sense of an
individual's history.

From Country to City

The significance of "Dame Deborah" is informed by the story's position as
the penultimate piece in Cooper's collection. By the time Joe sets forth to
study the "great book" of man, the reader has encountered four stories
about youths who seek fortune by leaving rural communities. As these
pieces each end in failure, Cooper creates a devastating irony: the reader is
more aware than either protagonist or narrator that Joe's painstaking
preparations for his adult endeavors might be wasted effort. The possibility
of future calamity shadows the child's first steps.

"London 'Venture; or the Old Story Over Again," as its title implies,
reflects on the conventions of narratives about emigration to urban centers,
the literary rite of passage in which adulthood is defined as the ability to
navigate the social space of the metropolis, which is presented as a location of
freedom, possibility, and culture. The story is a striking counterpart to
"Dame Deborah." Whereas the latter gives meticulous attention to the
contradictory influences that shape Joe's inner life, "London 'Venture"
provides little interiority and only the barest of histories for its protagonist,
Ingram Wilson, a young man "who had forsaken an engagement on a
thriving newspaper in an opulent agricultural district, and had 'come up
to London' . . . chiefly through a vivid persuasion, that London was the only
true starting point for 'a man of genius'" (2:42). Offering a rapid account of
Wilson's failure to find employment, the expenditure of his savings, and his
decline into poverty, the story glides over the writer's education and world
view. In fact, economic contingency reduces the hero's intellectual accomplishments to so many irrelevancies, detritus both figurative and literal. By
the end of the third paragraph the aspiring *littérateur* has sold his library:

> His books none of the pawnbrokers would have: they were an article that
> could be turned to no account, if not redeemed. So Ingram pawned his

> watch ... When six months were gone, part of his books were gone likewise; but they were *sold* at comparatively wastepaper price at the second-hand booksellers ... He had ... not half-a-dozen books left that would fetch him the value of another week's subsistence at the book-stalls. (2:44)

Thus stripped of the paraphernalia of intellectual biography, Wilson reflects on scenes at the margin of London's economy: "He was driven to moralise ... as he wandered about from street to street; and he had many a notch in his mind about costermongers riding in front of their dog-carts" (2:44). A variation of Baudelaire's *flâneur*, but lacking the latter's freedom, Wilson suffers not existential but material deprivation. The narrator juxtaposes the hero's education, the evidence for which emerges as fragmentary quotations recalled desultorily, with the degraded circumstances of his present; to complete the previously cited passage, Wilson compares the suffering of Tantalus with that of a costermonger's dog. An ironic and bleak portrait of a "poverty-stricken philosopher," the protagonist is a parodic reflection of Cooper's own celebrated feats of learning, his hard-won classical education proudly on display in *The Purgatory of the Suicides*.[6]

At times "London 'Venture" reads as an outline of its genre. The mentor whom Wilson befriends, a retired half-pay naval officer, can only warn him of the fate of the thousands who come to London, his description criticizing literary convention as well as the hero's decision:

> It is not merely through the persuasion that they shall be able to attain eminence in literature that the young come on adventure to London. A sort of universal romantic idea pervades the minds of most young people with regard to the capital; and, indeed, it is the same almost all over Europe ... All young people imagine, if they can only struggle up to London, they shall make something out in the world. Alas! thousands reach this overgrown hive, merely to starve and die in it; and they are fortunate who can find their way back into the country. (2:51)

Wilson ignores his friend's recommendation to seek employment as a copyist in the British Museum, anxiously insisting on the originality of his project. But the narrator describes his protagonist in stereotyped language, treating the youth from the provinces as the cliché he is. The phrases that pervade the literary marketplace bleed into the narrator's idiom. When Wilson finds work, it is with "a small publisher, who had commenced a small periodical, and wanted a young man of genius, and all that, to edit it" (2:55). This development is described in a perfunctory manner: "Ingram went to work in that quarter: – helped to bring out four weekly numbers of the periodical – received one sovereign for his month's labour – and then the thing was stopped, like hundreds of similar ephemera, because 'it did not sell'" (2:55). Mooting the emotional significance of the protagonist's failure, the narrator makes clear that no matter Wilson's particular efforts, the paper is doomed by an overcrowded publishing market. The very typicality of Wilson's story, the fact that hundreds of young writers produce "similar ephemera," is what ensures defeat. Trapped in an individualism he does not recognize as structured in advance, Wilson sinks into the atomized crowds the narrator repeatedly evokes ("He began to feel himself in a desert, even amidst thousands") (2:43).

Cooper depicts Wilson's ambition as derivative, originating in an unspecified body of literature about feats of genius in the metropolis. This corpus is bitterly criticized by the failure of Wilson's plans: the hero sells his library to sustain a poor facsimile of the life the volumes describe. Wilson also fails to discover an embodied model for the career he wants to pursue. The elderly officer who tries to rescue the protagonist occupies the position of a benefactor but cannot fill out the role. Having abandoned the ambitions of his youth, the old soldier "embarrasses" his finances by sharing a nightly dinner with the protagonist, who eventually declines to accept even this support when he learns of the pinched circumstances of his friend. When a "literary M.P." from Wilson's home district refuses the writer assistance, the Balzacian project of social mapping is left stillborn, the doors to polite society closed. The youth from the hinterlands can find no route to maturity in the city, and Cooper's genre outline remains a hollow contour.

A Dialogic *Bildungsroman*

Of Cooper's formal experiments, the most dramatic and successful occur in "'Merrie England' – No More!" This story revisits a central tableau of the novel of development, the moment a youth departs the stultifying existence of his village or town. Set pieces in continental and British fiction, such scenes typify the "transcendental homelessness" Lukács ascribes to the nineteenth-century novel, "the inadequacy that is due to the soul's being wider and larger than the destinies which life has to offer it" (*Theory* 112). Cooper's innovation is profound: from a chronicle of this event, he displaces and silences the putative protagonist, recounting the attempted departure of a young man from Leicester, but from the perspective of the community he seeks to leave behind, which is instantiated in a confusing welter of voices. Delineating the cost of the celebration of exceptional individuals and a definition of maturity predicated on the rupture of early relationships, "'Merrie England' – No More!" is a *Bildungsroman* in search of its protagonist.

Relentlessly dialogic, the story relies on direct discourse, often unattributed, to advance its action (Kuduk 174). It begins with "a group of five or six destitute-looking men" conversing around a Roman milestone marker. The unemployed laborers discuss the prospects of Tom, a youth who has gone missing the previous day. One member of the group tries to reassure the boy's father John about his son's fate: "He can't be worse off than he would have been at home, let him be where he will. What's the use of grieving about him? He was tired of pining at home, no doubt, and has gone to try if he can't mend his luck. You'll hear of him again, soon, from some quarter" (1:202). Though others chime in to defend Tom's right to "mend his luck," dismissing John's worries that he might become a thief or be transported, the substantive action of the group will be to frustrate Tom's effort to leave. Judged from these characters' standards, Tom's action is particularly troubling; the youth has decided to enlist in the army, a decision all recognize will endanger him and harm the community, making him at once a "sold slave" and active agent of oppression.

The climax of the story occurs when someone spies the "pale, tall stripling" with a recruiting sergeant, whom a crowd surrounds:

> The father ran toward the soldier and his child; and every group on the Coal-hill was speedily in motion when they saw and heard the father endeavouring to drag off the lad from the soldier, who seized the arm of his prize, and endeavoured to detain him. An increasing crowd soon hemmed in the party, – a great tumult arose. (1:206)

What follows is a near riot against military recruitment, the only representation in *Wise Saws* of a direct confrontation between "the people" and state authority. Though the mass implicitly threatens violence, it also articulates a coherent position. The crowd invokes communal responsibility and derides the sergeant's celebration of individual constancy, reminding Tom that soldiers lack personal freedom. Here again, the story criticizes fantasies of self-making, illustrating how seemingly decisive assertions of personal agency might involve individuals in even more restrictive structures. As Tom has not yet accepted payment, the mob eventually forces the recruiting officer to release him. The discussion that follows analyzes Tom's actions in terms of their political implications. One member of the chorus is proud that "the bloody rascals have not had two Leicester recruits these two years" (1:208). Another wonders if the refusal of "all workingmen ... to go for soldiers" would be a viable option to win political rights, a strategy advocated by certain Chartists under the slogan "No Vote, no Musket!" A third doubts the efficacy of such a plan because of the "Johnny Raws ready to list in the farming districts." Though the commotion is about Tom, the story remains decentered. Indeed, the youth's only contribution to the dialogue – and his only speech in the whole story – is to explain how the recruiter had "been at me this three months; but I never yielded to this morning, when I felt almost pined to death and he made me have some breakfast with him, – but he'll not get hold of me again!" (1:207–8).

The narrator's refusal to arbitrate between competing perspectives during the group's discussion measures the distance between *Wise Saws* and didactic fiction. The story itself points up this difference in an angry conversation between John's family and another destitute couple about a tract left by "a piety-monger" at the couple's home. The characters object equally to the tract's quiescent politics, its condescending tone, and its simplistic language. The narrator warns Christian missionaries that they "must expect to find the deepest subjects of theology, and government, and political economy, taken up [by the urban poor] with a subtlety that would often puzzle a graduate of Oxford or Cambridge" (1:216). This polemical claim has already been demonstrated by the conversation about Tom's prospects, which ranged lazily over such topics as the underlying similarity between environmental determinism in Owenite socialism and the role of providence in Calvinist theology. But unlike secular sermons in didactic fiction, such as Harriet Martineau's *Illustrations of Political Economy*, the dialogue in "'Merrie England' – No More!" remains casual, idiomatic, and liable to break off at a moment's notice.

Although the crowd's victory demonstrates the potential power of collective activity, "'Merrie England' – No More!" retains the critical, pessimistic outlook of Cooper's collection, which, like so much Chartist fiction, anatomizes present economic, social, and political crises, rather than imagining their resolution. After all, the effect of the crowd is only to cancel the displaced hero's single action and return him to a barely sustainable existence in depressed Leicester. But "'Merrie England' – No More!" also negates a narrative structure that articulates freedom and self-realization in terms of an individual's escape from community life. The story's evocative close makes explicit the violence Cooper does to received form:

> There is no "tale" to finish about John or his lad, or Jem and his wife. They went on starving, – begging, – receiving threats of imprisonment, – tried the

"Bastile" for a few weeks, – came out and had a little work, – starved again; and they are still going the same miserable round, like thousands in "merrie England." What are your thoughts, reader? (1:217)

Considering the finality common to the endings of much Victorian fiction, Cooper's conclusion startles. Jagged phrases degenerate into a rote list, epitomizing the disjointed, repetitive cycle of lives ruled by economic contingency and political repression. A distant and alienated overview, in which characters merge back into an unnamed mass, explicitly refuses the conventions of closure – "there is no tale to finish" – in favor of the evocation of what Lauren Berlant terms "crisis ordinariness," an endemic, ongoing condition that can be interrupted, if at all, only by the engagement of the reader addressed in the final sentence.[7]

The Impossibility of Nostalgia

In addition to stories about childhood and young adulthood, Cooper's collection features several narratives in which elderly characters play prominent parts. These figures are often portrayed as remnants of an earlier time, castaways whose habits and attitudes modern society renders incomprehensible. "Last Days of an Old Sailor, or, 'Butter your Shirt; Sing Tantara-Bobus, Make Shift!'" is explicitly about nostalgia, but its setting, the same desiccated landscape of "'Merrie England' – No More!" transposed to a more rural locale, swallows the best efforts of the title character to conjure the experiences of youth or recover a bygone spirit of possibility. The central episode of "Last Days" is a reunion between the retired sailor Matthew Hardcastle and his former shipmate Paul Perkins. Meeting accidently on a street in Gainsborough, they retire to Matthew's cramped quarters, which are decorated with portraits of the "gallant faces" of admirals as well as curios from the South Seas, "odd fragments of a sailor's fondness" (1:165). The comrades share grog, recollect old stories, and honor "the bravery and virtues of the dead" (1:166). Late at night the conversation turns political. Paul points out how wars have saddled the nation with exorbitant taxes, linking militarism with the country's endemic poverty and, implicitly, with his and his friend's straitened circumstances. He describes, moreover, "this setting of poor Englishmen on to fight poor foreigners [as] only a deep scheme, on the part of the rich abroad and the rich at home, to keep the poor down" (1:171). Even as "Last Days" delivers this message, however, the sailors' dialogue reflects on the limits of didacticism as a formal strategy for politically engaged literature. The argument breaks down "with a hearty laugh on both sides" when Matthew wearies of serious talk and exclaims, "Blow me! . . . if I can see the use of all your palaver" (1:174–75).

The story, however, is political in another sense. In staging the alcohol-soaked retelling of the sailors' hijinks, Cooper takes aim at a triumphalist vision of the national past promoted by the "naval novelists" Frederick Marryat and Frederick Chamier and the many hack writers who imitated their tales of adventure at sea. Marryat's novels, some of the most widely read fiction of the 1830s (Parascandola 10), synthesized antiradical politics with episodes about the exploits of junior naval officers during the Napoleonic Wars. *Mr Midshipman Easy*, for example, describes a young Briton sympathetic to Jacobin principles who joins the navy because he believes that "although the whole earth has been so nefariously divided among the few . . . the waters at least are the property of all," only to be cured of this mad philosophy by naval experience and discipline (38). Of all Cooper's reinterpretations of popular genres, "Last Days" is the most easily traceable, for it slips in and out of Marryat's own idiom.

The second half of the story's title "Butter your Shirt; Sing Tantara-Bobus, Make Shift!" refers to a pet phrase Matthew invokes as a kind of charm to ward off ill fortune. The reader learns its origin when Paul tells a waitress from the local public house an anecdote which is itself a send-up of naval fiction:

> It was during a severe engagement with the Dutchmen that Mat and I were ordered to the main-top, – but hardly had we reached it, when a shot from the enemy cut our mainmast fairly in two, and hurled us both on to the enemy's deck, in the midst of more than a hundred heavy-bottomed Dutchmen! To dream of fighting against such odds, ma'am, you'll understand was, of course, out of all question; so we quietly walked our bodies, to the tune of "donner and blitzen," down below, to become close prisoners under hatches . . . The only fellow-prisoners we found in the hole where they crammed us were cheeses and queer big tubs . . . Clambering up some o' these huge tubs at one end of the hole, we both lost footing together, and fell head over heels into the midst of something that was remarkably soft; and there we struggled, and struggled hard, too, – but 'twas all in vain, we could not flounder out, – and so were content to remain closed on all sides up to the neck, with just our heads bobbing out, and gasping for breath . . . At length the Dutchman was taken; and . . . Mat and I were discovered up to the neck in one of the Dutchmen's big butter firkins. (1:167–68)

In this escapade and its condensation into a talismanic saying, Cooper captures essential components of Marryat's prose. First, there is a comedy made up of cataclysmic circumstances, a lightheartedness authorized by the hero's ability to land on his feet. The narrator of *Mr Midshipman Easy* exclaims, "There certainly is a peculiar providence in favour of midshipmen . . . always in the greatest danger, but always escaping from it" (142). Matthew's increasingly frustrating reiteration of his formula (which he uses to counter Paul's exposition about the troubled state of the country) calls to mind Marryat's happy-go-lucky characters and mocks the repetition at the heart of a potentially infinite series of picaresque adventures.

Finally, "Last Days" reinterprets Marryat's valuation of personal bravery. In Patrick Brantlinger's description, the characters in Marryat's novels exhibit "a spirit of 'altruistic suicide.'" While praising individual endeavor, the novels lose sight of individuality in an onrushing staccato of action: "the hero is he who can swim with the tide of events, which threatens at every moment to overwhelm mere selfhood" (Brantlinger, *Rule* 50). The selfhood of Cooper's characters is similarly cast in doubt, but with a key difference. Instead of becoming transcendent figures subsumed into heroic activity, they are reduced to passive objects, social atoms at the mercy of unseen political and economic forces, a passivity foreshadowed even in youth by the sailor's ludicrous confinement. Matthew is shocked to learn that a sailor who served with him at Trafalgar recently died in a poorhouse, though "he used to rush into a gun-boat like a ravenous wolf." (1:173). Nor can he anticipate that a similar fate awaits himself: "In proportion to Matthew becoming helpless, people were wearied with waiting upon him; and, disgraceful to relate! the old warrior-seaman was, at length, neglected till his aged body swarmed with filth" (1:175). The story's irony extends beyond the discrepancy between Matthew's providentially touched life in the navy and his experiences on shore, for the old sailor has unwittingly helped author his own fate, though in a circuitous fashion he cannot recognize. His poverty, Cooper suggests, stems from the burdens placed on the civilian economy by the wars he fought in, while his neglect by the community is a result of the diffusion of an individualistic ideology that can only advise the downtrodden to "butter your shirt; sing tantara-bobus, make shift!"

A spiritual biography in which the hero on setting out from the "City of Destruction" doubts the meaning of his pilgrimage; a truncated *Künstlerroman* that refuses to sublimate youthful ambition into an aesthetic project, insisting that literature is a problem of markets and surplus labor as well as of creativity and genius; an archetypal scene from the novel of development retold to displace the protagonist from his position at the center of the narrative; and a naval picaresque that remains landlocked in order to hold in one frame the larks of young adulthood and the limits of old age – Cooper's hybrid stories indicate a more innovative relationship between Chartist authors and popular and middle-class forms than is recognized by typologies that consider the radical oeuvre in terms solely of melodrama or popular romance.[8] Stories of exclusion, displacement, and loss, Cooper's fiction is at war with itself, at once deeply reliant on the patterns of the most individualistic of genres, but sharply critical of those same genres' conventions. The longing for self-realization, the dream of autonomy and individual purpose, becomes so many traps for Cooper's heroes. But the desire that animates and propels the collection remains starkly individuated. There is little sense of the possibility of social trans-formation in these prison-house compositions. The task of integrating the aspiration for personal improvement and the dream of a more just society fell to Cooper's epic and to other Chartist authors, such as William Lovett, John Collins and Peter McDouall, writing on education, working-class culture, and collective forms of self-help, a body of literature that will be considered in the next chapter.

CHAPTER 4

Questions from Workers Who Read: Education and Self-Formation in Chartist Print Culture and Elizabeth Gaskell's Mary Barton

Although the Chartist organ the *Northern Star* was a careful observer of literary developments, especially concerning social problem fiction, it failed to comment on the publication of Elizabeth Gaskell's *Mary Barton*, today the best-known novel to treat Chartism. This popular and controversial work about the consequences of an assassination committed by a disillusioned activist slipped by the radical paper unnoticed in the tumult of the fall of 1848. But the *Star* was not as unfamiliar with *Mary Barton* as its initial silence suggests. Two years later, when the paper reviewed *The Moorland Cottage*, it praised Gaskell's earlier book as "a powerful and truthful exposition of the evils inherent in the factory system," adding that "the graphic manner in which the writer placed before the public the domestic, moral, and social results of factory life, brought down from the upholders of the factory system many sneers at her political economy and her sentimentalism; but none denied the unquestionable genius and superior discrimination of character and motives which pervaded the work" (December 28, 1850).

How could the *Star* endorse *Mary Barton* with such unstinting enthusiasm given the obvious ambivalence – even occasional hostility – Gaskell's work shows toward working-class political organization? One answer may be found in the significant but unrecognized ground shared by Gaskell and the Chartists. Beyond the novel's sometimes heterodox political economy, the confluence between Gaskell's and Chartists' thinking is most apparent in the novel's representation of education, which adapts and is shaped by a variety of radical ideas. Even as Gaskell utilizes common novelistic conceits about individual ambition, upward mobility, and interclass reconciliation, *Mary Barton* echoes the radical suggestion that education might provide a space of independence and resiliency for the working classes rather than act as the means of winning their assent to the established political and economic order. Gaskell's negotiation with Chartist theories of learning demonstrates the complexity of ideas about self-improvement in the 1840s, suggesting a political malleability that made certain versions of self-help compatible with challenges to the status quo and others with more conservative ideologies.

Contemporary critics have often found *Mary Barton* exceptional among the social problem narratives of the 1830s and 1840s for the respect it shows working-class characters, for its grounding in personal observation, and for its avoidance of the reifying language of sociology and political economy. At the same time, *Mary Barton*, like other Condition of England novels, has been faulted for turning away from its political story line and imagining narrowly individualistic solutions – marriage, emigration, education, and upward mobility – to the problems of inequality, poverty, and unemployment. The circumstances of the novel's composition and the nature of Gaskell's source material have underwritten both sets of interpretations, often advanced by the same critics. In these accounts, Gaskell's philanthropic work at the Cross Street Chapel, where her husband William was a minister, as well as her study of the reports of the Unitarian Domestic Mission Society, taught her that moral failings could not alone account for the degrading and dangerous conditions that afflicted the city's working classes. The Unitarian Mission sought to inculcate the values of rational individualism – thrift, self-help, sobriety, and diligence – in the population to which it ministered. But its reports, which provided factual material for the most harrowing scenes in Gaskell's novel, documented over and again that squalor and penury visited the virtuous as well as the improvident.[1] Shot through with these same contradictory attitudes toward liberalism, *Mary Barton* advances a significant challenge to the ideology that considers poverty a question of individual responsibility (Seed 19). But its narrative resolution, which permits the most respectable characters' escape from the Mancunian underworld, undermines this critique. Affiliating *Mary Barton* with a liberal philanthropy deeply divided about its own project helps explain why Gaskell's narrator oscillates between sympathy and judgment, hopefulness and despair.

Despite the insights this reading provides, its emphasis on the power dynamic implicit in philanthropy has tended to disguise other vectors of contact between Gaskell and the working classes and to obscure the extent to which she herself might have learned from working-class culture and politics, an interpretive irony given how concerned *Mary Barton*, like *North and South*, is to model interclass dialogue and show middle-class characters profiting from the exchange.[2] In general, critics of social problem fiction have more successfully contextualized the orthodox views of novelists than accounted for authors' moments of heterodoxy (Guy 33–36).

Nevertheless, Gaskell's thinking about education shared affinities with ideas widely disseminated in radical print culture in the 1840s, especially in Chartist periodicals, ideas which were taken up by a circle of left-wing Unitarians to which she was closely connected. Gaskell's work is an important example of the way working-class writing helped mold a genre of middle-class fiction seemingly premised on the cultural gulf separating rich and poor. Like the Chartists, Gaskell was skeptical of ideas that treated knowledge as instrumental, a view propagated by several utilitarian thinkers, including prominent Manchester dissenters. By contrast, *Mary Barton* celebrates the wide-ranging, eclectic, and humanistic obtainments of her working-class characters even as the narrator occasionally repeats the Carlylean idea of the inarticulacy of the poor. The recognition of the diversity of working-class accomplishments and the belief that middle-class observers would not be able to perceive them because of their narrow, class-bound view of culture are further similarities linking *Mary Barton* and Chartist writing. Most significantly, Gaskell's novel departs from many middle-class depictions of self-help that stress the achievements of exceptional individuals who surmount personal obstacles through feats of diligent application. Gaskell documents instead how learning is socially embedded by evoking patterns of mutual support that include the sharing of a wide variety of knowledge. In this light, education and improvement seem less thoroughly individualistic in *Mary Barton* than much criticism assumes. Appreciating the connections between Gaskell and the world of Chartism renders more coherent the perceived antimonies in Gaskell's politics between the public and private spheres as between individual and collective forms of action. Indeed, Gaskell recognizes, though more ambivalently than the Chartists, that working-class learning might lead to political radicalization, not quiescence.

Beyond Philanthropy: Gaskell and the Chartists

How did a minister's wife at a prestigious chapel, which numbered bankers, factory owners, aldermen, and MPs in its congregation, come into contact with Chartist ideas? I would suggest three modes of contact, the most direct of which was Gaskell's and her husband's philanthropic work, which embodied the widespread Unitarian commitment to education as a means of individual and social reform (Watts 162–97). As is well known, Gaskell married at the age of twenty-one, leaving behind her maternal aunt and rural childhood home to join her new husband in Manchester. Her career as an author began gradually as she balanced writing with child rearing and active participation in the Cross Street Chapel. Gaskell's involvement included performing home visits for the Unitarian Domestic Mission and teaching in the chapel's Sunday school, which provided free instruction for the children of the poor (Brill 32–33; Thiele 266). William served as secretary of the Domestic Mission, held English classes at the Mechanics' Institute and Working Men's College, and helped manage these and other organizations. Gaskell's letters leave ample evidence of the impression encounters in these contexts made upon her. In 1838, she wrote to Mary Howitt about her husband's lectures on "The Poets and Poetry of Humble Life," presented in Miles Platting, "the very poorest district of Manchester":

> You cannot think how well they have been attended, or how interested people have seemed. And the day before yesterday two deputations of respectable-looking men waited on him to ask him to repeat those lectures in two different parts of the town. He is going on with four more in the winter, and meanwhile we are *picking up* all the "Poets of Humble Life" we can think of. (*Letters* 33; see also Brill 46–47)

Perhaps remembering these earnest visitors, Gaskell makes inverted home visits (i.e., by workers, not middle-class philanthropists) a structuring device in *Mary Barton*. Whereas laborers call on the mill owner Carson, he remains ignorant of his workers' domestic lives.

No matter the paternalistic assumptions common in educational philanthropy, instructing Manchester operatives in the 1840s and 1850s involved dialogue with a politicized population, potentially exposing the teacher to radical notions. At the end of the 1850s, the Chartist W. E. Adams enrolled in the Rev. Gaskell's Mechanics' Institute course. In Adams's telling, the participatory nature of William's class was striking. Students prepared themes to be read and discussed in class, including one by Adams on "the republican idea." Though we cannot know the contents of this essay or the discussion that ensued, Adams had become notorious a short time earlier when the publisher of his 1858 tract *Tyrannicide*, which justified attempts on Napoleon III's life, was prosecuted during a scare about violence by radical émigrés. Years later, Adams recollected the class appreciatively: "Our literary evenings under Mr. Gaskell were ambrosial evenings indeed" (390–91).

Even home visits to the impoverished might involve more equal communication than is usually assumed (Elliot 135–36; Siegel 4–6). Elizabeth's friend Susanna Winkworth's description of encounters with a family of Chartists evokes the give and take of argument, not the imposition of ideas from on high, even if Winkworth had expected passive acquiescence: "[Having] despaired of getting them to listen to reason ... quite to my surprise last Tuesday, the man began to praise me and said that if all the middle classes took as great an interest in the working classes as I did, they could soon come to an understanding with each other and get their grievances redressed" (qtd. in Uglow 163). In *North and South*, Gaskell captures the fraught nature of philanthropic visits, depicting conversations arising in that context as dynamic and surprisingly egalitarian (Elliot 150–53). Indeed, the protagonist Margaret Hale, an ex-minister's daughter, learns more from the working-class family she visits than what she imparts, including the crucial insight that they resent her presumption in assuming the role of benevolent visitor. When Margaret counsels Christian resignation to the family's daughter, the father reproaches her: "Now, I'll not have my wench preached to. She's bad enough as it is, with her dreams and her methodee fancies" (91). In *The Life of Charlotte Brontë*, Gaskell records similar skepticism toward charitable visits among the Reverend Brontë's Haworth parishioners. Their dislike of being "preached to," like Nicholas Higgins's in *North and South*, made them appreciate Charlotte's father's desultory attitude toward house calls: "many of the Yorkshiremen would object to the system of parochial visiting; their surly independence would revolt from the idea of any one having a right, from his office, to inquire into their condition, to counsel, or to admonish them" (42).

Gaskell's own letters tell us little about the circumstances of her conversations with the Manchester poor, but they say more about the influence they exerted on her than the uplift she provided. Indeed, a local Chartist helped inspire *Mary Barton*: "Nobody and nothing was real ... in M. Barton, but the character of John Barton; the circumstances are different, but the character and some of the speeches, are exactly of a poor man I know" (*Letters* 82). And: "'John Barton' was the original title of the book. Round the character of John Barton all the others formed themselves; he was my hero, *the* person with whom all my sympathies went, with whom I tried to identify myself at the time, because I believed from personal observation that such men were not uncommon" (*Letters* 74).[3]

A second way that Gaskell would have been exposed to Chartist ideas is through contact with a circle of radical Unitarians. Understanding Gaskell's relationship with this network contextualizes the novel's sharp questioning of common middle-class assumptions about the market, the nature of poverty, and the rights of the poor. While Unitarianism as a whole was defined by a reforming zeal that led members of the religion to play important roles in the abolition of slavery and Catholic emancipation, a left wing of the church was committed to causes more radical still, including Chartism at home and republicanism in Europe.[4] More skeptical about orthodox political economy than many coreligionists, this group centered on W. J. Fox's South Place Chapel in London and included in the forties John Humphreys Parry and the young lawyers William Shaen and James Stansfeld. Reforming authors and publishers who were not themselves Unitarians also moved in Fox's orbit, including Douglas Jerrold, Eliza Cook, and William and Mary Howitt. Not only did the radical Unitarians endorse the Chartists' program, they actively participated in radical organizations, especially William Lovett's National Association in London.[5] This Chartist organization emphasized education, self-improvement, peace, and women's rights, issues all resonant with the commitments of Fox's circle. In lectures at the association's National Hall in Gate Street, Holborn, William Shaen discussed phrenology and Sabbath legislation, James Stansfeld talked about educational reform and the need for teachers' colleges, and W. J. Fox spoke regularly on "literary and other topics," including giving a lecture on Cooper's *Purgatory of the Suicides* (Cooper, *Life* 280–81). John Humphreys Parry edited the *National Association Gazette*, to which Fox contributed.

Nor did influence flow only from middle-class philanthropists to working-class protégés. A treatise on education by William Lovett and John Collins, titled *Chartism*, so impressed William Shaen that he wrote his sister of plans to use it as the basis for the curriculum of the Unitarian Sunday school he superintended (Gleadle 76). Lovett contributed articles about Chartist activities to Howitt's *People's Journal*, and he acted as the magazine's publisher after debates about religion prompted him to resign his position as secretary of the National Association.[6] Jerrold, Fox, and Howitt were enthusiastic enough about the writings of the "laureate of labour" Thomas Cooper to contribute letters to a soiree honoring him (*NS* May 9, 1846). The *Chartist Circular*, in turn, excerpted Howitt's writings on the colonies while the *Northern Star* reprinted poetry from *Howitt's Journal* and included a poem that puffed the journal's namesake in the form of an acrostic: "Wonder no more! ye Tyrant men, / If 'gainst you wields the patriot's pen" (*NS* October 24, 1846). In a biographical sketch of W. J. Fox (accompanied by a half-page portrait), *Reynolds's Political Instructor* remarked that "in political opinions [he] is a Chartist – and something more" (December 3, 1849). Chartists and Unitarians also came together in two organizations dedicated to promoting the cause of republican émigrés, Lovett's People's League and the People's International League (Cooper, *Life* 300; Finn 71–72; Prothero 225). In sum, Fox's circle celebrated working-class literature and culture, supported Chartism as a movement seeking political and intellectual liberation, and actively built alliances with working-class radicals.[7]

Although Gaskell was not directly involved in this London-based and mostly masculine network, outspoken and politically minded women connected to it were some of her most intimate friends. In late 1847, when Gaskell was completing the novel, she hosted Annie Shaen, William's sister, in Manchester, and visited the Shaen family at Crix, near Colchester, where she talked politics for several hours. Gaskell also knew William Shaen through Emily Winkworth, who lived with the Gaskells while being tutored by the Rev. Gaskell. Winkworth, herself a committed reformer, became engaged to the radical lawyer over Christmas 1848. The Howitts, longtime advocates of abolition and peace, were especially important in the context of *Mary Barton*. Correspondents from the 1830s, the Gaskells met the pair – to both parties' surprise – while vacationing in Heidelberg in 1841, where they spent some time touring together. The Howitts published Gaskell's first works in their journal, helped place *Mary Barton* at Chapman and Hall's, and offered advice on the contract. Although Gaskell only met Eliza Fox, W. J. Fox's bohemian daughter, on a trip to London after the publication of *Mary Barton*, the two artists formed a close and lifelong friendship.[8] Gaskell's affectionate letters to "Tottie" brim with enthusiasm for radical émigrés and describe the author's divided sense of her personality, including "one of my mes ... a true Christian – (only people call her socialist and communist)," language echoed in *North and South* when the protagonist is teasingly described as "a democrat, a red republican, a member of the Peace Society, a socialist" (*Letters* 86, 108; *North* 323).

Finally, Gaskell might have encountered Chartist ideas by reading Chartist periodicals, a possibility curiously neglected in the critical literature, though *Mary Barton* depicts them as an important part of working-class culture. They were, moreover, easily available in Manchester, which was a longtime center of radical publishing and the headquarters of the National Chartist Association until 1844. Scholars are familiar with Gaskell's friendship with Samuel Bamford, the author of *Passages in the Life of a Radical*, for whom she acquired from Tennyson a signed copy of his works.[9] Although the aging Bamford grew increasingly conservative in the 1840s, the *Northern Star* excerpted his memoir (August 8, 1840). Abel Heywood, a printer, proprietor of an important radical bookstore, and member of the national executive committee of the National Charter Association, was also a "freelance Unitarian" and visited the Cross Street

Chapel.[10] At Heywood's shop and many others, Gaskell would have found *McDouall's Chartist and Republican Journal*, the *National Association Gazette*, and the *Northern Star*, which evidence from *Mary Barton* strongly suggests she read.[11] Not only was she aware of the *Star*'s frequently communal consumption (she shows Barton reading and discussing a copy of it borrowed from a public house), but she also accurately represents the kind of material found in it from the mid-1840s when it became increasingly concerned with the factory question (John Barton reads an editorial supporting "short time" – legislation limiting the workweek). More speculatively, the publicity around the lottery for the Chartist land plan might have inspired the novel's use of the figure of the lottery to describe the conditions of the poor and to designate John Barton the secret assassin of Henry Carson. In a drawing conducted in Manchester on Easter Monday, 1846, the Chartist Co-operative Land Society chose at random from among its thousands of members the "fustian landlords" who would receive homes on the first of five farms purchased with society funds.[12] Finally, Gaskell had a good grasp of the canon of authors promoted by the radical press. In Jem Wilson's climactic confrontation with Henry Carson, she has the artisan intone a line of Burns, whose poetry Chartist journals ubiquitously reprinted. The narrator later speculates that the operatives representing the strike know their Carlyle, who was also widely excerpted. These instances of working-class reading will be examined in detail later in this chapter.

Philanthropy among a politicized population, diverse connections with the radical Unitarians, and exposure to working-class print culture all suggest Gaskell's access to Chartist ideas, especially on themes central to *Mary Barton*, including education, self-help, and mutual improvement. The following two sections explore a range of Chartist viewpoints by examining Lovett and Collins's *Chartism* as well as writing in *McDouall's Chartist and Republican Journal*, a weekly published in the Manchester region in 1841 and 1842. Although there is no evidence Gaskell was familiar with this specific material, together they describe the radical milieus with which she came into contact. The unstamped, one-penny *McDouall's* was the type of writing John Barton's original would have read – like the *Star* it was full of the kind of polemics about the factory system which Gaskell's hero quotes to his daughter's suitor. But *McDouall's* was also preoccupied with questions surrounding self-help and literacy. It reported contemporary debates about education and aimed to rebut middle-class stereotypes that justified a monopoly on political privilege with claims of working-class ignorance. Its diverse contents themselves integrated a curriculum about political rights with a more general program of learning. Lovett and

Collins's *Chartism*, which, as already mentioned, was influential among the radical Unitarians, called for a national system of schools while suggesting a theory of pedagogy that would transform classrooms into laboratories of local democracy. *Chartism* and *McDouall's* show a foundation in radical thought for Gaskell's celebration of the liberatory potential of learning and the novel's vision of self-help based on collective activity and mutual support.

"A System of Education Which Puts Their Useful Knowledge to Shame"

As much as the now more commonly discussed issues of poverty, inequality, and social strife, a debate about education defined the Condition of England question in the 1830s and 1840s. Education was seen as a sign of division between the nations of rich and poor but also held out as a potential remedy for that divide. Whig politicians and middle-class philanthropists hoped Mechanics' Institutes and a newly decorous penny press would foster a culture of respectability and invest the working classes in the emerging industrial order by promoting the virtues of thrift, sobriety, and diligence. But working-class activists sharply contested these limited notions of improvement. They challenged what should count as education, the context in which instruction should occur, and the ultimate goal of learning. Considering the fierceness of the debate, the term "education" poses terminological problems, a difficulty Dickens complained of in 1848 when he noted that "that ill-used word might, quite as reasonably, be employed to express a teapot" (*Amusements* 93–94). Risking imprecision, I use "education" in the expansive sense favored by the radical press, in which any formal or informal efforts by individuals or groups to acquire or share knowledge counted as education.[13] Stressing the informal nature of working-class learning countered middle-class educational reformers who emphasized the poor's ignorance and proposed schools as a means to mitigate the negative influence families and communities supposedly exerted on children. The radical press defined education as inherently political, true education the movement toward liberation (Harrison xiv; Haywood, *Revolution* 24). In this light, the press saw itself as a crucial agent of learning, the proper educator of the people. This notion animated the Chartist press throughout the 1840s. Indeed, as Richard Altick points out, the London Working Man's Association (LWMA), which drafted the text of the Charter in 1837, was founded to assist in paying the fines of editors and printers convicted in the "war of the unstamped," the campaign that

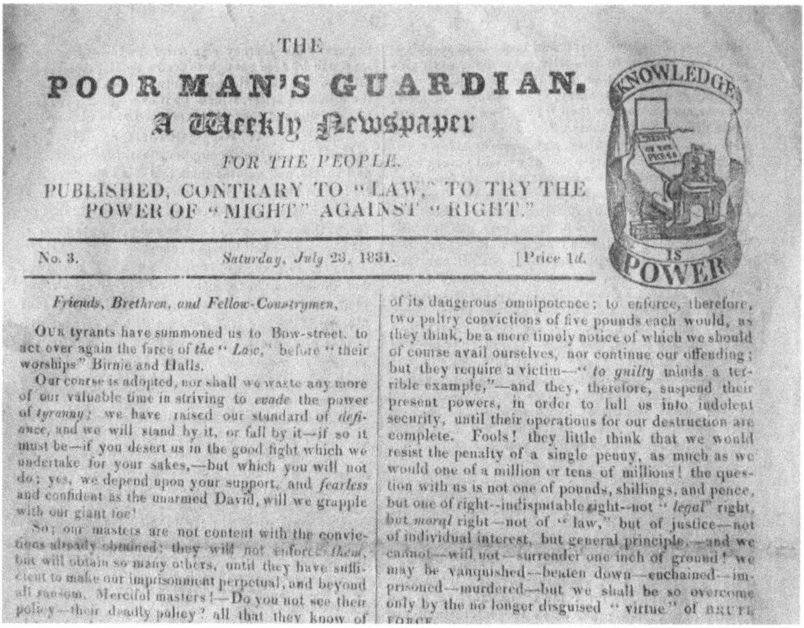

THE

POOR MAN'S GUARDIAN.

A Weekly Newspaper

FOR THE PEOPLE.

PUBLISHED, CONTRARY TO "LAW," TO TRY THE POWER OF "MIGHT" AGAINST "RIGHT."

KNOWLEDGE IS POWER

No. 3. *Saturday, July* 23, 1831. [Price 1*d.*

Friends, Brethren, and Fellow-Countrymen,

OUR tyrants have summoned us to Bow-street, to act over again the farce of *the* "*Law*," before "their worships" Birnie and Halls.

Our course is adopted, nor shall we waste any more of our valuable time in striving to *evade* the power of *tyranny*: we have raised our standard of *defiance*, and we will stand by it, or fall by it—if so it must be—if you desert us in the good fight which we undertake for your sakes,—but which you will not do; yes, we depend upon your support, and *fearless* and confident as the unarmed David, will we grapple with our giant foe!

So; our masters are not content with the convictions already obtained; they will not enforce *them*, but will obtain so many others, until they have sufficient to make our imprisonment perpetual, and beyond all ransom. Merciful masters!—Do you not see their policy—their deadly policy? all that they know of of its dangerous omnipotence; to enforce, therefore, two paltry convictions of five pounds each would, as they think, be a mere timely notice of which we should of course avail ourselves, nor continue our offending; but they require a victim—"*to guilty* minds a terrible example,"—and they, therefore, suspend their present powers, in order to lull us into indolent security, until their operations for our destruction are complete. Fools! they little think that we would resist the penalty of a single penny, as much as we would one of a million or tens of millions! the question with us is not one of pounds, shillings, and pence, but one of right--indisputable right--not "*legal*" right, but *moral* right—not of "law," but of justice—not of individual interest, but general principle,—and we cannot—will not—surrender one inch of ground! we may be vanquished--beaten down—enchained—imprisoned—murdered—but we shall be so overcome only by the no longer disguised "virtue" of BRUTE FORCE.

Figure 4 The masthead of *The Poor Man's Guardian*, July 23, 1831, with its assertive "counter-stamp."

aimed to repeal the "taxes on knowledge." As the LWMA expanded its agenda, a free press remained an intrinsic element of the radical program and a part of a vision of the democratic potential of education (Altick 341). Reflecting these ideas, the *Poor Man's Guardian*'s motto proclaimed "Knowledge is Power." In a self-authorizing gesture, which prefigured the change the paper claimed "knowledge" would bring about, the *Guardian* defiantly replaced the red government stamp with a black one showing a printing press (see Figure 4).

The career of William Lovett embodies the central role of education in radical culture. A cabinet maker, longtime activist, and founder of the LWMA, Lovett had himself undertaken an arduous program of study, reading widely on politics, language, and religion before becoming involved in various mutual improvement endeavors including the London Mechanics' Institute and a radical discussion group called the Liberals.[14] His pamphlet, *Chartism, a New Organization of the People* (1840), written with John Collins, was the most extensive treatment of educational theory the Chartist movement produced. Attentive to the material basis of knowledge, *Chartism* grapples with the constraints placed on learning by poverty and labor, challenges typically glossed over in middle-class publications celebrating working-class achievement, including George Craik's popular *The Pursuit of Knowledge under Difficulties*, despite the latter's title.

Lovett and Collins composed *Chartism* during their twelve-month confinement in Warwick Gaol on a conviction for seditious libel resulting from the incendiary Manifesto of Ulterior Measures of the Chartist convention of 1839. This document urged that should Parliament reject the Chartist petition for suffrage reform, the people respond with consumer boycotts, the withdrawal of currency from banks, and a "national holiday" or general strike. Though conditions in the prison were harsh and Lovett suffered poor health for years from bronchial and intestinal issues arising there, the confinement provided the working-class activists enforced leisure and a room of their own, allowing them, paradoxically, the freedom to write:

> Being in a prison, we have found some difficulty in proceeding as far as we have, for the want of such books and facilities as our liberty would have enabled us to obtain; but, in all probability, if we were in the enjoyment of that inestimable blessing, the pressing demands of our families, and the active pursuits of life, would have so far engaged our attention, as to have prevented us from ever writing anything on the subject. (Lovett and Collins 110)

Lovett and Collins argue that the Chartist rank and file should direct their efforts to creating a network of democratic educational institutions. They suggest that if the million plus signatories of the first Chartist petition would subscribe a small sum to a central body, the association could maintain a vast range of services: 710 circulating libraries, a press that would distribute 20,000 tracts per week, and 80 district halls. The halls would offer evening programs for adult instruction and amusement and free nondenominational schools for children of all ages and both sexes (25–26). Relying on the cultural wealth indigenous to the class, these schools would include small museums "furnished . . . by the collections and contributions of the members" (54).[15] Finally, the organization would award prizes for essays that advance an enlightened pedagogy, a topic badly in need of development: "Though much has been written on the subject of education, we think that very little of it has been to the purpose" (54).

Chartism itself lays out a set of pedagogical practices designed to bring radical ideals into the classroom. In the words of the *Northern Star*, the pamphlet creates "a system of education which puts their useful knowledge to shame" (October 17, 1840; qtd. in Simon 244). Lovett and Collins continually stress the importance of democratic structures and cooperative learning. Adult education should focus on discussion groups and reading circles, forums that depend on the involvement of all. The education of children should eschew lecture and recitation in order to foster active and creative participation. In this regard, *Chartism* departs from most educational initiatives in the 1830s, the heyday of the monitorial system, which emphasized discipline and rote learning (Simon 262). A faith in cooperative self-help contrasts starkly with the educational establishment, which often saw the school's role in educating the poor as "redeeming the mischief wrought in generations of a vicious parentage" (Kay-Shuttleworth, "First" 295). Even Owenite educational theory considered students raw material rather than equal participants in a shared endeavor (Simon 265).[16] Lovett and Collins, on the other hand, denigrate the idea of students passively acquiring a set body of knowledge, emphasizing instead the realization of the student's own capacities: "'EDUCATION,' to be useful, such as will tend to make wise and worthy members of the community, must comprise *the judicious development and training of* ALL *the human faculties*, and not, as is generally supposed, the mere teaching of '*reading, writing, and arithmetic*'" (67). To this end, the authors suggest a model curriculum which includes literature, music, science, dance, and the appreciation of nature. Recognizing individual enjoyment as both a goal of education and a spur to greater learning, they keep in view which activities children will find the most stimulating. A measure of Lovett and Collins's heterodoxy is their emphasis on play for the youngest classes, for whom time outside the classroom should be paramount, because in "the air and exercise of the play-ground . . . all their faculties are in full activity" (38).

Lovett and Collins's approach to discipline represents another departure from contemporary norms. A pedagogy of the oppressed, the essay stresses that power inequalities between teacher and student reflect and perpetuate wider injustice. Lovett and Collins condemn corporal punishment for its brutality as well as the way it promotes a "slavish subjection" (41). Along similar lines, they insist that schools welcome girls while opening the National Association's membership to women. Linking political oppression with subjugation in the domestic sphere, the authors argue that women's exploitation demands their political education (61). Although *Chartism* goes on to justify female education in terms of women's duties within the family (63), feminism featured prominently in Lovett's National Association, separating it from most Chartist organizations. Subtitled "The Rights of Man and the Rights of Woman," the association's *Gazette* published essays on political and educational inequality by Harriet Martineau, Mary Wollstonecraft, and W. J. Fox (January 8, January 15, and February 12, 1842).

Upon founding the National Association in March 1841, William Lovett promoted it as an alternative to Fergus O'Connor's National Charter Association, an effort that led to a schism within Chartism and resulted in Lovett's marginalization from the mainstream movement. Although the National Hall became an important center in London, Lovett's organization had little reach outside the capital, and its membership never exceeded five hundred. Nevertheless, as Kathyrn Gleadle has shown, alliances forged between middle- and working-class radicals under the auspices of the National Association made significant contributions to the early feminist movement (77–81). The association also helped nurture Chartism's cultural front. Although the O'Connorite *Star* condemned the organization as a source of disunity and lampooned "Knowledge Chartism" as a poor substitute for political organizing, it did not reject Lovett and Collins's educational program in itself (April 17, 1841).[17] Indeed, as local organizations followed the *Star*'s lead by passing resolutions censuring the "New Move" to a politics emphasizing religion, learning, or temperance, they pursued the direction Lovett and Collins advocated (Epstein, "Some" 235–40). The early 1840s witnessed an explosion of working-class cultural and educational activity as radicals organized schools, churches, temperance societies, and libraries; conducted camp revivals; and went on lecture tours. Poetry readings, political tea parties, and soirees took their place as fixtures of Chartist life beside "monster" rallies, branch meetings, and debates. By 1840, Chartist adult classes had spread throughout much of the country, including a dense network of study groups in Manchester and Salford (Chase, *Chartism* 144–45; Pickering, *Chartism* 45; Silver 82). The Halifax Chartists established a reading room in their party headquarters; in Leeds a debating society aimed "to cultivate that talent which, for want of opportunities, has lain as long dead" (*Northern Star* March 27, 1841). O'Connor praised as "a great intellectual hotbed" an enormous Manchester hall outfitted with a Sunday school, library, and massive amphitheater, which became a center of Mancunian culture (qtd. in Simon 244). The Sunday school served "seventy children of various ages," whose parents, according to the *Star*, were delighted at the "arrangements made for carrying out an effective system of education, so much at variance with the generally adopted plan of conducting Sunday schools" (June 24, 1843). The rich working-class tradition of politicized education, then, would have been available to Gaskell in writing *Mary Barton*.

"Useful Knowledge" Is Power? The *Penny Magazine* and the Chartist Press

Lovett and Collins's tract appeared in a publishing market saturated with educational material for the poor, which presented a variety of perspectives on the significance of working-class learning. By the 1840s, the stamp duty had been substantially lowered but penalties for violating it made more draconian. At the same time, a new kind of periodical literature strenuously competed with the radical press for working-class audiences. Useful knowledge magazines such as the *Penny Magazine* and *Chamber's Edinburgh Journal* were part of a concerted effort by middle-class philanthropists to shape working-class reading by providing a politically safe alternative to the unstamped press.[18] The Society for the Diffusion of Useful Knowledge (SDUK), which published the *Penny Magazine* as well as inspirational biographies and tracts on a variety of subjects, embodied this program. A postscript in the opening number of the SDUK's magazine imagines how orthodox reading will replace illicit material: "We are called upon to pour into [the channel opened by other papers] clear waters from the pure and healthy springs of knowledge" (March 1, 1832). Thirty years later, the *Penny Magazine*'s publisher recalled his paper's effort to supersede "contraband newspapers ... dangerous in principle and coarse in language" (Knight 2:180).

A weekly miscellany superintended by Charles Knight, the *Penny Magazine* achieved the extraordinary circulation of 200,000 in 1832, its popularity attributable to several factors including its innovative use of woodcut illustrations. Sales declined to 40,000 by the mid-1840s, but even this figure matched the *Northern Star* at its height.[19] The *Magazine* included frequent articles on industrial processes and other technical and scientific topics, making it a literary analog to the Mechanics' Institutes movement, which the SDUK also supported. But it also touched "rapidly and lightly upon many subjects" (Knight 2:182). Travel writing, anthropology, historical essays, pieces on the colonies, and sketches of famous writers all appeared regularly. Though imaginative literature was putatively excluded, the *Magazine* skirted its own prohibition with ample quasi-fictional material, including summaries of the *Canterbury Tales* and epic poetry about El Cid throughout 1841. Aligning learning with entertainment rather than politics was characteristic. The paper's first issue outlines a theory of leisure reading that makes this bias clear:

> There are a very great number of persons who can spare half an hour for the reading of a newspaper, who are sometimes disinclined to open a book. For these we shall endeavour to prepare a useful and entertaining Weekly Magazine, that may be taken up and laid down without requiring any considerable effort; and that may tend to fix the mind upon calmer, and, it may be, purer subjects of thought than the violence of party discussion, or the stimulating details of crime and suffering. (March 31, 1831)

While eschewing "the violence of party discussion," the *Magazine* never-theless sought out controversial topics but treated them in a non-polem-ical, putatively objective manner. Essays on industrial technology and on the colonies were presented absent the debates about emigration, colonial rule, and the "factory question." The *Magazine* avoided advocating laissez-faire, but its illustrations and enthusiastic prose promoted the benefits of industrialization (Bennett 132). In this way, the *Penny Magazine* taught its audience to read apolitically what was divisive elsewhere while articulating a vision of politics as a sphere separable from the broad and diverse realms of knowledge it claimed as its subject.

The framework of useful knowledge similarly bleached controversy out of historical writing. Once again, the *Magazine* attempted to recontextualize material common in the radical press. Histories of the Norman Conquest and of seizures of monastic properties during the Protestant Reformation, both leitmotifs in radical discourse, featured prominently, but the optimistic tone of travel writing bled into this contentious subject matter. In the inaugural issue, for instance, an article recounts improvements in Charing Cross brought about by "clearing away decaying houses" (March 31, 1831). Rather than justifying the clearances, the paper offers a history of the neighborhood, including the sixteenth-century seizure of a Catholic hospital, a precedent for the latter-day urban renewal. The off-handed presentation of interesting but decontextualized facts converts the privatization of Church property and the destruction of charity for the poor into a piece of local color. Accounts of the Norman Conquest likewise promote a touristic sensi-bility: "Whatever our individual opinions may be as to the object or necessity of any particular battle, or even of battle and warfare more generally, who can look upon the scene of a 'well-foughten field' with-out finding themselves drawn, as it were, into its influences" (January 16, 1841).

If radical topics reemerged as a kind of political unconscious in the *Penny Magazine*, the conventions of useful knowledge influenced Chartist periodicals as well. Struggling over a mutually conditioning field, radical papers responded to the useful knowledge fad by incorporating writing on an ever-widening range of subjects. They gave substantial space to science, biography, history, and literature. This new emphasis characterized the whole range of genres that defined Chartist print culture, evidencing a commitment to a democratic and communitarian variant of the improvement ethic. News weeklies like the *Northern Star* and the *Northern Liberator* offered reports on the reading groups, Sunday schools, and lectures that were part of the fabric of daily life in Chartist branches. Literary magazines such as the *Labourer* included improving stories with democratic twists. Educational journals such as the *Chartist Circular* and the *National Association Gazette* presented extended series on a range of subjects, including educational experiments in other countries and debates concerning national education. And radical miscellanies like the *Western Vindicator* and *McDouall's Chartist and Republican Journal* offered an alternative to useful knowledge publications such as the *Penny Magazine*.

A member of the "uneasy classes," Peter Murray McDouall was a Scottish doctor who became politicized as a young man when he conducted a survey on the living conditions of the working classes in Bury, where he had established his first medical practice in the mid-1830s.[20] The poverty, sickness, and degradation he discovered amid Lancashire operatives made him a vehement critic of the abuses of the factory system and, eventually, a Chartist.[21] At the Chartist convention of 1839, McDouall represented the left wing by urging the right of the people to bear arms and advocating a general strike in the event of Parliament rejecting the National Petition, the position that provided grounds for Lovett and Collins's imprisonment. Arrested himself in 1839, McDouall was described by the attorney general as "one of those individuals who made it his business to travel over various parts of the kingdom, for the purpose of inflaming the minds of the lower orders against the existing laws" (McDouall 3). After serving a year sentence in Chester Castle, McDouall suffered chronic financial difficulties, supporting himself, like a number of activists, through paid lecturing and journalism. He wore a black suit and "long cape" when he spoke in public, a costume that gave him, according to a fellow Chartist, "the appearance of a hero of melodrama," a persona that seemed only to increase his popularity (W. E. Adams 212). His journal, based seven miles east of Manchester in Ashton, combined articles on republicanism and the factory system with topics further afield from radical politics. Over a run of twenty-seven issues, it printed travel stories from the American West; a history of the corruption of the Roman Republic; a series of letters by William Aitken on hydrostatics (the subject also of an SDUK tract); jokes and humorous anecdotes; reflections on the French revolution; fables set in Turkey and Arabia; and weekly mathematical problems, to which solutions appeared in subsequent numbers.

But *McDouall's* also distinguished itself from useful knowledge magazines, criticizing middle-class educational provision in ways common to radical papers. The Chartists asserted that useful knowledge, despite its apolitical pretensions, promoted a politics in favor of the status quo (Johnson 78–79). The poet John Watkins wrote in the *Star*: "We ask for the Charter, and they give us a reading-made-easy" (February 11, 1843). For Lovett and Collins, philanthropic educational initiatives were "[training] up the youthful mind of our country to be submissive admirers of 'things as they are'" (vi). In *McDouall's*, Bronterre O'Brien directly addressed Lord Brougham, the founder of the SDUK, complaining he encourages education that would not "*enable* [the people] to resist their oppressors, but one that would teach them to be '*content with their station*,' that is to say, to remain passive paupers and slaves. You would teach them the difference between a camel and a dromedary, but you would not teach them the difference between the natural and the artificial rights of property" (July 3, 1841).

While deriding the irrelevance of useful knowledge material, the Chartist press liked to point out that learning of any stripe could be put to purposes beyond the schoolmaster's intent. Following an outbreak of incendiarism, the *Star* made hay with Brougham's claim that his educational initiatives had mitigated the Luddite spirit of the working classes. The *Star* suggested instead that arsonists might have acquired their expertise in the middle-class's own papers: "Have the *Penny Magazine, Chambers' Journal* . . . and the *Saturday Magazine* existed for nothing [?] Has all the stuff we have heard about fire-balls, and air-guns, and mixtures for spontaneous combustion, been all humbug?" (January 25, 1845). The insurrectionary-minded McDouall likewise played on assumptions about the pacifying nature of education by urging that adult classes be used as a front for seditious organizing: "To be safe from the fangs of the law, subdivide your association into reading clubs of any number . . . and, above all, *profess only to aim at the spread of knowledge*" (19). This suggestion had a distinguished pedigree in British radicalism, a tradition with which Gaskell would have been acquainted from reading Bamford's *Passages in the Life of a Radical*. Bamford recounts how during the governmental repression of

1816, "open meeting thus being suspended, secret ones ensued; they were originated at Manchester and assembled under various pretexts. Sometimes they were 'benefit societies;' sometimes 'botanical meetings' . . . but their real purpose divulged only to the initiated, was to carry into effect the night attack on Manchester" (40).[22] In the context of discussions of adult schooling in *McDouall's*, criticism of the pap provided in Brougham's "blue-coat slave training nurseries," the advice for forming Chartist cells disguised as reading circles, though intended literally, becomes pointed satire (July 3, 1841). The image of armed study groups turns on its head the notion of self-improvement through education as politically safe.

As Chartist papers mercilessly criticized useful knowledge publications, they also attempted to meet the demand for interest in the genre. Though readers of *McDouall's* failed to learn the "difference between a camel and a dromedary," they did encounter a biography of Archimedes and a pair of articles on panther attacks in America. Even McDouall's polemical "Lectures on the Factory System" and his articles on Roman and British history might be found, slightly modified, in the *Penny Magazine*. In the Chartist press, however, a radical sensibility could frame the most ordinary content. Thus William Aitken introduces his series on hydrostatics in a utopian key: the study of science will dispel "the unhallowed influence [of] a venal and hypocritical priesthood" and conduct "the world at last to freedom" (*McDouall's* April 10, 1841). The *Western Vindicator*, which featured a science column with articles on sound, astronomy, the atmosphere, and anatomy, distinguished its program from the offerings in Mechanics' Institutes, where the curriculum is like the play "'Hamlet' with the part of Hamlet left out . . . The earth, the air, the heavens are explored . . . but MAN – his nature and relations, the action of the external world upon him, his condition in society, his physical constitution – are neglected, or only honoured with an occasional and trifling notice" (December 7, 1839).

Substantial differences also separated Chartist biographical and historical writing from those genres in useful knowledge papers. Chartist history underlined the contemporary significance of events, situating current crises in entrenched institutions. The *National Association Gazette* prefaces a history of taxation with the promise that the admittedly tedious subject will place its readers "in a better condition to understand the financial proceedings of the government, and to exercise a greater check upon its extravagance" (January 15, 1842). Accounts of revolutionary movements were also common, including the French

Revolution and the plebeian revolts in ancient Rome, the latter in Ernest Jones's *Notes to the People*. Needless to say, the *Penny Magazine* ignored these inflammatory topics. Along similar lines, Chartist biography promoted a pantheon of revolutionary heroes. William Tell, Toussaint L'Ouverture, and Percy Shelley feature in the *Chartist Circular* and George Washington and the orators of the French Revolution in the *National Association Gazette*. Emphasizing the role of "the great mass of population in history," these profiles present their subjects as exemplary leaders of various movements rather than accomplished individuals (Robert Hall 236).

A dramatic example of the merger of educational and editorial functions occurs in a series in the *Northern Star* on state trials, which began while John Frost and the other leaders of the Chartist rising in Newport awaited trial for treason during the winter of 1839–40 and continued during their hearings. Three prisoners were ultimately condemned, but a massive petition campaign succeeded in saving their lives. As the country anticipated the trials, the *Star* educated its readers on British justice by recounting Anne Boleyn's execution by Henry VIII, prosecutions for witchcraft in the time of Queen Elizabeth, and the scapegoating of Catholics in the aftermath of Guy Fawkes.[23] In the place of the SDUK's "Whig history" in which superstition had been superseded by technology, reason, and liberal values, the *Star* shows irrationality and tyranny continuing into the present. Announcing that one issue's proceeds will go to the defense fund of the Welsh prisoners, and claiming that its series aims to rectify the "willful errors [of] bigoted historians," the paper casts education and resistance as synonymous acts (December 14, December 21, 1839).

Beyond mocking the content of useful knowledge or reimagining the genre in ways that configured learning as a terrain of ideological struggle, the Chartist press challenged a fundamental assumption of philanthropic educational initiatives: the supposed ignorance of the working classes. A series of articles in *McDouall's* critical of knowledge tests as a voter qualification defend the breadth of working-class learning by arguing that all labor involves intellectual activity. McDouall suggests, for instance, that demonstrating the use of a plow or loom might replace a contemplated literacy test as an appropriate assessment for the right to vote: "if you make the tools of labour the standard … then the least of the labourers would make a fool of the greatest of your aristocrats" (May 8, 1841). A later essay propounds a materialist vision of learning in which reading contains within it several types of craft labor, anticipating Michael Denning's "labor theory of culture" with a labor theory of knowledge (Denning 91–94). In a polemical inversion of middle-class educational schemes, McDouall insists that the working classes educate the rest of society, not vice versa:

> [Any journalist who advocates a knowledge test] forgets, in his boundless ignorance, that the trades have to supply him with the very materials, without which manufactured articles he would be as illiterate as a Hottentot. The paper-makers supply one medium of communicative instruction; the type founders another; the compositors a third; the book-binders a fourth, and so on through every department of education. (August 28, 1841)

Images of weavers reduced to rags or colliers suffering exposure were a standard part of the radical idiom of the 1830s and 1840s. Carlyle's *Past and Present*, Marx's *Paris Manuscripts*, and the radical press used such images to embody poetically the labor theory of value, asserting that the fruits of labor had been lost to those who perform it.[24] McDouall's innovation is to link this language to learning, to suggest that literacy has been torn from the class which creates it, because the workers who enable widespread reading are themselves barred from the enjoyment of knowledge (August 28, 1841). The question of the poor's claim on the world of culture and the implication of their exclusion from that world also animates Gaskell's novel, which like Chartist writing is attentive to the political stakes and material circumstances of education.

Collective Agency and Domestic Melodrama in *Mary Barton*

Raymond Williams vexed appreciation of *Mary Barton* in *Culture and Society* helped establish the novel's place in the modern canon while delineating a set of terms through which it is still commonly discussed. For Williams, *Mary Barton* begins a powerful reconstruction of working-class life but ends a disappointing fable, in which the intractable problems of the two nations are displaced onto a fantasized space beyond the borders of England (*Culture* 99–103). Following the murder of a Manchester mill owner, the Chartist John Barton all but disappears from the novel as the narrator turns her attention to private life and Mary's efforts to exonerate the falsely accused Jem Wilson. Williams's framework of a retreat from collective action to domestic regeneration, as well as his idea that this divide is marked formally with Gaskell's initial realism giving over to melodrama, remains influential. Catherine Gallagher stresses that self-contradictory ideological imperatives, rather than Gaskell's artistic failings or the limits of the social problem genre, lead to the novel's formal divisions (*Industrial*

33–34; see also Stone 176). She describes how the competing conventions of tragedy (associated with John Barton's struggle) and melodrama (affiliated with the domestic plot around his daughter) shape the narrative (*Industrial* 72–77).[25] Deirdre d'Albertis likewise focuses on political tensions in Gaskell's thought, arguing that her novels "ricochet almost uncontrollably between orthodoxy and radicalism ... even as each is ultimately resolved through an uncomfortable or, alternatively, an excessive resort to conservative ideologies of the State, Christianity, science, or the home" (13). Chris Vanden Bossche suggests that by turning to Jem's upward mobility story Gaskell excludes forms of working-class agency other than individual improvement (173–74). Ruth Yeazell and Josephine Guy broaden Williams's framework to other works of social problem fiction. Yeazell contends that industrial novels commonly substitute a "conventional heroine" for a male figure associated with political violence, thereby shifting "from the public history of class conflict to the private story of an individual courtship" (243). Guy goes further, arguing that the individual was the horizon of possibility for all "mid-Victorian writers (of whatever political persuasion)" and that every social issue was inevitably "addressed by recommending changes in *individual behaviours*" (10).

These interpretations identify an important structure in social problem fiction, one undeniably present in *Mary Barton* with its dramatic shift from Chartist hero to his apolitical daughter. Considering Gaskell's engagement with the Chartist program of education and self-improvement, however, complicates the dichotomies upon which much of this criticism rests. Education in the 1840s was politically multivalent, supported as a prescription to resolve various social issues by both radicals and liberals, though in dissimilar ways. Appreciating this multivalence enables us to see *Mary Barton* as a thoroughgoing exploration of the relationship between individual and collective improvement. Radical ideas about education circulate freely in the novel. Lovett's emphasis on mutual improvement is instantiated in the circuit of cultural and intellectual sharing Gaskell describes. McDouall's complaints about the denigration of working-class intellectual accomplishments are echoed in the satirical portrait of the younger Carson's contempt for Jem and the striking operatives. And like the Chartists, Gaskell rejects the view of education as a simple antidote to social ills, a way to teach the lower orders respect and docility. Instead, the novel presents learning as oppositional and democratic, a surprising arena of working-class autonomy and authority. Rather than simply abandoning Chartist themes in the novel's second half, then, Gaskell isolates the ideological currents within the movement which in her view hold out the best hope for the resolution of the crises she portrays. Indeed, the achievement of working-class political power is not the solution Gaskell advances. She continues to suggest that the task of advocacy for the poor should fall to well-meaning members of the middle classes, a position that starkly separates her from both the Chartists and the radical Unitarians who supported the demand for working-class civil rights. Nevertheless, the novel delineates the limits of an upward-mobility plot based on individual success, so that Jem and Mary's happy ending remains shadowed by and connected to the collective struggles that the novel details.

Narrative focalization has often been taken as an index of the separation between the novel's two halves with their various thematic emphases. Detailed attention to focalization, however, troubles the supposedly neat division between the Chartist and domestic sections of the novel.[26] Mary's perspective becomes central after the death of Carson, but the narrator initially aligns herself with multiple viewpoints, including Mary's. In fact, the reader first learns of John's political life through his daughter's limited perspective: "she was aware that he had joined clubs, and become an active member of the Trades' Union, but it was hardly likely that a girl of Mary's age . . . should care much for the differences between the employers and the employed" (23). By intermingling political and domestic themes, the chapter goes on to indicate the importance of politics to even "a girl of Mary's age." In the space of a few pages, the reader learns of John's beliefs, the death of his son by scarlet fever, and Mary's desire to seek work as an apprentice dressmaker, a decision informed by her father's attitudes which hold "domestic servitude a species of slavery" (26).

Domestic and political themes remain interwoven throughout the early part of the novel. Even John's visit to London as a Chartist delegate is embedded in a chapter about Jem's frustrated attempt to propose to Mary. In a humorous scene, the would-be lover is made to listen to John's perspective on the factory question while his daughter hides in her room. The very appearances of Mary's competing suitors have been marked by history – Jem Wilson's face is scarred by childhood smallpox, a fact notable in a novel that understands the exposure to disease as an essential inequality between the two nations. Similarly, Jem's mother Jane was maimed in an industrial accident and feared her husband would retract his promise to marry. As these examples indicate, the personal lives of Gaskell's characters unfold in a world suffused with political and economic conflicts. The novel's original title, *A Manchester Love Story*, highlights the ironic disjunction between the quotidian nature of Mary's romantic adventures and the world-historic pressures brought to bear upon them.

Although the narrator leavens her account of her heroine's work with details of frivolous gossip, Mary is cast in the iconic role of the sweated seamstress, a figure that recurs in mid-century fiction as a symbol of the abuse of female labor and one to which Gaskell returns in *Ruth*. The repeated scenes of Mary and her friend Margaret sewing late into the night are the only depiction of work in the novel, a fact rarely noticed in critical interpretations, perhaps because the treatment of their labor differs markedly from the exposé-like descriptions of the impoverished home life of the Bartons, Davenports, and Wilsons. Nevertheless, Mary's sexual vulnerability arises out of her subordinate economic position. The narrator underlines how Carson's attempted seduction of Mary derives from his class privilege, his threatening behavior paralleling his militancy in the face of the strike.[27]

In Williams's account, Henry Carson's murder is the hinge between the novel's focus on politics and its sensational story line of romance and upward mobility. Williams's emphasis, however, has tended to obscure the novel's delicate interlacing of the Chartist and domestic plot. Participating in a union lottery to decide who will revenge the mill owner's lockout, Barton chooses "the lot of the assassin," an inspired device worthy of the melodramatist Boucicault (190). This fated resolution decrees Barton commit an act of personal *and* political revenge: the tyrannical cotton lord is simultaneously Mary's seducer. The elegant logic of the hero's action, however, is not the end of the story, as it would be in stage melodrama, for neither Barton nor any other character recognizes the poetic justice of his deed. Mary, in fact, is dumbfounded at her father's involvement; she has kept her romantic entanglement hidden from him and so cannot imagine what motive he might have. The knowledge the reader shares with Mary as she pursues the contradictory goals of exonerating Jem and protecting her father creates a peculiar effect where the narrative generates suspense around Jem's guilt or innocence after the question has been settled. By foregrounding the counterfactual possibility of Jem's guilt, the novel explores the implications of two crimes, the actual assassination and a hypothetical murder resulting from a real love triangle. It explores, in other words, the very divide which dominates critical discussion of the novel: the difference between stories about politics and about private lives.[28]

Mary's correct but confused perspective views her father's participation as essentially random. His seemingly capricious violence is contrasted to the hypothetical involvement of Jem, who has an easily understandable connection to the victim. The elder Carson's suspicions, the doubts of

Jem's friends, and the sympathy the public shows the wronged lover all highlight the legibility of romantic melodrama, the mode through which Mary's workmate Sally Leadbitter describes the events. Sally confesses to Mary that she would not "think much the worse of a spirited young fellow for falling foul of a rival – they always do at the 'theater'" (359). Gaskell sharpens the comparison of the crimes' relative legibility by having Barton fail to recognize his personal link to Carson when he rebuffs his sister-in-law Esther, who tries to warn him about the danger menacing Mary. By ignoring Carson, Barton has neglected his responsibilities toward his daughter, a failing he unwittingly rectifies with the murder.

Caroline Levine has alerted us to the high stakes of suspense in Victorian realism. For Levine, the creation of doubt functions as a kind of "political and epistemological training, a way to foster energetic skepticism and uncertainty rather than closure and complacency" (2). Levine's framework is particularly suggestive for *Mary Barton* where suspense is "anomalous," involving a mystery that has already been resolved (Abbott 62). What question, then, does the murder investigation consider? We have noted that Mary's confusion about the crime creates a sense of chance ruling Gaskell's characters' lives. The excruciating scenes of Job and Jem's mother waiting as Mary races to save Jem likewise pit human agency against a fatal mechanism, the machinery of the law. These effects are consonant with the feeling of powerlessness in the face of the economy the first half of the novel emphasizes, a sense rendered more complete by Gaskell's willingness to leave unspecified the origin of the economic crisis that shutters Manchester's mills. Unlike Dickens, who typically traces crises to the wrongdoing of specific characters (i.e., Mr. Merdle's malfeasance in *Little Dorrit*), Gaskell precedes with broad overviews, seemingly unconcerned to enclose her characters' universe as they are pummeled by abstractions beyond their range of sight. Taking seriously the purpose of suspense, the murder plot explores from a different angle themes central to the novel's first half, rather than simply abandoning them.

The novel's climax in the union's fatal lottery invokes Gaskell's framing metaphor for economic contingency and the helplessness of the poor. The introduction describes Gaskell's imaginative identification with belea-guered strangers buffeted by circumstances they cannot control:

> I bethought me how deep might be the romance in the lives of some of those who elbowed me daily in the busy streets of the town in which I resided. I had always felt a deep sympathy with the care-worn men, who looked as if doomed to struggle through their lives in strange alternations between work and want; tossed to and fro by circumstances, apparently in even a greater

degree than other men … The even tenor of [the rich's] seemingly happy lives appeared to increase the anguish caused by the lottery-like nature of their own. (3)

When a real lottery dooms both Carson and Barton, Gaskell renders literal this figure for economic determination. The eschatological language of the preface describes in advance the hero's plight, who, to borrow a phrase from Jacques Rancière, is "exposed to a precariousness that [takes] on the visage of prison" (155). In the event, however, it is not only the economic system that transforms Barton into a plaything of chance. Ironically, the Chartists' attempt to shape a collective destiny by imposing human will on anonymous economic forces completes the hero's degradation. The narrator marks Barton's loss of freedom with repeated reference to the fixity of his expression, his "involuntary motions" and "measured clockwork tread" (*Mary Barton* 346; Graziano 144–48). Despairing of mass politics, *Mary Barton* turns to education as an alternative way to imagine agency in the face of crushing social forces. The following section analyzes the implications of this turn.

Education, Self-Help, and Mutual Improvement in *Mary Barton*

In the novel's penultimate chapter, the elder Carson asserts the importance of individual responsibility to answer Job's claim that the rich as Christians owe the poor generous treatment: "Facts have proved, and are daily proving, how much better it is for every man to be independent of help, and self-reliant" (385). This laissez-faire version of self-help anticipates the use to which liberals put the ideology in the 1850s when a gospel of individual transformation and the cult of the self-made man became important arguments against the need for the social amelioration of economic conditions.[29] Carson ultimately becomes a quiet reformer, but does the novel affirm his perspective on the need for self-reliance? In other words, how does Gaskell negotiate the divergence between the liberal assumptions of the Unitarian Domestic Mission, in which fostering individual virtues would ameliorate social harms and Chartist ideals that saw education in terms of mutual support, solidarity, and political engagement?

The novel is structured around a chiasmus. Initially, Mary's romantic daydreams appear selfish and vain, whereas John's political involvement seems noble and self-sacrificing. Ultimately, however, John's political enthusiasm severs his ties to the community, and Mary demonstrates her altruism in the effort to rescue Jem. The changing evaluation of Mary and her father, however, is complex. The narrator treats Mary sympathetically only after her romantic attachment transfers to Jem, for it is the selfish nature of Mary's dreams, as much as her sexual naïveté, which the narrator condemns. Mary fantasizes about providing a condescending patronage to her spurned working-class lover once she becomes Henry Carson's wealthy wife. Worried that "kindness from me, when I'm another's, will only go against the grain," she imagines rescuing her father from "the old dim work-a-day court" and installing him in her "grand house," a fantasy made humorous not least because she envisions her father perusing "newspapers and pamphlets ... everyday – and all day long if he liked," enjoying, in other words, a political literature that condemns exactly such scenes of idleness and luxury (80).

The increasing financial stability of the Wilson family allows the narrator to revisit earlier motifs in a changed context, as when the terrifying scenes at Ben Davenport's deathbed, which include scathing social commentary, are reworked through the representation of Alice Wilson's peaceful death and Mary's illness and recovery. But even as an aura of prosperity replaces images of destitution, the Wilsons' relative affluence depends on a telling irony. Jem keeps his job though his factory is "all the while turning off hands" (122), only because he has invented an engine that will enable his employer to replace a less efficient crank. The *Penny Magazine* and similar useful knowledge journals endlessly celebrated these kinds of devices without considering their social implications. On one level, Gaskell treats Jem's invention similarly, narrowly focusing on his ingenuity and the good fortune that results. But the novel has also intimated that such innovations might depress the demand for labor and exacerbate the effects of the economic crisis, as when Barton's neighbors suggest the Chartists should demand regulation of spinning jennies to mitigate their impact on employment and wages.[30]

If Jem and Mary become self-reliant at the end of the novel, they do so in a manner different from what the elder Carson imagines. Jem's upward trajectory does not entirely separate him from his class, either by elevating him into the ranks of the masters or cordoning off his family's fortunes from those of the community. In Raymond Williams's account, Jem's emigration epitomizes Gaskell's failure to find a solution to the narrative's conflicts, for his success occurs outside the framework of the factory system, and, indeed, outside England. However, emigration as a closural gesture has a range of meanings in Victorian fiction. The Micawbers' voyage to Australia at the end of *David Copperfield* acts mostly as an escapist fantasy, though one ironic in its excess. Thomas Martin Wheeler's *Sunshine and Shadow* and Frances Trollope's *Michael Armstrong*, on the other hand, feature protagonists who seek asylum abroad as political and economic refugees. In these novels, emigration indicts British society by highlighting the intractability of the antagonisms that define it. Though Gaskell's idealized closing is less critical than Wheeler's or Trollope's, the narrator in the final pages turns back to an untransformed Manchester and the shared grave of John Barton and his sister-in-law, marking the limits of the proffered solution. Jem and Mary's success is also less individualistic than it might seem. A family carving a home out of the Canadian wilderness resembles the emigration propaganda the Chartists press repeatedly debunked, a topic taken up in Chapter 6. Yet even this vision of hardy pioneers includes the ghost of collective liberation: Jem achieves "independence" through his immersion in an institution loosely related to the radical politics depicted in the novel's first half. He obtains a position at an agricultural college in Toronto, his continued involvement in a culture of education and self-help signaling that the passage to Canada is more than a personal escape from the class structure.[31] Duncombe, the name of the factory master who secures Jem's new position, affiliates this character with a famous ally of working-class radicalism. T. S. Duncombe, an MP for London, sponsored the Chartist petition of 1842, worked to ameliorate conditions for several Chartist prisoners and had his portrait distributed by the *Northern Star*.

Margaret Jennings, the other character who prospers economically over the course of the novel, likewise remains loyal to the aspirations of the community as her fortunes improve. Just as Mary helps Margaret complete her sewing outwork, Margaret insists on sharing with her friend the wages from her recitals at the Mechanics' Institute. This mutual aid is part of the moral economy the novel reconstructs, a network of support notably different from the conflict-ridden system that binds masters and men. In the novel's first chapter, John Barton scolds Jem "that it's the poor, and the poor only, as does such things [as providing help during illness] for the poor" (11). Tellingly, Gaskell elides the association of the Mechanics' Institute with middle-class philanthropy, an irony given her and her husband's deep involvement in educational initiatives for the laboring classes. In *North and South*, the middle-class protagonist's father does prepare lectures for working-class audiences at a "neighbouring Lyceum," but he does so badly, selecting his subject of "Ecclesiastical Architecture ... in accordance with his own taste and knowledge" rather than his hearers' interests (140). In *Mary Barton*, Gaskell renders the

Mechanics' Institute a working-class space where a popular audience enjoys politicized folk songs free from elite involvement. Similarly, the narrator consistently foregrounds the extent to which the poor pool their resources: characters share food, money, shelter, and work, as well as newspapers, poetry, medicine, and advice. This web of shared possessions, experiences, and knowledge comes to define Gaskell's characters in a way that defies novelistic convention. In Anne Graziano's account, John Barton too closely embodies the sociological conditions of Manchester to function effectively as a protagonist because he lacks the openness and possibility Bakhtin has highlighted as essential characteristics of novelistic heroes (144–48). Graziano helps explain why Gaskell dispenses with John in favor of Mary. But looked at another way, Gaskell shows how Barton depends upon a dense system of relationships for his existential ground, stretching the possibilities of a fictional protagonist's character space. Mary's developmental plot tracks whether and to what degree she will remain connected to or become independent of this network.

The complexity and ambivalence of the upward mobility plot is an indication of the way competing ideological imperatives shape *Mary Barton*. The novel likewise presents tangled viewpoints when it considers the nature and extent of working-class learning. The preface borrows the Carlylean motif of Chartism as an inarticulate expression of grievances by an ignorant population: "I became [anxious] to give some utterance to the agony which, from time to time, convulses this dumb people" (3).[32] This judgment resurfaces intermittently and relates to the political failure the novel chronicles. Nevertheless, Gaskell gives the reader ample grounds to distrust it. First, the narrator presents herself as a naïve observer who cannot understand the science of political economy, affiliating her perspective with that of the "dumb people." Second, just as textual developments frequently negate explicit affirmations of political and economic orthodoxy, the novel's detailed reconstruction of the intellectual pursuits of the working-class flatly contradicts the assertions of their ignorance.[33] The puzzling cleavage between the narrator's explicit commentary and the way the narrative frames events instantiates the inability of the middle class to comprehend working-class experience, a theme the novel considers at length.

Job Legh, an amateur naturalist who is Barton's friend, is the novel's most vivid embodiment of working-class learning. Realizing many readers will not credit the accomplishments of the autodidact, Gaskell defends his verisimilitude by recounting an anecdote from the botanist Sir J. E. Smith's autobiography that encapsulates the incredulity she anticipates:

Being on a visit to Roscoe, of Liverpool, he made some inquiries from him as to the habitat of a very rare plant … Mr Roscoe knew nothing of the plant; but stated, that if any one could give him the desired information, it would be a hand-loom weaver in Manchester … Smith proceeded by boat to Manchester, and on arriving at the town, he inquired of the porter who was carrying his luggage if he could direct him to So-and-So.

"Oh, yes," replied the man. "He does a bit in my way"; and, on further investigation, it turned out, that both the porter, and his friend the weaver, were skillful botanists; and able to give Sir J. E. Smith the very information which he wanted. (39)

What Smith assumes is the specialized knowledge of an exceptional individual is shown to be the common property of a broad culture of learning (King 257). The narrator affiliates Job's science with Jem's industrial invention and Alice Wilson's "considerable knowledge of plants and herbs" (16). This emphasis distinguishes Gaskell's portrait of working-class achievement from the biographical sketches of isolated persons that populate the *Penny Magazine* and Craik's volume.[34] For Gaskell, working-class knowledge encompasses both formal subjects (natural history and "mathematical problems," the latter taken up by "many a broad-spoken, common-looking factory hand") and topics middle-class observers "are accustomed to call valueless," such as Alice Wilson's herbal remedies (16, 39). Even Margaret's singing is praised as a species of "really scientific knowledge" (37). Gaskell is also attentive to the informal spaces in which education occurs. The narrator describes "common hand-loom weavers" reading Newton's Principia at the "loom" and presents characters reciting poems in working-class residences, where they also discuss newspaper articles and dispute questions of marine biology (39). Finally, the text's footnotes valorize the intelligence native to the Manchester poor. Answering an editor's demand to make working-class dialect understandable to a middle-class audience, Gaskell in a polemical gesture glosses the operatives' language with quotations from high literature.[35] The reader discovers that working-class colloquialisms derive from Shakespeare, Spenser, Ben Jonson, the *Canterbury Tales*, and the Wickliffe Bible. Dialectal language, far from its typical function as comic relief, demonstrates the popular share of a universal cultural inheritance (Poole 99–101). *North and South* similarly troubles derogatory associations with working-class speech when the middle-class protagonist justifies her use of slang to her scandalized mother: "If I live in a factory town, I must speak factory language when I want it"

(233). In *Mary Barton*, the reader's presumed unfamiliarity with the vernacular highlights his or her ignorance of the elite literary canon, calling out anticipated condescension.[36]

Yet the narrator also repeatedly notes the lack of education of her working-class characters, particularly around questions of economics. This stance becomes, in fact, part of the novel's case for reform, for the narrator attributes the alienation between the classes to ignorance of political economy. If the operatives understood the tenuous circumstances of their masters in the international market, the narrator suggests, it would dull the conflict between the groups. In the novel's penultimate chapter, a conversation between Job, Jem, and the stricken Carson models the kinds of relationships Gaskell envisions superseding the violent strife the narrative records. In this regard, *Mary Barton* echoes the view common in the 1830s and 1840s that education might remedy class conflict, an idea popularized by among others Gaskell's Manchester acquaintance James Kay-Shuttleworth. The first secretary of the newly established Privy Council on Education, Kay-Shuttleworth wrote several influential essays on working-class learning, at least one of which his wife loaned to Gaskell.[37] In an 1832 treatise about Manchester, Kay-Shuttleworth claims that unionism and machine-breaking stem from ignorance of political economy and that education would guarantee domestic peace by suppressing radical organization.[38] By the rise of the Chartist movement in 1839, his prognosis had become desperate. An essay from that year argues that only a national system of schools can stem the rising influence of demagogues who "teach the population to seek a remedy for the evils they endure by violent attempts at social change" (Kay-Shuttleworth, "Recent" 89).

The union meeting at the Weaver's Arms, where Henry Carson's murder is decided, repeats several aspects of Kay-Shuttleworth's stereotyped view of radicalism. Gaskell presents the London orator as an intellectual arriviste manipulating a benighted population: "As the man who has had his taste educated to love reading, falls devouringly upon books after a long abstinence, so these poor fellows, whose tastes had been left to educate themselves into a liking for tobacco, beer, and similar gratifications, gleamed up at the proposal of the London delegate" (185). But the image of the London radical betrays ambivalence toward the idea of education as a social sedative. He not only plays on the strikers' ignorance and intemperance but also flatters their aspirations for culture – classical allusions dapple his incendiary speech. Whereas Kay-Shuttleworth describes a universally ignorant population, *Mary Barton* recognizes that learning is *already* an integral part of a militant working-class milieu. Explaining that Barton's politics stem from a lack of knowledge, a few sentences later the narrator details how his intellectual abilities serve the Chartist movement: "He had a sort of practical power, which made him useful to the bodies of men to whom he belonged . . . He had a pretty clear head at times, for method and arrangement; a necessary talent to large combinations of men" (170). It is therefore appropriate that the narrator turns to that most famous subaltern autodidact, Frankenstein's monster, to describes her hero: "The actions of the uneducated seem to be typified in those of Frankenstein, that monster of many human qualities, ungifted with a soul, a knowledge of the difference between good and evil" (170). The monster crystallizes Gaskell's ambivalence about working-class learn-ing, for Shelley's creation is, after all, not uneducated, but self-educated. And it is precisely the monster reading Milton, Plutarch, and Goethe at the Delaceys' cottage that transforms him from an innocent brute into a wronged individual intent on revenge.

Literature likewise politicizes Barton. On his deathbed, the penitent murderer describes his first effort learning to read and his subsequent confusion trying to "make folks' actions square wi' th' Bible" (371). Earlier, we encounter Barton reading the *Northern Star*. His justification to Jem of short-time legislation includes an anecdote that illustrates the radicalizing effect of reading. Barton recounts how he was allowed addi-tional time to recuperate from a fever in his factory's infirmary because he could transcribe medical reports. Literacy earns Barton the privilege of food, rest, and medical attention, but these fail to purchase his loyalty. He describes to Jem how he informed the company surgeon that the docu-ments made clear that "by *far th' greater part o' the accidents as comed in happened in th' last two hours o' work*, when folk getten tired and careless" (84). Years later, the example buttresses the *Star*'s case for a shorter work-day. Barton's critical use of the Bible to reveal injustice and his education by the radical press resemble the Chartists' view of learning as a means of social struggle.

Several other characters read a political canon, including some see-mingly uninterested in politics. Job's penchant for natural history is far from Bamford's image of artisans studying insurrection under cover of botanical societies, but he shares with Mary and John a poem written by Bamford himself, which espouses a militant Christianity and expresses the hope that "God will yet arise and help the poor" (112). Both the poem's thematic emphasis and the fact that its author is "a weaver like oursel" validate working-class culture (111).[39] Similarly, in the key confrontation between Jem and Henry Carson, the words of "the Ploughman Poet" Robert Burns give the operative courage to challenge his romantic rival about the latter's mistreatment of Mary: "He seemed to the poor smith so elegant, so well appointed, that he felt the superiority in externals, strangely and painfully, for an instant. Then something uprose within him, and told him, that 'a man's a man for a' that, for a' that, and twice as much as a' that'" (176). More is at stake here than the contrast between Carson's pretensions and Jem's democratic philosophy. The conflict between masters and men plays out not least in the cultural realm; working-class literature nourishes a set of values that permits a critical judgment of the "superiority in externals" of the masters in a way that calls to mind the debunking of a knowledge qualification for the franchise in *McDouall's*. In fact, a poem by Robert Nicholls in the latter journal anticipates the use to which Gaskell's operative puts Burns's verse: "Burns! thou hast given us a name / To shield us from the taunts of scorn" (June 12, 1841).[40]

When the narrator turns to Carson, she explores the deficiencies of his own class-bound view of culture, how miseducation warps his perception:

> He looked at Jem from head to foot, a black, grimy mechanic, in dirty fustian clothes, strongly built, and awkward (according to the dancing-master); then he glanced at himself, and recalled the reflection he had so lately quitted in his bedroom. It was impossible. No woman with eyes could choose the one when the other wooed. It was Hyperion to a Satyr. That quotation came aptly; he forgot "That a man's a man for a' that". (177)

A short while later another misapplication of Shakespeare dooms this would-be Hyperion. He appends a quotation from Falstaff to the caricature he sketches with his "silver pencil" of the "famine-stricken" union delegates, which circulates among the masters (184). Not realizing the dubiousness of affiliating his perspective with Shakespeare's "fat knight," Carson makes a more serious mistake: when he attempts to discard the torn halves of the drawing, he is "careless whether they reached their aim or not [and] did not look to see that they fell just short of the consuming cinders" (184). This carelessness, as much as the drawing itself, evokes Carson's contempt for the operatives, his assumption of their cultural or real illiteracy. But the narrator has already speculated that the delegates are readers of a literature of which the masters know nothing. In describing the dilapidated clothing of the operatives, the narrator wonders if they have read Carlyle's "Sartor Resartus," because they value eloquence and intelligence over appearance.[41] And of course – although Carson never knows it – they understand the implications of the caricature all too well.

Gaskell's view of education in *Mary Barton* is multi-sided and contradictory, but the aim of this chapter has been to ground her dissident ideas in a rich but largely forgotten canon of radical writing. If the narrator repeats at times the cliché of the inarticulate and unlearned poor, the portraits of Job, Jem, Margaret, Alice Wilson, and John Barton dispel those stereotypes. Besides the affirmation that education will mitigate tension between the classes are examples of readers learning to assert their rights. Self-improvement leads to individual prosperity, but it does so within a system of mutual support. A last aspect of Gaskell's treatment of working-class education, the stress on the private enjoyment of study, might also have been gleaned from Lovett and Collin's curriculum, which emphasized engaging and inspiring "all the human faculties" or from the enthusiastic eclecticism of Chartist miscellanies like *McDouall's* (67). This emphasis distinguishes Gaskell's perspective from that of many middle-class observers, including Kay-Shuttleworth who advocated broadening the curriculum for children in workhouse schools mainly in terms of the "practical utility" of a diverse subject matter (*First* 335). Richard Altick's study of the common reader underlines how debates about the dangers of mass literacy, the advantages of public libraries, and the necessity of a politically orthodox cheap literature emphasized again and again questions of public usefulness while ignoring the individual's pleasure in reading. While parsing the political implications of workers who read, Gaskell shares her character Margaret Jenning's wonder at how much satisfaction learning provides: "Well, I'm often downright glad grandfather is so fond of his books, and his creatures, and his plants. It does my heart good to see him so happy, sorting them all at home, and so ready to go in search of more" (42). The cultural movement of Chartism similarly possessed a broad and humanistic sense of the possibilities of working-class intellectual life, insisting on education as a democratic right and celebrating it as a tool in the struggle for individual and collective self-realization.

CHAPTER 5

Revenge in the Age of Insurance: Villainy in Theatrical Melodrama and Ernest Jones's Fiction

The fiction of Ernest Jones – the dashing barrister, poet, and novelist who joined the Chartist cause in 1845 – marks a significant departure from the narrative of feminine vulnerability protected by working-class manhood depicted in an array of radical rhetoric throughout the 1840s and 1850s. Whereas most Chartist authors and orators present as idealized a version of the home as any middle-class moralist, demonstrating how far-reaching the ideology of separate spheres had become at mid-century, Jones's tales of flawed protectors and dangerous families disclose the drudgery and inequality that define domestic life for women. Chartist politicians, anti-New Poor Law activists, and members of the factory movement all lionized the efforts of male reformers on behalf of distressed femininity. The militant preacher J. R. Stephens's jeremiads against the Bastardy Clause of the New Poor Law, Peter McDouall's polemics against the factory system's mistreatment of female operatives, and Feargus O'Connor's invocations of the Chartist land plan as a restoration of a traditional sexual division of labor founded on an agricultural economy cast the radical movement as the heroic protector of vulnerable womankind (Zlotnick 184–87). But Jones's fiction, a staple of the radical press in the 1840s and 1850s, reshapes the narrative pattern that stands behind this political rhetoric, marking an important intervention in the debate about women's rights in the working-class agitation for reform. Whereas radicals borrowed heavily from literary and theatrical seduction plots, in which male heroes rescue female victims from the clutches of elite libertines (Clark, "Rhetoric" 65), Jones's sensational stories show the efforts of men on behalf of women as self-interested, ineffectual, and painfully unheroic. They feature female protagonists capable of protecting themselves and depict the suffocating dynamics of the patriarchal home as the true threat menacing women's well-being. Jones's corpus thus demonstrates the complexity of a movement that involved thousands of female activists while seeking democratic rights for men under the banner of universal suffrage.[1] By undermining the image of the home as a domain independent of the strife of the public sphere, Jones's fiction challenges the endorsement of *couverture*, the idea that a wife's political life is subsumed into her husband's, which was common both to radicalism and mainstream politics.

Jones's fiction is also an example of the flexibility of melodrama, long seen as a "dominant modality" in Victorian thought, a style recognizable in journalism, oratory, and the visual arts, as well as in drama and fiction (Hadley, *Melodramatic* 3; McWilliam, "Melodrama" 59–60). In recent decades, feminist scholars of working-class literature have described the way melodrama focuses attention on the family, sexual relations, and domestic life, offering a politicized view of key areas of female experience. Synthesizing archetypal motifs and contemporary concerns, melodrama utilizes an enclosed dramatis personae drawn from primary psychic relationships but sets these figures wandering through a realistically drawn landscape that vividly embodies the disruptions and dislocations of an industrializing society (James, "Time" 182; Vicinus, "Helpless" 128). Melodrama has frequently been seen as a mythic response to the rise of factory labor, an argument "for the preservation of the family and its traditional values – a binding in of the errant son or unforgiving father or wayward daughter."[2] In a similar vein, historians have discerned in radicalism's use of melodramatic tropes anxiety about industrial change, the image of the seduced maiden condensing the fears of men losing control of the labor of their wives and daughters as domestic economies dissolved into new patterns of female employment (Clark, "Rhetoric" 48–49; *Struggle* 220–32; Schwarzkopf 64).

To specify fully the originality of Jones's fiction, then, it is necessary to describe it against the backdrop of both Chartism and the factory movement and of melodrama and the early Victorian stage. As Rohan McWilliam points out, although historians have utilized categories suggested by melodrama in creative ways, too often their discussion has been divorced from detailed attention to specific literary works ("Melodrama" 70). Critics of Jones's oeuvre, on the other hand, have focused on the novelist's relationship to popular fiction, making only passing reference to Jones's sustained engagement with the theater. But Jones's challenge to commonplace assumptions about the family, female sexuality, and women's work becomes most evident in the ways he revises theatrical formulas. Looking at Jones's fiction can clarify in turn overlooked aspects of melodrama, which, as much recent criticism has shown, was a dynamic mode with a complex history in several generic instantiations.[3] In particular, this chapter takes up how stage and fictional melodrama addresses and critiques institutional forms of power, a tendency sometimes obscured by the genre's penchant for emotional climax, its polarized view of good and evil, and it formulaic happy endings. Rather than focusing on individual villainy, Jones's melodrama scrutinizes an array of unjust social structures, including the workplace, the legal system, and the patriarchal home. His fiction thus expands our notions of a key Victorian mode and of the range of possibilities of working-class gender politics.

Ernest Jones and Popular Culture

The entry of a fashionable young lawyer and aspiring author into Chartist politics in the winter of 1845 caused a stir in both radical and polite circles. Casting his image in the tradition of a gentlemanly "friend of the people," Jones used his writing to win a prominent place in the movement's leadership, displacing the schismatic Thomas Cooper as "labour's laureate." After serving a two-year term in Tothill Fields Prison for incendiary speeches made during the crisis of 1848, Jones became the most important Chartist leader and theoretician during the decade of the movement's decline following the repression of the late 1840s. He remained a politician of national stature until his death in 1869, which followed shortly on his election to Parliament as a candidate on the left fringe of the Liberal Party.[4] Between 1847 and 1852, Jones produced a substantial corpus of fiction that spanned a range of popular genres: adventure and crime stories, romantic fables, a fictionalized account of the Chartist movement, and a group of five novellas (which themselves incorporated a variety of forms).[5] These efforts appeared alongside Jones's poetry, literary reviews, and essays on miscellaneous topics in the *Labourer* (1847–48) and *Notes to the People* (1851–52), journals edited by Jones himself.

A joint effort with Feargus O'Connor, *The Labourer* appeared monthly for the relatively inexpensive price of 6d. It provided the Chartist movement with a format that could accommodate expansive essays and serial fiction, genres excluded from the *Northern Star* for want of space. Besides copious material (mostly by O'Connor) on the Chartist land plan, a popular scheme to resettle urban families in small agrarian communities, the *Labourer* introduced readers to the national literatures of Germany and Poland and entertained with picaresques and historical fiction.[6] *Notes to the People*, a weekly, was likewise a Chartist miscellany. It featured a survey of world religions and mythologies, histories of ancient Rome and Sparta, a memoir of the Hungarian revolutionary Kossuth, extensive reports on union agitation, and selections from German and American poets, especially Edgar Allen Poe, whom Jones claimed as a fellow internationalist and radical. A victim of the splintering of democratic politics following 1848, the journal never sold more than three thousand copies per issue and failed after a year. Nevertheless, *Notes to the People* contains Jones's most ambitious literary endeavors, including the anti-imperialist verse "The New World, a Democratic Poem"; an uncompleted novel about Chartism, *De Brassier, A Democratic Romance*; and the novellas *Woman's Wrongs*, which stand as some of the most incisive studies of gender inequality of the mid-Victorian period.

Like Thomas Martin Wheeler and other Chartist journalists of the late 1840s and early 1850s, Jones turned to popular fiction out of anxiety that new commercial periodicals such as *News of the World* and *Lloyd's Weekly Newspaper* were siphoning off the readership of the radical press.[7] The preface to the second volume of the *Labourer* proclaims that the publication will be "based on a more elevated literature than that of the generality of 'popular serials'" (ii). Jones promotes *Notes to the People* in similar terms, but his tone has turned truculent:

> *In starting and continuing these "Notes," at a time of peculiar political and social apathy, I have . . . had more than ordinary difficulties to contend against . . . They were started with a determination not to pander to the sensuality of the public by meretricious writing – not to degrade the literature of democracy to the level of the street-walker.* (iii)

Given that pirates, criminals, arsonists, and indeed streetwalkers crowd Jones's stories, this holier-than-thou posturing seems another example of the "skin deep" respectability Rohan McWilliam discerns in G. W. M. Reynolds's pornographic and politically radical penny bloods, which "helped construct an audience that had 'high' cultural aspirations but 'low' desires at the same time" ("Mysteries" 183). Jones's contradictory posture, however, is more than hypocritical role playing: skepticism toward popular formulas penetrates the heart of the material, which exaggerates and ironizes the "meretricious writing" Jones condemns while reproducing.

Jones's contorted attitude toward popular fiction reflected an anxiety about the ability of radicalism to compete with the allure of mass culture. The popularity of the Great Exhibition of 1851 was particularly troubling to him, and the massive crowds that haunted its fairgrounds and enjoyed the "artistical display" and "national pomp" sponsored by an anti-democratic government seemed to parody the political ferment of a few years earlier.[8] Reflecting this sense of competition between radicalism and a conservative mass culture, political and nonpolitical crowds jostle in the opening chapters of Jones's *De Brassier*. Elsewhere in his fiction, Jones uses theater to reflect on the politics of spectacle. In *A Romance of the People*, the popularity of the Polish revolution among the English finds expression in playbills "from Sadler's Wells to Surrey" (*Labourer* 2.79). In "The Working Man's Wife," debauched onlookers enjoy the sorry show of the heroine's execution: "They came, as they had gone the previous evening to the playhouse, to get the amusement of one excitement more!" (*Woman's* 37). Beyond competing inscriptions of drama as a democratic form capable of inspiring solidarity with the oppressed and a sensationalist medium that desensitizes the public to actual violence, a theatrical sensibility inheres in the tissue of Jones's stories.

An inveterate consumer of the theater, Jones served his literary apprenticeship as an unsuccessful playwright, authoring eight plays that went unperformed and largely unpublished.[9] *St. John's Eve*, the only extant play in Jones's oeuvre, appeared serially in the *Labourer* in 1848.[10] Written before Jones became a Chartist, it nevertheless anticipates important aspects of his later fiction. A cut above much Victorian melodrama, the play recounts a Faustian story about the lovestruck Rudolf, who traffics with a Mephistophelean stranger in order to peer into the future and discern whether or not the tyrannical elderly father of Gemma, his beloved, will die in the next year. Seeing instead a ghostly vision of Gemma's own funeral, the hero in his agitation lets slip to his lover that while her father is safe "death has daintier work in hand" (*Labourer* 4:188). Rudolf's moral ambiguity coupled with his counterproductive efforts on Gemma's behalf looks ahead to Jones's fiction, in which male protagonists often unwittingly menace the women they would protect. In *St. John's Eve*, Rudolf's séance doubly threatens Gemma. First, the vision becomes nearly self-fulfilling as his cryptic warning terrifies his lover, causing her health to decline. Second, when Gemma's father discovers that Rudolf has engaged in sorcery, he blackmails his daughter with her suitor's life, coercing a promise to marry a wealthier rival (who turns out to be the stranger who inveigled the hero into black magic). That Gemma ultimately rescues herself also resonates with Jones's later writing, though the means by which she breaks her fiancé's power – declaring her eternal love for Rudolf – is more conventionally melodramatic than Jones's Chartist fiction.

Although his ambitions as a dramatist were frustrated, Jones turned to melodrama for the basic technical elements and paradigmatic concerns of his fiction.[11] Jones's plots borrow freely from domestic and temperance plays, featuring scenes of seduction, domestic violence, evictions, and the seizure of property by creditors, all told in a heightened idiom that finds cosmic oppositions in day-to-day occurrences. His characters are a catalogue of stage types: poachers, landlords, sailors, thieves, well-to-do rakes and aggrieved maidens. And his narratives hinge on *coups de théâtre* while deploying diverse melodramatic devices: extraordinary coincidences that bring antagonists together in a fatal hour; lurid depictions of anguish, pyrotechnic catastrophes; returns from the dead; and tableaux that freeze action at its climax, crystallizing insoluble conflicts into living paintings.[12] Jones's fluency translating the vocabulary of the melodramatic stage into serial fiction casts light on the political import of Victorian popular theater, rereading the field from which the stories emerge. In particular, his fiction demonstrates how melodramatic elements can be utilized to represent entrenched structures of power, a tendency that challenges assumptions about the genre. Even critics who emphasize the connections between political radicalism and melodrama sometimes characterize the latter as stories of individual oppression surmounted by personal heroism. By seeing villains as individuals removed from "a larger pattern of injustice," melodrama appears to offer a consoling vision in which social wrongs, though powerfully embodied by the calamities that afflict the hero and heroine, can be easily righted (Vicinus, "Helpless" 139). But Jones's stories disclose the institutional forces supporting the machinations of seemingly isolated malefactors. The strong continuities between his fiction and contemporary theater suggest that in stage melodrama as well we will find villains acting not merely as personalized embodiments of antisocial evil but also affiliated with everyday structures of power.

Seduction and Male Rescue on the Melodramatic Stage and in Jones's Early Fiction

Jones must have witnessed dozens of staged seductions in his fifty or so visits to playhouses between 1841 and 1846, for the tribulations of daughters, sisters, lovers, and wives at the hands of rakes of all kinds were a fixture of early Victorian drama. W. T. Moncrieff's *The Lear of Private Life* (1820) bequeathed to the dramatists of the 1830s and 1840s including George Dibdin Pitt and Douglas Jerrold a sensibility that rendered sexual dalliance a philosophical crisis threatening to blot out the world. In Moncrieff's play, the seduction of Agnes by an unscrupulous officer precipitates her father's descent into madness. Incapable of reconciling his image of his daughter with her transgression, the deranged Fitzarden compulsively sketches a tomb he plans to erect. Although the play portrays the father as a victim of his daughter's disgrace, his eulogies to Agnes's lost purity rhyme eerily with his drawings, suggesting that his idealization of chastity is life negating: "She was as pure as are those seraphs who stand the nearest heaven's eternal throne. She was as chaste as marble in its strata" (9).

In later drama, the heroine's virtue usually remains intact, but *The Lear of Private Life* is typical in presenting the possibility of female infidelity as worthy of existential crisis. In Douglass Jerrold's *The Rent Day*, which was enormously popular for years following its 1832 debut (Rahill 162), the honest farmer Martin Heywood is beset by a series of financial calamities that culminate in the threatened eviction of his family from his childhood home. The hero breasts misfortune until he mistakenly learns that his wife has sold her virtue to pay his debts. Lamenting that "All's gone! – I cannot carry with me even a hope of better days," Martin resolves to pull up stakes and emigrate to the West Indies where a position awaits him as the manager of a slave plantation (56). By translating Heywood's failure to provide for his family into sexual jealousy, *Rent Day* illustrates the conjunction between seduction plots and a crisis in masculinity precipitated by the disruption of family-based cottage industries. In Dibdin Pitt's *The Beggar's Petition* (1840?), questions of female virtue similarly displace a story line about the inadequacy of a male breadwinner, in this case concerning a father's reckless speculations. The impecunious man laments his daughter's elopement with the son of the family's landlord: "My child, my hope, my prop, my comfort, she has proved weak and faithless. Oh, misery! What is poverty to this?" (17). From John Walker's *The Factory Lad* (1833), a play about unemployment and incendiarism, to T. P. Taylor's *The Bottle* (1847), a riveting piece of temperance propaganda, a wide range of drama communicates the sense of patriarchal economies unraveling, but more often than not stories about errant female sexuality embody the uncomfortable adjustment to new gender roles demanded by changing economic realities.

As in stage melodrama, the central conflicts in Jones's fiction revolve around infidelity, but Jones uses this material in surprising ways. Ironizing the stakes men place in the question of female chastity, his stories surround adulterous women with an aura of purity. At the same time, his fiction upends the motif of men rescuing threatened virtue by suggesting heroes and villains share underlying attitudes toward female sexuality. Lastly, in the place of the stage's self-denying exemplars of virtue, Jones inserts passionate female characters who are intent on avenging the wrongs they suffer at the hands of men.

An unwieldy mixture of styles, "The Confessions of a King" welds the radical gothic of monarchical exposé with a Romantic-fantastic idiom in which identities merge and cross and desire seems to move independently through an abstract landscape. At times evoking the French Revolution and the career of Napoleon, it chronicles the rise of a "child of toil" to courtier, governmental minister, and despot (83). Despite this vague historicism, "The Confessions of a King" offers no substantive account of historical development, staging instead a dream world, in which ambitions and fears, once intimated, are suddenly and drastically realized. The heroine Myrrha is the one stable point in this psychologized setting; the protagonist's rise and fall are told in relation to her. Myrrha's first appearance introduces the theme of male rescue that defines so much of Jones's fiction. The hero intervenes when he spies a beautiful young woman in the street struggling with her father, who he learns has threatened to marry her to the hero's mentor to cancel a debt. The protagonist offers to resolve the man's bill himself in exchange for his daughter's hand. Despite a limp apology, the crassness of the hero's proposition discloses how the logic of male rescue threatens to entrap women in a new captivity.[13]

This threat is realized later in the story after the hero has turned to outlawry to support Myrrha and his infant child. Eventually imprisoned, the protagonist – who is never named – prostitutes his wife to the king to purchase his freedom, a repetition of the exploitation she suffered at her father's hands. The hero then avenges his cuckolding by stoking a popular revolt that topples the monarch and installs himself on the throne. This absurd plot is far from Jones's best, but it anticipates later attempts in three ways. First, the protagonist's drift from rescuer to victim to tyrant distinguishes the story from the morally legible universe of stage melodrama where characters are fixed as good or evil integers. Second, the hero's struggle on behalf of Myrrha is revealed as part of his desire for power, which becomes as menacing as any earlier danger. Finally, although Myrrha engages in an affair, Jones never considers her fallen, a rare attitude in Victorian literature, though less uncommon than literary histories which exclude working-class fiction assume (Breton 117–19; Rosenmann 15–18). Stacking the deck by having Myrrha submit to save her child, the story points up the protagonist's hypocrisy in benefiting from adultery. In an echo of the Queen Caroline affair of 1820, a radical *cause célèbre*, the hero seeks a divorce by trumping up charges of a second liaison. When the clergy follows popular opinion by declaring Myrrha "untainted and innocent," the country rises in revolution to vindicate the queen (*Labourer* 2:70).

Even with the extraordinary tumult around Myrrha, however, she remains locked in the passive role of stage heroine. In Peter Brook's account, melodramatic virtue cannot raise its voice against its persecutors "for to do so would be to violate its nature as innocence" (*Melodramatic* 31). The leading women of melodrama are self-abnegating to the point of repenting crimes they have not committed (Vicinus, "Helpless" 136). If falsely accused, they beg compassion from the men who judge them wrongly (e.g., Rachel in *The Rent Day*). Immobilized by goodness, they await rescue at the hands of husbands, brothers, and fathers (Jerrold's eponymous *Black Ey'd Susan*) or pledge suicide rather than submit to a relationship that would violate their attachment to the hero (Princess Olinska in Milner's *Mazeppa*). Though social injustice is commonly shown the cause of sexual disgrace, fallen women die to atone their transgressions (Clark, "Politics" 64). A compound of these figures, Myrrha is murdered by the villain even as a revolutionary crowd attempts to come to her aid (pointedly reversing Burke's sexualized account of Jacobins plundering Versailles). Skeptical of stories of men liberating women, Jones cannot imagine the alternative in "The Confessions of a King," because he has rendered his heroine a suffering angel defenseless in the face of male violence. The women in Jones's other fiction, however, depart from the stereotypes to which Myrrha succumbs. Three stories in the *Labourer* and *Notes to the People* feature heroines who commit acts of arson to protect their virtue or avenge its loss. Sexual and aggressive, these figures are extraordinary variations on melodrama's seduced maiden.

Influenced by the popular subgenre of naval melodrama, "The Pirates' Prize" is less topical than most fiction in the *Labourer*.[14] Another story about female seduction, it elicits the reader's desire for the hero to save the heroine from a nightmare confinement but then shows the disastrous consequences of his actions (Breton 107). "The Pirates' Prize" tells the story of the looting of Mobile, Alabama, by the crew of the Spanish vessel the *Spirito del Mar*. The reader's point of entry is Audrey, a British sailor who has been conscripted into the band of outlaws. Audrey's qualms allow the reader to participate vicariously in a Schillerian fantasy of rebellion and sexual excess while standing safely aloof.[15] After burning the city and massacring a group of refugees who seek asylum in a church, the pirates drag young women back to their ship and engage in drunken orgies. Audrey slows this savagery as best he can and saves an English girl "mal-treated" by members of the crew. Following the logic of heroic rescue, however, he claims the girl as his own. Back on ship, he defends her through the night from the advances of the others but is powerless the following morning as he witnesses "these monsters, who called themselves men, [hurl] those wretched females, mostly beautiful young girls, some of the first and most affluent families, one by one, into the fathomless deep" (*Labourer* 3:149). Intervening again to save his prize, Audrey fights off hungover shipmates until the captain Clarron puts an end to the half-comedic struggle by shooting Audrey and taking the girl to his cabin.

The second installment of the story recounts Audrey's plot to rescue the heroine, who remains sequestered with Clarron and his black cabin boy. Conspiring with the other Englishman aboard the ship, a gentleman-bandit named Dyke, Audrey plans to betray the *Spirito del Mar* into the hands of local planters as it moors off the Mexican coast. At this point, the tale seems an unproblematic celebration of cross-class alliance in the face of foreign and racial villainy along the lines of Dickens's and Collins's *The Perils of Certain English Prisoners*. The story's conclusion, however, upends Audrey's and the reader's previous interpretation of events. As the Englishmen's efforts to betray the ship continue, the narrator reveals that Clarron is the girl's father and that his reunion with his daughter has transformed him from "the fiend into the man" (175). This improbable development falls squarely in the melodramatic tradition of providential coincidence and transformative familial reunions, but the effect in Jones's piece is unsettling, not integrative. First, dramatic irony persists with Audrey never realizing the true identity of the man he assumes is his antagonist. Clarron, moreover, does not simply slough off his villainous past. Rather, a new framework reveals his crimes as righteous vengeance for larger injustice. In an extended flashback, the reader learns Clarron, a poor English emigrant, settled as a small farmer in Mexico "and there, scorning prejudice, had loved and married a runaway slave." The narrator celebrates interracial marriage and describes Clarron's wife in heroic terms. When a slave owner uses the "summary power" of the law to reclaim her and their child, Clarron becomes an avenging angel of the oppressed: "he leagued with a band of desperate men, and the fierceness of his revenge almost amounted to an insanity, as he wreaked it on the world in the scourge of piracy . . . especially in those districts inhabited by the planters" (176). The looting of Mobile is thus revealed as a semi-legitimate form of rebellion, an appropriate answer to a society founded on the institution of slavery.

If the story's ending topples the reader's assumptions about a stable moral order, it challenges other hierarchies as well. Clarron's intimate reliance on the "hideous black boy" – termed so through Audrey's focalization – now signifies the pirate's racial egalitarianism. Audrey's prejudices, on the other hand, are revealed as disastrously hypocritical. In obtaining help from local planters to defeat the pirates, Audrey repeats the slavers' capture of his lover's mother. It is fitting, then, that the same slave owner who pursued Clarron's family heads the group of masters who seize the ship and kill Clarron. By the final scene, Audrey is a mere spectator as his diabolical double claims the "pirate's prize." But if the hero unwittingly fulfills the work of the planters, it is the heroine who completes her father's vendetta against the slave-owning class: "'I come!' answered a silvery voice from below, and she came! She came like an avenging spirit in a hurricane of fire! By the powder store she had watched, like a fairy over a priceless treasure ... and at the fatal summons of Andorio she fired the magazine" (179).

The figure of virtuous woman turned incendiary appears in different guises throughout Jones's oeuvre. In *The Romance of a People*, a historical novel about the Polish Revolution of 1830, "the thrilling summons" of Lady Sandomir, a Polish noblewoman, rallies her tenants to resist Russian oppression. When Lady Sandomir's family estate is threatened by foreign occupiers, she exchanges kindling oratory for propaganda of the deed, translating herself into a fiery element as she burns down her home. Like Charlotte Brontë in *Jane Eyre* or Mary Elizabeth Braddon in *Lady Audley's Secret*, Jones uses the figure of arsonist to upend the ideals of "unchallenging womanhood" (Brantlinger, "What Is 'Sensational'" 12), but Jones does so through the lens of romantic martyrdom, not madness:

> It was the Maniac Lady. The flames rushed after her, pouring out through the windows and shattered roof, till they played around her like a robe, pure, bright, and beautiful, as though angels were busy arranging her in the garments of heaven, that her soul might appear in festal guise before the Eternal gate. Her form seemed dilated beyond the human stature with the kindled atmosphere; wildly she raised her arms towards heaven, and, as she waved, their dark shadows sailed across the land, as though she showered visible curses from her burning throne. (116–17)[16]

If flame in the shape of a woman is a specter and monster, it is also the power of light against the dark, a dilation of self, and transcendence of the human form. Self-immolation is rendered stellification. "The Maniac Lady" becomes a Marian figure, but she sits on a burning throne and her illuminated speech remains curses, promising neither victory nor justice, only revenge. Jones's uncanny fusing of angelic and diabolic imagery is typical of his reworking of the melodramatic concept of suffering womanhood. An act of power and violence wins Lady Sandomir a robe of purity and beauty, but her action, like that of the heroine of "The Pirate's Prize," is self-consuming.

Maline, a betrayed heroine who revenges herself upon her seducer in the political novel *De Brassier*, is a final instance in Jones's series of incendiaries, but she turns from the pattern of her predecessors in several key respects. Unlike her pyromaniacal sisters, Maline commits violence not as a blow against tyranny but to settle a personal vendetta. Additionally, whereas Clarron's daughter and the Lady Sandomir use arson only when threatened with imminent danger, Maline seeks out the lord who slept with her a decade earlier. After herself seducing a servant to secure entry to Walter De Brassier's country estate, she performs a reenactment of her fall by confronting the now crippled man in his bedroom as the fire she set closes around him. By accepting the initiation into the night world of desire and power her tempter has offered, Maline extravagantly inverts aspects of the melodramatic heroine. The most explicitly sexual of Jones's female characters, she alone survives the commission of her crime. As flames consume Walter's bed, she leaps from his second floor window to safety and freedom.

The Villain or the Institution? *De Brassier* as Structural Melodrama

Although Jones encourages the reader to take sadistic pleasure in Walter's death, the revenge plot in *De Brassier*'s is more complex than that of *The Romance of a People* or "The Pirate's Prize." For Maline's vengeance plays off of an explicitly political act of violence, a pairing that allows Jones to reflect on the efficacy of force as an activist strategy (Ledger, "Chartist" 53). If Maline can avenge the individual wrong she has suffered and escape unhurt, the anarchic actions of a working-class crowd that loots and burns an estate owned by the factory magnate Dorville discredit the movement seeking to ameliorate conditions in the district. In political terms, the industrialist's death matters little because his property passes to his banker and creditor, who rescues deeds, mortgages, and contracts from the burning house. By staging this transfer of power, *De Brassier* considers the limits of melodramatic revenge in a capitalist society where villainy is embodied in institutions and capital. Dorville, having anticipated that locked-out workers in the district would target the businesses of the most hated masters, insures his property at double its value: "They'll burn some factories, level a few houses, kill a few people, drink a few hogshead, destroy a good deal of property, get themselves knocked on the head, and all will go on the same as before" (332). Dorville's predictions prove substantially correct, though ironically he is one of the "few people" the rioters kill. Rituals of defiance targeting particular masters are shown insufficient to an age where insurance apportions risk among the whole class.

That Dorville's death solves nothing for his workers points to Jones's most significant innovation in his use of melodramatic form: his demotion of the villain. Following Frank Rahill and Peter Brooks, several critics emphasize that good and evil are highly individuated in the genre: "They are assigned to, they inhabit persons who . . . have no psychological complexity but who are strongly characterized" (Brooks, *Melodramatic* 16–17; see also Joyce, *Democratic* 177). In accounts informed by Brooks, the defeat of the villain restores order to a troubled social sphere, but it also leads to a paradoxical effect. Although melodrama, introduced to Britain by the Jacobin Thomas Holcroft, maintains a sensibility celebrating the "humble of the earth," the personalization of villainy forecloses analysis of social problems by indicating that these problems are questions of individual morality).[17] Indeed, the transparency of melodramatic characters means that even as plays stage crises, they carry within themselves, in the words of Martin Meisel, "an assurance of reassurance, of obscurities dispelled, ambiguities resolved, of a vigorously marked binary pattern of coherence" (67). The role of Jones's villains is markedly different. While they remain melodramatic in terms of their passion, power, and vindictiveness, they are not moral freaks, aberrations whose cruelty derives from their isolation. Instead, Jones's villains are consummate insiders who rely on mainstream institutions – the courts, the police, structures of the workplace – to commit their outrages.

Jones's innovation, however, should not be viewed as a complete break from the conventions of melodrama so much as a calling to the surface tendencies present, if submerged, within the mode. The critical emphasis on the dominant personality of stage villains has tended to eclipse the ways that their activity is embedded in larger structures.[18] In George Dibdin Pitt's *Marianne, the Child of Charity* (1844), the villain manipulates the courts in an effort to defraud the eponymous heroine of her just inheritance. Pitt's *Beggar's Petition* likewise features trials for poaching and theft at which a landowner influences the court against penniless defendants. Not only poisons and dirks but also a knowledge of the legal apparatus are tools of the trade of Victorian villainy. In Douglas Jerrold's *Black-Ey'd Susan* (1829), "the most popular play of the era," the proliferation of dangers that surround the heroine sheds light on the way even seduction plots can examine institutional power (James, "Time" 183; C. Williams 99).[19] Susan staves off eviction at the hands of her uncle until her husband William returns from sea. He pays her debts and also fends off an assault on her virtue by the smuggler Hatchet. The play's decisive crisis, however, arises only when the honest sailor interrupts a second would-be seducer. By striking the man before he realizes who he is – William's commanding officer Crosstree – the loyal tar commits an act of mutiny that carries a capital penalty. An inflexible state authority stands behind Crosstree (whose very name evokes the gallows), so it is his lust, not Hatchet's, that is truly menacing. An earlier jeremiad by William against "the Law" in the person of the bailiff who distrains Susan's goods functions as a fitting motto for the climactic court martial from which the hero narrowly escapes: "His Beelzebub's ship, the Law! . . . She's built of green timber, manned with lob-lolly boys and marines; provisioned with mouldy biscuit and bilge water, and fire nothing but red hot shot" (18). John Walker's *The Factory Lad* is a final example of a melodrama in which focus on a charismatic villain magnifies instead of eclipses the view of unjust social conditions. The play portrays an attack on a factory arising when the son of the recently deceased owner throws operatives out of work by introducing new machinery. Although the generational plot individuates the villain (by comparing his actions to his father's paternalistic consideration), *The Factory Lad* makes clear that the son, who mouths the formulas of political economy, is an avatar of broader change.

The critical judgment that the villain remains an isolated individual removed from any "larger pattern of injustice" is insufficient to each of these cases (Vicinus, "Helpless" 139). Nevertheless, the deindividuation of villainy in *De Brassier* is extreme, making a subordinate impulse of the genre an organizing principle. The novel shares with theatrical melodrama a penchant for relatively independent episodes punctuated by pyrotechnic climaxes (the volcanic eruptions, fires, naval engagements, and earthquakes that were a staple of so many plays).[20] But even as *De Brassier* seeks the literary equivalent of stage disasters, it frustrates the reader's desire to witness a decisive clash that will settle the antagonisms propelling the plot. The novel evokes climactic moments but suggests they cannot resolve the underlying crises which bring them about. An early sequence outlines this pattern. After being fired from a factory for joining a labor union, Charles Dalton stands on the edge of indigence and inanition. He and his sister are denied poor relief when Agnes rebuffs the sexual advances of a parish overseer, so Dalton sets out into London seeking work to stave off eviction and homelessness. Spying his former employer in a crowd of spectators awaiting an appearance by the royal family, the operative makes a final, desperate appeal. While the scenario is melodramatic, Jones unsettles the stark opposition between master and man by introducing the crowd as a third element. The narrator cuts repeatedly between the pivotal encounter to the undulating mass in which it is lost:

> There was a struggle and a turmoil on the spot – the rich merchant was assisted to his carriage by eager and obsequious friends – suddenly the deep booming of artillery shook the ground – all eyes were drawn in a different direction – a stretcher was hastily procured – the ghastly and motionless form of the outcast was hurried out of sight, as an unseemly object – the crowd opened to let it pass, and turned away with disgust – but speedily their aspect brightened – a man, and woman, and two little children had appeared on the distant platform of the railway station, all praised their rosy looks and pretty faces . . . martial ranks presented arms . . . – God save the queen! (48)

Not merely a reflection on the compensatory nature of state spectacle, this banal and distant view of the figures on the platform problematizes melodramatic causal narratives in which social harm is authored by individuals who can be easily identified and defeated. Not only the master, but his "obsequious friends," the indifferent crowd, the military display, and the barely glimpsed monarchy are implicated in Dalton's despair.

Indicating Jones's shift from villains as charismatic individuals, several chapters of *De Brassier* are named for institutional spaces – including "The Stock-Exchange," "The Court," and "The Town Hall" – or for parallel zones of poverty and neglect such as "The Garret" and "The Street." Jones's effort to narrate the institutional causes of harm leads to dramatic revisions of melodramatic plotting. Following Dalton's arrest for assault, while the laborer awaits his turn in the dock, the reader witnesses a discussion between lawyers about how to dispose of a case of forcible seduction. Although the evidence is damning, all agree the accused should be acquitted because his counsel, the nephew of a prominent judge, is setting out on his career. A jarring retelling of the archetypal melodramatic violation, the scene omits the villain and practically the crime, focusing instead on the system of privilege that surrounds and protects it.

If the assailant in the preceding case remains out of view, the introduction of Walter De Brassier allows Jones to explore the clichés of stage villainy more directly. Walter is the brother and rival of the protagonist – the penniless aristocrat Simon, who throws his lot in with the Chartists. This character affords Jones the opportunity to reflect on the stereotypes of "Old Corruption," the image of predatory elites preying on the people. As if aware of his prescribed role, Walter aspires to but cannot fill out the theatrical type of libertine:

> He kept his hounds and hunters, though he never hunted . . . he stored his
> cellar, though his physicians would not allow him to drink his wine; he kept
> his mistress, though he had no passions to gratify . . . He had all these things,
> because it was customary to have them . . . His grooms were the enjoyers of
> his stud . . . his servants rioted on his cellar . . . and his dearest friend had the
> benefit of his mistress. (48)

Complicating formulas of the debauched profligate, Jones demonstrates
how the stereotype fails to comprehend a system that invests a wide class in
the maintenance of the ruling clique. Nevertheless, the pattern of social
organization Walter represents is more insidious than the deeds of diabolic
supermen: "There was no particular vice in him – but he was the encour-
ager of vices in others . . . The people hated him . . . in their eyes he was
represented as a monster of excess, rioting in sin and luxury . . . Some huge
modern ogre . . . The individual obtained the obloquy due to the system
only" (48).

   Jones had completed six chapters of the second volume of his novel
when financial difficulties bankrupted *Notes to the People*. Never returning
to *De Brassier* or seeking to publish it separately, he was content to allow it
to trail off in defeat, a final testament to the fracturing and enervation of
the movement that it chronicled and upon which it depended for an
interpretive community to make its project vital. But *De Brassier* is fragmentary in senses other than its abrupt ending. Subplots are only tenuously
linked to the main action and some story lines drop out entirely.
Compounding the splintering plot, the novel adopts a variety of styles.
Chapters about a Chartist meeting are made up entirely of direct discourse
while the narrator's account of life on Walter De Brassier's estate resembles
good-humored Trollopian satire (a resemblance heightened by a focus on
rural sports and the disposal of sinecures). The novel's original title, "The
History of a Democratic Movement, Compiled from the Journal of a
Demagogue, The Confessions of a Democrat, and The Minutes of a
Spy," draws attention to the novel's "heteroglot form," an effect marked
typographically by the different fonts used in each line of the title (Ledger,
"Chartist" 50).

   One might consider this fragmentation artistic failure: Jones never
achieves the labyrinthine interweaving of G. W. M. Reynolds's *Mysteries
of London* or the delicate social maps of Dickens's urban panoramas. But
utilizing principles of hybridity and serial discontinuity learned at the
theater and in the radical press, Jones shifts melodramatic narrative away
from personified evil to social harm. In this light, fragmentation seems an
effect of Jones's commitment to show the insufficiency of the old

antagonists. Attempting to narrate villainy diffused throughout the social structure and embodied in institutions, *De Brassier* arrives at several dead ends: clashes that are not climactic, acts of vengeance that right no wrong, still-born conspiracies that mistake the nature of their opponents.

"Begin at Home": Jones's Challenge to Separate Spheres

Woman's Wrongs, which appeared alongside *De Brassier* in the second volume of *Notes to the People*, gives the most sustained attention to questions of gender of any work in Jones's corpus, enlarging the picture from melo-dramatic seduction plots, which inevitably resurface, to encompass women's family relationships and working lives. Whereas *De Brassier* is a fictional history recounting the failed struggle for democracy and the cost of the exclusion of the laboring population from the institutions of government, *Woman's Wrongs* seeks to "pourtray [*sic*] the working of our social system in the *domestic sphere*" (*Notes* 514). In a series of five novellas, it traces female exploitation and oppression through the different social classes.[21] While *Woman's Wrongs* never explicitly calls for female suffrage, a fact for which Ella Dzelzainis faults it (89), the preface glosses the stories that follow as effects of women's lack of political power: "Society counts woman as nothing in its institutions, and yet makes her bear the greatest share of sufferings inflicted by a system in which she has no voice! Brute force first imposed the law – and moral force compels her to obey it now" (1). The form of loosely linked narratives proved more congenial to Jones's imagina-tion and the exigencies of his journal than the novelistic structure of *De Brassier*. But the full significance of the work emerges only when the stories are regarded as a composite piece (Ledger, "Chartist" 60). By showing female dependence extending from sweated milliners to titled elites whose fortunes nevertheless hinge on the exigencies of the marriage market, Jones isolates gender as a specific category of oppression, imbricated with social class for its expression but also functioning independently.

It should be stressed again that Jones's writing breaks from most Chartist discourse, which rarely addresses the subordination of women as a central political concern. Jones joined Chartism after women's participa-tion in the movement had declined from its highpoint in the late 1830s. Between 1838 and 1848, women organized nearly two hundred local female Chartist groups in England and Scotland, some numbering as many as three thousand members (Chase, *Chartism* 42; Clark, *Struggle* 228; Rogers 85–123). Where *The Times* and other middle-class papers decried female participation in activist politics, Henry Vincent remarked in the *Western*

Vindicator that women's organizations "may be justly ranked as one of the most important features in the present political movement."[22] Nevertheless, the proportion of female signers of the Chartist petitions fell significantly between 1839 and 1848 (from between 13 percent and 20 percent of the 1.28 million signers in 1839 to 8 percent in 1848) (Chase, *Chartism* 359). These figures track a decline in women's overall participation brought about by a complex set of causes, including the increasing formalization of activist culture in which the Chartists turned from a "heritage of community mobilization" to a greater reliance on party political structures (Clark, *Struggle* 220; D. Thompson, *Chartists* 122). As importantly, women's subordinate role in the movement and the Chartist commitment to a middle-class vision of domesticity and the male breadwinner ideal may also have led to women's alienation from Chartism.[23] Against this backdrop, *Woman's Wrongs* is striking for its criticism of sentimental versions of separate spheres and domesticity – and of these ideologies' inflection within radical politics.

The title of Jones's series affiliates it with Charlotte Elizabeth Tonna's *The Wrongs of Woman* (1843–44). The distance between Tonna's didactic tales and Jones's fiction, however, illustrates the way Jones departs from central assumptions of the factory movement. The agitation for factory legislation framed its argument for the need to reduce working hours in ways that cast home as a woman's proper sphere, presenting industrial labor as a threat to female virtue, marital bonds, and the moral education of children (Zlotnick 188–95). Closely aligned to the efforts of the parliamentary leader Lord Ashley, Tonna's stories instantiate claims about the disruptive and degrading effects of waged female employment.[24] In "The Forsaken Home," the farmer John Smith emigrates to an urban center with his wife Alice and their five children. His failure to obtain employment and the consequent necessity of Alice becoming a factory hand deranges family life, a process Tonna chronicles more fully than workplace experiences. Alice neglects her domestic duties, the "natural employment of woman" and John, having lost self-respect granted by "honestly labouring for the support of his family," turns violent drunkard (98, 119). Deprived of maternal care, the children become sickly and disobedient. That they too join the industrial workforce at the story's end illustrates how the factory system's destruction of the family extends across generations. For Tonna, as often for advocates of factory reform, the effect of capitalist exploitation of women is viewed through an idealized lens that celebrates patriarchal authority as divinely ordained: "It is the monstrous abuse of forcing the female to forsake her proper sphere that gives rise to such deplorable wretchedness: no previous acquirements can remedy this evil . . . the effects will be both seen and felt of such a wicked outrage on God's providential government."[25]

The Wrongs of Woman provided a limited model for Jones's series, which also treats the intersection of women's work, family life, and romance, but pointedly omits scenes of female labor in factories. If Tonna depicts women's employment outside the home as destructive and corrupting, Jones's fiction details how family relationships are themselves exploitative, connected to the marketplace rather than independent from it. One strategy Jones uses is to dramatize how the Victorian home was in fact often a workplace. Like Henry Mayhew's *Morning Chronicle* articles about outworkers in the London millinery, dress-making, and tailoring indus-tries, which conceptualize private dwellings as a crucial space of capitalist production, demonstrating how life in the home is connected by so many threads to the factory system, *Woman's Wrongs* relentlessly overlays the domestic sphere and the degraded world of work.[26] By describing the drudgery of chores and exploitation within home-based industry, Jones upends cherished notions about the necessity of women remaining insu-lated from the compromises of a market economy. In this regard, *Woman's Wrongs* departs from most Victorian writing about female labor, which, as Helsinger, Sheets, and Veeder have shown, misconstrues woman's work by failing to recognize how much occurs within the home mediated by familial relationships (111).[27] Jones's series takes aim at precisely these occlusions. The opening installment describes reformers' blindness to women's domestic plight:

> Many a battle is fought by the dim circle of the household hearth, as noble, or as terrible, as that with crowned brigands on the fields of "glory." Oh! many a suffering is endured in the still bosom of familiar life, as bitter or as hopeless as that of the unlaurelled martyr at the bigot's stake! (1)

Focusing on suffering in the "bosom of familiar life," three stories represent labor in domestic contexts (Haywood, "Introduction" xxiv). In "The Tradesman's Daughter," Laura Trenton's (unpaid) employment in her father's grocery has reduced her existence to that of "a human counting machine" (69). Her toil, however, is hidden from view:

> A white little hand might be seen driving a large steel pen at a rapid rate, behind a crimson curtain – while, against the rails of a high placed desk lay the top edge of a ponderous ledger, over which, ever and anon, some delicate silken tresses were sweeping to and fro, from a face, invisible to the customers of the counter. (69)

This fetishized juxtaposition of Laura's feminine delicacy and the masculine instruments with which she works might imply a kind of life more appropriate to the young woman, one in which her "little hand" and "silken tresses" could captivate a suitable lover. Jones, however, criticizes romantic relationships along parallel lines as Laura's work for her father, revealing once again the home as a domain in which women's economic and affective labor is exploited and erased.

When her cousin Edward becomes apprenticed in the shop, flirtation and courtship disturb the monotony of Laura's existence, but she soon agrees to complete his bookkeeping tasks, doubling her work so he can pursue his vocation as a poet. Edward's use of Laura's accounting, moreover, parallels the division of labor between writer and muse. After Laura is forced to marry her father's partner, Edward sublimates his love into a story that shares the title of Jones's novella. What follows is self-critical scrutiny of social problem fiction. Edward's version of "The Tradesman's Daughter" is plagiarized in turn by the unscrupulous author Sucknoodle, who publishes it to great success. This dizzying sequence of appropriations – Laura's life becoming Edward's raw material, Sucknoodle's hit, and, metaleptically, Jones's magazine copy – highlights women's exclusion from the literary marketplace. Although the story repeatedly foregrounds Laura writing (making bookkeeping entries or composing letters), it is men who tell her story: "Such solace was not Laura's. [Edward] could fly out in the sunshine – she, like a brooding dove, must fold her wings, and sorrow in the shade" (89). By situating authorship with a discredited poet and the best-selling plagiarist, Jones points out the limits of his own project, a final, self-referential twist on his sustained criticism of the trope of male rescue: social problem fiction renders women passive objects of suffering dependent on self-interested authors rather than agents of their own liberation.

Where "The Tradesman's Daughter" documents industry based within the home, a second story takes aim at ideologies that would sanctify the sexual division of labor, consigning women to housework and childcare and men to waged employment. If Tonna portrays the forces of industrialism disturbing the protective and nurturing space of the family, for Jones, women's subordinate position at home reinforces their degradation in the social world. "The Working Man's Wife" describes the dangers a union activist poses to the well-being of his wife and children, suggesting a skeptical stance toward Chartism's own vision of male prerogatives. A capsule summary of the story, which recounts the downward trajectory of a working-class London family, will prove helpful for further analysis. Shortly after the birth of John and Margaret Haspen's second daughter Mary, John loses his position as a bricklayer in the employer Barrowson's manufacturing firm. To make ends meet, the husband conspires with his former workmate Latchman to steal from the company warehouse. The thieves are caught and sentenced to ten years hard labor followed by transportation for life. Playing against type, Barrowson aids the penniless Margaret by hiring her as a porteress. She keeps this position until the employer has an affair with her older daughter Catherine, at which point he sets Margaret up as an inn-keeper outside of London. The soon-abandoned girl descends into a life of vice. Meanwhile, John and Latchman escape and make their way to Margaret's inn. There, in fulfillment of the perverse counter-providence that rules Jones's fiction, the escaped criminals meet and murder their former employer. In another parodically melodramatic coincidence, the repentant Catherine happens upon her father, which leads to his discovery and death at the hands of the police. Margaret is arrested as John's accomplice and, wrongly convicted, hanged in sight of her daughters.

The stuff of penny bloods or the "bombastic sublimity" of the melodramatic stage (Brooks, *Melodramatic* 40), this prurient story is far from Tonna's morally improving didactic fiction. Its sensational form, however, should not distract from the argument it advances. "The Working Man's Wife" anticipates melodramas of the 1860s and later, in which focus shifts from outside threats menacing the family to troubling dynamics within domestic life itself (Kaplan 34). The real threat to the well-being of the titular character is not primarily the villainous employer, but the father and husband whose masculine authority has been undermined and who goes to increasingly extreme measures to reclaim it. If external pressures, such as John's loss of work and Catherine's seduction, set in motion the Haspens' downfall, these forces activate possibilities implicit in the nuclear unit. From the opening scene, Jones presents a ruthlessly unsentimental view of home life, which is defined for the wife by "toil, domestic duties, [and] the painful care of her child" but for John as a cynical version of separate spheres, in which he can look "on his house merely as a resting-place – at his wife merely as a servant without wages, whom he found convenient to prepare his meals, and make and share his bed" (4).

Frightening violence erupts in this context after John loses his employment and begins to drink, but the power dynamics of marriage condition John's response to the erosion of his authority grounded on his role as breadwinner. In a stark challenge to the readers of *Notes to the People*, the narrative repeatedly characterizes John as a union militant, a gesture that suggests the complicity of the radical paper's audience in the attitudes and actions the story criticizes. John's commitment to working-class solidarity coupled with his embrace of gender hierarchy echo Jones's confrontational preface, which underlines how often "the well-wishers of mankind" ignore women's wrongs (1). John's union loyalties are particularly striking in the context of *Notes to the People*, which included a weekly column "Trades Grievances," featuring reports on ongoing strikes and accounts from union activists of acts "of oppression or injustice" (*Notes* 579).

"The Working Man's Wife" exposes the hypocrisy of Chartist discourse that fashions a masculinist radicalism the protector of womankind. As the danger John represents to his family becomes clear, his invocations of its members' well-being ring increasingly hollow. In a scene immediately following an altercation between John and Margaret, in which the father accidently burns his youngest daughter, John strikes a defiant pose: "I tell you from the time bread fell short – my children fell sick – they'll never recover it! It's the life of my wife and children the thieves have robbed me of!" (14). While Barrowson's portion of blame is undeniable, John's scape-goating is off, for the story presents the family's self-destructiveness. Indeed, after John's conviction, Margaret wants to escape her relationship but realizes she can neither remarry nor divorce. Margaret's various occupations during John's imprisonment ironize the story's title, which becomes increasingly ill fitting for the economically independent woman bound legally to the convict. Her efforts at autonomy are thwarted by the supremacy of her marital identity, even as her relationship degenerates into naked antagonism and enforced separation. In this regard, "The Working Man's Wife," like "The Tradesman's Daughter," anticipates an 1859 essay by Harriet Martineau, which argues that familial categories disguise female employment, because women often perform marketplace work at home to support the ventures of husbands and fathers ("Female").

Although Haspen's working-class background is far from Jones's own, it is tempting to view this story about a radical's destructive marriage as an effort to grapple with inequities in the author's own life. Such inequities appear in flashes in Jones's correspondence. A pair of autumn 1850 letters from his mother-in-law informed Jones, traveling on a lecture tour following his release from prison, of his wife Jane's miscarriage and convalescence, then noted two weeks later that Jane "was a little disappointed in seeing in the Star last week that your engagements would keep you in the country longer than you at first thought they would."[28] A cramped and cross-hatched letter from Jane Atherley Jones offers a similarly devastating glimpse of the dissatisfactions she suffered as the wife of an activist-writer jailed for a cause for which she had little sympathy.[29] Addressed to Jones in

Tothill Fields Prison, the letter reports news of the publication of a double issue of the *Labourer* and a pamphlet concerning Jones's trial as well as her efforts to coordinate a lobbying campaign to improve his conditions. After giving an update on family life, including how a son remarked "the other evening 'what a long walk Papa is making that he does not come home all the time,'" the note slips into another key: "My health is as usual . . . You tell me You tell me not to brood over the present to look to the future – what has the future ever done for me! . . . You may look to the future with more satisfaction for your future . . . is in your own hands – mine is not."[30] Without speculating further on Jones's capacity for self-reflection, it is notable that his most scathing indictment of marital inequality features a radical, formerly imprisoned protagonist.

Barrowson, Haspen's libertine tormentor, is strongly cast as a stage villain, but in a surprising twist on melodramatic convention he also provides solutions for Margaret's financial difficulties, including establishing her as a proprietor of a public house. Jones's displacing and complicating the villain's guilt continues the trend we observed in *De Brassier*. Where *De Brasier* looks at institutional structures which dwarf the actions of individuals, *Woman's Wrongs*, which likewise examines institutions, including marriage, work, and the courts, further details a broad pattern of male participation in female disempowerment. In the series, louche aristocrats are not the only men to benefit from the subordination of women. Negative romantic relationships occur between characters from the same class, a crucial difference with stage melodrama. Although Jones likens men in these pairings to aristocratic seducers, the rhetoric has been loosened from its class referent to describe gender relations throughout society. Emily's shop boy lover in "The Girl with the Red Hands" goes to "masked balls and casinos – where sensuality panders to sin and the foundations of ruin are laid for so many and so many!" (102). The porter Frederick Treadstone, who harasses the heroine of "The Young Milliner," is a half-life version of an aristocratic sensualist. If "decay and perdition" are traceable to the "moneyed classes," Jones's stories insist that women face endemic violence from men in their own milieu (41).

The voyeuristic quality of the stories, which several critics emphasize, is unsettling in a series that insists on widespread complicity in the abuse of women. Jones's preface warns the reader that the stories that follow represent "the world that surrounds you – such is the world that made you – such is the world you help to make – go! try to alter it, and BEGIN AT HOME" (1). As if to call out, then humiliate, the male reader's desire, several novellas begin with a fetishizing look at the female protagonist, only to affiliate the narrator's gaze with that of a suspect character.[31] The first scene of "The Young Milliner" observes the eponymous heroine through her garret window, but on the next page the reader learns that the disreputable Treadstone has also "noticed the beauty of Anna, the young milliner – and the libertine was aroused within him" (41). "The Young Milliner," like "The Working Man's Wife," ends with the public death of the heroine: Anna's pauper corpse is dissected for a group of medical students, reducing her body to a literal object. As one of the young men in the class is her ex-lover Charles, who abandons her when she becomes pregnant, the narrator calls to mind the novel's opening sequence, in which the hero watches and daydreams about his beloved. In a morbid version of the narrator's/the reader's/Charles's/Treadstone's objectifying gaze, the students in the gallery respond excitedly to the macabre spectacle: "All heads were raised – the words 'young woman' had riveted attention – all eyes were fixed on the body" (68).

Jones's fiction looks ahead to the sensation genre that came to dominate the literary marketplace in the 1860s, signaling a major break in realist fiction and a challenge to mid-century gender politics. The relationship between stage melodrama, working-class literature, and sensation fiction has been long appreciated, beginning with contemporary reviewers who remarked disconcertedly that authors such as Mary Elizabeth Braddon made "the literature of the Kitchen the favourite reading of the Drawing-room" (*North British Review* September 1865). Nevertheless, critics of sensation fiction frequently only gesture toward working-class fiction rather than analyze particular connections (Law, "Memoir" 203). Jones's stories of female passion, exploitation, and revenge would be one productive starting point.[32] So many of the startling aspects of Braddon, Collins, and their peers – the combination of romance and realism, the translation of a Gothic sensibility to domestic settings, the depiction of heroines actively involved in crime, and the intense scrutiny of women's proper roles – are on full view in Jones's work. Like the sensation novelists a decade later, Jones highlights the contradictions in the principle of *couverture* by depicting the home as a place of peril and potential violence and by making marriage an enabling problem of the narrative rather than its resolution (Pykett 55–58).

PART III

Radical Internationalism in the 1840s and 1850s

CHAPTER 6

"Outworks of the Citadel of Corruption": The Chartist Press Reports the Empire

Over the past decade and a half, a gradual but marked shift has taken place in our understanding of the relationship between Victorian literature and culture and the British Empire. The once widespread assumption that support for the colonial endeavor, faith in Britain's civilizing mission, and belief in European racial superiority inevitably marked the era's cultural artifacts has given way to increased recognition of the diverse and conflictual responses colonial issues provoked. This reevaluation has proceeded on several fronts. Recent studies on cosmopolitanism have analyzed the ideology's dialectical nature, the way it underwrote support for a globalizing capitalism but was also turned against dominant cultural norms as a critical discourse celebrating peace and international cooperation.[1] In these accounts, the empire destabilized British culture and provoked complex literary responses that grappled with the "antithetical scales and perspectives" demanded by a global political and economic system (Agathocleous 14).

Other critics have demonstrated how literature about foreign cultures intervened in domestic controversies around such issues as industrialism and the "woman question." Feminist scholars in particular have emphasized the importance of parsing the social position of British writers who looked at the colonies, arguing that the marginal location of women and the conflation of racist and sexist stereotypes made female authors more likely than their male counterparts to regard racial hierarchies with skepticism and to celebrate cultural difference as a way to criticize gender inequality at home (Meyer 9–11; O'Gorman 230–35). Patrick Brantlinger's *Victorian Literature and Postcolonial Studies* highlights the field's recent evolution. Whereas his own groundbreaking *Rule of Darkness* evoked a culture effectively unanimous in support of colonialism, Brantlinger's later work has emphasized debate and fracture, foregrounding domestic opposition to the empire and pointing out how even explicitly imperialist texts sometimes "weave Oriental and occasionally contestatory voices into their accounts" (81).

The recognition of divisions within British society has led to important reevaluations of the significance of such landmark events as the Great Exhibition and the Indian rebellion of 1857. In particular, Christopher Herbert has upended conventional wisdom about the aftermath of 1857, long considered a moment of near complete consolidation of support for jingoistic imperialism. In Herbert's account, far from uniting the public, the rebellion provoked a sustained cultural crisis that shattered Britons' image of a benevolent empire. In a series of sensitive readings of contemporary histories of the rebellion, Herbert depicts a society strenuously debating the proper response to the revolt as it tried to come to terms with the abuse, racism, and violence of the colonial regime. Restoring a sense of contest to this crucial episode, Herbert's work takes issue with Foucauldian-inflected scholarship by showing the insufficiency of models in which "all the mechanisms of imperialist society, political, cultural, psychological, work in concert to reinforce and to rationalize domination" (5).

In light of these studies, metropolitan culture vis-à-vis the colonies has come to seem more dynamic, but we are only beginning to appreciate the full diversity of opinion on the many issues the empire raised. The perspectives of key groups are still largely missing from our account, including the voices of working-class people and the radical movements that tried to represent their interests, a striking absence given that these groups offered some of the period's most searching criticism of the empire. Even Herbert's study is marked by the class divide that bedevils scholarship. Herbert contends that explicit support for the rebels' cause was an insuperable barrier journalists and historians of the conflict never dared cross and claims that "to call for so much ideological consistency would be to wish for a book that could not possibly have been written and published in England at that moment" (168). Such prominent figures as the Chartist politician Ernest Jones and the radical newspaper editor G. W. M. Reynolds, however, crossed this very boundary, trying to rally their working-class constituencies to support the rebels' effort to overthrow British rule. Moreover, Jones's and Reynolds's responses were not the result of a traumatic shock that, in Herbert's telling, gripped the middle-class public in the wake of the rebellion. Rather, they grew out of a tradition of writing in the radical press skeptical of the colonial system, a tradition that provided a coherent framework with which to understand unfolding events and in certain instances had predicted them. The inclusion of radical and working-class perspectives on the colonies thus changes our understanding of the nature of dissent, revealing new fault lines in metropolitan society while broadening the focus from individual voices and internally divided texts to the institutions and traditions that nourished criticism of the empire.

Focusing on two of the most popular papers of the 1830s and 1840s, the *Northern Star* and the *Chartist Circular*, this chapter analyzes the treatment of colonial questions in Chartist print culture. With the following chapter, which takes up post-Chartist responses to European revolution, it examines internationalist currents in radical thought while considering how the category of citizen translated to contexts outside Britain. As the Chartists defined themselves by their exclusion from key aspects of national life, their perspective on Britain's aggressive and expanding mid-century colonialism was unique. From the vantage point of critics of the state, they variously described the colonial endeavor as the usurpation of the popular rights of native peoples, the extension of an exploitative economic system under which the working classes suffered, and an ideological matrix designed to distract from the pressing need for domestic change. The movement press synthesized a utilitarian tradition skeptical of militarism and colonial rule, an evangelical universalism opposed to slavery, and a radical analysis of the metropolitan class structure to forge a scathing critique of British imperial ambitions.

Studies of Chartism and radicalism by social historians have challenged received ideas about nationalism in several crucial respects, but they have had less to say about the empire.[2] Following the formidable example of E. P. Thompson, social historians have placed more emphasis on local institutions, customs, and struggles than on international and colonial contexts in constituting ordinary people's sense of self. In the words of Susan Thorne, "History from the bottom up has been preeminently a history of everyday lives whose horizons are invariably local" (3). This chapter describes how Chartist print culture brought colonial controversies and domestic crises into the same analytic frame for tens of thousands of working-class readers. Chartist papers and journals spilled copious ink commenting upon the abolition of West Indian apprenticeship in 1838, the six major colonial wars fought in the 1830s and 1840s (in Afghanistan, China, India, and southern Africa), the expanding network of Christian overseas missions, and the idea that emigration to the colonies could heal social divisions at home by providing the poor opportunities denied them in Britain. The Chartists drew connections between domestic misrule and poverty and famine in India, between the state's suppression of internal dissent and military interventions around the globe, and between an inhumane industrial system and the degraded condition of freed blacks. Ireland's immiseration, its rejection of Protestant missionaries, and the draconian measures with which the state met Irish protest made the Chartists wary of claims that the empire would bring civilization to backward peoples. Named for the 1798 journal of the United Irishmen, the *Northern Star* put forward a brief for rapprochement between the Chartists and Irish nationalists. This priority, as well as the concerns of thousands of Irish Chartists, inflected coverage of coercion, the Repeal movement, and the famine.[3]

Consistently celebrating colonial revolts and military resistance to British aggression, Chartist writers inverted Orientalist discourse by casting their own rulers in stereotypical images of pagan natives while rendering colonial subjects as democratic patriots. At the same time, a language of development and nationhood left Chartist ideology vulnerable to more pro-imperialist perspectives, especially when reporting conflictual relations between working-class emigrants and indigenous inhabitants of the settler colonies. Nevertheless, Chartist writing makes clear that just as patriotism remained a fluid, negotiated category throughout the 1830s and 1840s, at times critical of the status quo and at other times underwriting conciliatory politics, imperialist ideology was not always passively consumed or blindly accepted. If the colonies were, as in Catherine Hall and Sonya Rose's formulation, "part of the given world that had made [the British] who they were," this world was one the Chartists questioned, challenged, and sought to transform (3).

Coverage of Empire in the *Northern Star* and *Chartist Circular*

As the most widely read Chartist periodicals, the *Northern Star* and *Chartist Circular* represent important resources for understanding what working-class readers learned about the empire in the 1830s and 1840s. The *Star*, a stamped weekly priced at four and a half pence, was founded by the Chartist politician Feargus O'Connor in Leeds in 1837 and remained there until 1844 when it moved to London. Its most important editors were the Swedenborgian minister William Hill (1837–43) and the young ultra-radical and internationalist George Julian Harney (1845–51). The *Star* was the only financially solvent publication of the more than one hundred Chartist journals and papers, but despite its commercial success and a professionalism that allowed it to employ seven reporters in 1842, it maintained the defiant ethos of the radical press of the 1830s. Profits were plowed back into expenses associated with the movement, and the paper relied heavily on the personnel of the "War of the Unstamped" – Harney had been a newsboy for the *Poor Man's Guardian* – and on submissions from readers, who contributed poetry, editorials, and reports on local events. The *Chartist Circular* was established in 1839 by the Universal Suffrage Central Committee for Scotland, a leadership organization for the movement in the north. Modeled on the *Anti-Corn Law Circular* and edited by the union activist William Thomson, the educational journal cost only one halfpenny, avoiding the stamp tax by omitting news items. It reprinted articles by such middle-class activists as the abolitionist and peace lecturer George Thompson and the militant Quaker William Howitt, an editorial practice that reflected ties between Scottish Chartism and middle-class radicalism.

The two publications shared wide popularity. The *Circular* sold 20,000 copies per issue; although it failed to survive the depression of the early 1840s, Thomson claimed that he had sent "two million little agitators abroad in the world" over the journal's first two years (September 18, 1841). The *Star* had a circulation of 36,000 in 1839 – exceeded only by the combined sales of *The Times*'s six weekly issues – and between 7000 and 13,000 for most of the next decade. But these figures fail to indicate the extent of the papers' audience, given the degree to which copies were shared and read aloud in a variety of contexts, including Chartist discussion groups, radical public houses, and working-class reading rooms (Chase and Vargo 459; Epstein, "Feargus O'Connor" 69–70). Nor do raw numbers express the cultural authority the publications enjoyed as semiofficial organs of the Chartist movement. The *Star* in particular was praised in countless poems, toasts, and speeches for its role in fostering a critical working-class culture. These weekly best sellers drew disparate and local struggles into a single movement and created a national "community in anonymity," similar to those Benedict Anderson's seminal work on nationalism describes but composed overwhelmingly of working-class readers (36).

Part of the popularity of the *Star* stemmed from its encyclopedic ambition, its desire to function as a "universal press," which unlike other radical sheets could rival the breadth of middle-class dailies (Pickering, *O'Connor* 76). Its survey of the contemporary scene included regular reports from the colonies, often grouped in weekly columns entitled "Foreign Intelligence" and "The Imperial Parliament." The literature page published excerpts from *Simmond's Colonial Magazine* throughout 1844 and recommended monographs on China, Australia, and New Zealand as well as a novel set in southern Africa. Letters to the editor frequently evinced interest in the empire, and the *Star* republished articles on colonial topics taken from middle-class newspapers, such as an account of a tiger attack in India; reports about the exploration of Africa; and a satire from *Punch*, which described the unjust military conquests of Rome and Greece as models for the latter-day British empire.[4] In addition, the paper regularly reported shipwrecks and other travails suffered by emigrants (September 9, 1843; March 20, 1847; June 2, 1849), and it printed letters written by emigrants themselves warning their countrymen of the hardships of colonial life (April 1, 1843). Finally, fiction in the *Star* took up questions of empire. Thomas Martin Wheeler's *Sunshine and Shadow* (1849–50), which alternates between England and a West Indian island, expands the atlas of the mid-nineteenth-century British novel, challenging the "spatial-moral order" that in Edward Said's formulation relegates Britain's colonial possessions to the textual margins (Said 64). Wheeler's peripatetic *Bildungsroman* suggests instead that any imaginative map of contemporary Britain need encompass the places it rules over the sea. The final section of this chapter examines *Sunshine and Shadow* as an experimental *Bildungsroman* that looks ahead to proto-modernist versions of the genre and a forceful intervention in debates about post-emancipation society in the Caribbean.[5]

While the *Star*'s coverage of the colonies was largely unsystematic, the format of the *Circular* as an educational journal allowed room for more comprehensive analysis. A serialized biography of Toussaint L'Ouverture recounted the slave revolts in St. Domingo, a group of essays on British involvement in India lambasted a history of misrule, and an abbreviated encyclopedia introduced readers to the nations of the world. As in the *Star*, the correspondence and poetry columns included accounts of the problems emigrants confronted. And coverage of protest meetings, the only kind of current event to feature regularly in the *Circular*, included several reports of lectures opposed to the Opium and Afghanistan Wars. In short, coverage of the empire was an integral part of both papers, and their critique of the colonial system developed out of a wide-ranging frame of reference.

Colonial Tyranny and Domestic Misrule in the Chartist Press

The first decades of Queen Victoria's reign saw the rapid expansion of the empire, but they also marked a period of sharp questioning of the government's foreign policy. Although middle-class writers from Edward Gibbon Wakefield to Thomas Carlyle trumpeted emigration as a safety valve that would heal domestic strife by allowing the poor opportunities overseas, support for emigration did not translate into unanimous endorsement of all aspects of empire building. In particular, British military adventures were exposed to an unprecedented degree of criticism by the small but newly politicized Peace Society, a broad-based anti-militia movement, and the American autodidact Elihu Burritt's League of Universal Brotherhood, the first pacifist group to obtain a mass membership in England or elsewhere. The Peace Society alone held 270 lectures in 1844 and distributed more than a half million tracts against the militia two years later (Ceadel 345; *NS* May 23, 1846). This broader movement nurtured Chartist journalism, but skepticism toward Christian missions and the supposed benefits of free trade distinguished Chartists from middle-class pacifists.[6]

From 1839 to 1842, items about the wars in Afghanistan and China dominated news coverage of imperial issues in the *Star* and *Circular*. Starting from the assumption that their government was illegitimate and abusive, the Chartists imagined the British state acting with the same coercive power around the globe. The wars, pursued in the Chartists' view to enrich British opium merchants and prop up unpopular figureheads, became a lens with which to regard a metropolitan society founded on political exclusion and economic competition. At the same time, reporting events thousands of miles away posed significant problems for the Chartist press. The *Star*'s writing about European radicalism and the revolutions of 1848 was aided by diverse connections with political exiles in England, including Friedrich Engels, whose articles appeared under the byline "Our Foreign Correspondent." But besides occasional eyewitness reports from disaffected soldiers and emigrants, most factual information about the colonies came from sources sympathetic to British policy: clippings from colonial newspapers and *The Times*, governmental circulars, and parliamentary debates. To remedy this difficulty, the Chartists adopted two strategies: criticism of mainstream reports and attention to domestic protest against the wars.

Analyzing the practices of other publications was a mode of media criticism with a long lineage in the radical press's treatment of domestic issues. Critiques of colonial policy might be delivered with a simple, ironizing headline, such as "More Robbery – The Annexation of the Punjuab," which introduced a reprinted announcement of a military victory (*NS* May 26, 1849). But occasionally the *Star* made the stamped press's coverage the central story:

> The unrighteous quarrel of the "Shopkeepers" with the Chinese empire has afforded food for all the newspapers during the past week; and, with marvellous ingenuity, the hired hacks of the "shopkeeping" fraternity have laboured to mystify the whole matter, by talking contemptuously of the Chinese as the "celestials" – by prating of the injuries which *we* have received. (April 4, 1840)

Biased and class bound in the *Star*'s view, the middle-class press deployed an Orientalist rhetoric to disguise the divisions embodied by a war for free trade. Only by regarding the Chinese as a mystified other could restrictions on opium smugglers appear an injury "which *we* have received."

The *Star* and *Circular* gave as much attention to domestic criticism of the wars as to the conflicts themselves. Over a space of two months in the summer of 1841, the *Star* reported a Chartist meeting at Bradford which denounced the government's interventions in China, Canada, Portugal, and the Levant (June 12, 1841), a lecture by Harney in Sunderland on Whig foreign policy (July 24, 1841), and a speech by Thomas Cooper in Leicester that excoriated overseas entanglements, including "that most iniquitous war which had no other professed object than a determination to slaughter people with the sword who were unwilling to be poisoned with opium!" (July 10, 1841). The next year, the *Circular* published portions of a "brilliant speech" about the "Affghan Crusade" by George Thompson at a Peace Society meeting in Houndsditch (June 11, 1842), as well as a Manchester and Salford Auxiliary Peace Society resolution condemning the Afghanistan War (July 12, 1842). An address by Arthur O'Neill's Christian Chartist Church of Birmingham called upon the town's citizens to refuse to enlist in the army or serve in the militia (*CC* June 4, 1842). O'Neill himself had founded a Peace Society branch in Birmingham, and his activism included disrupting a recruiting parade at the Birmingham fair and publicly promising to pay no income tax to a government at war, a pledge for which he was arrested (*NS* September 3, 1842; Tyrrell 85). O'Neill's advocacy continued a tradition of Chartist anti-militarism and "counter recruitment," which extended from the early addresses of the London Working Men's Association to the National Anti-Militia Association organized during the Oregon controversy of 1846 (Ceadel 331–32, 358–59; Goodway 56).

Turning from media criticism and reports of domestic protest to writing about the empire itself, homology served as the central rhetorical structure the Chartists used to analyze events overseas. Knowing little about life or politics in the colonies, the Chartists described events there as a repetition of the misrule they suffered at home. This stance was in some sense problematic because it allowed the Chartists to dispense with specific aspects of colonial power and elide internal divisions in indigenous society; yet it also enabled them to transcend negative ideas of racial and cultural difference. A *Star* editorial about the Opium War asserted that economic exploitation in Britain and a war to enforce free trade were the reverse sides of the same coin:

The circumstances which have brought about our new position, in regard to China, are but parts and consequences of that general system, which, for years and years, has been prostrating the glory of our name and fame yet lower and lower into the dust before surrounding nations; while it has, at the same time, being gradually beating down, to a depth of suffering and slavery unparalleled, the sons of our own soil on their native hearths. We now bring those circumstances before the people as an useful illustration of the system which they must destroy. (January 18, 1840)

Both the *Star* and the *Circular* evaluated Chinese society in ways that indicted the failings of Britain (*CC* April 11, 1840; *NS* February 11, 1843). A reviewer in the *Star* recommended a "splendid" book on China, because it showed "the powers and capabilities, of a people who have learned how to keep and feed a population of 300,000,000 without having to deem the working portion of it 'surplus'!" (February 11, 1843).

Criticism of Malthusian philosophy formed an important link between accounts of the empire and analysis of the domestic scene. By justifying inequality as a natural phenomenon, Malthus's theories of overpopulation and resource scarcity provided a philosophical basis for the program of social austerity instituted by the New Poor Law of 1834, a law vociferously decried in the radical press. This controversy formed the subtext for a group of articles about India that appeared in the *Circular* from December 1839 to April 1841 and provided a historical assessment of the effects of British rule.[7] A year later, John Cleave's *English Chartist Circular* published a parallel if slightly narrower series, "India – Her Own – and Another's," which recounted episodes from the conquest of India, a process it claimed "which for rapacity, wantonness, and cruelty, stands without likeness or example in the history of man."[8] The Scottish *Circular* conceived of its study in terms of a broader effort to demystify symbols of "national power and grandeur":

Since the Chartist agitation began, our "time-honoured" institutions have underwent a scrutiny that have stripped them of all pretensions of respect or esteem, and shown them to be utterly destitute of any other aim than the misery and degradation of the people.

As forming part and parcel of those same plundering institutions – as constituting the outworks of the citadel of corruption, the Colonies are worthy of some notice. Like the rest, the one pervading principle, by and for which they live, move, and have their being, is gross selfishness, the miserable selfishness of the few, with a superlative contempt for the rights and interests of the many. (March 27, 1841)

The remaining articles focus on the violent conquest of the region and offer an account of the origins of Indian famine. Reversing imperial progress narratives, the *Circular* argues that British rule has brought barbarism, not civilization. "British Tyranny in India" details how extortionate taxes have caused cultivated farmland to devolve into unproductive nature, making farming "almost profitless" and forcing "thousands upon thousands of acres [to be] relinquished to the possession of wild beasts and venomous reptiles" (December 21, 1839). By emphasizing the social origin of famine, the *Circular* counters the Malthusian idea of the intractability of poverty. The magazine heaps scorn on theories of environmental determinism that explain scarcity outside a political context. "Result of English Tyranny in India" rejects the racialized idea that the innate characteristics of inhabitants of tropical climates make them vulnerable to natural calamities. In fact, the stereotyped attributes ascribed to the Indian people originate in a predatory economic system, which demoralizes the population by taking the fruits of their labor: "The rapacity of the English had reduced the natives to that condition of poverty, apathy, and despair, in which the slightest derangement of the season might superinduce famine" (April 3, 1841). Neither "the uncertainty of seasons," nor a static and oppressive culture, nor individuals' psychology shaped by a punishing environment make famine inevitable. India, like England, is not ruled by the inverted providence of a cruel Dame Nature. Its catastrophes, "impiously attributed to the government of the Divine Being," are the products of political and economic rule (December 21, 1839).

The majority of articles in the *Circular*'s series treat the effects of British governance on India. "Our Colonies" on the other hand deals with the consequences of the empire for British society, making visible connections between colonial and domestic misrule that the magazine usually left implicit. The article rehearses positions inherited from the utilitarian critics of empire: the colonies do not support themselves and therefore increase domestic taxes; they prop up corruption by creating sinecures for the aristocracy; and they provide no benefit to the people, "immediately or remotely" (March 27, 1841).[9] Class politics, however, infuses the latter argument. Not the people in general but the "working classes . . . steeped to the lips in poverty and wretchedness" bear the financial and human burden of supporting a colonial regime.

Orientalism Inverted: British Pagans and Virtuous Natives

A factor that distinguishes Chartist writing on the empire from much middle-class journalism is the relative absence of the study of native peoples, an effect of the priority given to political reporting and of the tendency to conceive of the empire as a reflection of British society. Given the lack of anthropological forays in the *Star* and *Circular*, Chartist conceptions of native peoples must be discerned in brief references in other kinds of writing, including reportage and editorial essays. Immediately apparent, however, is the rejection of the language of exoticism, especially in descriptions of India, China, and the West Indies. As we saw in the *Star*'s blistering attack on the caricature of the Chinese as "the 'celestials,'" Orientalist tropes were sometimes explicitly scrutinized. A more common strategy was to parody such discourse by depicting British officials as rapacious, sensual tyrants and colonial subjects as heroic patriots or quasi-Christian martyrs. The imaginative leap that found common cause with victims of the empire across the boundaries of race, nationality, and religion ("colour, clime, or creed" in Harney's formulation) starkly contrasted with the pseudo-scientific theories of racial difference that became increasingly prominent over the course of the 1840s, although this ideology also surfaced in the Chartist press by the end of the decade.[10]

The *Star*'s coverage of the Opium and Afghanistan Wars consistently inverts the language of Christianity and heathenism, casting the rulers of Britain as exotic foreigners. Whereas British merchants in China attempted to erect "an altar to Mammon and Moloch, their most favourite deities," the Chinese scorned the profits of an illicit trade with England, because their "kindly and benevolent religion" condemned the "whole sale butchery" caused by opium addiction. Surveying the cause of the conflict, the *Star* asks, "Have we anywhere on record a finer rebuke administered by Pagan integrity to Christian degeneracy?" (January 18, 1840). This motif emerges repeatedly in coverage of this and other wars. The leniency of the Chinese to British smugglers "contrasts strongly and strangely with the barbarian-like ferocity of 'civilized' and 'Christian' nations" (*NS* April 4, 1840). Chinese victims were "murdered by the devotees of the English Juggernaut – the god, wealth" (*NS* October 31, 1840). A British massacre in India is described by a veteran as a "novel and modern suttee, unequalled in atrocity, and which casts into shade the car of Juggernaut or the doctrines of Brama!" (*NS* April 16, 1842). The conflicts thus afforded the Chartists a Swiftian inversion of perspective, in which the imaginary viewpoint of colonial others illuminated the contradictory objects of the imperial endeavor: "The Chinese and the Affghans must certainly think us an odd sort of people to send among them one set of men to proclaim 'peace on earth and good will towards men,' and another set armed with murderous weapons to cut them up at the word of command" (*NS* July 16, 1841).

Besides turning upside down the Evangelical *cause célèbres* of suttee, juggernaut, and idol worship, this rhetorical role reversal criticized Christian justifications of empire. The venal ends of British wars, the immoral conduct of the army, and the celebration of violence, exposed empire's "higher purpose" as mere cant. The *Circular* excerpted William Howitt's *Colonization and Christianity*, a jeremiad aimed at the use of Christian ideals to disguise "lawless and domineering" expropriation: "forth they went singing the *Te Deum*, and declaring that they went to plant the cross among the heathen . . . However, it turned out to be the cross of one of the two thieves" (February 1, 1840). In 1838, the *Star* contained several neutral or positive articles about missionary lectures; by the fall of 1840, however, a series of letters from a Norfolk reader echoed the paper's editorial stance in maintaining that missions could not win "true convert[s]," because preachers in the colonies, as in Ireland, offered the people "the word in one hand, and fire, blood, and misery in the other" (October 31, 1840).

A sense of competition pervades Chartist writing on Christian missions. Missionary propaganda was an alternate source from which the public learned about the colonies, and missions were central institutions in working-class culture. The Norfolk letter writer instructs the *Star*'s readers when "preachers [ask] your pence for the poor souls in India and China request of them a history of both countries; ask them to detail to you the oppressions in India, and the murders in China" (October 31, 1840). A series of articles in the *Star* looks jealously at Christian fundraising successes in the economic depression of the early 1840s, a period during which Chartist "missionaries," as itinerant activists and lecturers were called, received diminished support.

The *Star* was also apt to point out the hypocrisy of concern for suffering overseas given how frequently injustice in Britain was ignored. Such criticism of "telescopic philanthropy" will be familiar to readers of Dickens's *Bleak House* or Carlyle's *Past and Present*, but the implications here were different. For Dickens and Carlyle, though the metropolitan poor were worthier objects of charity than savage pagans, negative associations linked the groups.[11] The *Star* repurposed the analogy, reversing its class thrust. Having no desire for Mrs. Jellyby's ilk to turn their telescopes toward the domestic poor, it invokes the trope of British paganism and foreign virtue to recommend that the London Missionary Society redirect its proselytizing fervor

to convert our worse than heathen rulers from the error of their ways . . . Now, we would seriously ask the Society to commence their work on a new plan. If they really desire to promote the well-being of the idolatrous nations, let them labour a little at home in prevailing upon our Christian Government to withdraw their man-butchers from amongst the "savage" tribes and the "obstinate" people of China. (July 16, 1841)

Juxtaposing the fetishistic worship of material things in British culture and the Christ-like attributes of peacefulness and charity in foreign society undermined the assumption that free trade, Christianity, and British rule were synonymous with cultural progress. The *Star*'s polemic against the London Missionary Society calls into doubt the nation's right to spread gospels worldly or divine: "We tell them ... that the system under which we live is worse than that which obtains in any pagan land – that it generates more ignorance, vice, and woe, than that of any other on the surface of the earth" (July 16, 1841). This style of Podsnappery in reverse was frequent in Chartist writing, forming a counterpoint to the patriotic pride in England's constitutional tradition often associated with British radicalism (Weisser, "Role" 86–89). The *Circular* declared that "in the science of taxation, tyranny, and oppression, every nation to which we ... can advert, whether their government is despotic or monarchical, their religion Christian, Pagan or Mahometan, are immeasurably behind us" (December 7, 1839).

We have seen how the Chartist press applied an Orientalist vocabulary to colonial rule and the elites it benefited. Its representation of colonial subjects followed logically from this depiction. If British rulers were decadent, tyrannical, and heathen, the natives they governed were cast in the mold of a heroic and masculine radicalism that resembled the Chartists' self-image. A movement that reiterated the historical precedents for the right to bear arms could frame colonial resistance to British power as a patriotic assertion of popular rights. Indeed, by defending the right to political violence in the face of oppressive power, support for colonial revolt intervened in Chartist debates about "physical" or "moral" force as a radical strategy. A remarkable denunciation of British military action occurred along these lines in an 1847 debate in Tiverton, Devon, between George Julian Harney and Britain's foreign minister Lord Palmerston. Knowing the encounter would afford a national platform from which to polemicize against Whig foreign policy, Harney contested Palmerston's parliamentary seat (with, of course, no chance of winning) "teeth to teeth on the hustings" (Schoyen 150). Although Harney stopped short of supporting the dissolution of colonial ties, fearing that other European powers would fill the vacuum left by the British, he lambasted the suppression of the Canadian rebellion of 1837 and the invasion of Afghanistan while excoriating the Opium War as elevating the principles of free trade to acts of international brigandage. Harney's speech transformed Afghanis into persecuted Englishmen and fashioned Akhbar Khan, who routed British forces at Kabul and was demonized in the mainstream press, a veritable folk hero:

> I say my country when right, but the right always, and may the right triumph though my country may perish. (Enthusiastic cheering.) . . . Akhbar Khan was justified in doing as Bruce and Tell had done before him. (Loud cheers.) . . . Suppose Englishmen subjected to the insults and outrages that the Affghans were, should we not be justified in doing as they did? (Cheers.) Well then, does not the right exist for them as well as for us? . . . (Great cheering.). (*NS* August 7, 1847)

Trumpeting resistance to colonial rule, the Chartist press contested the idea that native subjects were passive pawns of British governance. In the *Circular*, George Thompson's "Origin of British Power in India" stresses that order in the colony is maintained only by a massive military occupation, "a circumstance somewhat unintelligible, when viewed in connection with the oft repeated assertion, that our government in India is a government of opinion" (January 1, 1840). The *Star* punctured celebrations of the defeat of Sikh forces in 1849 by pointing out that "discontent, popular risings, [and] conspiracies" would inevitably result: "That [the victory] has put an end to war, or that it will prevent the brave and patriotic natives of those wide realms from attempting to wrest from us the power which we have usurped, we do not believe" (April 28, 1849). This speculation echoed a series of letters in 1842 by an antiwar veteran, who prognosticated that British military adventures ultimately would bring about the collapse of the empire in India:

> We have no chance of success in Cabul or in the East, eventually. The natives are getting civilised; the chain that has bound them is broken; they hate us; there is a fearful debt of retribution against us; they have feared us; they never loved us. From Affghanistan to Cape Comorin, from Malabar to Bengal, the spirit will arise which will drive the Towrs, the Feringhess into the sea or into their factories. Fresh defeats and disasters will be followed by fresh mutinies. (April 2, 1842)

Although the *Star* ceased publication five years before its predictions of Indian revolt came to pass in 1857, several former Chartists, including Patrick Brewster, Ernest Jones, and G. W. M. Reynolds, all explicitly supported the rebel cause (Chase, *Chartism* 55; A. Taylor, "Little"). Their response departed significantly from the jingoistic reaction of the mainstream press. Herbert has shown how the rebellion led to intense questioning of the imperial endeavor, but the conflict initially strengthened nationalistic currents and undermined the cause of humanitarian reform. Thomas Macaulay described with satisfaction the transformation of domestic politics: "The cruelties of the sepoys have inflamed the nation to a degree unprecedented in my memory. Peace Societies, and Aborigines Protection Societies, and Societies for the Reformation of Criminals are silenced. There is one terrible cry for revenge" (Trevelyan 2:366).

In the midst of this nationalistic fervor, the Chartist writer and politician Ernest Jones republished his 1851 poem *The New World* as *The Revolt of Hindostan or the New World*. The poem recounts colonial crimes and imagines a peaceful revolution overthrowing the Indian empire. Jones also gave a series of highly publicized lectures on foreign affairs at St. Martin's Hall in central London to "bespeak the sympathy of the English people for their Hindu brethren." Jones articulated an internationalist politics that fitted the Indian rebels into a tradition of nationalist patriots extending from the Chartists to the oppressed nations of Europe.[12] Tracing rebel atrocities to violence by British "robbers and miscreants, who stamped the impress of cruelty and torture on the native mind, and who sowed the seeds of that sanguinary harvest," Jones argued the English should support the rebellion as they had European revolutions of the previous decade ("England's" 221).

The Limits of Internationalism: Chartist Conceptions of Race in Settler Regions and Other Colonies

The complicated legacy of the Chartist critique of empire in the post-1848 era is illustrated in the later writings of Jones and Harney, the movement's two most significant internationalists. Both remained skeptical of Britain's imperial project, but Harney drew markedly different implications than Jones from the Chartist brief against the colonial system. "Chartism and something more," the platform developed after the setbacks of 1848 in an effort to revitalize the agitation for democracy, insisted on the necessity of social and economic reforms to complete the political revolution begun with universal male suffrage (*Red Republican* June 22, 1850). Along with an array of social welfare policies, delegates at the 1851 Chartist convention sought the abolition of standing armies: a policy they recognized might lead to the emancipation of the colonies (*NS* April 5–12, 1851).

Yet in terms of Harney's writing, "Chartism and something more" represented a diminished vision. From within a broken and scattered movement, Harney could no longer imagine resistance to the imperial state and sought only to improve the position of the working class within the established order. Whereas his speech at Tiverton focused on British oppression, four years later Harney demonstrated an increased commitment to empire. The history of colonial injustice, if "long to tell and sad to trace," was a completed, inevitable fact. Rebutting calls by the "Manchester School" for retrenchment, Harney outlines why "the integrity of the British empire must be maintained; but the advantages of that empire must be no longer monopolized by privileged usurpers, and Moloch-like mammonites" (*Red Republican* August 31, 1850). Here is a case for empire in the radical idiom. Since the people have born the cost of colonial wars with their taxes and lives, their sacrifice should be redeemed by a more equitable distribution of the spoils.

How did aspects of a polemical critique of the colonial system reemerge as a call to preserve the empire? First, although the *Star* and *Circular* focused on the negative consequences of British rule, they rarely outlined what the Chartist alternative would look like. Moreover, the universalism of Chartist internationalism was fractured by a developmental view of the nation state. Within a framework focused on European movements for self-determination and democratic government, support for (non-British) colonial subjects depended on a recognition of common identity based on a set of interlocking terms: as fellow citizens, as an extension of "the people," as members of the working classes. These identifications were by no means automatic when translated to colonial settings. While the radical press articulated forceful denunciations of racism, at other points it replicated hegemonic racial discourse, particularly concerning colonies where numbers of working-class emigrants encountered large native populations. For the Chartists, the aristocratic rulers of the West Indies and the merchants governing India exaggerated the worst traits of Britain's government, but the settler colonies presented more complicated issues. Although the Chartist press actively opposed emigration as social policy, it remained supportive of emigrants, a population drawn largely from the poor and politically disaffected, groups that comprised Chartism's core constituency.

Although Chartist periodicals frequently challenged the pervasive colonial discourse that described native societies as living anachronisms, versions of this language also surfaced in radical writing. The *Communist Manifesto*, the first English translation of which appeared in Harney's *Red*

Republican, reproduced in inverted form the idea that the empire would rescue backward, atavistic peoples:

> Through the incessant improvements in machinery and the means of locomotion, the Bourgeoisie draw the most barbarous savages into the magic circle of civilization. Cheap goods are their artillery for battering down Chinese walls, and their means of overcoming the obstinate hatred entertained towards strangers by semi-civilized nations. (November 9, 1850)

Marx's example shows how pro-imperialist assumptions could penetrate a radical milieu skeptical of the imperial project. In the place of earlier media criticism that highlighted the racism of the "hired hacks of the 'shopkeeping' fraternity" during the Opium War, the "unilinear narrative" of the *Manifesto* renders the colonial world an anachronistic space *tout court* (*NS* April 4, 1840; Shilliam 195).

In the *Star*, representations of native populations in Africa, Canada, New Zealand, and Australia veer between a mixture of clichés and scrutiny of those same stereotypes. The paper polemicizes against "atrocities that have been committed upon this 'ignorant' and 'savage' people [in Australia], by those of our countrymen, who have 'settled' down in the lands of the natives, and tried to extirpate the former and rightful owners; atrocities that make humanity sicken" (February 11, 1843). But it also republished without comment accounts describing aboriginal violence. The *Star* even praised a book by the colonial administrator W. Fox, which predicts the extinction of New Zealand Maoris as a result of the "depression of spirits and energy, which in the mind of the savage ensues upon his contact with civilized men" (August 9, 1851).

Notably, the Xhosa (or Kaffir) War of 1846–47 was the only major conflict where the paper sided, at least implicitly, with the British cause. The *Star* excerpted jingoistic accounts from settler newspapers reporting the "outrages" of the "ruthless savages" and the "smart successful" maneuvers of British forces (July 25, 1846; January 19, 1847; May 1, 1847). By the Second Xhosa War, the editorial posture of the *Star* was in line with its treatment of other conflicts. Whether Harney's departure in 1851 or increasing disillusionment with the protracted hostilities was responsible for the shift, the *Star* derided supposed British victories (June 14, 1851), condemned a policy of ethnic cleansing (July 19, 1851), and sympathetically reported a Peace Society meeting (December 6, 1851). Even in accounts condemning the war, however, writers alternated between rejecting the rhetoric of barbarism and deploying it to deflate celebrations of British success: "We can gain no glory, even in the vulgar acceptation of that term, by shooting down a host of almost naked savages" (September 13, 1851).

The Chartist press was more consistently critical of dominant racial discourse when analyzing other contexts, especially the West Indies. A hatred of slavery and its planter aristocracy made radical writers wary of the increasingly prevalent image of lazy and shiftless freemen most notoriously presented in Carlyle's "Occasional Discourse on the Negro Question." At a moment when widespread disappointment at the moral progress of emancipated slaves was weakening support for the Evangelical model of "Christian-humanitarian" colonialism (Lester 80–81), the Chartists repeatedly lauded the political accomplishments of freed blacks and others of mixed ancestry. The *Star* celebrated the election of a "brown man" to the Jamaican assembly and the editorship of two leading newspapers in Jamaica and Barbados by "gentlemen of colour" (March 29, May 3, 1851), hailed a protest movement in Jamaica (asking "What if we find them agitating for the 'Charter' next?" October 14, 1843), and dubbed the cooperative effort of "seventy native labourers" to purchase their former plantation "the Chartist land plan in Guiana" (May 15, 1847). As such language makes clear, the progress of liberty in the West Indies argued for its expansion at home:

> [Our opponents] contend that the people must be prepared for freedom by previous intelligence; we affirm, on the contrary, that nothing fits the people so much for liberty as the enjoyment of it ... Look to the negroes of Jamaica. Until their recent emancipation they were the most degraded of their species. Now, in a few short years, they may safely be compared for intelligence, for morality, for order, with any population in the world. (September 26, 1846)

In the Chartist view, political and social relationships, not inborn racial characteristics, were determinants of conditions in the West Indies. A three-part biographical sketch of Toussaint L'Ouverture, serialized in the *Circular* in 1841, commemorates the early nineteenth-century slave uprising in French St. Domingo for the way it transformed culture and art as well as economic and political life. Published the year of the failed Niger expedition, the *Circular*'s biography takes aim at language that used the abolition of slavery as a humanitarian justification for colonial expansion (Brantlinger, *Rule* 174–78). A counter-narrative of self-emancipation depicts heroic revolutionaries fully capable of governing themselves:

> The revolution of St. Domingo ... soon furnished ample proof, that, among those whom European injustice had stigmatised as an inferior race

of beings and doomed to perpetual servitude, were heads endued with legislative wisdom, hearts pregnant with heroic energies, and hands capable of holding the sword of war, or swaying the rod of empire. (February 27, 1841)[13]

Like common invocations of the French Revolution, this celebration of the second independent republic in the Western Hemisphere attempts to inspire belief in the people's ability to transform British society. But the ubiquitous trope of slavery in radical writing inflects the discussion of life in post-revolutionary St. Domingo. Whereas the language of bondage in Chartist oratory and poetry describes grievances afflicting Britain's wage and political "slaves," here, real enslaved people serve as a model for the domestic poor and disenfranchised.[14]

The *Circular* series also highlights the differences separating Chartist internationalism from the evangelical universalism underpinning both abolitionist ideology and Protestant overseas missions. Chartism's linking of British radicals, black Jacobins, and rebels in arms against the British empire asserted a common humanity while avoiding the condescension often present in philanthropy. Rather than present suffering slaves in need of uplift, the Chartist press was drawn to moments when colonial people became shapers of history. The temporal imagination of the two ideologies also differed. Christian universalism offered only a future possibility of communion: the evangelical agenda depended on an "acrobatics of identification and differentiation" that saw foreign peoples both as degraded exotics and brothers and sisters in Christ (Rai 117). If the Chartist press integrated little understood foreigners into stock figures of "freeborn Englishmen," it also encouraged its readers to relate struggle in the colonies to their own future. Praising cooperative ventures among ex-slaves in Guiana, the *Star* urged: "We quite agree with Mr. Barmby that in all this 'the image of God in ivory might take a lesson from the image of God in ebony.' The 'ivories' are at length beginning to learn this lesson, but it appears that the 'ebonies' are in advance of them" (November 14, 1846).

The variety of racial discourse in the Chartist press resulted from the competing perspectives of various authors and editors and from the different sources from which they gathered news. But a discernable pattern separated the treatment of the settler colonies from other areas. Following the utilitarian critics of empire's equivocal approach, the Chartists were more likely to vindicate the rights of working-class emigrants than of upper-class administrators or West Indian grandees. Yet the Chartists were stridently critical of emigration as a solution to the problems of poverty and overpopulation in

Britain, sensing that this policy might undermine their own vision of social transformation. Hobson's theses (later taken up by Lenin) about the political effects of the empire on working-class movements were rooted in debates from the 1840s and 1850s. In 1848, *The Times* posed the question starkly: "The choice ... we are called upon to make [is] Colonisation or Revolution – a peaceful increase of the empire into its colonies or an overthrow of authority and order at home" (qtd. in Flett 41). Ernest Jones attacked *The Times*'s view of emigration, arguing that the labor markets of Australia, New Zealand, and Canada were as glutted as England's, that native occupants possessed historical and natural rights to their land, and that emigration schemes were promoted "to thin the discontented spirits out of England" (Claeys 6:294). Jones's lectures built on traditions of Chartist journalism. The *Star* published or excerpted at least three series discrediting the claims of emigration companies, including a piece of muckraking travel writing in which the activist Lawrence Pithkeithly joined a group of poor emigrants bound for America in order to recount their hardships and scrutinize "the 'thousand and one' flattering statements circulated" about the country (April 8, 1843). Yet even as the *Star* condemned the idea that emigration could solve the problems of poverty, overpopulation, and political strife, offers of passage to America, Canada, or New Zealand appeared almost weekly in its advertising column, sometimes cheek by jowl with articles debunking emigration company propaganda. Even Pithkeithly's letters indicated the ambivalence the Chartist press maintained toward emigration: they also provided advice on how best to make the trip.

The Colonies as Prison House – Thomas Martin Wheeler's Colonial *Bildungsroman*

The debate about emigration extended beyond journalistic exposés to the only original novel to appear in the *Northern Star*, Thomas Martin Wheeler's *Sunshine and Shadow*, which was serialized from March 1849 to January 1850.[15] Much middle-class fiction, including Gaskell's *Mary Barton*, Dickens's *David Copperfield*, Braddon's *Lady Audley's Secret*, and Edward Bulwer-Lytton's *The Caxtons*, presents emigration as an opportunity for dramatic refashionings of the self. Wheeler, on the other hand, represents it as coerced and constraining. To do so, he draws on discursive links Chartist journalism made between the experiences of economic refugees and the conditions of political prisoners. The radical press gave significant attention to the transportation of John Frost and the other leaders of the Newport rising of 1839 as well as to the exile of William Cuffay, who was sent to Tasmania for his role in the stillborn Orange Tree conspiracy of 1848. These *cause célèbres* became points of reference for describing the travails of ordinary emigrants, whom like Chartist prisoners were said to be driven from their homes.[16] To the *Northern Liberator,* "'Emigration' ... is only another name for forcing working men to *transportation*" (December 22, 1838). *Sunshine and Shadow* similarly collapses political repression with the confining circumstances of poverty and inequality, rendering the colonies a prison house rather than a theater of reinvention.

Structured around the three high-water marks of Chartist revival, Wheeler's political *Bildungsroman* attempts to provide a history of the movement's successes and failures "to clear it of prejudice and calumny" (96). The dedication declares the novel a literary as well as political intervention: "The fiction department of literature has hitherto been neglected by the scribes of our body, and the opponents of our principles have been allowed to wield the power of imagination over the youth of our party" (72). The novel follows the career of Arthur Morton, orphan graduate of "a second-rate boarding school" and unemployed printer, as he is swept into the tumult of Chartist agitation. A capsule summary reveals a back-and-forth structure, which alternates between Arthur's biography and historical events. Covering the years 1831–39, the narrator recounts Arthur's time in school, his friendship with Walter North (a future commercial magnate and member of Lords), and his apprenticeship as a printer in a London suburb. Unable to find employment in the capital, Arthur travels to Birmingham, which is in the grip of political ferment. Inspired by platform oratory, the hero plunges into the world of politics, but internal dissension soon dissolves the Chartist National Convention. When the government uses the Bull Ring riots as a pretext to arrest many of the movement's leaders and activists, Arthur, falsely accused of arson, flees England.

The middle portion of the novel tracks Arthur's experiences in an unnamed colony in the Caribbean, where he arrives after being rescued from a shipwrecked vessel bound for America. A Crusoe who discovers an outpost of empire instead of virgin nature, Arthur works in a counting house, considers the condition of recently emancipated men and women, and engages in an ill-starred romance with Walter's sister Julia, now the wife of the island's governor. After Julia's death and Arthur's arbitrary arrest and eventual pardon, the Chartist sojourns in America before returning to England. In 1842 Arthur is in Manchester amid the stilled factories of a general strike, but following the strike's defeat and a wave of arrests, Arthur once more pursues his individual course. He marries a fellow Chartist; within a few years, sickness and poverty claim one of their two children. Arthur turns to drink and crime, robbing a wealthy stranger, whom he belatedly recognizes as his childhood friend Walter. When the country reawakens a third time in 1848, a repentant Arthur joins the cause in London, but military repression again condemns the hero to exile. The novel ends with Arthur on the Continent, separated from his wife and awaiting "that national jubilee, which shall commemorate the downfall of oppression" (192).

At the novel's center, Wheeler rereads the emigration plot in ways that typify Chartist anti-imperialism. The Chartists had inherited from Bentham and James Mill the concept of the colonies as schoolhouses of despotism, which cautioned that the empire might exert deleterious effects on English political life by serving as an incubator for autocratic rulers and tyrannical institutions. Working-class radicals crucially adapted these notions. Instead of seeing the colonies as a corrupting space that threatened to transform British government, they described them as the location where the real nature of the existing British state was made most manifest. Along these lines, the colonies in Wheeler's novel disclose the relationship between inequality, political exclusion, and state repression present but kept out of view at home. In London, Arthur lacks a defined antagonist and is denied the decisive clash which will resolve the oppositions structuring the narrative. The hero cannot even approach his childhood friend after the latter's rise. In the capital, power is diffuse and inaccessible; in the West Indies, on the other hand, the hero confronts the tyrannical British governor directly. The colonial context calls to the surface antagonisms implicit but remote in the more mediated social system of the metropolis.

Grafting social problem themes onto a *Bildungsroman* constituted an important early Victorian subgenre, which included Frances Trollope's *Michael Armstrong*, Dickens's *Hard Times*, Gaskell's *Mary Barton* and *North and South*, and Disraeli's *Sybil* and *Coningsby*. Wheeler's novel calls to mind these more familiar examples, especially *Coningsby*, which Wheeler would have encountered in the *Star* in 1844–45. Using an unusual format, the *Star* serialized the future prime minister's novel, combining weekly excerpts with interpolated commentary, possibly written by Wheeler himself, the *Star*'s London correspondent, but more likely by Harney.

Like *Coningsby*, *Sunshine and Shadow* traces the careers and conflicted relationship of two schooltime friends as an allegory for the shifting political configurations of the 1830s and 1840s. In Disraeli's novel, the grandson of a peer marries the daughter of a factory owner (and sister of a fellow Etonian), resolving a homosocial romance and signaling the need for a middle- and upper-class alliance in the post–Reform Bill era. Disraeli's traditional closural gesture of marriage heals the fractured relationship of the schoolfellows from different class backgrounds. Wheeler's characters, on the other hand, experience only increasing alienation. While Arthur descends into poverty, Walter rises through the commercial ranks and eventually secures both a seat in Parliament and noble title. Arthur's and Walter's estrangement culminates with a chance robbery of the commercial magnate by the Chartist hero, an encounter between virtual strangers. This sequence reverses a dominant pattern in social problem fiction, which often concludes with antagonists from the two nations coming face to face and discerning their common interest. But the marriage that concludes *Coningsby* is unavailable to Wheeler's hero: Walter has cemented his ascendency by forcing his sister Julia to marry the governor of the unnamed island. This rapprochement between a member of an ascendant middle class and a colonial representative of old corruption discloses the disastrous consequences of Disraeli's marriage plot, a settlement that excludes the working classes (Vanden Bossche 113–16).

Wheeler's most dramatic departure from *Coningsby* (and from most contemporary examples) is his choice to make the colonies an important setting in their own right rather than a place of offstage transformation. In *Culture and Imperialism*, Edward Said describes the paradox of a literature that ubiquitously alludes to the empire but leaves it beyond the text's margins. For Said, the casual ease with which the nineteenth-century novelist refers in passing to "massive [colonial] appropriations" is symptomatic of an order that subordinates the colonies to British concerns (66). Wheeler's choice to follow his hero into the colonies and back is particularly surprising given that *Sunshine and Shadow* synthesizes social problem fiction and the novel of development, two genres deeply invested in the idea of the nation and typically enclosed by its borders. In effect, Wheeler's colonial setting displaces the Condition of England question from England itself while reimagining the familiar map of the *Bildungsroman*.

Franco Moretti stresses the central role national capitals assume in the latter genre, which typically traces a youth's journey from the provinces to the center, then dwells on his experiences there (*Atlas* 65).[17] David Copperfield's and Pip's travel to London, like Julien Sorrel's and Lucien Chardon's to Paris in *The Red and the Black* and *Lost Illusions* affiliate the project of self-formation with metropolitan culture. With the

Bildungsroman's streamlined route from village backwater to national capital in mind, the rootless nature of *Sunshine and Shadow* comes as a shock. Over the novel's serial run, the reader accompanies the Chartist protagonist from his childhood home in a London suburb to a town thirty miles distant; then back briefly to London; on to Birmingham and Liverpool; to Dominica and an unnamed Caribbean island; to the United States; to England and Manchester; twice more to London; and, ultimately, to an anonymous location in Europe. At one point, the narrator apostrophizes London as the "giant heart of the mighty centre of the world's civilization" (81), but the metaphor of center and periphery is insufficient to the itinerant map Wheeler traces, a restless wandering that transforms the geography of development and recasts the capital as a point of departure rather than destination. More than one-third of the narrative unfolds outside of England, and crucial episodes occur at sea, an index of the novel's lack of center.

Although *Sunshine and Shadow* shares the characteristic restlessness of the *Bildungsroman*, it challenges an organizing myth of the genre: that travel allows and necessitates radical transformation. The novel describes exotic locales that repeat the cramped circumstances of home, movement over vast spaces felt as confinement, and the paradoxical experience of placeless-ness within a global system. Removing the geographic telos from the process of *Bildung, Sunshine and Shadow* dissolves other traditional markers of development. Closural gestures come too early, only to be taken away: careers misfire before begun; children perish; husband and wives are forced apart. The social problems of poverty, inequality, and unemployment appear intractable, dooming the hero's efforts to navigate a world in which "industry cannot secure success; talent oft times is only a burthen to its possessor" (135).

Wheeler's combination of a colonial setting with a narrative about a hero's frustrated efforts to arrive at a stable adult role looks ahead to what Jed Esty has termed the "anti-developmental fictions" of late nineteenth- and early twentieth-century colonial *Bildungsroman*. Esty follows Jameson's influential argument about the connection between modernism and late nineteenth-century imperialism (Esty 416–17). In Jameson's account, formal experiments in such areas as point of view, chronology, and narrative decoding instantiate the "unrepresentable totality" of life in a world system in which individual experience is insufficient to comprehend the massive determinants structuring daily existence (Jameson, "Modernism" 58). Focusing on Olive Schreiner's experimental style, Esty describes how "the conspicuously imperial frame[s]" of *Story of an African*

Farm (as well as of *Kim* and *Lord Jim*) disarrange the protagonist's efforts at self-formation. Growing up in contexts defined as anachronistic, Kipling's, Conrad's, and Schreiner's heroes become trapped in versions of perpetual childhood. Other critics extend Esty's and Jameson's framework, rightly pointing out that Britons struggled to comprehend connections between their daily lives and the empire's global system long before the closing decades of the nineteenth century (the 1790s sugar boycott being one signal example) (Agathocleous 13; Goodlad, "Cosmopolitanism's" 405). *Jane Eyre* and *Great Expectations* provide the most famous instances of how the unseen determinants of empire take strange shapes in Victorian fiction. Pip's psychological breakdown after meeting Magwitch and the eruption of the Gothic in Rochester's mansion index the difficult endeavor of giving narrative form to Jameson's "unrepresentable totality."

For these reasons, Jameson's and Esty's analysis of literature from the *fin de siècle* provides a compelling model for *Sunshine and Shadow*, suggesting overlooked continuities between early modernism and the Victorian novel. Like Brontë's and Dickens's masterpieces, *Sunshine and Shadow* takes up the question of subjectivity in an age of massive determinants from across the sea. Not a narrative of moral crisis and personal transformation, Wheeler's novel chronicles lives defined and circumscribed by political institutions, persons adrift on the currents of international trade. Returning to England, the hero reflects on steam, that "annihilator of space, that clasps the whole world in the embrace that joins island to island, continent to continent" (142). The disjunction between an individual's experience and that experience's determining structures is effectively registered in the novel's tonal shifts, experiments in points of view, and picaresque plot. The novel is episodic, its action scattered over a wide geography as the narrator follows the tenuous thread of "Cause and Effect," "fragments of one mighty chapter of accidents" across diverse and far-flung settings (170).

If the novel's scattered locales index its revision of the plot of development, the peripatetic nature of *Sunshine and Shadow* also separates it from contemporary social problem fiction, in which a claustrophobic city instantiates the suffocating conditions that threaten the hero's or heroine's aspirations. Dickens's Coketown and London of *Hard Times* and *Bleak House*, like Gaskell's Manchester and Milton, function as microcosms, condensing the divisions between the two nations. At the same time, these novels' unity of place underwrites the authors' project of narrating buried social connections while holding out the hope of reconciliation between the classes. Social problem fiction, as Kate Flint writes of Dickens, often begins with the "seemingly random" proximity of characters in urban milieus, "but below this surface, as [the] plots gradually reveal, there is a vast networks of interconnections" (Flint, "Victorian" 30). In line with Wheeler's expansive and varied settings, *Sunshine and Shadow* allows only a highly mediated approach between the classes, which remain locked in separate social milieus. Though characters from different economic strata cross the same literal ground, they experience it differently, their relationships to geography marking another effect of social division.

Wheeler utilizes a back-and-forth structure, which alternates between Arthur Morton's biography and description of the condition of England in which Chartism forms a part. This alternation aims to show the hero as multi-sided, countering common literary caricatures of working-class radicals: "Our novelists – even the most liberal – can never draw a democrat save in warpaint. 'Sincere, but stern and hard-hearted' – . . . 'ignorant, dogmatic, and fierce, but a lover of principle'" (99). To correct these stereotypes, Wheeler presents politics not as a limiting sphere but as the necessary outgrowth of the desire for self-realization. Notably, the narrator waxes most poetic recounting Arthur's public activity, appropriating Romantic imagery to describe his political awakening: "the mute lyre of his soul had been touched by the finger of popular emotion" (95). Nevertheless, the alternation between episodes from the historical record and anecdotes from the protagonist's biography follows a noticeable pattern that indicates an unresolved tension separating Arthur's endeavors as an individual from his activity as a member of a protest movement. When political prospects are at low tide, the focus remains steadily on Arthur's private life. At moments of political upsurge, on the other hand, Arthur's activity drops largely from view, submerged, as it were, in the energetic confusion of a mass movement. Focalization and temporal arrangement shift as the point of view ascends to encompass a broad sweep of events over a protracted time frame. These sections whipsaw Arthur between protagonist and an anonymous participant in a collective endeavor. Describing a crowd moved by political oratory, the narrator glosses the wrenching adjustment in character space the hero undergoes: "All sense of individuality is annihilated – the unit is lost in the mass – the solitary billow merged into the raging ocean, which swells and foams as if in disdain of the laws which regulate its motion" (93). When Arthur speaks before the crowd, he becomes disassociated from himself: "Unknowing what he did, and scarce conscious of his own identity, he sprang to the centre at the close of one of the speakers' harangue" (94).

Point of view continues to shift, especially in periods of retreat following political high points. As the movement recedes, Arthur resumes the role of a more traditional protagonist. Some critics have complained that Wheeler and

Chartist fiction more generally awkwardly combine radical plots with derivative story lines from popular fiction (Mitchell 257–58; Vicinus, "Chartist" 9–12). The transition between different kinds of writing can seem jarring as the novel varies between the use of journalistic conventions (including editorial comment, broad overviews, and direct address) and more familiar novelistic modes.[18] However, one might understand this stylistic fracture on its own terms. Just as Schreiner turns to a host of forms and styles to dissolve the familiar contours of the female *Bildungsroman*, the disorienting alterations in Wheeler's prose point to his scrutiny of the conventional plots of individual advancement and social integration. Arthur's pursuit of a career, his voyages abroad, and the retreat to the domestic hearth each evoke commonplace solutions to narrative conflict. In Wheeler's version, political crises invade and distort seemingly private domains and repeatedly push Arthur toward public life: "The love of home, which once characterised him, existed no longer, it reminded him too bitterly of the past, and he flew with avidity to the excitement of politics" (176).

Wheeler's text becomes more conventionally novelistic in its colonial setting where it features a romance plot and remains consistently focalized with the protagonist with only brief discursive overviews. Yet in the West Indian episodes, Wheeler recasts the plot of individualistic transformation often present in emigration stories. By granting the destitute protagonist economic and social chances unavailable in England, Wheeler demonstrates the colonies' role in Britain's imaginative life as a domain putatively open to meritocratic achievement. The hope that such a sphere would suture Britain's divisions was held out by middle-class commentators from Carlyle to Edward Gibbon Wakefield as well as the social problem novelists (Carlyle, *English* 214; Wakefield 761). Wheeler depicts his protagonist as himself susceptible to fantasies of the colonies as a compensatory realm of national greatness. Recently unemployed and sleeping in the open en route to Birmingham, Arthur dreams of Oriental luxury and power: "in the visions of the night we can lose sight of the harsh realities of the day. So it was with Arthur; he was no longer a poor friendless outcast ... but an eastern monarch, surrounded with gold and silver ore, which his slaves around were casting into dazzling type" (90). The hero's failure abroad dispels this vision. Far from making him a king, emigration takes on the character of penal transportation as Arthur discovers in the West Indies a nightmare synthesis of Asiatic despotism and British tyranny (97).

The geographic dispersal and centrifugal energy of *Sunshine and Shadow*, its quasi-Oriental setting, and its improbable coincidences align the novel with the genre of romance. Arthur's shipwreck and rescue call to mind

Prospero's enchanted island as much as Crusoe's quotidian one. In romance, however, the hero's wanderings allow an escape from the laws of home. Overlaying Britain and its colony, Wheeler makes clear that Arthur's journey permits no such escape. As if called forth by the hero's earlier dream, the island appears the domain of an Oriental monarch. The governor's mansion is "erected after the Eastern fashion" and his pleasure garden filled with exotic plants (117). If the landscape looks foreign, however, the colonial regime replicates the most corrupt aspects of British society: economic exploitation, a marriage market, and arbitrary political power. At the same time, the novel deploys stock motifs from colonial settings to render strange the class relations and sexual mores of the metropole.[19] Commenting on economic inequality in England, the narrator remarks "that classes sprung from the same root, and not one generation removed, are as effectually separated . . . as the god-descended Brahmin from the outcast pariah" (77). Arbitrary colonial power also shapes relations between the sexes. The governor's career supervising plantations conditions his pursuit of Julia: he approaches her parents to arrange the match "with the promptness of a West Indian – in all that related to dealings in human flesh" (86). Julia's coerced acceptance is described in term of a suttee, "an immolation of her soul on the altar of Mammon" (113). This language challenges feminist justifications of empire, which were commonplace from the 1820s (when James Mill linked the condition of women and the progress of civilization) and present in Wollstonecraft a generation earlier.[20] Rather than rescue native women from archaic and oppressive customs, the tyranny of colonial relationships infects society at home. A description of Parliament echoes the account of Julia's feverish decline in the languid tropics: "its atmosphere has become vitiated by stagnation . . . its constitution has become torpid and emaciated by age and indulgence" (132).

Finally, Wheeler's colonial episodes puncture British self-satisfaction regarding the abolition of slavery. The narrator argues that the institution's continuation in America is a legacy of British rule and warns that an emigration scheme designed "to entrap the poor East Indian from his native home" threatens to reduce black freemen to wage peonage and "the level of the British artisan" (116). The controversy around black labor and East Indian emigration dominated discussions of the West Indies in the late 1840s, most famously in Carlyle's and John Stuart Mill's debate in *Fraser's Magazine* in the winter of 1849–50, which Wheeler's colonial chapters anticipated by a few months.[21] Wheeler's view departs from both Carlyle's virtual advocacy of a return to slavery as well as Mill's effort to rehabilitate liberal colonial reform. Like Mill, Wheeler counters the planters' and their allies' assertion about blacks' natural indolence by suggesting that reluctance to return to the plantation indicates only that laborers are "not properly remunerated for [their] toil" (115). At the same time, Wheeler rejects the humanitarian imperialism Mill propounds. Significantly, Wheeler's hero accomplishes no reform on behalf of the black workers other than advising them to organize themselves against economic and political repression (117). The narrator goes so far as to call for political and economic self-determination for the island's black population. Whereas the rule of "great proprietors and legislators in England" perpetuates an economic system that resembles slavery in crucial respects, black West Indians, if freed from the burdens of empire, could establish a just society:

> If [the freed slaves'] energies had fair play, their habits of industry, their adaptability to the climate, and their system of brotherly co-operation, would speedily render them proprietors of those islands which they had so long tilled as slaves, and the Black Republic of the New World [would] become, perhaps, as famous as the White. (115)

Given the context of the virulent racism Carlyle's diatribe announced, Wheeler's egalitarian celebration of the capacity of freedmen is striking.[22] The emerging orthodoxy that saw race as the primary source of national character also bears on Wheeler's anti-racist portrait of William Cuffay, a descendent of West Indian slaves who became an important Chartist leader in London and nationally – *The Times* once dubbed the movement in the capital "the Black man and his party."[23] Cuffay, who was Wheeler's personal friend, features prominently in the novel, the only historical figure to receive more than passing reference. Scapegoated by *The Times* as an exotic outsider, lampooned by *Punch* in a series of racist caricatures, and ultimately transported to Tasmania for his participation in the Orange Tree Conspiracy (Gossman 60–64), Cuffay, in Wheeler's novel, transcends nationality but inherits the best attributes of the free-born Englishman:

> Though the son of a West Indian and the grandson of a slave he spoke the English tongue pure and grammatical, and with a degree of ease and facility which would shame many who boast of the purity of their Saxon or Norman descent. Possessed of attainments superior to the majority of working men, he had ... that day been elevated by the unsought voices of his fellow-men to the highest office in the Chartist ranks ... I acknowledge that it was madness that brought thy fate upon thee but it was a noble, a god-like madness – a spark of that electric fire which shook the dynasties of Europe

REYNOLDS'S POLITICAL INSTRUCTOR.

EDITED BY GEORGE W. M. REYNOLDS,

AUTHOR OF THE FIRST AND SECOND SERIES OF "THE MYSTERIES OF LONDON," "THE MYSTERIES OF THE COURT OF LONDON," &c. &c.

No. 23.—Vol. 1.]   SATURDAY, APRIL 13, 1850.   [PRICE ONE PENNY.

Figure 5 The Chartist leader and internationalist William Cuffay. Referencing his birth aboard a merchant vessel, *Reynolds's Political Instructor* remarked, "cradled on the vast Atlantic he became by birth a citizen of the world, a character that, in after life, he well maintained" (April 3, 1850).

> ... – that created, by its magical breath, a race of free men and free institutions. (151)

Cuffay's fluent tongue shames racial ideas of the nation as it takes on the "unsought voices" of his "fellow-men" and the "magical breath" of the divine to create a world in which the enchaining logic of biological inheritance dissolves into "a race of free men." (See Figure 5.)

Conclusion

The occasional adoption by the Chartist press of racist language describing indigenous populations in conflict with white settlers forecast a more complete embrace of the colonial enterprise later in the century by radical reformers, labor unions, and Fabian socialists. But the Chartist archive also demonstrates that the empire was sharply debated and that its acceptance was by no means easy or automatic. Far from being passive consumers of imperial ideology or willing participants in the colonial project, the Chartists included the colonies in their critique of the dominant structures of early Victorian society. Emigration, the army, and missionary activity came under special scrutiny as facets of the empire that demanded significant working-class participation. Most significantly, the Chartist press undermined a bifurcated geographical imagination that insisted on the otherness of colonized peoples and the unitary completeness of the metropole vis-à-vis foreign societies. The colonies offered instead a crystallized image of the worst injustices of British society: plutocratic rule in defiance of the popular will, military repression, and a hierarchical social order that excluded the producers of wealth from the rewards of their labor.

The utilitarian critics of empire had bequeathed the Chartists a tradition linking domestic and colonial tyranny. They warned that the colonies might be used to justify standing armies and train corps of petty despots, who, returning home, would undermine British institutions. But the *Star* and *Circular*, like Wheeler's novel, describe a different geography. For the Chartists, tyranny at home was already realized: the colonies were less a schoolhouse of despotism than an integral part of a completed system. Oppression and vice emanated outward from the metropole as much as returned from the tropics.

CHAPTER 7

Two Nations Revisited: The Refugee Question in the People's Paper, Household Words, and Charles Dickens's A Tale of Two Cities

By the 1850s, Chartism was in retreat. The mobilization of 1848 had been quelled by an overwhelming deployment of police and military force, and a series of trials had led to the imprisonment and transportation of key leaders, including Ernest Jones and William Cuffay. How would the previous decade of working-class rebellion be remembered? This chapter explores how the defeat of Chartism was understood in relation to social and political developments at the end of the 1850s concerning Britain's relationship with France, a topic made especially controversial in 1858 when a series of debates about the rights of political refugees living in Britain culminated in the resignation of Palmerston's government. For the previous decade, the rise and fall of the French Second Republic had been a crucial locus in British thought around questions of nation and social class. Looking at these controversies beside Dickens's *A Tale of Two Cities*, I argue that the sustained crises of the 1840s continued to trouble later Victorian narratives of constitutional progress and gradual reform, challenging an island story that underwrote ideas of British exceptionalism. Propagated by organs of the mainstream press as by Macaulay and other historians, the island story reinterpreted the events of 1848 by describing how British institutions had ensured political and social stability while monarchies throughout Europe tottered and fell (Saville, *1848* 226–27). Suggesting Chartism's failure was an inevitable result of the national character (and thus eliding the government's use of force in the face of the Chartist mobilization), the island story sought to sever the connections between London and revolutionary Paris contemporaries had remarked at the height of the Chartist agitation.

Recent accounts of *A Tale of Two Cities* explore how the novel, written "in the shadow" of the Indian Rebellion of 1857, meditates on British national identity by using insurgent Paris as an allegory for colonial upheaval.[1] Building on these analyses of nationalism and foreign otherness, this chapter traces evolving British reactions to the divergent history of England and the continent in 1848. *A Tale of Two Cities* takes up issues raised in the 1850s debates about refugees, a context rarely mentioned in the critical literature, though one integral to Dickens's exploration of British exceptionalism in the context of European insurrection. Published a decade after 1848, *A Tale of Two Cities* imagines an extreme crisis of social authority but sutures the divisions it recounts, asking how social order can be reconstructed after historical rupture. Although the novel reiterates Whiggish ideas about British exceptionalism, stability, and progress, it also departs from "Whig history" by dramatizing how narratives of steady, gradual progress downplay and elide social antagonisms.

Recent Dickens criticism has also renewed a long-standing debate about the relationship between Dickens's fiction and radical politics. Documenting how radical satire and melodrama informed Dickens's writing, Sally Ledger has argued that his corpus continued a project exemplified by the Regency writers William Hone and William Cobbett (*Dickens* 2–3). Sambudha Sen perceives a similar influence but stresses how the "entertainment-oriented" media in which Dickens's work appeared involved a crucial shift from Hone's and Cobbett's polemical satire (Sen 16).[2] Where Sen and Ledger focus on Dickens's relationship to an earlier tradition, this chapter explores how Dickens attends to a set of pressing contemporary questions about Chartism, its aftermath, and a style of internationalism that defined an important strand of working-class radicalism in the 1850s, a politics embodied in the *People's Paper* of Ernest Jones. The anti-Jacobinism of *A Tale of Two Cities*, which presents revolutionaries as animalistic and demoniacal by turns, distinguishes Dickens from Chartist perspectives. At the same time, by vividly representing the possibility that England might not be immune from Jacobin politics, Dickens's novel reconsiders the island story that had come to underwrite theories of Victorian equipoise. Looking at Dickens's ambivalent response to working-class internationalism suggests Chartism's continued cultural importance and clarifies Dickens's divided perspective.

The Refugee Question and British Exceptionalism

In the latter half of the 1850s, a set of disputes around foreign political dissidents roiled British domestic politics and international relations. For many commentators, Britain's open-border policy evidenced political virtue. Following Louis Napoleon's coup d'état in December 1851, as many as forty-five hundred French refugees found asylum in England, including in the words of George Sala in *Household Words*, "Prolétaires, Fourierists, Phalansterians, disciples of Proudhon ... professors of barricade building; men yet young, but two-thirds of whose lives have been spent in prison or exile" (March 12, 1853). For the middle-class press, the presence of refugees eloquently testified to the virtues of British liberalism against Continental autocracy (Porter 111). Erasing the persecutions of the Chartist decade, the *Morning Advertiser* remarked in 1853, "it is because there is no other spot in Europe hallowed by the perpetual presence of Freedom, that our soil swarms with refugees. Imprisonment, transportation, or death would have been the doom of these unfortunates, had they remained in their own countries" (March 1, 1853). Similarly, Sala's March 12, 1853, account in *Household Words* embraces the island story, celebrating Britain as a haven from despotic rule and revolutionary upheaval: "The natural place of refuge for a hunted man is an island ... Patmos was the elected asylum of St. John the Apostle ... The isles of Greece were the eyries of poetry, and art, and liberty, when the mainland groaned beneath the despotism of the thirty tyrants."

Though a source of pride, Britain's lenient refugee policies precipitated conflicts with Continental governments uneasy about expats proclaiming revolutionary gospels from the modern Patmos. Louis Napoleon's regime repeatedly lobbied for the expulsion of French dissidents from Britain and Jersey, a British territory off the coast of Normandy, whose émigré community engaged in jeremiads against the autocratic ruler. The controversy reached a high point in 1855 when Félix Pyat encouraged the assassination of the emperor and suggested that Victoria had sacrificed political principle and sexual virtue by welcoming him to England with a ceremonial kiss. When the local journal *L'Homme* reprinted Pyat's speech, the lieutenant-governor of the island expelled three refugees connected with the paper, then thirty-six more who signed a declaration supporting the journalists, among them the novelist Victor Hugo (Finn 177–80; Porter 164–69). Middle-class liberals and working-class Chartists organized protest meetings condemning Palmerston's capitulation to French demands.

A more serious fracas arose in 1858 when the Italian nationalists Felice Orsini and Giovanni Pierri killed eight soldiers and civilians in a failed bomb attack on Napoleon III near the Place de l'Opéra in Paris (Finn 181–83; Porter 170–99). Because the assassins lived in England, had worked with English accomplices, and employed explosives manufactured in Birmingham, aftershocks of the bombing reverberated across Britain. Indeed, thanks to publicity around Orsini's escapes from a series of Austrian prisons, the revolutionary was welcomed as a celebrity during a lecture tour which took him from Brighton to Edinburgh (Orsini 187–94; Sutcliffe 104–6). In the wake of the bombing, Britain faced renewed pressure from France to change its policies toward political exiles.

Palmerston's government considered restoring the Alien Bill to allow the deportation of émigrés or extending the definition of treason to include violence against foreign sovereigns, but it settled instead on a Conspiracy to Murder Bill, which sought to strengthen provisions against plots to commit homicide in foreign territory. Popular demonstrations in several cities, however, greeted even this comparatively moderate measure, denounced as the "French Colonel's bill" in Ernest Jones's *People's Paper* (February 20, 1858).

Held up as an example of French dictation restricting English liberty, the legislation was defeated in Commons, forcing Palmerston's resignation. Writing a French acquaintance, Dickens celebrated the bill's rejection: "There is great excitement here this morning, in consequence of the failure of the Ministry last night, to carry the Bill they brought in, to please your Emperor and his troops. I, for one, am extremely glad of their defeat" (*Letters* 8:521). In a letter to John Delane, the editor of *The Times*, Dickens went so far as to express sympathy for the recently condemned assassin: "I think the attitude of that miserable man Orsini, on his trial, as sad a picture, almost, as this world has to shew at the present time" (*Letters* 8:525–26). The radical press went further, lauding Orsini as a martyred hero. Though half-heartedly rejecting "the doctrine of assassination," the *People's Paper* looked forward to "the death of despots at the barricades, in front of a conquering people" (January 23, 1858).

In April 1858, Orsini's compatriot and fellow refugee Simon Bernard stood trial in the Old Bailey on a capital indictment for his role in the murder of one of Napoleon's guards. Like the opposition to the Conspiracy to Murder Bill, Bernard's defense promulgated the idea that the institutions of British liberty were an exceptional but vulnerable inheritance that had to be protected from European despotism. Bernard's advocate Edwin James summed up in the idiom of patriotic radicalism:

> The object of this prosecution was to destroy the great principle of English liberty afforded to exiles, and he earnestly appealed to the jury not to allow the laws of England to be violated at the bidding of a neighbouring despot . . . Tell [Napoleon] that on this spot your predecessors have resisted the arbitrary power of the Crown, backed by the influence of crown-serving and time-serving judges. (*People's Paper* April 17, 1858)

Although the judge's summary urged a conviction, the jury acquitted Bernard, provoking "wild enthusiasm" among the courtroom audience (*People's Paper* April 24, 1858).

The Orsini affair participated in ongoing debates about the revolutions of 1848 and the subsequent reactions, both of which flooded England with political exiles. Several ex-Chartists were prominent defenders of Orsini, and prosecutions included an action against Edward Truelove, who published Chartist W. E. Adam's *Tyrannicide*, a pamphlet that justifies the assassination of despotic rulers (Ashton and Pickering 132). Radical support for Orsini renewed once common associations between Chartism and French republicanism, a connection obscured by the divergent course of Britain and Europe from the middle of 1848. The refugee question thus had a paradoxical significance. It foregrounded England's isolation from the Continent as a haven from tyranny *and* highlighted links between European revolutionaries and homegrown militants as between the French and British governments. Rejecting notions of British exceptionalism, the *People's Paper* declared that the exiles' "hearts bleed from the same wounds as our own" (January 23, 1858).

Throughout the Chartist period, France had served as a touchstone for understanding domestic unrest, in both the radical and the mainstream press (Saville, *1848* 97, 163). A movement that blended indigenous traditions with an eclectic cosmopolitanism, Chartism incorporated the iconography and vocabulary of 1789 into its public ritual and print culture (Finn 115–24; Saville, *1848* 55–56; Weisser, *Movements* 4). Caps of liberty adorned the mastheads of the *Red Republican*; the *National Association Gazette* provided sketches of French revolutionary orators (April–May 1842); and George Julian Harney, editor of the *Northern Star* from 1845, signed articles with Marat's pseudonym *L'ami du Peuple*. A decade earlier, Harney's mentor Bronterre O'Brien published a biography of Robespierre, which sought to "destroy, by anticipation, the credit of similar calumnies which may be levelled against the would-be-Robespierre of my own country" (16). Celebrations of revolutionary France extended to Chartist fiction, especially in the *Chartist Circular*, which used historical stories to reconstruct an international revolutionary tradition (Breton, *Oppositional* 62–67). In a story set in the 1790s, the *Circular* described in detail "the character, plan, and operation of a French revolt as we are well aware that many of our readers have no means . . . of ascertaining more of the characteristic features of republican France than what the pleasure or policy of a government-paid 'historian' may condescend to grant" (August 22, 1840).

Beyond celebrating the Jacobin legacy, Chartist newspapers promoted the journals of republican émigrés, offered their works in English translation, and reported on foreign events. Harney's *Democratic Review* featured frequent essays by Louis Blanc and Giuseppe Mazzini as well as letters "from our own correspondent" in Paris. William Lovett, who founded the Democratic Friends of All Nations, which included German, French, Polish, and Italian refugees, embarrassed the government in the "Post Office Incident" of 1844, which exposed the monitoring of émigrés' mail. Like the Orsini affair a decade later, this scandal around domestic surveillance revealed ways the British government supported repressive Continental regimes.[3] The resulting uproar made Mazzini and his cause popular in liberal intellectual circles.[4] The Fraternal Democrats, another organization made up of Chartists and émigrés, propounded a "revolutionary internationalism" that informed Chartist critiques of the British empire (see Figure 6; Goodway 58). Notably, the *People Paper*'s extensive commentary on Italian nationalists working to unseat Napoleon III ran side-by-side with articles in support of the Indian rebellion of 1857.

Chartist Francophilia only increased after the February 1848 revolution in Paris, which precipitated an upsurge in Chartist (and Irish nationalist) agitation (Saville, *1848* 15, 79). The *Star* reported that when the news reached London, "the greatest excitement prevailed in the metropolis. Several men on horseback rode up some of the leading thoroughfares shouting, 'The Republic for ever'" (March 4, 1848). Years later, Harney recalled in a letter to Friedrich Engels how "seeing *the news* placarded at Charing Cross, I ran like a lunatic and pulled the bell at Schapper's like a bedlamite" (Harney 355). Chartist organizations across Britain sent congratulations to the French people. After being deputized at an ebullient indoor meeting of ten thousand, Harney, Jones, and Philip McGrath traveled to Paris to deliver a laudatory message to the Provisional Government (Chase, *Chartism* 294–96; Goodway 68; Saville, *1848* 57, 79). Throughout the spring and summer of 1848, demonstrations featured French iconography, speakers invoked the tree of liberty, and crowds sang the *Marseillaise* or shouted "Vive la République" (F. B. Smith 104–8). The pageantry of April 10 also evoked Jacobinism; the procession to Kennington Common included women outfitted in the tricolor and a group of cordwainers carried a silk banner inscribed "Liberty, Equality, Fraternity. The Charter and No Surrender" (Flett 32). In short, if the Chartists required the lineaments of the past to step onto the stage of history, they donned the costumes of Marat, Danton, and Robespierre as readily as those of Hamden, Cromwell, and Wat Tyler.

Household Words, the Island Story, and 1848

Given widespread French iconography in Chartist display, it is not surprising that observers of the movement framed British developments with

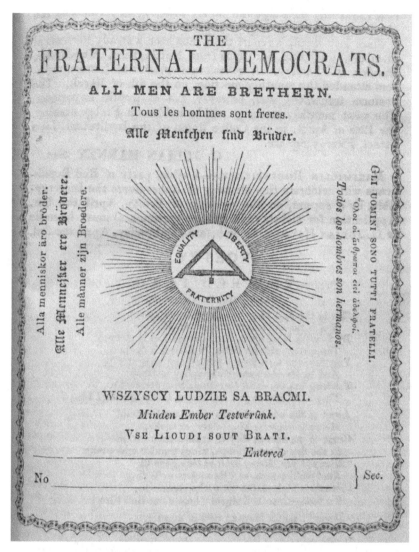

Figure 6 The Fraternal Democrats' membership card, which proclaimed "All men are brethren" in twelve languages. Reproduced in Harney's *Democratic Review*, April 1850.

reference to current and historical events in France. Opponents of radicalism condemned Chartist tactics as imports from the Continent and characterized the Chartists as foreign subversives (Finn 62–65). Thomas

Carlyle in his essay *Chartism* uses "sansculotte," "Jacobin," and "Chartist" as virtual synonyms. Dickens himself stressed the importance of properly understanding French history to contextualize the Chartist movement. In an article in the *Examiner* from the end of 1848, Dickens scolds a judge for his misuse of the historical record at a trial of Chartists in Cheshire. Though characterizing the Chartist prisoners as "enemies of the common weal," who have done "much damage to the cause of rational liberty and freedom all over the world," Dickens dissents from the optimistic assessment of life in prerevolutionary France the presiding judge offered the jury (*Amusements* 139). Anticipating a dominant theme in *A Tale of Two Cities*, Dickens argues that revolutionary violence in France expressed the systematic oppression of the ancien régime (141).

Like many middle-class liberals, Dickens responded with initial enthusiasm to the February Revolution, pledging to his friend John Forster that henceforth "Citoyen Charles Dickens" would cast off his national tongue for the language of the republic: "MON AMI, je trouve que j'aime tant la République, qu'il me faut renoncer ma langue et écrire seulement le langage de la République de France – langage des Dieux et des Anges – langage, et [en] mot, des Français!" (*Letters* 5:256; see also 5:259).[5] But Dickens also suspected that official support for the deposed Louis-Philippe might stoke further unrest: "All the intelligence and liberality, I should say, are with [the revolution], tooth and nail. If the Queen should be marked in her attentions to old Papa Philippe, I think there will be great discontent and dissatisfaction expressed, throughout the country" (*Letters* 5:254).

That in 1848 Dickens could conceive of France and England as closely related has resonance in the novel a decade later. As significant a context for *A Tale of Two Cities*, however, was the widely propagated idea that popular patriotism and Britain's political tradition had preserved the island from the flames of revolt. If throughout the 1840s democrats in France could be styled "French Chartists" and British radicals described as home-grown Jacobins, following the defeat and suppression of Chartism, commentators frequently worked to distinguish British and Continental politics. The disavowal of France as an analogous case was part of the erasure of the extreme challenge Chartism posed the state, the systematic forgetting that April 1848 had appeared to many contemporary observers a near revolutionary crisis. Already by summer, the *Ashton Chronicle*, edited by the ex-Chartist preacher J. R. Stephens, argued against drawing facile distinctions between the countries: "France is not more at war with herself, rich against poor, than England is. She has rushed earlier to the onslaught, but we are following fast in the same terrible career ... They are fools who look at

France and . . . hug themselves with the belief that we have wiser teachers, better soldiers, and more cowardly mobs" (July 8, 1848).

Decoupling British and French radicalism played an integral part in the process John Saville and Ian Haywood describe, in which Chartism, once defeated, "was submerged, in the national consciousness, beneath layers of false understanding and denigration" (Saville, *1848* 202; Haywood, *Revolution* 218–39). Attributing the failure of Chartism to liberal institutions and the national character rewrote the fact that only concerted repression broke the movement (Goodway 72–74). In the *Economist*, a survey of 1848 offered a Whig version of history to explain contemporary developments: "England has been peaceful because, through the long, plodding, patient industry of centuries, she had already gained all which other nations thought to arrive at *per saltum* in a year" (December 30, 1848). At times, *Household Words* propounded a similar view of British exceptionalism. Though usually hesitant to define attributes of the "national character," the magazine consistently held up the hatred of revolution as a shared national trait (Clemm 61–62). The island story animates a November 16, 1850, piece by the magazine's most prolific contributor Henry Morley. Complacently surveying the year of revolution, Morley pooh-poohs commentators who proclaim crises still menace England:

> There is a readiness in [British] politics to find out and to follow right, there is an active spirit of enquiry [in the press] . . . Therefore, we tranquilly content ourselves with the continual progress which this country makes, and have no faith in any man who tells us that it must be saved or ruined. (Household Words November 16, 1850)

France remained an important topic in *Household Words* throughout the 1850s. As Dickens's fiction of the period became increasingly international in its settings and characters, *Household Words* likewise sought to understand British identity in relationship to Europe and the world (Clemm 1–6, 48–79; Grossman 154–217). Despite Dickens's initial enthusiasm for the Second Republic, however, his magazine stressed that the gains won by the revolution were ephemeral, whereas its negative consequences appeared permanent. Morley and William Duthie's "The French Workman" assumes the composite voice of three French laborers to chronicle what was lost by the upheaval, ventriloquizing workers to give voice to antiradical sentiments in a gesture Dickens's own journalism sometimes used.[6] The synthetic narrator of Morley and Duthie's piece resents Louis Blanc's regulation of labor and is satisfied that thirteen hours are again considered "a fair day's work" (October 29, 1853). The article conflates aspects of Louis Napoleon's repressive government with the revolution itself, blaming the latter for Napoleon's restrictions on benefit societies and "even ... singing clubs." George Sala's "Liberty, Equality, Fraternity, and Musketry," which concerns Napoleon III's coup, similarly confounds the aims of revolution with the bloody consequences of reaction, "liberty" with "musketry." Although the piece recounts atrocities committed by Napoleon's soldiers, it maintains an ironical tone and denigrates both soldiers and democratic partisans, describing republicans as "a mob of the lowest riff-raff; thieves, *gamins* – vagabonds of every description – flying before the gendarmes" (December 27, 1851). Following Sala's report, the coup disappears as a topic from *Household Words*. Politics gives way to articles about Parisian hotels, theaters, and Bohemian life. Addressed to a tourist class (providing, for example, advice on choosing responsible servants), these articles betray how the magazine's "implied audience was rather more narrowly defined than the all-inclusive, class-transcending community" imagined in the preface to the first issue (Clemm 12, 107; Lohrlil 15).

The increasing hostility of *Household Words* to the French Revolution of 1848 likewise illustrates the distance between the magazine's politics and Chartist periodicals of the 1850s, which promoted radical internationalism. In contrast with the *People's Paper*'s unapologetic solidarity with those seeking the death of Napoleon III, *Household Words* celebrated the improvements Napoleon's regime effected in Paris, including its program of "Haussmannisation," which cleared impoverished neighborhoods by displacing thousands of poor residents (*Household Words* November 17, 1855). During the Crimean War, Dickens insisted on changes to articles critical of Britain's French ally (Blake 115). Most notably, Dickens's leader in the first issue of *Household Words* utilizes Jacobin iconography to stigmatize the kinds of papers Dickens hopes his venture will displace: "there are other [papers] here – Bastards of the Mountain, draggled fringe of the Red Cap, Panders to the basest passions of the lowest nature – whose existence is a national reproach" (March 30, 1850). G. W. M. Reynolds, Dickens's primary target, responded in kind, calling Dickens a "lickspittle hanger-on to the skirts of Aristocracy's role" and (falsely) asserting that he "was sworn in as a special constable on the 10th of April" (*Reynolds's Newspaper* June 8, 1851). Sometimes taken by critics as a merely personal attack, this article, amid a stream of *ad hominin* insults, delineates keys ways Dickens and *Household Words* depart from the radical program: the rejection of universal suffrage as the central demand for reform, tacit or explicit support for European monarchs, a tendency to ridicule Chartist activists, and the characterization of French republicans as "seditious." Clear ideological differences, then, separate Dickens's magazine from the

People's Paper, Reynolds's Newspaper, and other working-class radical journals. Nevertheless, Dickens's 1859 novel engages the perspective of radical internationalism, continuing to consider "the draggled fringe of the Red Cap" residing in Britain, an engagement that makes the novel more skeptical of notions of British exceptionalism and the island story than much contemporary writing, including in *Household Words* itself.

A Tale of Two Cities and the Refugee Question

In Raymond Williams's account, the animating dynamics of historical fiction became generalized in "the new novel of social change" of the 1840s even as the historical novel was consigned to the status of subgenre (*English Novel* 13–14). *A Tale of Two Cities* stands as an interesting variation on this paradigm in that it reclaims the vocabulary and syntax of the two nations for historical fiction. The project of mapping a split social universe is, as it were, outsourced in Dickens's novel: the seemingly isolated but mutually determining worlds of Jacobin Saint Antoine and middle-class Soho replace the geography of a divided England. Just as Condition of England fiction brings together the nations of rich and poor, *A Tale of Two Cities* overlays and confuses its structuring dichotomies: England and France, the experience of aristocrats and sans-cullotes, private life and historical catastrophe. Notably, however, Dickens's novel inverts a key plot structure of the earlier genre. Where Condition of England fiction slowly reveals a series of submerged connections linking different parts of the dramatis personae, *A Tale of Two Cities* establishes such connections quickly, then recounts increasingly desperate attempts to escape them. In this way, the novel replays in miniature the identification between French radicalism and Chartism observers remarked in the 1840s as well as the subsequent disavowal of that recognition.

That the novel will participate in the debate over the meaning of revolutionary France for British political culture is signaled before the famous opening of the first chapter. The dedication of the volume edition to "Lord John Russell in remembrance of many public services and private kindnesses" recalls both Russell's efforts steering the Reform Bill of 1832 through Commons and his prime ministership in 1848 when the state smothered the Chartist challenge. The noticeable disregard the novel shows to details of eighteenth-century dress, language, food, and customs reinforces its topical relevance. Dickens's story of revolutionary possibility latent in an exploitative social structure seems immediate and pressing, not only because Dickens has imbibed Carlyle's cyclical view of history but also because the novel draws inspiration from crises linking Britain and France more recently than 1789 (Gilbert; Andrew Sanders, *Victorian* 252–53).

A story about political émigrés in London and Paris, *A Tale of Two Cities* adapts contemporary controversies around foreigners in England. Charles Darnay's plot reworks key elements of the Orsini affair: an assassination attempt in which a radical émigré is implicated, a British trial of the émigré, and debate about the implications of Britain as a haven for political dissidents. An acquaintance of Mazzini and supporter of Italian refugees, Dickens might well have read Orsini's memoirs published in English translation in 1857. He may also have seen an 1856 letter by Orsini in the *Daily News*, which describes his confinement and escape from an Austrian prison in Mantua (Orsini 167–72). Orsini's memoirs anticipate crucial aspects of Dickens's novel, including hidden prison writing, a narrowly escaped death sentence, a flight to England, and a prisoner seeking revenge against his persecutors (Orsini 149–77). Beyond these thematic connections, an intriguing biographical link suggests the relevance of the controversy to *A Tale of Two Cities*. Dickens's friend Edmund Yates describes how he introduced the novelist to Simon Bernard's advocate Edwin James shortly after the celebrated acquittal. According to Yates, this "fat florid man with a large red face" served as the model for Darnay's bullying "stout, loud, red, bluff" Stryver:

> One day I took Dickens . . . to one of these consultations. James laid himself out to be specially agreeable; Dickens was quietly observant. About four months after appeared the early numbers of *A Tale of Two Cities*, in which a prominent part was played by Mr. Stryver. After reading the description, I said to Dickens, "Stryver is a good likeness." He smiled. "Not bad, I think," he said, "especially after only one sitting". (2:30–31)

If Stryver resembles Bernard's advocate, Dickens's refugee protagonist collates anxieties about political émigrés. Though not explicitly republican, Darnay renounces his dead uncle's title, earning the contempt of the royalists who gather at Tellson's bank as someone "infected with the new doctrines" (230). Even Stryver, not realizing that Evrémonde and his former client are the same person, speculates, "after abandoning his worldly goods and position to this butcherly mob, I wonder he is not at the head of them" (230). Indeed, such suspicion seems reasonable considering the circumstances of Darnay's uncle's death: the marquis is assassinated the night his nephew arrives at his estate. Although the culprit is Gaspard, whose child was killed by the Marquis's carriage, the French nobleman calls out a murderous undercurrent in his nephew's fantasy that he will one day relinquish the family property. Hours before the marquis's death, Darnay describes the nobleman's wealth as "a crumbling tower of waste, mismanagement, extortion, debt, mortgage, oppression, hunger, nakedness, and suffering" (119). Darnay's pledge to renounce his title – "a sacred object, [which] if it had carried me to death I hope it would have sustained me" – ironically anticipates the Jacobin cult of sacrifice from which the reformed aristocrat narrowly escapes at the novel's end (115).

Although never put in the dock for this displaced parricide, Darnay faces trial in the Old Bailey on the charge of spying on British troops to assist the French campaign in support of the American Revolution. As critics have noted, Darnay's British trial links the French ancien régime with the brutality of unreformed England and foreshadows the hero's encounters with Jacobin injustice (Glancy 45–50; Petch). This ambiguity echoes central themes of the Orsini affair. While the controversies around the refugees underlined differences between French arbitrary rule and a British system of constitutional protections, they also illustrated, especially in the radical press, the possibility that unchecked the British government would support autocracy. In Dickens's novel, the French and English systems are likewise intertwined. Darnay accuses his uncle of interfering in his trial "to give a more suspicious appearance to the suspicious circumstances that surrounded me" (115).

Lukács and later critics describe the opposition in *A Tale of Two Cities* between a private "human" sphere and the unfolding public catastrophe.[7] Less commonly remarked is how the trope of home as sanctuary is bound up with broader notions of England as asylum. The encounter between Darnay and his uncle delineates the theme:

> "England is very attractive to you, seeing how indifferently you have prospered there," [the marquis] observed . . .
> "It is my Refuge."
> "They say, those boastful English, that it is the Refuge of many. You know a compatriot who has found a Refuge there? A doctor?" (119)

The overlay of sheltering domesticity and Britain as refuge of the nations condenses the contradictory attitudes the novel adopts toward its structuring juxtaposition of England and France: just as the idealized Manette and Darnay family will turn against itself (when Manette's diary condemns his future son-in-law), Dickens celebrates Britain as a safe-haven from continental oppression while considering threats to that legacy. On the one hand, the novel depicts refugees in terms familiar from post-1848 treatments of political exiles in Britain, which used their presence to distinguish British liberalism and stability from European extremism and upheaval. The novel highlights how England welcomes refugees of all politics: royalists (who gather at Tellson's to plot counterrevolution) and the more democratic circle in Soho. Furthermore, the reader observes the purgative effect of British domestic life on exiles as Dr. Manette recovers from the trauma of his imprisonment in the Bastille. An 1853 piece in *Household Words* on the refugee community anticipates both these themes. The article celebrates how England embraces "the oppressor and the oppressed, the absolutist and the patriot, the butcher and the victim, the wolf and the lamb, the legitimist as white as snow and the *montagnard* as red as blood" (March 12, 1853). It also describes how the country transforms and softens its guests: "The very climate seems to have a soothing and mollifying influence on the most savage foreign natures ... Hangers of men and scourgers of women forego blood-thirstiness; demagogues forget to howl for head."

Despite *Household Word*'s embrace of the island story, *A Tale of Two Cities* never definitively decides whether the two cities of the title represent opposed or analogous cases. Instead, Dickens balances between overlaying and disambiguating the two settings. Descriptions of parallel institutions, numerous plot developments, symbolic connections, and an alternating structure that cuts between the two locales join England and France through much of the novel. Yet the concluding chapters are premised on a strict dichotomy as one nation descends into anarchy and the other embodies a secure haven, a juxtaposition underlined by the concluding flight from Paris.

For a critic in the *Saturday Review*, Dickens depicts the French and British ancien régimes in similarly irresponsible terms. James Fitzjames Stephen complains of Dickens's exaggerated portrait of "the faults of the French aristocracy" and the novel's attacks on British Old Corruption, singling out the first trial scene as unfair criticism of the British penal system (44). Linked to the mob justice of the revolution as well as the decadence of the ancien régime, the transactions at the Old Bailey feature paid informers, intoxicated advocates, and a debauched crowd awaiting the brutalizing spectacle of punishment. The allegorized description of the attorney general's efforts "to spin the rope, grind the axe, and hammer the nails into the scaffold" anticipate the nightmarish scene where the sans-culottes sharpen their weapons at a grindstone in Lorry's courtyard (Dickens, *Tale* 62).

Dickens heightens such thematic links with a series of spatial homologies in which locales in England come to resemble their French counterparts. In particular, the novel plays images of the Bastille off those of

Tellson's bank, ironically parallel institutions that uphold the established order. The buildings share barred windows, locked chambers, and secreted documents, affinities that emerge in the banker Lorry's dream during his voyage to secure Manette's release from one institution on behalf of the other (Glancy 45). Reminiscent of the diptychs so prominent in Condition of England fiction, chapters seven and eight of Book Two likewise associate French and British settings. The chapters shift between Dr. Manette's retreat in Soho to the residence of a generically composite aristocrat. Contrasting the simplicity of the doctor's dwelling with the nobleman's luxurious suite, the chapters indicate how the approaching revolution makes both interiors vulnerable. Finally, the climactic Book Two, chapter twenty-one, the sole chapter to house both French and English scenes, uses the recurrent metaphor of echoing footfalls to collapse the distance separating Paris and London: "Headlong, mad, and dangerous footsteps to force their way into anybody's life . . . the footsteps raging in Saint Antoine afar off, as the little circle sat in the dark London window" (206). This pivot is made more surprising given the chapter's arrangement of time. In the first half, six years pass in domestic reverie. The second half transports the reader to the single, apocalyptic afternoon of July 14, 1789, a day in which history has coalesced, "as if there were an eternity of people, as well as of time and space" (208).

Beyond the various homologies the novel establishes between British and French society, *A Tale of Two Cities* describes a series of richly textured cultural links joining the nations. Stryver and Carton study in Paris in their youth; Manette and Darnay emigrate to England as political dissidents; elite émigrés flee the revolution; Darnay makes his living in London teaching children his native tongue (the occupation of Orsini's coconspirators Bernard and Pierri during their residences in Britain); even the eminently British Tellson's has served French clients for one hundred and fifty years. Besides answering why the novel's ensemble should gravitate to revolutionary Paris and speak fluent French once there, these mechanics create a sense of a cosmopolitan culture bridging the national divide, a culture Dickens himself enjoyed and celebrated. In the *Household Words* article "A Flight," Dickens marvels how modern rail travel overthrows both a traditional sense of space and modes of subjectivity grounded on it: "A voice breaks in with 'Paris! Here we are!' / I have overflown myself, perhaps, but I can't believe it. I feel as if I were enchanted or bewitched" (August 30, 1851; rpt. in *Amusements* 34).

British Jacobins and French Chartists

The novel's intimations of transnational radicalism establish a final set of bonds tying England and France. Dickens inscribes British motifs into the depiction of French sans-culottes while evoking the Jacobin potential in British society. Although republican cabals never surface in London, the opening scene of a night coach traveling to Dover inaugurates the motif of betrayal from within, as passengers suspect one another of murderous plotting. This theme becomes central with Manette's unwitting condemnation of his son-in-law, a moment in which the structures of family and home threaten rather than protect. Nor are Jacobin possibilities in Britain merely metaphoric. The novel opens in 1775 with the looming American Revolution ironizing the confidence of the "State preservers of loaves and fishes that things in general were settled for ever" (7). This context returns at Darnay's trial when he is accused of aiding the French military by the attorney-general, whose blustering patriotism betrays concern that the jury might not share his high-flown sentiments. As we have seen, the trial calls up associations with Simon Bernard and radical émigré culture; it also suggests earlier political trials, such as those of the British Jacobins and the Chartists (Ledger, "Old" 77–78; Andrew Sanders, *Dickens* 160). By far the most famous treason trial in Dickens's life concerned the leaders of the Newport rebellion of 1839, during which thousands of armed colliers and iron workers marched on the Welsh town, probably attempting to precipitate revolution (David Jones 203–7). Three Chartists, John Frost, William Jones, and Zephaniah Williams, were sentenced to death, but a massive petition campaign succeeded in having their punishment commuted to transportation for life. Granted free pardons in 1856 in the general amnesty at the conclusion of the Crimean War, only Frost returned to England. He was welcomed to London by a procession witnessed by at least twenty thousand. Ernest Jones's *People's Paper* describes the parade's Jacobin pageantry, which included horsemen wearing silk scarves adorned with the tricolor and bands "pouring forth . . . the inspiring notes of the glorious Marseillaise hymn" (qtd. in Finn 127).[8]

The novel's confusion of French and British politics extends to its depiction of the revolution itself. As political toasts and the oral sharing of newspapers were fixtures in London's scene, the practices of British radicalism might easily have provided Dickens's incidental images of French revolutionary culture (282, 325). More importantly, the fatal discovery of Manette's manuscript draws on Chartist motifs. This document's preface, which describes its composition with soot and charcoal mixed with blood, echoes Ernest Jones's gothic claim that he used his own blood to write verse in prison (Ledger, *Dickens* 63). A parliamentary investigation led to considerable publicity of Jones's mistreatment, which included a significant period in solitary confinement.[9] The *Northern Star* linked Jones's case with France by publishing his translation of "The Marseillaise" while he suffered "imprisonment in Tothill Fields Dungeon . . . for the 'crime' of demanding Justice for the people" (February 24, 1849). Both the mainstream and radical press compared the political prisoner's plight to that of the victims of European despotism: "The prison over which [the jailor] is represented to possess so lawless and unbounded a control is worse than the Bastiles of Continental tyrants" (*York Herald* June 7, 1851, in *NP* 210). In Mme Defarge's metaphor of the coming revolution as a long-preparing earthquake or lightning bolt (a motif discussed below), one can almost hear echoes of Jones's prison poem "We are Silent":

> All in silence glides the larva [sic]
> Thro' its veins of red-hot ore;
> All in silence lightnings gather
> Round the mountains glacier hoar;
> Weight on Weight, and all in silence
> Swells the avalanche's snow,
> Till a scarce-heard whisper hurls it
> Crushing on the world below.   (*NP* 92)

Dickens further links French and British political persecution by having the reader first encounter the idea of secreted prison writing in England. After Darnay tours the Tower of London, he recounts a story of papers turned to ash beneath a cell's floor (96–97). This sequence foreshadows the novel's conclusion in which Manette's manuscript endangers Darnay. Ernest Defarge, the Jacobin who discovers and eventually publicizes Manette's text, shares Jones's first name, affiliating Dickens's revolutionary leader with the most prominent politician in late Chartism. In particular, Jones was important in the agitation for the rights of émigrés, translating the protest writings of French expatriates in Jersey and hosting the French socialist Armand Barbès in 1855 after the latter was released from prison (M. Taylor, *Ernest* 175).

The writing of another Chartist might also have inspired the conceit of Manette's imprisonment. Several critics suggest that the plot around Manette's documents derives from a short passage in Carlyle.[10] As John Forster points out, however, Dickens conceived of elements of Manette's story line more than a decade before his study of *The French Revolution*. Forster excerpts a July 1846 letter he received from Dickens, which includes the kernel "afterwards used in a modified shape for the *Tale of Two Cities*": "Good Christmas characters might be grown out of the idea of a man imprisoned for ten or fifteen years: his imprisonment being the gap between the people and circumstances of the first part and the altered people and circumstances of the second, and his own changed mind" (Forster 1:419).

The year preceding July 1846, Dickens was in intermittent contact with the Chartist ex-prisoner Thomas Cooper. In fact, Dickens read in manuscript Cooper's poem *The Purgatory of the Suicides*, which was composed in Staffordshire gaol. Douglas Jerrold, whom Cooper approached to help find a publisher, forwarded the manuscript to Dickens, who was sufficiently impressed with the epic to pass it along to Jeremiah How, who published it (Thomas Cooper, *Life* 274–76; Paz 126–27). Cooper's imprisonment, like Jones's, was a radical *cause célèbre*. The *Star* published a smuggled letter by Cooper describing his isolation and lack of reading and writing materials: "I am sure I was nearly mad yesterday, and could not forbear shouting 'murder.' For God's sake, alarm – alarm!" (May 27, 1843). Throughout the country, protest meetings condemned Cooper's mistreatment, and Thomas Duncombe raised the issue in Parliament, efforts that led to improved conditions for Cooper and other political prisoners. Cooper's "Prison-Rhyme" amply treats the themes of political dissent and unjust imprisonment, central concerns of Dickens's novel. The exordia that begin each of the epic's ten books recall the reader to the site of the poem's composition in Cooper's cell, a device that Manette's manuscript uses when the prisoner describes his difficulties writing (307, 314). Cooper's preface goes so far as to credit incarceration as the poem's condition of possibility: "An individual who bent over *the last* and wielded *the awl* till three and twenty ... could scarcely have constructed a fabric of verse embodying more than a few poetical generalities. My persecutors have ... the merit of assisting to give a more robust character to my verse" (iii). Beyond detailing life in prison, Dickens's novel evokes the importance of former political prisoners in radical culture, the celebrity that arose around victims of persecution including Cooper, Jones, and Frost. Manette repeatedly tries to exploit his hard-won celebrity to protect his son-in-law, an intention he declares to Lorry: "There is no patriot in Paris ... who, knowing me to have been a prisoner in the Bastille, would touch me, except to overwhelm me with embraces, or carry me in triumph" (250).

A self-critical reflection on the automatism that defines many of Dickens's characters, Manette struggles to surmount his monomaniacal desire to make shoes, a condition stemming from his time in prison. Three full chapters describe a cycle of recovery and regression, which is only short circuited when Lorry and Miss Pross destroy his workbench and tools. Always on the verge of falling back into his obsession, Manette instantiates the interconnections between French and English politics, his life in Soho simultaneously evoking a refuge from history, a revolutionary garret, and a prison cell. In a novel that systematically pairs mirrored personalities, "the shoemaker of the garret of Paris" shadows the doctor as a kind of doppelganger. His "dull mechanical perception" while cobbling anticipates the stilted, routinized expressions of the Parisian revolutionaries (*Tale* 40). Lorry's effort rescuing him from his monomania becomes the ground upon which the novel stages the struggle of prying individuals free from the determinants of history.

As overdetermined as Mme Defarge's fateful knitting, Manette's activity is defined by the novel's symbolic system that links manual labor and revolution. The traumatized doctor's hobby as shoemaker, moreover, calls upon a proverbial belief in the militancy of that profession. These artisans enjoyed a reputation for political engagement that made the radical shoemaker a stock literary figure from Shakespeare's *Julius Caesar* (where an anonymous cobbler leads a riotous crowd) to William Cobbett's *Surplus Population, an Anti-Malthusian Comedy* (where an artisan intellectual bests a political economist).[11] Thomas Cooper himself began his working career as a shoemaker, a circumstance to which the preface of *The Purgatory of The Suicides* alludes. These specific connotations surrounding "the gentle craft" explain why Manette's hobby appears dangerous to his friends and family. But his compulsion is rendered uncanny by broader associations the novel traces between labor and revolutionary possibility. From the opening chapters, the narrator describes violence latent in everyday tools: "[On the trade signs] nothing was represented in a flourishing condition, save tools and weapons; but, the cutler's knives and axes were sharp and bright, the smith's hammers were heavy, and the gunmaker's stock was murderous" (33). Critics often highlight Dickens's naturalistic metaphors for revolution (Baldridge 648–49; Baumgarten 166); running beside these figures is a repeated motif affiliating work and political upheaval: "Every lean bare arm, that had been without work before, had this work always ready for it now, that it could strike ... The image had been hammering into [Saint Antoine] for hundreds of years, and the last finishing blows had told mightily" (213). In fact, Mme Defarge reclaims naturalistic metaphors for the realm of labor when she urges her husband to continue their patient preparation for the coming outbreak:

"It does not take a long time to strike a man with Lightning," said Defarge. "How long," demanded madame, composedly, "does it take to make and store the lightning? . . ."

"It does not take a long time," said madame, "for an earthquake too swallow a town. Eh well! Tell me how long it takes to prepare the earthquake?" (171)

Work that reshapes the physical world suggests other dangerous transformations: "It is likely enough that in the rough outhouses of some tillers of the heavy land adjacent to Paris, there were sheltered from the weather that very day, rude carts . . . which the Farmer, Death, had already set apart to be his tumbrils of the Revolution" (8). Such images recur throughout the novel: The roof of Monseigneur's chateau is transformed into bullets, the bells of parish churches are melted for cannon (reversing the biblical imperative to beat swords into plowshares), and the walls of Saint Antoine are pulled down to furnish missiles.

The Re-emergence of the Island Story

As we have seen, diverse formal and rhetorical strategies draw Dickens's two cities together, upending any easy narrative about the peculiar advantages of British social and political institutions. Nevertheless, by the end of the novel England appears a refuge from the tumult of France. In this light, Dickens recapitulates the evolution of middle-class attitudes toward the relationship between Chartism and French radicalism, a process by which a perception of deep commonalities gave way to self-congratulatory assertions of difference. The novel, in other words, stages the *formation* of the island story. If Dickens ultimately embraces notions of British exceptionalism, however, the novel simultaneously demonstrates how the repression of historical memory underwrites such claims and how such acts of repression can prove dangerous.

The novel's conclusion most clearly distinguishes the two societies, but certain earlier events do as well. Darnay's acquittal is one crucial pivot. If the British penal code reminds the reader of the arbitrary power of the ancien régime, an independent jury holds the state in check. Manette's testimony at Darnay's first trial, which describes his "long imprisonment, without trial, or even accusation," sharpens the distinction between the two systems (70). Moreover, the narrator's bruising satire of prosecutor and judge invokes a public sphere capable of scrutinizing the activities of the state. As Sally Ledger has shown, Dickens's fictional trials mobilize a carnivalesque tradition that transforms courtrooms into the realm of the absurd (*Dickens* 39–64). In *A Tale of Two Cities*, the satire is hardly farcical, but the episode's macabre humor modulates into a romance plot when the trial's three most important figures propose to Lucie Manette in quick succession. Due process, it seems, has preserved a realm free from the pressures of history.

Markers of British exceptionalism remain an undercurrent until the novel's final book. A new orientation is signaled via focalization, which for most of the novel alternates between French and English characters, but in Book Three remains consistently with the English. This formal shift abandons a hallmark of Condition of England fiction, which program-matically moves between the perspectives of two or more sets of characters. The change encourages a reevaluation of the relationship between England and France. The servant Pross's xenophobia becomes typical. In language worthy of a Podsnap, Pross tells Mme Defarge, "I little thought ... that I should ever want to understand your nonsensical language" (352). Notably, Pross's patriotism replaces a homely cosmopolitanism, which had prompted the servant to seek out French recipes and develop a cuisine "half English and half French" for her émigré mistress (95). Reminiscent of Duthie and Morley's use of ventriloquized working-class voices (or Dickens's condemnation of railway strikes in the persona of an engineer), Pross and Jerry Cruncher give most explicit voice to anti-revolutionary politics. The working-class characters' loyalty toward their employers stages cross-class solidarity as an integral component of the island story.

As Pross and Cruncher declare the patriotism of British proles, the novel's geography also changes. Earlier cuts between England and France give way to literal crossings that are used to distinguish the previously overlaid settings. Darnay's voyage toward Paris defines his birthplace as the negation of his adopted country: "Not a mean village closed upon him, not a common barrier dropped across the road behind him, but he knew it to be another iron door in the series that was barred between him and England" (237). Along with this changed textual geography, the final book alters the way characters are inscribed into the story. A letter from Dickens to Forster provides a telling account of the driven, onward-rushing sequences that characterize the revolution: "I fancied a story of incident might be written ... pounding the characters in its own mortar, and beating their interest out of them. If you could have read the story all at once, I hope you wouldn't have stopped halfway" (Forster 2:281). This gloss, which Forster cribs in an unsigned review in the *Examiner*, sugges-tively captures the way the novel subordinates other elements to plot.[12] The description, however, elides the British scenes. The proposals to Lucie, the dissipation of Carton, the home life in Soho, and even the treason trial, emphasize portraiture, dialogue, and comedy, more than controlling incident. In revolutionary France, on the other hand, the narrator's mode of characterization drastically shifts, marking how the deterministic forces of history exceed the personality of individual agents. The fall of the Bastille is narrated as nominalized predicates lacking human subjects: "Cannon, muskets, fire and smoke ... Flashing weapons, blazing torches, smoking wagon-loads of wet straw ... shrieks, volleys, execrations, bravery without stint, boom, smash and rattle" (207). Similarly, revolutionaries hide their identities behind the ubiquitous pseudonym "Jacque," and the Jacobin Defarge speaks in a "reserved and mechanical way" (255). By traveling to France, Darnay has fallen into the gear works of history.

With the escape of Lorry, Darnay, and the Manettes, the novel ends how it began: with England providing a refuge for the persecuted of the Continent. The flight is narrated in the present tense and first-person plural, as if the refugees and the reader both rush toward the future promised in Carton's prophetic vision:

> I see the lives for which I lay down my life, peaceful, useful, prosperous and happy, in that England which I shall see no more. I see her with a child upon her bosom, who bears my name ... I see that child ... a man winning his way up in that path of life which once was mine. I see him winning it so well, that my name is made illustrious there by the light of his ... I see him, foremost of just judges and honoured men. (360–61)

If the novel's conclusion invokes the Whiggish idea of gradual progress in order to project a resolution across generations, this vision of social peace is out of keeping with much that has preceded it. In particular, Carton's fantasy calls to mind Mme Defarge's very different version of the work of time. For the Jacobin woman, slowly accumulating effects issue only in cleansing catastrophe, apocalyptic breaks: if "the earthquake" takes long to arrive, she reassures her husband, "it is always preparing, though it is not seen or heard" (171). The novel, moreover, has been at pains to demonstrate the vulnerability of the institutions Carton evokes as the guarantors and fruits of stability, an untroubled domestic sphere and a fair judicial system. Finally, Carton's prophecy of a stable future elides the French and British experience of 1848, an act of historical erasure *A Tale of Two Cities* often thematizes. The ritualistic interment of Manette's tools, Lorry's effort to "bury" Tellson's French books (273), and the manuscript hidden in the Bastille are so many instances of social forgetting. Yet the novel also repeatedly stages returns from the dead: Manette's release from prison, the government informer Barsad's reincarnation as a Jacobin spy, Darnay's unwitting escape. And Dickens is equally concerned to bring to light the repressed history of the cross-pollination of British and French radicalism while exploring how the dangers endured by Darnay, Lucie, and Manette stem not simply from devilish foreigners but from Pross's traitorous sibling and Manette's former self. Indeed, the novel's title page shows an old man writing furtively in a cell, collapsing Manette's manuscript with the testimony of the novel, a conflation made complete by Book Three, chapter ten, in which the narrator's voice gives over to the words of the shoemaker of Beauvais. Even as the novel insists on the potentially fatal consequences of unearthing Manette's narrative, it recalls that history to life.

This study of *Household Words* and *A Tale of Two Cities* has endeavored to suggest that radicalism continued to influence social problem fiction and the cultural sphere more generally long after Chartism's decline following its suppression in 1848. The events of the 1840s shape *A Tale of Two Cities* in diverse ways. Engaging the world of working-class radicalism, it echoes the themes of contemporary crises around republican émigrés, incorporates Chartist iconography into its portrait of Jacobinism, and reflects at length whether the fire next time will encompass London as well as Paris. In dialogue with a movement that challenged so many aspects of the political, economic, social, and cultural status quo, and bearing continued witness to the ruptures of the 1840s, Dickens's novel calls into question both the island story and the narrative of national progress and peaceful change it underwrote.

Notes

Introduction: Can a Social Problem Speak?

1. The *Star*'s circulation was roughly 11,000 in 1838 and 7400 in 1845, but historians estimate that the paper's readership was several times higher given the communal contexts in which it was read (Epstein, "Feargus" 56, 69–70, 96–97; Vernon 143–45). In volume format, *Coningsby* rapidly went through three editions, selling 3000 copies of the first edition (Braun 79).

2. The accessibility of this literature has greatly improved over the past decade thanks to Ian Haywood's and Peter Scheckner's anthologies of Chartist literature as well as digitization projects that make several radical journals available online. See also my and Rob Breton's *Chartist Fiction, a Digital Resource* (forthcoming in early 2018) for a bibliographic index of fiction and literary reviews printed in Chartist periodicals: chartistfiction.hosting.nyu.edu.

3. Vanden Bossche, Sen, and Ledger (*Dickens*) coordinate the radical corpus with more canonical literature. My analysis pursues new directions in considering institutional networks linking middle-class authors to radical politics and by focusing on contemporaneous connections rather than, as in Sen and Ledger, relationships to an earlier tradition.

4. *Cooper's Journal*, January 5, 1850. See also "Literary Reform," *Chartist Circular*, January 30, 1841.

5. This argument intervenes in a historiographic debate about the prevalence and significance of the language of Old Corruption in Chartist discourse. For Stedman Jones (1–30) and Joyce (*Visions* 31–40), the discourse of Old Corruption typified how the Chartists eschewed the language of class. Old Corruption emphasized the exclusion of the people from the ancient right of self-rule while avoiding analysis of economic exploitation. It described politics not through a tripartite class division but as a contest between a corrupt aristocracy and the virtuous people or the "industrious classes." Joyce further argues melodrama embodied working-class populism, seeing the genre's villains as figures of Old Corruption and identifying its endings as the celebration of a stable, hierarchical world (*Democratic Subjects* 176–92). I suggest alternative readings of melodrama in Chapters 2 and 5.

6. Earlier criticism of Chartist fiction stresses its derivative qualities, particularly the way it is warped by conventions of popular romance and improving fiction

(Mitchell; Vicinus, "Chartist" 9–12, *Industrial* 118). Recent scholarship emphasizes its experimental nature and complex relationship with popular forms. See Breton 1–10; Haywood, *Revolution* 146–91; Ledger, "Chartist" 46–53; and Loose passim.

7. This formulation was suggested by Agathocleous's description of the decentering of London in contemporary postcolonial texts (26).

8. W. Hughes 9, 16. Brantlinger, "Sensational" 27. For the influence of working-class literature on sensation fiction, see Law; Pykett 53; W. Hughes 41–42.

9. Curran 63; James, *Fiction* 13; Williams, "Radical" 18. For the war of the unstamped and radical publishing in the 1830s, see Hewitt 4–14; Hollis, *Pauper*. For the class character of the battle for a free press, Hollis passim; E. Miller 5; E. P. Thompson, *Making* 719–20.

10. Aled Jones's discussion of how the nineteenth-century newspaper was "imagined and theorised" informs this and the following paragraph (*Powers* 28–46).

11. Feltes 11–12; Hayward 29; Hughes and Lund 4–7; E. Miller 90; Payne 9. For serialization in the radical press, see Haywood, *Revolution* 172, 176.

12. 23. For another example of the group consumption of the Chartist press, see Dunning 125, 135.

13. Roberts, "Who Wrote" and M. Sanders, "Jackass" provide excellent studies of the interaction between the *Star* and its readers.

14. Loose 151–72 brings long overdue attention to female Chartist writers.

15. Following Gareth Stedman Jones's influential 1983 essay "Rethinking Chartism," Joyce (*Visions* 31–40), M. Taylor (*Decline* 99–108 and *Ernest Jones* passim), and others argued that Chartism was a populist rather than class-based movement. Disputing Marxian typologies, they discerned in Chartist discourse a persistent kind of rhetoric that was "inclusive and universalising … in contrast to the exclusive categories of class" (Joyce, *Visions* 11). Historians critical of this interpretation – known as the linguistic turn for its use of discourse analysis – have emphasized how it ignores the way context shapes discourse; how it mutes questions of power and force in explaining the defeat of Chartism; how it fails to recognize that populist language itself was often class based; and how it glosses over continued friction along class lines within the supposed consensus of the mid-Victorian period. See Janowitz, "Class"; Pickering, "Class"; Saville, *1848* 219–20; Scott, *Gender*; D. Thompson, "the People?" Broader histories that stress the movement's class politics include Chase, *Chartism*; Flett; Finn; Rogers; D. Thompson, *Chartists*.

16. Jones's paper, Seligman Collection, Columbia University. See correspondence with Edward Eldred and numerous letters in box 8, especially from T. M. Wheeler and Evan Williams.

17. Dickens, of course, had direct experience with gaol in childhood when his whole family save himself joined his father in debtor's prison.

18. The *Charter* has nearly a dozen reviews of works inspired by Dickens between February 1839 and March 1840. See, for example, February 24, 1839.

19. Carlyle's writing was a part of wider Chartist print and educational culture. The *Chartist Circular* (August 1, 1840) and the *Northern Liberator* (October 5, 1839) excerpted his work. At a London lecture on Byron, Thomas Cooper, who dedicated his epic poem *Purgatory of the Suicides* to Carlyle, concluded his presentation with passages from *Past and Present* (*NS* November 1, 1845).

20. *CC*, February 15, March 7, and April 18, 1840.

21. Mayhew was Jerrold's son-in-law. A correspondent for the *Chronicle* series Agnus Reach had worked at the *Shilling Magazine*.

22. I discuss this question further in "Literature" (448–50) from which the preceding two sentences are adapted.

23. Exceptions include Ledger (*Dickens*) and Sen on Dickens, Vanden Bossche on a wide range of social problem fiction, and Gallagher (*Industrial* 127–46) on the factory movement and industrial novels.

24. Jones slyly advertised a cycle of poems with Carlyle's "endorsement": "My countrymen! Thomas Carlyle ... congratulated me on my imprisonment, because Tothill Fields was just the place to write a book in" (*NS*, July 27–August 17, 1850).

25. "On Strike," *Household Words*, February 11, 1854, rpt. in *"Gone Astray,"* 196–210.

26. *Alton* 247; Brantlinger, *Reading* 94; Salmon 174. Vanden Bossche provides an excellent introduction to the novel's relationship to Chartist conceptions of agency 150–63.

27. *Northern Liberator*, March 9, 1839; *Northern Star*, March 2, 1839. See also *Champion and Weekly Herald*, July 8, 1837.

28. Williams, *Culture* 99–103; Guy 9–10, 33–36; Yeazell 243. Bodenheimer and Zlotnick both suggest ways seemingly "'private' plot[s]" sometimes engage public questions (Bodenheimer 5–7; Zlotnick 127).

29. D. A. Miller 162. Goodlad, "Cosmopolitanism's" offers a succinct overview of this tradition from which she dissents (404).

30. Bodenheimer 28. Critics debate whether Trollope's novel endorses or rejects charitable paternalism. Betensky 36, 43–44; Bodenheimer 23–25; Brantlinger, *Spirit* 44 emphasize Trollope's ultimate inability to imagine working-class agency. Heineman, *Mrs. Trollope* 174; Kestner 51–52; Priti Joshi, *Michael Armstrong* 49; and Zlotnick 137 emphasize the novel's rejection of individual philanthropy. As discussed later, my reading sides with the latter critics. However, the controversy itself keys into the novel's conflicted posture about how to resolve its narrative problems.

1 Social Inheritance in the New Poor Law Debate: William Cobbett, Harriet Martineau, and the Royal Commission of Inquiry

1. Useful introductions to poor law debate include Englander; Poynter; Lees; Himmelfarb 155–75; Poovey 9–13; Hadley, *Melodramatic* 77–132; Goodlad, *Victorian* 33–45.

2. See Edsall and Knott for histories of the anti–New Poor Law movement. Where Knott elucidates the ideology animating the cause, Edsall tends to dismiss protest as incoherent and riotous.

3. Assistant commissioners visited a fifth of the 15,000 parishes in England and Wales (Englander 10). See Hamilton for the procedures of the Royal Commissions and the rhetorical tendencies of their reports.

4. On Brougham and the SDUK, see Webb, *Working-Class* 67–73; Altick 188–212; and James, *Fiction* 14–16.

5. Himmelfarb 169–70; Brundage 44. The four novellas were *The Parish* (May 1833), *The Hamlets* (October 1833), *The Town* (March 1834), and *The Land's End* (August 1834).

6. Poynter 175–76; Himmelfarb 216–29; E. P. Thompson, *Making* 746–62; Hollis, *Pauper* 204.

7. E. P. Thompson, *Making* 757. Thompson elsewhere applies the framework of Old Corruption directly to Cobbett's *History* in a passing reference (*Making* 440). For an example of Cobbett's text particularly susceptible to Thompson's reading, see *History* 1:102.

8. Important exceptions include Huzel 193; Williams (*Cobbett* 44 and passim); Dyck (*Cobbett and Rural* 4, 214, and passim).

9. The best introduction to Cobbett's career is Spater. See also Nattrass, Gilmartin, Green, Sambrook, and Baker. Certain sentences in this and the following paragraph are drawn from Vargo, "Cobbett's."

10. *History* was not paginated. Parenthetical references indicate volume and paragraph number. See M. Wheeler 77–110 for an account of pro- and anti-Catholic histories of the Reformation.

11. Ulrich 109–10; Jann 145; Chandler 81; D. Culler 157–58; M. Wheeler 142–43.

12. For Gothic's ambivalent anti-Catholicism, see Baldick 13 and O'Malley 16–22.

13. Chandler 61; D. Culler 165; Jann 141; Himmelfarb 215.

14. Raymond Williams in *William Cobbett* comes to an opposite conclusions from Thompson. He writes that although Cobbett saw parliamentary reform as a solution to a broad range of issues, he "continually broke through to the harder realization that there was a whole wide system of 'plunder' – of systematic exploitation" (44). See also Noel Thompson for the basis of Cobbett's thought in physiocratic critiques of the market (43–44).

15. See Hill for the evolution of the "Norman Yoke" over its three-hundred-year lifespan (50–122) and Cunningham for how this discourse eventually encompassed criticism of political economy (66–69).

16. Brundage 60; Edsall 22–23; Hollis, *Pauper* 95–96 and passim; Huzel 165–88.

17. *Western Vindicator*, October 19, October 26, 1839; *Northern Liberator*, March 3, October 12, 1839; Roberts, *Prisoners* 76. See also a series in the *National Vindicator* beginning January 1, 1842, concerning the "Origin and Establishment of the Church of England."

18. July 26, 1834. The *Poor Man's Guardian* greeted *Legacy* inconsistently. It reviewed the piece favorably as "the bitterest pill the aristocracy has ever had to swallow" but also expressed agreement "in the main" to an anonymous correspondent who argued that "Mr. Cobbett's ideas with regard to the rights of the industrious classes are quite erroneous . . . he goes back for perfection to 'our glorious ancestors' . . . The very height of perfection in society, according to his views, is for the great bulk of the working classes to be able to obtain leave to labour for others, retaining for themselves bacon and pots of beer, and for the rest to have the right of being kept in pauperism" (December 6, 1834 and December 20, 1834).

19. Himmelfarb 232–52 includes an excellent discussion of *The Poor Man's Guardian* and the New Poor Law, to which my ideas in this paragraph and the previous are indebted. However, Himmelfarb overestimates the conservative aspects of Cobbett's writing on the law and exaggerates the gulf between Cobbett and the *Poor Man's Guardian.*

20. Charlotte Tonna's collaboration with Lord Ashley and the factory movement, discussed in Chapter 5, counts as another example.

21. Huzel 55; Freedgood, "Banishing" 36; Himmelfarb 169. *Illustrations of Political Economy* sold approximately 10,000 copies per book, but as many of these went to mechanics' libraries, Charles Fox claimed 144,000 read each story, a falsely precise but numerologically significant number (in the seventh chapter of Revelations 144,000 elect souls appear before Yahweh's throne).

22. *The Poor Man's Guardian* makes this connection more explicit: "Miss Martineau, the anti-propagation lady, a single sight of whom would repel all fears of surplus population as regards himself, her aspect being as repulsive as her doctrines" (August 16, 1834). Logan aptly discusses the *Guardian*'s sexism (39), but it should be noted that the *Guardian*'s *ad hominem* attacks were not limited to Martineau; the same paragraph accuses Malthus of fathering "a host of bastard children" and claims Brougham's "juiceless body of bones has been impoverished in fathering one."

23. As a maneuver to dampen opposition to the New Poor Law's passage, the bill only established the administrative structure for relief, rather than specifying policy changes, which were left to the Poor Law Commission to develop (that

the commission would follow a program of retrenchment to render relief "less eligible" than independent work, however, was widely known). Three main changes sought to replace the variable parish-based relief with a uniform policy (Edsall 8–11). First, the act established a central authority overseeing relief, shifting ultimate responsibility for the administration of the Poor Law from local communities to a national bureaucracy. Second, it mandated the consolidation of parishes into larger administrative units. Whereas under the Old Poor Law, each parish was responsible for raising its own rate, dispensing relief, and hearing appeals, the Poor Law Commission united a total of 2066 parishes into 112 unions in its first seven months (*Annual Report*, 1834, 42). Last, the act sought to professionalize poor law governance, replacing parish vestries (usually made up of volunteers) with elected Boards of Guardians aided by paid overseers and assistants.

24. See Huzel 55–98 for Martineau's relationship to Malthus.

25. Martineau's interest in this subject persisted until the 1860s. "Sister Anna's Probation," which appeared in *Once a Week* in March and April 1862, follows the life of a novitiate nun during the period of the dissolution of the monasteries.

26. This paragraph is indebted to Klaver's excellent account of Martineau's popularization of political economy. Especially see the introduction and chaps. 1 and 3.

2 Books of (Social) Murder: Melodrama and the Slow Violence of the Market in Anti-New Poor Law Satire, Fiction, and Journalism

1. Media criticism remained central throughout the nineteenth century. See Elizabeth Miller for socialist journals' media criticism in the 1880s and 1890s (40).

2. The Chartist press also sometimes used information gleaned from Poor Law Commission reports to indict the New Poor Law and the political system more generally. See the *Charter*, August 18, 1839 and the *Northern Star*, March 3, 1849.

3. The story appeared anonymously in the *Northern Liberator*. Haywood persuasively supports Klaus's attribution of the story to Doubleday, the *Liberator*'s editor (*Chartist* 1:1–4). On the *Northern Liberator*, see Hugman. An ad in the *Liberator* claimed that a separate volume edition sold 6000 copies in England and was "reprinted at New York" (October 26, 1839).

4. See the *Northern Star*, December 12, 1840, for a similar critique of self-interested testimony by employers.

5. *CWH*, May 20, June 16, August 19, 1837.

6. My account of radical satire is indebted to Sen, who highlights William Cobbett's efforts to undermine the polite conventions of Malthus's discourse with colloquial effects (25).

7. 1:16–17. Reprinted in Haywood (ed.), *Literature*.

8. A notable exception was John Cleave's extraordinarily successful *Weekly Police Gazette*. See Crone 211–12, 228–42 for an excellent account of crime reporting in Cleave's journal and elsewhere.

9. Cleave was an important radical publisher. Published from 1837 to 1844, *Cleave's Gazette of Variety* "pioneered the deft mingling of romance, sensation and radical politics that Edward Lloyd and G. W. M. Reynolds would soon make their own" (Chase, "Cleave" 127). "The Widow and the Fatherless" is reprinted in Haywood (ed.), *Literature*. References refer to this edition.

10. J. R. Stephens frequently reflects on this passage in his sermons (cf. *Northern Star*, March 16 1839). Lees discusses how poor law unions typically classified men based on employment status and women based on "life-cycle issues" such as pregnancy, desertion, and widowhood (144, 204–5).

11. See in particular: "The Convict" (December 28, 1839); "Mary Lyle. A Tale of the Game Laws" (April 11, 1840); "The Tanner of Mascara" (February 6, 1841); and "The Poacher" (January 8, January 15, 1842).

12. This story is also reprinted in Haywood (ed.), *Literature*. References refer to this edition.

13. See also Gallagher's discussion of melodramatic family plots in J. M. Rymer and G. W. M. Reynolds (*Industrial* 131–33).

14. Ledger also counters Hadley's depiction of melodrama as a nostalgic mode locked into a politics of deference ("Chartist" 49).

15. Gray 48–58 describes a variety of other theories of paternalism, including Tory, Liberal, and Whig versions.

16. For Stephens's biography, see Edwards.

17. See Knott 237–42 and McDonagh 102–6 for accounts of the pamphlet and the controversy it sparked. Knott, however, is unsure if the pamphlet is serious or satirical. McDonagh makes a reasoned guess that writers from *The Northern Liberator* wrote the pamphlet, a hypothesis she supports by the unusual amount of attention the newspaper gave the piece and other satirical writing that appeared in the paper's orbit. Gregory Claeys, the editor of *The Chartist Movement in Britain, 1838–1850*, which reprints the Marcus pamphlet, tentatively attributes the work to George Mudie, an anti-Malthusian cited in the introduction to William Dugdale's *The Book of Murder*.

18. *The Times*, January 15, 1839. Reprinted in the *Northern Star*, January 19, 1839.

19. The *Northern Star* discusses the political import of publishing the pamphlet in the face of government censorship (February 9, February 23, 1839).

20. Reprinted in *The Times*, June 8, 1837. The original story appeared in *The Times*, April 6, 1837.

21. *CWH*, August 19, September 2, 1837; *NS*, March 30, 1839.

22. *Northern Liberator*, September 21, 1839. See also *The Times*, June 8, 1838, for an anti–New Poor Law meeting in Bradford at which a speaker urges the prosecution of government officials for the rash of infanticides.

23. Deeply enmeshed in specifics of the poor law debate, the early chapters of *Oliver Twist* attend to many of the characteristic themes of anti–New Poor Law journalism, such as diet and discipline in workhouses (Ledger, *Dickens* 90–92). An example of Dickens's topical satire is Sowerberry's description of how the trade in coffins has increased since the adoption of the new law. This episode answers the utilitarian reformers' complaints about jobbing under the Old Poor Law – jobbing persists under the new system but only in such macabre articles as coffins.

24. The arrangement of the original serial publication in *Bentley's* differed significantly from the volume publication in ways that bear on this point. In *Bentley's*, Dick's death appears at the end of a short part that is not a full chapter (whereas nearly all other parts contain two chapters). Having Dick's death conclude the part in which Oliver learns of his kinship with the Maylies highlights the lack of full redress the happy ending provides. However, some of the effect of the volume publication is lost in that it separates the death of the pauper child from the trial of Fagin.

25. Englander 7; Himmelfarb 126; Huzel 20; Poynter 144.

26. Digby 165–66; Edsall 2, 21; Himmelfarb 158; Poynter 325–27. See Huzel 42–43 for a useful historiographical summary of the question.

27. In the *Northern Liberator*'s satirical news report about a "Marcusian Experiment on the Sleeping Infant," Marcus scoffs at "the utter futility of the 'moral checks' of his predecessor. 'Restraint,' exclaimed he; 'how can I pronounce the word amidst such a dazzling galaxy of female beauty … as I now behold [in the audience].'" Malthus himself considered infanticide a positive check that embodied the immorality that overpopulation encouraged. By facetiously arguing that newborns have not taken possession of life, Marcus makes infant murder a "preventive" check instead.

3 A Life in Fragments: Thomas Cooper's Chartist *Bildungsroman*

1. The name of the "Shakesperean Chartists" stemmed from the group's meeting place in Leicester's Shakesperean Hall, but it also expressed the centrality of

culture and literature in the group's activities. Cooper advocated making Shakespeare's birthday a national holiday (Roberts, *Chartist* 39). Claiming Shakespeare as the people's bard had a long tradition in radical politics (Antony Taylor, "Shakespeare"). In 1840, the *Northern Star* ran a series of articles, "Chartism from Shakespeare," which culled democratic passages from the national poet (Janowitz, *Lyric* 146).

2. Cooper, *Life* 165–70; *Northern Star*, April 17, 1841, December 3, 1842, January 21, 1843; Roberts, "Cooper" and *Chartist* 69–80; Patterson 318–24; Briggs 144; Dorothy Thompson, *Chartists* 124.

3. Cooper's *Life* relates his difficulties finding a publisher, the search for which brought him into contact with MPs Thomas Duncombe and Benjamin Disraeli, as well as with Dickens (263–79). See also Cole, *Chartist* 199–207.

4. Focus on the stories has been more limited, generally centering on the pieces Ian Haywood's 1995 anthology *The Literature of Struggle*. See Breton passim; Haywood, *Revolution* 158–59; Klaus, "Mrs. Rochester" 5–7.

5. E. P. Thompson, *Making* 31–35; Rose passim. Bunyan was especially important in nineteenth-century radicalism. Thomas Doubleday wrote a Chartist version titled *The Political Pilgrim's Progress*, and John James Bezer modeled his *Autobiography of one of the Chartist Rebels of 1848* partly on Bunyan.

6. See Cooper's *Life* for the biographical material used in "London Venture," including Cooper's ineffectual appeal to the novelist Edward Bulwer-Lytton (126–29).

7. This paragraph is indebted to Ian Haywood's excellent analysis in *The Literature of Struggle* (9).

8. See in particular Devereux 145–46 and Mitchel.

4 Questions from Workers Who Read: Education and Self-formation in Chartist Print Culture and Elizabeth Gaskell's *Mary Barton*

1. For the ideological tensions in the Domestic Mission reports, see Secord 35–38; Seed 14–19; Watts 178–80. For Gaskell's use of the reports and the impact of her work with the Manchester poor on her fiction, see d'Albertis 60; Foster 22–24; Thiele; Wyke; Parker.

2. An important exception is Stone, who considers "working-class languages, texts, and perspectives," including Chartist poetry, integral to the novel's dialogism (186).

3. Gerin hypothesizes that the original "John Barton" was the father of one of Gaskell's pupils (87–88). Gaskell's close relationship with her Sunday school students led her to invite them to her home for additional lessons (Watts 167).

4. For the tradition of reform in Unitarianism, see Millard 6–8; Watts 103–7. For the radical Unitarians, see Gleadle and Watts 203–5.

5. Gleadle 75–81; Hammond and Hammond 7–15; Joel Wiener 100, 113–14.

6. Lovett, however, was never listed for his work as publisher of the *People's Journal*, an indication of the frequently unequal nature of partnerships between working-class radicals and even the most progressive middle-class reformers.

7. Outside London, Chartists and the allied anti–New Poor Law Movement occasionally used Unitarian chapels as meeting places, including in the Lancastrian town of Elland (*NS*, July 7, 1838). In Bolton, a sermon was preached in the Unitarian chapel to raise money to found a Chartist Sunday school (*NS*, January 22, 1842).

8. For Gaskell's relationships with the Shaens, Howitts, Winkworths, and Eliza Fox, see Uglow passim; Gaskell, *Letters* passim; Watts 208–9.

9. See Poole for Bamford's influence on the novel.

10. Pickering, *Chartism* 30; Seed 16. See Maidment, "Manchester" for Heywood's place in local print culture and his role as an informant on working-class reading. See Reach 37–40 for Heywood's interview in the *Morning Chronicle* series.

11. *McDouall's* and the *National Association Gazette* list Heywood as their Manchester distributor. Gaskell's correspondence demonstrates her knowledge of the importance of working-class bookstores. An 1850 letter requests help distributing a tract by the Christian Socialist Frederick Maurice to workingmen "by getting some sellers of working men's papers to put them in their shops" (*Letters* 103–4).

12. For details on the land plan, see Chase, *Chartism* 248–61.

13. For the informal nature of working-class education, see Rose 57–58 and passim; Johnson 79–80; Sutherland 120–21; Vincent 98 and passim.

14. For Lovett's biography, see Lovett, *Life and Struggles* and Joel Wiener.

15. The emphasis on mutual aid, as well as the grandiosity of the scheme, marks the text's intellectual origins as Owenite, the milieu in which Lovett served his political apprenticeship (Wiener 18–35, 81).

16. Lovett and Collins's plan bears affinities with the extensive, though usually ephemeral networks of groups dedicated to self-help and mutual improvement in working-class culture (Harrison 51–52; Rose 65, 75–78). Lovett had also participated in Methodist Sunday schools, whose role fostering working-class education has been widely appreciated (Kelly 135–38; Laqueur 155–56; Rose 62; E. P. Thompson, *Making* 42).

17. For descriptions of the debate around the "New Move," see Chase, *Chartism*, 168–78; Epstein, *Lion* 242–46; Joel Wiener 36–37, 85–87.

18. Raymond Williams, "Radical" 22; Hollis, *Pauper* 137–38; Vincent 136–65; Simon 159–62; Haywood, *Revolution* 191.

19. The *Magazine*'s readership, however, was likely smaller than its circulation as its sales included bulk purchases by employers and philanthropists, who would distribute it to captive audiences (Webb, *Working-Class* 26–27; Hollis, *Pauper* 139–40).

20. Accounts of McDouall's career can be found in Ashton and Pickering 7–28; Pickering and Roberts.

21. Ironically, McDouall's movement from doctor to social critic followed a parallel track to that of Kay-Shuttleworth, the important Manchester education reformer whose experiences as a medical practitioner, in Poovey's account "led him to recast physiological disorders into more general social and political terms" (56).

22. See McCalman for an earlier example among the Spencean socialists (115).

23. The series ran from November 9, 1839, through January 25, 1840.

24. For an analysis of these motifs see Haywood, *Revolution* 199–214. Marx's theory of alienation in *The Paris Manuscripts*, now the most famous example of the use of such tropes, was not published until the twentieth century.

25. Although Gallagher elaborates a set of dynamic relationships between social problems and the "personal sphere" in Condition of England fiction, she insists that such fiction assumes a "deep rift" between "public and private fields of action" (*Industrial* 114 and passim). Elliot (157–58) and Bodenheimer (5–7) offer sympathetic critiques of Gallagher, suggesting a deeper interpenetration between public and personal realms in social problem fiction.

26. Several feminist critics have shown how the novel might be considered more coherent than in Williams's thesis. Stoneman points out the murder plot is part of a larger critique of patriarchal fatherhood (55); Surridge underlines how Barton's politics are grounded in the domestic sphere (337); Kestner remarks that themes of revenge and solidarity join the novel's two story lines (123); Nord argues that the novel consistently meditates on the "public role of women" (154); and Stone suggests that claims of the novel's inconsistencies overlook that it is thoroughly dialogic and works by juxtaposing contradictory standpoints (176). Melodramatic language also defines both halves of the novel. Though this language becomes more prominent after Henry Carson's murder, episodes in the first half, especially Aunt Esther's fall, her alienation from the family, and the seduction plot around Mary include melodramatic discourse.

27. Kestner discusses how seductions in industrial fiction frequently include elements of class exploitation (77).

28. Notably, in *North and South* the political plot enables the resolution of the personal story line, not vice versa. The mill owner Thornton's tentative friendship with the union activist Higgins untangles the identity of Margaret Hale's brother, whom Thornton had believed was a romantic rival.

29. Tholfsen offers a good account of conflicts about self-help and respectability in the 1850s and onward. This topic is a persistent theme throughout the study, but see in particular 125–43. Also, see Harrison 54–55.

30. *Mary Barton* 87. One imagines that the latter detail, though rendered parodically, likely derived from Gaskell's contact with working-class radicals in her philanthropic work or from reading Chartist newspapers. See Pickering, *Chartism* 29–30 on Chartist critiques of mechanization raised both in Manchester and nationally.

31. My reading departs from Vanden Bossche's contention that Jem's plot upholds Carson's vision of self-help (166–67, 173–74).

32. Carlyle praised *Mary Barton* for exactly this emphasis (Sabin 51–53).

33. There are several examples where ideological pronouncements by a character or the narrator are refuted by events or tableaux in the story (Nord 148–49). To cite one instance, shortly after Jem asserts to Barton that during economic slumps the rich share the poor's travails, Jem visits Carson's home to obtain medicine for the dying Davenport and is distracted by the delicious smells emanating from the master's kitchen. A more extended example concerns the murder plot in which the narrator condemns Barton for his wanton violence. For the editor of the novel's Penguin edition, the murder "[occludes] the emergence of 'social murder' as a valid concept" (Daly 22), but the narrative complicates the narrator's condemnation of the act by pairing Barton and Carson in ways that remind the reader of the social violence Barton and his class have suffered and by focusing on the threat of state violence against the innocent Jem.

34. My reading departs from Secord, who likens the depiction of Job to middle-class biographies of working-class naturalists, which render them bereft of their cultural context, omitting such institutions as popular scientific clubs that met in public houses. While Gaskell also excludes these groups, the inclusion of the anecdote from Smith, the narrator's introduction of Job, and the kinds of learning other characters exhibit indicate that Job while exceptional is not isolated in his endeavors.

35. Gaskell's husband provided the notes.

36. Freedgood suggests the footnotes mark the working-class characters' exclusion from a "common culture" and highlight their literary impoverishment vis-à-vis the narrator ("Novelist" 214). In this light, the footnotes might function analogously to McDouall's application of the labor theory of value to literacy.

37. The Kay-Shuttleworths, who introduced Gaskell to Charlotte Brontë, enjoyed a cordial relationship with the novelist, though Gaskell's letters express skepticism toward James's utilitarianism and record quarrels with Lady Shuttleworth about the factory system and the duties of employers (119, 130).

38. Kay-Shuttleworth, *Moral* 69–70; Simon 168; Silver 96–97. For the wider Whig belief that education would promote political stability, see Hollis, *Pauper* 8–10; Altick 271. For accounts of Kay-Shuttleworth's project, see Goodlad, *Victorian* 167–79; Poovey 75–88.

39. Freedgood, however, points out that Gaskell omits the poem's most polemical stanza ("Novelist" 214).

40. Burns was central to the radical canon. To cite a few other instances: Thomas Cooper lectured about the poet in Leicester and Scotland (Howel 115; Wilson 246). Banners at a Chartist protest in Newcastle in 1838 included quotations from Burns, as well as from Byron, Cowper, and Goldsmith (Phillip Collins, *Cooper* 19). Chartist dinners frequently toasted "the Ploughman Poet" and recited or sang his verse. In fact, a Female Political Union Democratic Festival in spring 1839 sang the air "A Man's a Man for a' that." And the *Chartist Circular* went so far as to claim the poet as "a republican, a democrat; and in principle and practice, an honest Chartist" (February 20, 1841; see also Janowitz, *Lyric* 140).

41. It seems Gaskell herself struggled to understand this notoriously murky text, a fact she confessed to Eliza Fox: "I never cd enter into Sartor Resartus, but I brought away one sentence which does capitally for a reference" (*Letters* 117).

5 Revenge in the Age of Insurance: Villainy in Theatrical Melodrama and Ernest Jones's Fiction

1. For women's roles in Chartism, see Dorothy Thompson, *Chartists* 120–51 and *Outsiders* 77–102; Clark, "Rhetoric" and *Struggle* 220–47; Chase, *Chartism* passim; B. Taylor 264–75; Rogers 80–123; Schwarzkopf; De Larrabeiti; Rose 126–53; and Gleadle 75–79. For literature by Chartist women as well as the treatment of gender issues by male Chartist authors, see Loose 111–72.

2. Vicinus, "Helpless" 141; Clark, "Politics" 48; Hadley, *Melodramatic* 100–101; Gallagher *Industrial* 127–46.

3. Melodrama has been recognized as especially important in radical and working-class discourses: see Rahill 165; Ledger "Chartist" 46–49; Rosenmann; Islemann; Shepherd and Womack 188–218; Hadley, *Melodramatic* 77–134; and James, *Print* 82–87.

4. Miles Taylor's hostile biography is the only modern book-length treatment of Jones's career. Also see Haywood, "Introduction" x–xii and Saville, *Ernest*; Flett 178–86 for an account of Jones's election to Parliament; and Janowitz, *Lyric* 159–94 for an account of the literary rivalry between Jones and Cooper.

5. Besides *Woman's Wrongs*, Jones's longer fiction has remained out of print since the nineteenth century. Haywood's recent edition of the former has brought overdue attention to Jones's work.

6. See Airey for an informative introduction to the journal.

7. Devereux 129–34; Ledger, "Chartist" 42–45; Haywood, "Introduction" xiv–xvi.

8. *Notes to the People* (hereafter *NP*) 15. Jones eventually decided that it was easier to swim with the tide of public opinion and published a boosterish poem praising the exhibition (*NP* 400).

9. See M. Taylor, *Ernest* 56–58 for Jones's stillborn career in the theater. Jones attended fifty plays between 1841 and 1846, during which time he became the friend or acquaintance of several prominent actors and playwrights, including Charles Kean and Dion Boucicault.

10. The play was accepted by the Lyceum Theater in 1844, but the company went bankrupt before the play could be staged. A rejection letter from Thomas Serle of the Drury Lane Company states that the house might have accepted Jones's play *St. John's Eve* if the theater had been a "melodramatic company" (M. Taylor, *Ernest* 57–58).

11. See James, *Fiction* 146–48 for broader connections between popular drama and fiction, including plagiarisms between the media.

12. Meisel, Shepherd and Womack, and Rahill provide helpful introductions to formal aspects of melodrama.

13. See Clark, "Politics" 65 for implications of male rescue in melodramatic discourse; Breton 102–8 for this motif in Chartist fiction; and DeLamotte 149–228 for the relationship between imprisonment and domesticity in the Gothic.

14. See Cox and Carlson for competing accounts of the politics of naval melodrama.

15. Jones featured Schiller's *Die Räuber* and *Fiesko* in a review of international literature in the *Labourer* (3:232–43). Schiller's early drama also strongly influenced Jones's *De Brassier* (in the figure of the poacher) and "Price of Blood. A Tale of the South" (1847, 2:129–41). A female revenge plot, "Price" narrates an aggrieved wife's betrayal and murder of the "Napoleon of robbers."

16. *Jane Eyre*, like Jones's novella, was published in 1847. "The Romance of a People," a serial in the *Labourer*, continued intermittently into 1848 until the magazine sputtered out shortly after Jones's imprisonment in June. Jones published a completed version of the story in 1854 as *The Maid of Warsaw*. Citations refer to the serialized edition. Ulrica's arson and self-immolation in chapter 31 of Sir Walter Scott's *Ivanhoe* is a likely source for Jones's scene.

17. Brooks, "Melodrama" 16. Rahill 166; Slater 29–30; Vicinus, "Helpless" 137–39; Gerould 185; Joyce, *Visions* 235; and M. Booth 160.

18. My argument follows recent criticism that suggests how melodrama sometimes explores social harm and institutions, especially Humpherys, "Encylopedia" 129 and Priya Joshi 83–87.

19. *Black-Ey'd Susan*, a sensation on its first appearance, remained quite popular into the 1840s (James, "Taking" 152; Slater 66–67). In March 1847, the play was performed at a Chartist benefit at the Royal Marylebone Theatre (*NS*, February 6, February 27, 1847). Robert Sheridan Knowles's *William Tell* also featured on the bill. Douglas Jerrold was regularly lionized by the *Northern Star* for his social problem fiction and his reforming *Shilling Magazine*. See especially March 8, 1845 and June 14, 1845. The London-based *Charter* rated Jerrold "one of the two or three dramatic writers whose sympathies are of the right sort, and whose genius and taste are so eminently fitted . . . to elevate the dramatic art" (August 25, 1839).

20. On serial discontinuity as a structuring style of Victorian theater, see Meisel 67 and von Rosador 99.

21. Jones added a fifth novella to the original four when he re-issued the stories in a penny format. Unless noted, parenthetical citations refer to Ian Haywood's *Chartist Fiction*, vol. 2. A more substantial body of criticism analyzes these pieces than Jones's other fiction. In addition to Haywood's introduction, see Haywood, *Revolution* 192–217; Devereux; Dzelzainis; and Ledger, "Chartist."

22. Qtd. in D. Thompson, *Chartists* 134. The *Vindicator* frequently printed addresses by such organizations (cf. August 31, 1839).

23. Clark, *Struggle* 220–47; B. Taylor 264–75. Rogers 81–82 offers a counter view pointing out that many female Chartist organizations echoed male celebrations of domesticity.

24. See Kestner 95–102 for an introduction to Tonna's series. See Gallagher, *Reformation* 114–46 for an account of the public and private spheres in reform discourse.

25. Tonna 126–27. Gray 24–37 offers an account of the factory movement, which "publicly represented [women] as beneficiaries of the desired reforms, rather than protagonists in the cause" (30). Also see Sophie Hamilton for an account of how the Royal Commission of the 1830s and 1840s grouped female workers with children in need of protection, a conflation Tonna's stories repeatedly make.

26. Mayhew's articles were reprinted in Chartist journals such as the *Red Republican*. For the impact of Mayhew's journalism, see E. P. Thompson, "Mayhew" and Yeo. Mayhew's investigation of the conditions of outworkers departed from the practice of official employment commissions (Rogers 169–74).

27. See Davidoff and Hall 149–92 and Helsinger et al. 109–64 for middle-class attitudes toward the sexual division of labor. For Chartist attitudes toward female work, see Schwarzkopf passim. Schwarzkopf views Jones's stories as

confirming the movement's sexism (41–43), an interpretation from which my reading dissents.

28. Jane Atherley to Ernest Jones, September 16, September 28, 1850. Seligman Collection, Columbia University.

29. On Jane's dislike of Chartism, see Taylor 103, 128–29.

30. Jane Atherley Jones to Ernest Jones, July 23, 1848. Seligman Collection, Columbia University.

31. Schwarzkopf 237; Devereux 137–38; M Taylor, *Ernest* 158; and Dzelzainis 92–93 argue that *Woman's Wrongs* offer up tortured female bodies as objects for consumption by a male readership. Only Breton 124–25 and Ledger, "Chartist" 56–59 take seriously the degree to which the stories undermine their own fetishizing descriptions.

32. Law's dynamic account of G. W. M. Reynolds's "Memoir" series suggests another.

6 "Outworks of the Citadel of Corruption": The Chartist Press Reports the Empire

1. Agathocleous 2–3; Amanda Anderson 267–68; Robbins, "Introduction" 1–4; and Goodlad, "Cosmopolitanism's" 400.

2. Accounts of Chartist internationalism focus on attitudes toward British foreign policy in Europe, the movement's support for European revolutions, and its collaboration with radical exiles living in England. Margot Finn's *After Chartism* is the indispensable starting point. See also Weisser, *British* and "Role"; Cunningham; Schoyen. Sutcliffe 31–57 counters earlier scholarship by showing internationalist currents extending beyond London, an argument this chapter affirms. Studies on Chartism and abolitionism engage an important colonial theme but generally do not speak to larger attitudes toward the empire; see Bradbury; Fladeland; Hollis, "Anti-Slavery"; and Mays.

3. Ireland was crucial in term of Chartist attitudes toward colonialism; news about Ireland, however, was also a special case – grouped with domestic issues and more politically urgent than stories from Jamaica, India, Africa, or Australia. For these reasons, this chapter focuses on Chartist attitudes toward the broader geography of empire. For the relationship between Chartism and Ireland, see Goodway 62–67; Saville, *1848* 69–74 and passim; Dorothy Thompson, "Ireland" and *Chartists* 15–18, 26–27.

4. *Northern Star* (September 30, 1843). Hereafter *NS*.

5. Criticism of *Sunshine and Shadow* largely overlooks its treatment of empire, including two recent illuminating studies: Vanden Bossche 113–25 and Loose 83–109.

6. M. Taylor, *Decline* 173–78 and van der Linden 287–315 stress organizational connections linking the Peace Society and the Chartists. For controversies between the groups, see Ceadel 325–35 and *NS*, November 14, 1840; January 24, 1846; January 29, 1848; and October 13, 1849. For pieces sympathetic to the society see August 6, 1842, and February 7, 1846.

7. The series included at least eight articles about India and three about the colonies in general: "British Tyranny in India," December 21, 1839; "Consequences of British Tyranny in India," December 28, 1839; "Origin of British Power in India," January 1, 1840; "Colonization not Consistent with Christianity," February 1, 1840; "Colonization not Consistent with Christianity (continued)," February 8, 1840; "Colonial Justice," March 14, 1840; "The Horrors Committed in India and our Colonies," June 27, 1840; "The English in India," September 12, 1840; "Our Colonies," March 27, 1841; "Our Aristocracy in India," March 27, 1841; "Result of English Tyranny in India," April 3, 1841.

8. Volume 2:96, p. 174. The series runs through issue 2:113.

9. For utilitarian theories of empire and their continuation in the Manchester School, see M. Taylor, "Imperium"; Semmel; Knorr 257–67; and Brantlinger, *Rule* 114–16. Semmel, Knorr, and Brantlinger point out how fear of a surplus population, widespread poverty, and the political unrest resulting from these conditions convinced Bentham, James Mill, and J. S. Mill of the usefulness of the colonies as a political and economic safety valve. The Chartists' rejection of the category of surplus population and their insistence on domestic solutions to poverty therefore constituted crucial differences from the utilitarians' understanding of the colonies.

10. For accounts of early Victorian racial attitudes, see Hall, *Civilising* 191–96; Fryer 165–90; West; and Meer.

11. See Grace Moore 31–35 for the wider association between the poor and "savage" populations.

12. See Flett 153–54 on the importance of the lectures for late 1850s radicalism. Claeys and Saville (*Ernest*) anthologize portions of Jones's writing on the rebellion, which appeared in the *People's Paper* throughout 1857. Pratt offers a sophisticated account of Jones's journalism about the rebellion. For a study of anti-colonialism in Jones's poetry, see Paul.

13. See also March 6, March 20, 1841.

14. Kelly Mays remarks that the worker-slave analogy in Chartist verse renders slavery "a trope so abstract and multivalent" that it obscures the plight of actual slaves (144). Similarly Shilliam 201–5; Wilderson 8–10; and Hartman 168 point out how the analogy (or other renderings of the enslaved "qua worker") ultimately obscures crucial aspects of the experience of enslavement, collapsing the violence and domination inherent in slavery to the conditions

of wage labor. These critics open an important line of critique. Reporting on the colonies, however, the Chartists sometimes reversed the thrust of the worker-slave analogy. Rather than using the moral capital of the enslaved to win sympathy to the Chartist cause, an expression such as the "Chartist land plan in Guiana" demands support for colonial movements through the metaphoric reduction of the Chartists' own activity. Furthermore, Mays's claim that Chartist journalism "suggested the interests of recently emancipated slaves [were] directly in competition with those of British workers" is scarcely supported by the evidence she adduces: the *Circular*'s polemical condemnations of the reimbursement of former slave owners. The *Circular* argued that the masters should not profit once more from former crimes, not that emancipation failed to justify the expense.

15. The *Star*'s circulation had fallen to 7000 by 1849, but this figure still represents a significantly larger audience than most early Victorian fiction enjoyed, especially given the communal consumption patterns of the radical press.

16. Mike Sanders, *Poetry* 119–23 and 148–53. Rudé 132–44 gives an overview of Chartist exiles and transportation as a tool of political repression. For analogous rhetorical conflations between emigration and transportation, see Hadley, "Natives" 414 and Huzel 44.

17. One should note that the female *Bildungsroman* often has a different and more complicated geography.

18. See Haywood, *Chartist Fiction* 1:68 for a gloss of Wheeler's use of journalistic devices.

19. In adapting images of Oriental despotism, Wheeler draws on a prominent tradition depicting Asian rulers as tyrannical, arbitrary, effete, and repressive toward women and simultaneously portraying the societies they rule as passive, stagnant, and outside history (Curtis 183–91; Tzoref-Ashkenazi 285–92). Part of these ideas' appeal, however, was their flexibility. The concept of Oriental despotism often helped justify empire, but it was occasionally put to subversive ends, as when it allegorized William Pitt's anti-Jacobin repression or was used to describe British rule in India (Curtis 107; Tzoref-Ashkenazi 293–94, 299–300).

20. For accounts of the relationship between feminism and colonialism, see Hall, "Of Gender" and Midgley.

21. In 1842, the *Star* extensively criticized two Parliamentary reports recommending an emigration plan to bring African laborers to post-emancipation plantations, cautioning that "it is not a fair remuneratory profit that is sought, but such a command of the labour market, as will enable the rich to trample upon the rights of industry, and to establish slavery in reality, though not in name" (September 3, 1842).

22. For racial attitudes in the Carlyle-Mill debate, see Hyam 161 and Gikandi 58–63.

23. Qtd. in *Reynolds's Political Instructor*, April 13, 1850. Cuffay was a director of the National Anti-Militia Society and involved in internationalist groups. In 1848, he became a member of the executive of the National Charter Association. A more ambivalent (though not racialized) portrait of Cuffay can be found in Jones's novel *De Brassier* (*Notes* 854–55). For sketches of Cuffay's life and analysis of his role in Chartist politics, see Chase, *Chartism* 303–11; Fryer 237–46; and Gossman.

7 Two Nations Revisited: The Refugee Question in the *People's Paper, Household Words*, and Charles Dickens's *A Tale of Two Cities*

1. Herbert 205–38; Priti Joshi, "Mutiny"; Grace Moore 136–54.

2. Sheckner, "Chartism" 93–95 and John 59–60 offer useful overviews of the long debate about Dickens's politics. See Vargo, "Literature" 447–50 for further discussion of Dickens's relationship to radicalism and a review of Sen and Ledger.

3. *Northern Star*, June 22–29, 1844; Sutcliffe 43–46; Denis Smith 41–43; van der Linden 302–3; Joel Wiener 110.

4. In the wake of the revelation, Dickens joked on the envelope of a letter that if "Sir James Graham [the official implicated in the scandal] should open this, he will not trouble himself to seal it again." Later, Dickens visited Mazzini's Italian school and helped raise money for Italian refugees in London (Dickens, *Letters* 4:151; 5:248, 579, 598–600).

5. Margot Finn provides an excellent account of evolving British attitudes toward the revolution of 1848, a "complex historical moment in which working- and middle-class reformers were alternately swept together and driven apart by patriotic radical convictions" (61).

6. Cf. "Railway Strikes" (*Household Words* January 11, 1850; *Amusements* 316–22); "A Poor Man's Tale of a Patent" (*Household Words*, October 19, 1850; *Amusements* 284–90).

7. Lukács, *Historical* 243–44; Lamb; Andrew Sanders, *Victorian* 18–19. Herbert 215 and Jones, Mee, and McDonagh 8 reject this interpretation.

8. For an account of the trial, see Chase, *Chartism* 134–37 and David Jones 175–98. A case could be made for the hubbub around Frost's return inspiring the central plot of *Great Expectations*.

9. See M. Taylor, *Ernest Jones* 112–36 for Jones's imprisonment. Frequently hostile to Jones, Taylor claims with scant evidence that the "ordinariness of his imprisonment tarnished his political reputation" (128). See Carlyle, "Model Prisons" 53 for a contemporary defense of Jones's treatment. See *Notes to the*

People 61–63, 203–12, 268–74 for diverse material written or collected by Jones relating to his and other Chartists' confinement.

10. Oddie 75; Collins, "*Tale*" 343; Andrew Sanders, "Introduction" viii.
11. See Hobsbawm and Scott for the reputation of shoemakers for radicalism in England, France, and elsewhere.
12. In Collins, *Dickens* 424–26.

Sources Cited

Nineteenth-Century Newspapers and Journals

Ashton Chronicle.
Athenaeum.
Bentley's Miscellany.
The Champion and Weekly Herald.
The Charter.
Chartist Circular.
Cooper's Journal: or Unfettered Thinker and Plain Speaker for Truth, Freedom, and Progress.
Douglas Jerrold's Shilling Magazine. Hathitrust.org. Web. July 7, 2016.
The Economist. Gale. Web. May 31, 2016.
Edinburgh Review. Proquest. Web. June 2, 2016.
Household Words.
Jerrold's Shilling Magazine.
The Labourer.
McDouall's Chartist and Republican Journal. New York: Greenwood Reprint Corporation, 1968.
Morning Advertiser. British Newspaper Archive. Web. June 22, 2016.
National Association Gazette. Gale Cengage. Web. Jan. 8, 2013.
National Vindicator.
North British Review. Hathitrust. Web. June 1, 2016.
Northern Liberator.
Northern Star. British Newspaper Archive. Web. June 5, 2016.
Notes to the People.
Once a Week.
Penny Magazine. Hathitrust. Web. May 21, 2013.
People's Paper.
Political Register. British Newspaper Archive. Web. June 22, 2016.

Poor Man's Guardian. New York: Greenwood Reprint Corporation, 1968.
Punch.
Quarterly Review. Proquest. Web. July 28, 2016.
Red Republican.
Reynolds's Newspaper. British Newspaper Archive. Web. June 21, 2016.
Reynold's Political Instructor.
The Times.
True Sun. British Newspaper Archive. Web. June 2, 2016.
Two-Penny Trash.
Western Vindicator.

Other Works

Abbott, H. Porter. *The Cambridge Introduction to Narrative.* New York: Cambridge University Press, 2008.

Adams, James Eli. *A History of Victorian Literature.* Malden, MA: Wiley-Blackwell, 2009.

Adams, W. E. *Memoirs of a Social Atom.* London: Hutchinson, 1903. Google Books. Web. Oct. 8, 2009.

Agathocleous, Tanya. *Urban Realism and the Cosmopolitan Imagination in the Nineteenth Century: Visible City, Invisible World.* New York: Cambridge University Press, 2011.

Airey, Glenn. "Feargus O'Connor, Ernest Jones and *The Labourer*." *Papers for the People: A Study of the Chartist Press.* Eds. Joan Allen and Owen Ashton. Bodmin, Cornwall: Merlin Press, 2005.

Allen, Joan and Owen R. Ashton, eds. *Papers for the People: A Study of the Chartist Press.* Bodwin, Great Britain: Merlin Press, 2005.

Altick, Richard. *The English Common Reader: A Social History of the Mass Reading Public, 1800–1900.* Columbus: Ohio State University Press, 1957.

Anderson, Amanda. *The Powers of Distance: Cosmopolitanism and the Cultivation of Detachment.* Princeton: Princeton University Press, 2001.

Annual Report of the Poor Law Commissioners for England and Wales. London, 1834.

Annual Report of the Poor Law Commissioners for England and Wales. London, 1838.

Ashton, Owen, and Paul Pickering. *Friends of the People: Uneasy Radicals in the Age of the Chartists.* London: Merlin, 2002.

Baker, William. "William Cobbett." *Biographical Dictionary of Modern British Radicals.* Eds. Joseph Baylen and Norbert Gossman. Atlantic Highlands, NJ: Humanities Press, 1979.

Baldick, Chris. "Introduction." *The Oxford Book of Gothic Tales.* New York: Oxford University Press, 1992. xi–xxiii.

Baldridge, Cates. "Alternatives to Bourgeois Ideology in *A Tale of Two Cities.*" *Studies in English Literature, 1500–1900.* 30:4 (Autumn, 1990): 633–54.

Bamford, Samuel. *Passages in the Life of a Radical.* New York: Oxford University Press, 1984.

Baumgarten, Murray. "Writing the Revolution." *Dickens Studies Annual.* 12 (1983): 161–76.

Ben-Israel, Hedva. *English Historians on the French Revolution.* New York: Cambridge University Press, 1968.

Bennett, Scott. "The Editorial Character and Readership of 'The Penny Magazine': An Analysis." *Victorian Periodicals Review.* 17:4 (1984): 127–41.

Berlant, Lauren. *Cruel Optimism.* Durham: Duke University Press, 2011.

Bezer, John James. *The Autobiography of One of the Chartist Rebels of 1848.* David Vincent, ed. Testaments of Radicalism: Memoirs of Working Class Politicians 1790–1885. London: Europa Publications, 1977.

Blake, Peter. *George Augustus Sala and the Nineteenth-Century Periodical Press: The Personal Style of a Public Writer.* Burlington, VT: Routledge, 2015.

Bodenheimer, Rosemarie. *The Politics of Story in Victorian Social Fiction.* Ithaca: Cornell University Press, 1988.

Booth, Michael. *Theatre in the Victorian Age.* New York: Cambridge University Press, 1991.

Booth, Wayne. *A Rhetoric of Irony.* Chicago: University of Chicago Press, 1974.

Botting, Fred. *Gothic.* New York: Routledge, 1996.

Bradbury, Richard. "Frederick Douglass and the Chartists." *Liberating Sojourn: Frederick Douglass and Transatlantic Reform.* Eds. Alan Rice and Martin Crawford. Athens: University of Georgia Press, 1999. 169–86.

Brantlinger, Patrick *The Spirit of Reform: British Literature and Politics, 1832–1867.* Cambridge, MA: Harvard University Press, 1977.

"What Is 'Sensational' About the 'Sensation Novel'?" *Nineteenth-Century Fiction.* 37:1 (June 1982): 1–28.

Rule of Darkness: British Literature and Imperialism, 1830–1914. Ithaca: Cornell University Press, 1988.

The Reading Lesson: The Threat of Mass Literacy in Nineteenth Century British Fiction. Bloomington: Indiana University Press, 1998.

Victorian Literature and Postcolonial Studies. Edinburgh: Edinburgh University Press, 2009.

Braun, Thom. *Disraeli the Novelist.* London: George Allen & Unwin, 1981.

Breton, Rob. *The Oppositional Aesthetics of Chartist Fiction: Reading against the Middle-Class Novel.* New York: Routledge, 2016.

Breton, Rob and Gregory Vargo *Chartist Fiction, a Digital Resource.* chartistfiction.hosting.nyu.edu.

Brierley, Ben. *Home Memories and Recollections of a Life.* Manchester: *Abel Heywood & Sons,* 1886.

Briggs, Asa. *Chartist Studies.* London: Macmillan and Co., 1959.

Brill, Barbara. *William Gaskel: A Portrait.* Manchester: Manchester Literary and Philosophical, 1984.

Brooks, Peter. *The Melodramatic Imagination: Balzac, Henry James, Melodrama, and the Mode of Excess*. New York: Columbia University Press, 1985 [1976].

"Melodrama, Body, Revolution." *Melodrama: Stage, Picture, Screen*. Eds. Jacky Bratton, Jim Cook, and Christine Gledhill. London: British Film Institute, 1994. 11–24.

Brundage, Anthony. *The Making of the New Poor Law*. New Brunswick, NJ: Rutgers University Press, 1978.

Buzard, James. *Disorienting Fiction: The Autoethnographic Work of Nineteenth-Century British Novels*. Princeton: Princeton University Press, 2005.

Carlson, Marvin. "He Never Should Bow Down to a Domineering Frown: Class Tensions and Nautical Melodrama." *Melodrama: The Cultural Emergence of a Genre*. Eds. Michael Hays and Anastasia Nikolopoulou. New York: St. Martin's Press, 1996. 147–66.

Carlyle, Thomas. "Model Prisons." *Latter-Day Pamphlets*. New York: Charles Scribner's Sons, 1901.

English and Other Critical Essays. London: J.M. Dent & Sons, 1915.

Past and Present. Berkeley: University of California Press, 2005.

Ceadel, Martin. *The Origins of War Prevention: The British Peace Movement and International Relations, 1730–1854*. Oxford: Clarendon Press, 1996.

Celikkol, Ayse. *Romances of Free Trade: British Literature, Laissez-Fare and the Global Nineteenth Century*. New York: Oxford University Press, 2011.

[Chadwick, Edwin.] "First Annual Report of the Poor Law Commissioners for England and Wales." *Edinburgh Review*. 63:128 (1836): 487–537.

Report on the Sanitary Condition of the Laboring Population of Great Britain. Edinburgh: Edinburgh University Press, 1965.

Chandler, Alice. *A Dream of Order: The Medieval Ideal in Nineteenth-Century English Literature*. London: Routledge and Kegan Paul, 1971.

Chase, Malcolm. *Chartism: A New History*. Manchester: Manchester UP, 2007.

"John Cleave." *Dictionary of Nineteenth-Century Journalism in Great Britain and Ireland*. Eds. Laurel Brake and Marysa Demoor. London: Academia Press and the British Library, 2009. 126–27.

"Cobbett, His Children and Chartism." *William Cobbett, Romanticism and the Enlightenment: Contexts and Legacy*. Eds. James Grande and John Stevenson. London: Pickering & Chatto, 2015. 123–35. ProQuest. Web. Feb. 17, 2016.

Chase, Malcolm and Greg Vargo. "*Northern Star* (1837–1852)." *Dictionary of Nineteenth-Century Journalism in Great Britain and Ireland*. Eds. Laurel Brake and Marysa Demoor. London: Academia Press and the British Library, 2009. 459–60.

Clark, Anna. "The Politics of Seduction in English popular Culture." *The Progress of Romance: The Politics of Popular Fiction*. Ed. Jean Radford. New York: Routledge: 1986. 47–70.

"The Rhetoric of Chartist Domesticity: Gender, Language, and Class in the 1830s and 1840s." *The Journal of British Studies*. 31:1 (1992): 62–88.

The Struggle for the Breeches: Gender and the Making of the British Working Class. Berkeley: University of California Press, 1995.

Clemm, Sabine. *Dickens, Journalism, and Nationhood: Mapping the World in Household Words*. New York: Routledge, 2009.

Cobbett, William. *A History of the Protestant "Reformation" in England and Ireland*. London, 1829.

"Surplus Population, A Comedy in Three Acts." *Two-Penny Trash*. 1:12 (1831): 266–91.

Legacy to Labourers; or, What Is the Right which the Lords, Baronets, and Squires, have to the Lands of England? London: Mills, Jowett, and Mills, 1835.

Rural Rides. Baltimore: Penguin, 1967.

Cole, G. D. H. *The Life of William Cobbett*. New York: Harcourt, Brace, and Company, 1924.

Chartist Portraits. London: Cassell Publishers Ltd., 1941.

Collings, David. *Monstrous Society: Reciprocity, Discipline, and the Political Uncanny, c. 1780–1848*. Lewisburg: Bucknell University Press, 2009.

Collins, Philip. *Thomas Cooper, the Chartist: Byron and the "Poets of the Poor."* Nottingham: University of Nottingham, 1969.

Dickens: The Critical Heritage. London: Routledge, 1971.

"*A Tale of Two Cities* and *Great Expectations* in Dickens' Career." *Dickens Studies Annual*. 2 (1972): 336–52.

Cooper, Thomas. *Wise Saws and Modern Instances*. 2 vols. London: Jeremiah Row, 1845.

The Purgatory of the Suicides: A Prison-Rhyme. London: Chapman and Hall, 1853 [1845]. Google Books. Web. Dec. 16, 2009.

The Life of Thomas Cooper. New York: Humanities Press, 1971.

Courtemanche, Eleanor. "'Naked Truth Is the Best Eloquence': Martineau, Dickens, and the Moral Science of Realism." *ELH* 73:2 (2006): 383–407.

Cox, Jeffrey. "The Ideological Tack of Nautical Melodrama." *Melodrama: The Cultural Emergence of a Genre*. Eds. Michael Hays and Anastasia Nikolopoulou. New York: St. Martin's Press, 1996. 167–89.

Craik, George Lillie. *The Pursuit of Knowledge under Difficulties*. London: Charles Knight, 1830. Hathitrust. May 21, 2013. Web.

Crone, Rosaline. *Violent Victorians*. Manchester: Manchester University Press, 2012.

Culler, A. Dwight. *The Victorian Mirror of History*. New Haven: Yale University Press, 1985.

Culler, Jonathan. *The Literary in Theory*. Stanford: Stanford University Press, 2007.

Cunningham, Hugh. "The Language of Patriotism." *Patriotism: The Making and Unmaking of British National Identity*, vol. 1. Ed. Raphael Samuel. London: Routledge, 1989. 57–89.

Curran, James. "The Press as an Agency of Social Control: An Historical Perspective." *Newspaper History from the Seventeenth Century to the Present Day*. Eds. George Boyce, James Curran, and Pauline Wingate. Beverly Hills, CA: Sage, 1978. 51–75.

Curtis, Michael. *Orientalism and Islam: European Thinkers of Oriental Despotism in the Middle East and India*. Cambridge: Cambridge University Press, 2009.

d'Albertis, Deirdre. *Dissembling Fictions: Elizabeth Gaskell and the Victorian Social Text*. New York: St. Martin's, 1997.

Daly, MacDonald. "Introduction." *Mary Barton* by Elizabeth Gaskell. New York: Penguin, 2003. vii–xxx.

Dames, Nicholas. "On Not Close Reading: The Prolonged Excerpt as Victorian Critical Protocol." *The Feeling of Reading: Affective Experience and Victorian Literature*. Ed. Rachel Ablow. Ann Arbor: University of Michigan Press, 2010.

Davidoff, Leonore and Catherine Hall. *Family Fortunes: Men and Women of the English Middle Class, 1780–1850*. Chicago: University of Chicago Press, 1987.

Davis, Lennard. *Factual Fictions: The Origins of the English Novel*. Philadelphia: University of Pennsylvania Press, 1983.

Denning, Michael. *Culture in the Age of Three Worlds*. New York: Verso, 2004.

DeLamotte, Eugenia. *Perils of the Night: A Feminist Study of Nineteenth-Century Gothic*. New York: Oxford University Press, 1990.

De Larrabeiti, Michelle. "Conspicuous Before the World: The Political Rhetoric of the Chartist Women." *Radical Femininity: Women's Self-Representation in the Public Sphere*. Ed. Eileen Yeo. Manchester: Manchester University Press, 1998. 106–26.

Devereux, Steve. "Chartism and Popular Fiction." *Writing and Radicalism*. Ed. John Lucas. New York: Longman, 1996. 128–49.

Dickens, Charles. *Oliver Twist*. New York: Penguin, 1985.

"The Chimes." *Christmas Books*. New York: Oxford University Press, 1988. 91–182.

The Letters of Charles Dickens. Eds. Graham Storey and Kathleen Tillotson. Oxford: Clarendon Press, 1995.

The Amusements of the People and Other Papers: Reports, Essays and Reviews, 1834–51. Ed. Michael Slater. Columbus: Ohio State University Press, 1996.

"Gone Astray" and Other Papers from Household Words, *1851–59*. Ed. Michael Slater. London: J.M. Dent, 1998.

A Tale of Two Cities. New York: Oxford University Press, 2008.

Digby, Anne. "Malthus and Reform of the English Poor Law." *Malthus and His Time*. Ed. Michael Turner. New York: St. Martin's Press, 1986. 157–69.

Disraeli, Benjamin. *Conigsby, or The New Generation*. New York: New American Library, 1962.

Sybil. New York: Oxford University Press, 2008.

Doubleday, Thomas. "The Political Pilgrim's Progress." *Chartist Fiction*. Ed. Ian Haywood. Aldershot: Ashgate, 1999.

Dunning, Thomas. "Reminiscences of Thomas Dunning." *Testaments of Radicalism*. Ed. David Vincent. London: Europa, 1977. 119–46.

Dyck, Ian. *William Cobbett and Rural Popular Culture*. Cambridge: Cambridge University Press, 1992.

"Cobbett, William (1763–1835)." *Oxford Dictionary of National Biography*. Ed. Lawrence Goldman. Oxford: Oxford University Press, 2004.

Dzelzainis, Ella. "Chartism and Gender Politics in Ernest Jones's *The Young Milliner*." *Famine and Fashion: Needlewomen in the Nineteenth Century*. Ed. Beth Harris. Burlington, VT: Ashgate, 2005. 87–97.

Edsall, Nicholas. *The Anti-Poor Law Movement 1834–44*. Totowa, NJ: Rowman & Littlefield, 1971.

Edwards, Michael. *Purge This Realm: A Life of Joseph Rayner Stephens*. London: Epworth Press, 1994.

Elliot, Dorice Williams. *The Angel out of the House: Philanthropy and Gender in Nineteenth-Century England*. Charlottesville: University Press of Virginia, 2002.

Englander, David. *Poverty and Poor Law Reform in Britain: From Chadwick to Booth, 1834–1914*. New York: Longman, 1998.

Epstein, James. "Feargus O'Connor and the Northern Star." *International Review of Social History*. 21 (1976): 51–97.

"Some Organisational and Cultural Aspects of Movement in Nottingham." *The Chartist Experience: Studies in Working-Class Radicalism and Culture, 1830–60*. Eds. James Epstein and Dorothy Thompson. London: Macmillan, 1982. 221–68.

The Lion of Freedom. London: Croom Helm, 1982.

Radical Expression: Political Language, Ritual, and Symbol in England, 1790–1850. New York: Oxford University Press, 1994.

Esty, Jed "The Colonial Bildungsroman: 'The Story of an African Farm' and the Ghost of Goethe." *Victorian Studies*. 49:3 (2007): 407–30.

Extracts from the Information Received by his Majesty's Commissioners as to the Administration and Operation of the Poor Laws. London: B. Fellowes, 1833.

Faulkner, Harold Underwood. *Chartism and the Churches: A Study in Democracy*. New York: Columbia University Press, 1916.

Feltes, Norman. *Modes of Production of Victorian Novels*. Chicago: University of Chicago Press, 1986.

Finn, Margot. *After Chartism: Class and Nation in English Radical Politics, 1848–1874*. Cambridge: Cambridge UP, 1993.

Fladeland, Betty. "'Our Cause being One and the Same': Abolitionists and Chartism." *Slavery and British Society*. Ed. James Walvin. Baton Rouge: Louisiana State University Press, 1982. 69–99.

Flett, Keith. *Chartism After 1848: The Working Class and the Politics of Radical Education*. London: Merlin Press, 2006.

Flint, Kate. "The Victorian Novel and Its Readers." *The Cambridge Companion to the Victorian Novel*. Ed. Deirdre David. Cambridge: Cambridge University Press, 2001. 17–36.

Ford, George and Lauriat Lane, eds. *The Dickens Critics*. Ithaca: Cornell University Press, 1961.

Forster, John. *The Life of Charles Dickens*, 2 vols. London: J.M. Dent, 1969.

Foster, Shirley. *Elizabeth Gaskell: A Literary Life*. New York: Palgrave, 2002.

Frankel, Oz. "Blue Books and the Victorian Reader." *Victorian Studies*. 46:2 (2004). 308–18.

States of Inquiry: Social Investigations and Print Culture in Nineteenth-Century Britain and the United States. Baltimore: The Johns Hopkins University Press, 2006.

Freedgood, Elaine. "Banishing Panic: Harriet Martineau and the Popularization of Political Economy." *Victorian Studies*. 39:1 (1995): 33–53.

"The Novelist and Her Poor." *Novel: A Forum on Fiction* 47:2 (2014): 210–23.

Fryer, Peter. *Staying Power: The History of Black People in Britain*. London: Pluto Press, 1984.

Gallagher, Catherine. *The Industrial Reformation of English Fiction: Social Discourse and Narrative Form, 1832–1867*. Chicago: University of Chicago Press, 1985.

The Body Economic: Life, Death, and Sensation in Political Economy and the Victorian Novel. Princeton: Princeton University Press, 2006.

Gaskell, Elizabeth. *The Life of Charlotte Brontë*. New York: Oxford University Press, 1996.

The Letters of Mrs. Gaskell. Eds. J. A. V. Chapple and Arthur Pollard. Manchester: Mandolin, 1997.

Mary Barton. New York: Penguin, 2003.

North and South. New York: Penguin, 2003.

Gerin, Winifred. *Elizabeth Gaskell, A Biography*. Oxford: Oxford University Press, 1976.

Gikandi, Simon. *Maps of Englishness*. New York: Columbia University Press, 1996.

Gilbert, Elliot L. "'To Awake From History': Carlyle, Thackeray, and *A Tale of Two Cities*." *Dickens Studies Annual*. 12 (1983): 247–65.

Gilmartin, Kevin. *Print Politics: The Press and Radical Opposition in Early Nineteenth-Century England*. Cambridge: Cambridge University Press, 1996.

Glancy, Ruth. "Introduction." *Christmas Books*. Charles Dickens. New York: Oxford University Press, 1988. ix–xxii.

A Tale of Two Cities: Dickens's Revolutionary Novel. Boston: Twayne Publishers, 1991.

Gleadle, Kathryn. *The Early Feminists: Radical Unitarians and the Emergence of the Women's Rights Movement, 1831–51*. New York: St. Martin's, 1995.

Goc, Nicola. *Women, Infanticide and the Press, 1822–1922: News Narratives in England and Australia*. Aldershot: Ashgate, 2013.

Goodlad, Lauren. *Victorian Literature and the Victorian State*. Baltimore: Johns Hopkins University Press, 2003.

"Cosmopolitanism's Actually Existing Beyond; Towards a Victorian Geopolitical Aesthetic." *Victorian Literature and Culture*. 38 (2010): 399–411.

Goodway, David. *London Chartism, 1838–1848*. Cambridge: Cambridge University Press, 1982.

Gossman, Norbert J. "William Cuffay: London's Black Chartist." *Phylon*. 44:1 (1983): 56–65.

Graff, Ann-Barbara. "'Fair, Fat and Forty': Social Redress and F.T.'s Literary Activism." *Frances Trollope and the Novel of Social Change*. Ed. Brenda Ayres. Westport, CT: Greenwood Press, 2002.

Gray, Robert. *The Factory Question and Industrial England, 1830–1860*. Cambridge: Cambridge University Press, 1996.

Graziano, Anne. "The Death of the Working-Class Hero in *Mary Barton* and *Alton Locke*." *JNT: Journal of Narrative Theory* 29.2 (1999): 135–57.

Green, Daniel. *Great Cobbett, The Noblest Agitator*. London: Hodder and Stoughton, 1983.

Griffin, Dustin. *Satire, a Critical Reintroduction*. Lexington: The University of Kentucky Press, 1994.

Grossman, Jonathan H. *Charles Dickens's Networks: Public Transport and the Novel*. New York: Oxford University Press, 2012.

Guy, Josephine. *The Victorian Social-Problem Novel: The Market, the Individual and Communal Life*. New York: St. Martin's, 1996.

Hadley, Elaine. "Natives in a Strange Land: The Philanthropic Discourse of Juvenile Emigration in Mid-Nineteenth-Century England." *Victorian Studies*. 33:3 (1990): 411–37.

Melodramatic Tactics: Theatricalized Dissent in the English Marketplace, 1800–1885. Stanford: Stanford University Press, 1995.

Hall, Catherine. *Civilising Subjects: Metropole and Colony in the English Imagination 1830–1867*. Chicago: University of Chicago Press, 2002.

"Of Gender and Empire: Reflections on the Nineteenth Century." *Gender and Empire*. Ed. Philippa Levine. Oxford: Oxford University Press, 2004. 46–76.

Hall, Catherine and Sonya Rose. "Introduction: Being at Home with the Empire." *At Home with the Empire: Metropolitan Culture and the Imperial World*. Eds. Catherine Hall and Sonya Rose. Cambridge: Cambridge University Press, 2004. 1–31.

Hall, Robert. "Creating a People's History: Political Identity and History in Chartism, 1832–1848." *The Chartist Legacy*. Eds. Owen Ashton, Robert Fyson, and Stephen Roberts. London: Merlin, 1999. 232–54.

Hamilton, Sophie. "Images of Femininity in the Royal Commissions of the 1830s and 1840s." *Radical Femininity: Women's Self-Representation in the Public Sphere*. Ed. Eileen Yeo. Manchester: Manchester University Press, 1998. 79–105.

Hamilton, Susan, ed. *"Criminal, Idiots, Women, and Minors": Victorian Writing by Women on Women*. Peterborough, ONT: Broadview, 1995.

Hammond, J. L. and Barbara Hammond. *James Stansfeld: A Victorian Champion of Sex Equality*. London: Longmans, Green, 1932.

Harney, George Julian. *The Harney Papers*. Eds. Frank Gees Black and Renee Métivier Black. Assen, Netherlands: Van Gorcum, 1969.

Harrison, J.F.C. *Learning and Living, 1790–1960: A Study of the History of the English Adult Education Movement*. Toronto: University of Toronto Press, 1961.

Hartman, Saidiya. "The Belly of the World: A Note on Black Women's Labors." *Souls*. 18:1 (2016): 166–73.

Hayward, Jennifer. *Consuming Pleasures: Active Audiences and Serial Fictions from Dickens to Soap Opera*. Lexington: The University of Kentucky Press, 1997.

Haywood, Ian, ed. *The Literature of Struggle*. Brookfield, VT: Ashgate, 1995.

"Introduction." *Chartist Fiction*, vol. 2. Ed. Ian Haywood. Burlington, VT: Ashgate, 2001.

The Revolution in Popular Literature. Cambridge: Cambridge University Press, 2004.

Heineman, Helen. *Mrs. Trollope: The Triumphant Feminine in the Nineteenth Century*. Athens: Ohio University Press, 1979.

Frances Trollope. Boston: Twayne, 1984.

Helsinger, Elizabeth, Robin Lauterbach Sheets, and William Veeder. *The Woman Question: Social Issues, 1837–1883*. New York: Garland Publishing, 1983.

Herbert, Christopher. *War of No Pity: The Indian Mutiny and Victorian Trauma*. Princeton: Princeton University Press, 2008.

Hill, Christopher. *Puritanism and Revolution*. New York: Schocken, 1958.

Himmelfarb, Gertrude. *The Idea of Poverty*. New York: Knopf, 1983.

Hobsbawm, Eric and George Rudé. *Captain Swing*. London: Phoenix Press, 2001.

Hobsbawm, Eric and Joan Wallach Scott. "Political Shoemakers." *Past and Present*. 89 (1980): 86–114.

Hollis, Patricia. *The Pauper Press*. New York: Oxford University Press, 1970.

"Anti-Slavery and British Working-Class Radicalism in the Years of Reform." *Anti-Slavery, Religion, and Reform*. Eds. Christine Bolt and Seymour Drescher. Hamden CT: Dawson, 1982. 294–315.

Holyoake, George Jacob. *The Last Trial for Atheism in England; a Fragment of Autobiography*. London: Trubner, 1871. Hathitrust. Web. June 1, 2016.

Howel, Phillip. "The Geography of Political Lecturing." *The People's Charter: Democratic Agitation in Early Victorian Britain*. Ed. Stephen Roberts. London: Merlin, 2003. 114–32.

Hughes, Linda and Michael Lund. *The Victorian Serial*. Charlottesville: University of Virginia Press, 1991.

Hughes, Winifred. *The Maniac in the Cellar: Sensation Novels of the 1860s*. Princeton: Princeton University Press, 1980.

Humpherys, Anne "Popular Narrative and Political Discourse in *Reynolds's Weekly Newspaper*." *Investigating Victorian Journalism*. Eds. Laurel Brake, Aled Jones, and Lionel Madden. London: Macmillan, 1990. 33–47.

"An Introduction to G.W.M. Reynolds's 'Encyclopedia of Tales.'" *G.W.M. Reynolds: Nineteenth-Century Fiction, Politics and the Press*. Eds. Anne Humpherys and Louis James. Burlington, VT: Ashgate, 2008.

Huzel, James. *The Popularization of Malthus in Early Nineteenth Century England: Martineau, Cobbett and the Pauper Press*. Burlington, VT: Ashgate, 2006.

Hyam, Ronald. *Britain's Imperial Century, 1815–1914* (3rd ed.). New York: Palgrave Macmillan, 2002.

Islemann, Hartmut. "Radicalism in the Melodrama of the Early Nineteenth Century." *Melodrama: The Cultural Emergence of a Genre*. Eds. Michael

Hays and Anastasia Nikolopoulou. New York: St. Martin's Press, 1996. 191–207.

James, Louis. *Fiction for the Working Man 1830–1850: A Study of the Literature Produced for the Working Classes in Early Victorian Urban England*. New York: Oxford University Press, 1963.

Print and the People 1819–1851. London: Allen Lane, 1976.

"Taking Melodrama Seriously; Theatre, and Nineteenth-century Studies." *History Workshop Journal*. 3 (1977): 151–58.

"Time, Politics and Symbolic Imagination in Reynolds's Social Melodrama." *G.W.M. Reynolds: Nineteenth-Century Fiction, Politics and the Press*. Eds. Anne Humpherys and Louis James. Burlington, VT: Ashgate, 2008. 179–98.

Jameson, Fredric. "Modernism and Imperialism." *Nationalism, Colonialism, and Literature*. Eds. Terry Eagleton, Fredric Jameson, and Edward W. Said. Minneapolis: University of Minnesota Press, 1990. 43–66.

Jann, Rosemary. "Democratic Myths in Victorian Medievalism." *Browning Institute Studies*. 8 (1980): 129–49.

Janowitz, Anne. "Class and Literature: The Case of Romantic Chartism." *Rethinking Class: Literary Studies and Social Formations*. Eds. Wai Chee Dimock and Michael Gilmore. New York: Columbia University, 1994. 239–66.

Lyric and Labour in the Romantic Tradition. Cambridge: Cambridge University Press, 1998.

Jenkins, Mick. *The General Strike of 1842*. London: Lawrence and Wishart, 1980.

Jerrold, Douglas. *The Rent Day*. London: Bradbury and Evans, 1854.

Black-Ey'd Susan. Nineteenth-Century Plays. Ed. George Rowell. London: Oxford University Press, 1969. 1–43.

John, Juliet. *Dickens and Mass Culture*. Oxford: Oxford University Press, 2010.

Johnson, Richard. "Really Useful Knowledge – Radical Education and Working Class Culture, 1790–1848." *Working-Class Culture: Studies in History and Theory*. Eds. John Clarke, Charles Crichter, and Richard Johnson. London: Hutchinson, 1979. 75–102.

Jones, Aled. *Powers of the Press: Newspapers, Power and the Public in Nineteenth-Century England*. Brookfield, VT: Scolar Press, 1996.

"Chartist Journalism and Print Culture in Britain, 1830–1855." *Papers for the People*. Eds. Joan Allen and Owen Ashton. London: Merlin, 2005. 1–24.

Jones, Colin, Josephine McDonagh and Jon Mee. "Introduction." *Charles Dickens, A Tale of Two Cities and the French Revolution*. Eds. Jones, McDonagh, and Mee. New York: Palgrave Macmillan, 2009. 1–23.

Jones, David. *The Last Rising: The Newport Chartist Insurrection of 1839*. Cardiff: University of Wales Press, 2013.

Jones, Ernest. "Price of Blood. A Tale of the South." *The Labourer*. 2 (1847): 129–41.

"The Confessions of a King." *The Labourer*. 1–2 (1847–48): 83–87, 131–33, 211–18, 253–59; vol. 2, 39–43, 67–77.

"The Romance of a People. An Historical Tale, of the Nineteenth Century." *The Labourer*. 1–3 (1847–48).

"St. John's Eve: A Romantic Drama, in Three Acts." *The Labourer*. 3 (1848): 203–18; 4 (1848): 183–92, 229–40.

"The Pirates' Prize." *The Labourer*. 3 (1848): 143–49, 168–80.

"England's Rule in India and the Cry for Vengeance." *People's Paper*. Oct. 31, 1857. *Ernest Jones: Chartist. Selections from the Writings and Speeches of Ernest Jones*. Ed. John Saville. London: Lawrence & Wishart, 1952. 221–22.

"De Brassier, A Democratic Romance." *Notes to the People*. New York: Barnes and Noble, 1968. celebrity

Woman's Wrongs. Chartist Fiction, vol. 2. Ed. Ian Haywood. Burlington, VT: Ashgate, 2001.

Joshi, Priti. "*Michael Armstrong*: Rereading the Industrial Plot." *Frances Trollope and the Novel of Social Change*. Ed. Brenda Ayres. Westport, CT: Greenwood Press, 2002. 35–52.

"Mutiny Echoes: India, Britons, and Charles Dickens's *A Tale of Two Cities*." *Nineteenth-Century Literature*. 62:1 (2007): 48–87.

Joshi, Priya. *In Another Country: Colonialism, Culture, and the English Novel in India*. New York: Columbia University Press, 2002.

Joyce, Patrick. *Visions of the People: Industrial England and the question of class 1848–1914*. New York: Cambridge University Press, 1991.

Democratic Subjects: The Self and the Social in Nineteenth-century England. Cambridge: Cambridge University Press, 1994.

Kaplan, E. Ann. "The Political Unconscious in the Maternal Melodrama: Ellen Wood's *East Lynne* (1861)." *Gender, Genre, and Narrative Pleasure*. Ed. Derek Longhurst. Boston: Unwin, 1989. 31–50.

Kay-Shuttleworth, James. "First Report on the Training School at Battersea to the Poor Law Commissioners." 1841. *Four Periods of Public Education as Reviewed in 1832, 1839, 1846, 1862* by Kay-Shuttleworth. Brighton: Harvester, 1973. 293–386.

"The Moral and Physical Condition of the Working Classes in Manchester in 1832." *Sir James Kay-Shuttleworth on Popular Education*. Ed. Trygve Tholfsen. New York: Teachers College Press, 1974. 41–79.

"Recent Measures for the Promotion of Education in England." *Sir James Kay-Shuttleworth on Popular Education*. Ed. Trygve Tholfsen. New York: Teachers College Press, 1974. 80–95.

Keating, P. J. *The Working Classes in Victorian Fiction*. New York: Barnes and Nobles, 1971.

Kelly, Thomas. *A History of Adult Education in Great Britain*. Liverpool: Liverpool University Press, 1962.

Kestner, Joseph. *Protest and Reform: The British Social Narrative by Women, 1827–1867*. Madison: University of Wisconsin Press, 1985.

King, Amy Mae. "Taxonomical Cures: The Politics of Natural History and Herbalist Medicine in Elizabeth Gaskell's *Mary Barton*." *Romantic Science: The Literary Forms of Natural History*. Ed. Noah Herringman. Albany: State University of New York Press, 2003. 255–270.

Kingsley, Charles. *Alton Locke*. New York: Oxford University Press, 1987.

Charles Kingsley: His Letters and Memories of His Life; Edited by His Wife. London: Kegan, Paul, Trench, 1882. 2 vols. Hathitrust. Web. Feb. 21, 2016.

Klaus, H. Gustav. "Mrs. Rochester and Mr. Cooper: Alternative Visions of Class, History and Rebellion in the 'Hungry Forties.'" *Literature and History*. 14:1 (2005): 1–13.

Klaver, Claudia. *A/moral Economics: Classical Political Economy and Cultural Authority in Nineteenth-Century England*. Columbus: Ohio State University Press, 2003.

Knight, Charles. *Passages of a Working Life*, vol 2. 1864. New York: AMS, 1973.

Knorr, Klaus. *British Colonial Theories, 1570–1850*. Toronto: University of Toronto Press, 1944.

Knott, John. *Popular Opposition to the 1834 Poor Law*. London: Croom Helm, 1986.

Koven, Seth. *Slumming: Sexual and Social Politics in Victorian London*. Princeton: Princeton University Press, 2004.

Kuduk, Stephanie. "Sedition, Chartism, and Epic Poetry in Thomas Cooper's *The Purgatory of the Suicides*." *Victorian Poetry*. 39:2 (2001): 165–86.

Lamb, John B. "Domesticating History: Revolution and Moral Management in *A Tale of Two Cities*." *Dickens Studies Annual*. 25 (1996): 227–43.

Laqueur, Thomas. *Religion and Respectability: Sunday Schools and Working Class Culture 1780–1850*. New Haven: Yale University Press.

Law, Graham. *Serializing Fiction in the Victorian Press*. New York: Palgrave, 2000.

"Reynolds's 'Memoirs' Series and 'The Literature of the Kitchen.'" *G.W.M. Reynolds: Nineteenth-Century Fiction, Politics and the Press*. Eds. Anne Humpherys and Louis James. Burlington, VT: Ashgate, 2008. 201–12.

Ledger, Sally. "Chartist Aesthetics in the Mid Nineteenth Century: Ernest Jones, a Novelist of the People." *Nineteenth-Century Literature*. 57:1 (June 2002): 31–63.

Dickens and the Popular Radical Imagination. Cambridge: Cambridge University Press, 2007.

"From the Old Bailey to Revolutionary France: The Trials of Charles Darnay." *Charles Dickens, A Tale of Two Cities and the French Revolution*. Eds. Colin Jones, Josephine McDonagh and Jon Mee. New York: Palgrave Macmillan, 2009. 75–86.

Lees, Lynn Hollen. *The Solidarities of Strangers: The English Poor Laws and the People, 1700–1948*. Cambridge: Cambridge University Press, 1998.

Legette, Casie. "The Lyric Speaker Goes to Gaol: British Poetry and Radical Prisoners, 1820–1845." *Nineteenth-Century Literature*, 67:1 (2012): 1–28.

Levine, Caroline. *The Serious Pleasures of Suspense: Victorian Realism and Narrative Doubt*. Charlottesville: University of Virginia Press, 2003.

Logan, Deborah Anna. "Introduction." *Illustrations of Political Economy: Selected Tales*. Harriet Martineau. Peterborough, ONT: Broadview, 2004. 9–50.

Lovett, William. *Life and Struggles of William Lovett, in His Pursuit of Bread, Knowledge & Freedom*. London: McGibbon & Kee, 1967.

Lovett, William and John Collins. *Chartism, a New Organization of the People.* 1840. New York: Humanities, 1969.

Lukács, Georg. *The Historical Novel.* Lincoln: University of Nebraska Press, 1983.

"Magazines of Popular Progress and the Artisans." *Victorian Periodicals Review* 17:3 (1984): 83–94.

The Theory of the Novel. Cambridge, MA: The MIT Press, 1996.

Malthus, T. R. *An Essay on the Principle of Population.* Cambridge, Cambridge University Press, 1992. [1803 edition.]

Marcus. *The Book of Murder. A Vade-Mecum for the Commissioners and Guardians of the New Poor Law Throughout Great Britain and Ireland, Being an Exact Reprint of the Infamous Essay on the Possibility of Limiting Populousness, By Marcus, One of the Three. With a Refutation of the Malthusian Doctrine.* London: William Dugdale, 1839.

Marryat, Frederick. *Mr Midshipman Easy.* New York: Henry Holt, 1998.

Martin, Meredith. *American Literature and the Culture of Reprinting, 1834–1853.* Philadelphia: University of Pennsylvania Press, 2013. Ebrary. Web. Dec. 7, 2015.

Martineau, Harriet. *The Hamlets.* London: Charles Fox, 1833.

The Parish. London: Charles Fox, 1833.

The Town. London: Charles Fox, 1834.

The Land's End. London: Charles Fox, 1834.

"Female Industry." *"Criminal, Idiots, Women, and Minors": Victorian Writing by Women on Women.* Ed. Susan Hamilton. Peterborough, ONT: Broadview, 1995.

Illustrations of Political Economy: Selected Tales. Peterborough, ONT: Broadview Editions, 2004.

Autobiography. Peterborough, ONT: Broadview, 2007.

Mays, Kelly. "Slaves in Heaven, Laborers in Hell: Chartist Poets' Ambivalent Identification with the (Black) Slave." *Victorian Poetry.* 39:2 (2001): 137–63.

McCalman, Iain. *Radical Underworld: Prophets, Revolutionaries and Pornographers in London, 1795–1840.* Cambridge: Cambridge University Press, 1988.

McDonagh, Josephine. *Child Murder and British Culture, 1720–1900.* Cambridge: Cambridge University Press, 2003.

McWilliam, Rohan. "The Mysteries of G.W.M. Reynolds: Radicalism and Melodrama in Victorian Britain." *Living and Learning: Essays in Honour of J.F.C. Harrison.* Eds. Malcolm Chase and Ian Dyck. Brookfield, VT: Scolar Press, 1996. 182–98.

"Melodrama and the Historians." *Radical History Review.* 78 (2000): 57–84.

Meer, Sarah. "Competing Representations: Douglass, the Ethiopian Serenaders, and Ethnic Exhibition in London." *Liberating Sojourn: Frederick Douglass and Transatlantic Reform.* Eds. Alan Rice and Martin Crawford. Athens: University of Georgia Press, 1999. 141–65.

Meisel, Martin. "Scattered Chiaroscuro: Melodrama as a Matter of Seeing." *Melodrama: Stage, Picture, Screen.* Eds. Jacky Bratton, Jim Cook and Christine Gledhill. London: British Film Institute, 1994. 65–81.

Menke, Richard. "Cultural Capital and the Scene of Rioting: Male Working-Class Authorship in 'Alton Locke.'" *Victorian Literature and Culture*. 28:1 (2000): 87–108.

Meyer, Susan. *Imperialism at Home: Race and Victorian Women's Fiction*. Ithaca: Cornell University Press, 1996.

Midgely, Clare. *Women Against Slavery: The British Campaigns 1780–1870*. New York: Routledge, 1992.

Millard, Kay. "The Religion of Elizabeth Gaskell." *Gaskell Society Journal* 15 (2001): 1–13.

Miller, D. A. *The Novel and the Police*. Berkeley: University of California Press, 1988.

Miller, Elizabeth Carolyn. *Slow Print: Literary Radicalism and Late Victorian Print Culture*. Stanford: Stanford University Press, 2013.

Milner, Henry. *Mazeppa. Victorian Melodramas*. Ed. Smith James. Totowa, NJ: Rowman and Littlefield, 1976 [1831]. 1–38.

Mitchell, Jack. "Aesthetic Problems of the Development of the Proletarian-Revolutionary Novel in Nineteenth-Century Britain." *Marxists on Literature. An Anthology*. Ed. David Craig. Harmondsworth: Penguin, 1975. 245–66.

Moncrieff, W. T. *The Lear of Private Life; Or, Father and Daughter*. 1820. In Chadwyck-Healey. English Prose Drama Full-Text Database. Web.

Moore, Grace. *Dickens and Empire: Discourses of Class, Race, and Colonialism in the Works of Charles Dickens*. Burlington, VT: Ashgate, 2004.

Moore, Sean. *Swift, the Book, and the Irish Financial Revolution: Satire and Sovereignty in Colonial Ireland*. Baltimore: Johns Hopkins University Press, 2010.

Moretti, Franco. *Atlas of the European Novel 1800–1900*. New York: Verso, 1998.
  The Way of the World: The Bildungsroman in European Culture. London: Verso, 2000.

Nattrass, Leonora. *William Cobbett: The Politics of Style*. Cambridge: Cambridge University Press, 1995.

Neville-Sington, Pamela. *Fanny Trollope: The Life and Adventures of a Clever Woman*. New York: Viking, 1997.

Nixon, Rob. *Slow Violence and the Environmentalism of the Poor*. Cambridge, MA: Harvard University Press, 2011.

Nord, Deborah Epstein. *Walking the Victorian Streets: Women, Representation, and the City*. Ithaca: Cornell University Press, 1995.

O'Brien, James Bronterre. *The Life and Character of Maximilian Robespierre*. London: J. Watson, 1837 (?). Hathitrust. Web. May 27, 2016.

O'Gorman, Francis. *The Victorian Novel*. Oxford: Blackwell, 2002.

O'Malley, Patrick. *Catholicism, Sexual Deviance, and Victorian Gothic Culture*. Cambridge and New York: Cambridge University Press, 2006.

Orsini, Felice. *Memoirs and Adventures of Felice Orsini*. Edinburgh: T. Constable and company, 1857.

Parascandola, Louis. *"Puzzled Which to Choose": Conflicting Socio-Political Views in the Works of Captain Frederick Marryat*. New York: Peter Lang, 1997.

Parker, Pamela Corpron. "Fictional Philanthropy in Elizabeth Gaskell's *Mary Barton* and *North and South*." *Victorian Literature and Culture* 25:2 (1997): 321–31.

Patterson, A. Temple. *Radical Leicester. A History of Leicester, 1780–1850*. Bath: Sir Isaac Pitman & Sons, Ltd, 1954.

Paul, Ronald. "'In louring Hindostan': Chartism and Empire in Ernest Jones's the New World, a Democratic Poem." *Victorian Poetry*. 39:2 (2001): 189–204.

Payne, David. *The Re-enchantment of Nineteenth-Century Fiction*. New York: Palgrave, 2005.

Paz, D. G. *Dickens and Barnaby Rudge: Anti-Catholicism and Chartism*. London: Merlin Press, 2006.

Petch, Simon. "The Business of the Barrister in *A Tale of Two Cities*." *Criticism: A Quarterly for Literature and the Arts*. 44:1 (2002): 27–42.

Peterson, Linda. "From French Revolution to English Reform: Hannah More, Harriet Martineau, and the 'Little Book.'" *Nineteenth-Century Literature*. 60:4 (2006): 409–45.

Pickering, Paul. "Class without Words: Symbolic Communication in the Chartist Movement." *Past and Present*. 112 (1986): 144–62.

Chartism and the Chartists in Manchester and Salford. New York: St. Martin's Press, 1995.

"'Mercenary Scribblers' and 'Polluted Quills': The Chartist Press in Australia and New Zealand." *Papers for the People: A Study of the Chartist Press*. Eds. Joan Allen and Owen R. Ashton. Bodwin, UK: Merlin Press, 2005. 190–215.

Feargus O'Connor: A Political Life. Monmouth, Wales: Merlin Press, 2008.

Pickering, Paul, and Stephen Roberts. "Pills, Pamphlets and Politics: The Career of Peter Murray McDouall (1814–54)." *Manchester Region History Review* 11 (1997): 34–43.

Pitt, George Dibdin. *Beggar's Petition, or, A Father's Love and A Mother's Care!* New York: Readex Microprint, 1967.

Plotz, John. *The Crowd: British Literature and Public Politics*. Berkeley: University of California Press, 2000.

Poovey, Mary. *Making a Social Body: British Cultural Formation 1830–1864*. Chicago: University of Chicago Press, 1995.

Porter, Bernard. *The Refugee Question in mid-Victorian Politics*. Cambridge: Cambridge University Press, 1979.

Poynter, J. R. *Society and Pauperism: English Ideas on Poor Relief, 1795–1834*. London: Routledge, 1969.

Pratt, Tim. "Ernest Jones' Mutiny: *The People's Paper*, English Popular Politics and the Indian Rebellion 1857–58." *Media and the British Empire*. Ed. Chandrika Kaul. New York: Palgrave, 2006. 88–103.

Pykett, Lyn. *The "Improper" Feminine: The Women's Sensation Novel and the New Woman Writing*. New York: Routledge, 1992.

Rahill, Frank. *The World of Melodrama*. University Park: The Pennsylvania State University Press, 1967.

Rai, Amit. *Rule of Sympathy: Sentiment, Race, and Power 1750–1850*. New York: Palgrave, 2002.

Rancière, Jacques. *Proletarian Nights*. New York: Verso, 2012.

Randall, Timothy. "Chartist Poetry and Song." *The Chartist Legacy*. Eds. Owen Ashton, Robert Fyson, and Stephen Roberts. London: Merlin Press, 1999. 171–95.

Robbins, Bruce. "Introduction Part I: Actually Existing Cosmopolitanism." *Cosmopolitics: Thinking and Feeling beyond the Nation*. Eds. Pheng Cheah and Bruce Robbins. Minneapolis: University of Minnesota Press, 1998. 1–19.

Upward Mobility and the Common Good. Toward a Literary History of the Welfare State. Princeton: Princeton University Press, 2007.

Roberts, Stephen. "Who Wrote to the *Northern Star*?" *The Duty of Discontent: Essays for Dorothy Thompson*. Eds. Owen Ashton, Robert Fyson, and Stephen Roberts. New York: Mansell, 1995. 55–70.

"Thomas Cooper in Leicester, 1840–1843." *The People's Charter: Democratic Agitation in Early Victorian Britain*. Ed. Stephen Roberts. London: Merlin, 2003. 133–51.

The Chartist Prisoners: The Radical Lives of Thomas Cooper (1805–1892) and Arthur O'Neill (1819–1896). New York: Peter Lang, 2008.

Rogers, Helen. *Women and the People: Authority, Authorship and the Radical Tradition in Nineteenth-Century England*. Burlington, VT: Ashgate: 2000.

Rose, Jonathan. *The Intellectual Life of the British Working Classes*. New Haven: Yale University Press, 2001.

Rosenmann, Ellen Bayuk. "The Virtue of Illegitimacy: Inheritance and Belonging in *The Dark Woman* and *Mary Price*." *G.W.M. Reynolds: Nineteenth-Century Fiction, Politics and the Press*. Eds. Anne Humphreys and Louis James. Burlington, VT: Ashgate, 2008. 213–26.

Royle, Edward. *Chartism*. New York: Longman, 1996 [1980].

Sabin, Margery. "Working-Class Plain Style: William Lovett vs. Carlyle, Gaskell, and Others." *Raritan* 18:2 (1998): 41–62.

Said, Edward. *Culture and Imperialism*. New York: Vintage, 1994.

Sambrook, James. *William Cobbett*. London: Routledge, 1973.

Sanders, Andrew. *The Victorian Historical Novel, 1840–1880*. New York: St. Martins Press, 1979.

"Introduction." Charles Dickens, *A Tale of Two Cities*. New York: Oxford University Press, 1988. vii–xviii.

Dickens and the Spirit of the Age. Oxford: Clarendon Press, 1999.

Sanders, Mike. "From 'Political' to 'Human' Economy: The Visions of Harriet Martineau and Frances Wright." *Women: A Cultural Review*. 12:2 (2001).

"'A Jackass Load of Poetry': The *Northern Star*'s Poetry Column 1838–1852." *Victorian Periodicals Review*. 39:1 (2006): 46–66.

The Poetry of Chartism. Cambridge: Cambridge University Press, 2009.

Sanders, Valerie. *Reason Over Passion: Harriet Martineau and the Victorian Novel*. New York: St. Martin's Press, 1986.

Saville, John "Introduction." *Ernest Jones: Chartist. Selections from the Writings and Speeches of Ernest Jones*. Ed. John Saville. London: Lawrence & Wishart, 1952.

1848, The British State and the Chartist Movement. Cambridge: Cambridge University Press, 1987.

Schoyen, A. R. *The Chartist Challenge: A Portrait of George Julian Harney.* London: Heinemann, 1958.

Schwarzkopf, Jutta. *Women in the Chartist Movement.* Houndsmill: Macmillan, 1991.

Scott, Joan Wallach. *Gender and the Politics of History.* New York: Columbia University Press, 1988.

Secord, Anne. "Elizabeth Gaskell and the Artisan Naturalists of Manchester." *Gaskell Society Journal* 19 (2005): 34–51.

Seed, John. "Unitarianism, Political Economy and the Antinomies of Liberal Culture in Manchester, 1830–1850." *Social History* 7:1 (1982): 1–25.

Semmel, Bernard. *The Liberal Ideal and the Demons of Empire: Theories of Imperialism from Adam Smith to Lenin.* Baltimore: Johns Hopkins University Press, 1993.

Sen, Sambudha. *London, Radical Culture, and the Making of the Dickensian Aesthetic.* New York: Columbia University Press, 2012.

Shannon, Mary. *Dickens, Reynolds, and Mayhew on Wellington Street: The Print Culture of a Victorian Street.* Burlington, VT: Ashgate, 2015.

Sheckner, Peter, ed. *An Anthology of Chartist Poetry: Poetry of the British Working Class, 1830s-1850s.* London: Associated University Presses, 1989.

"Chartism, Class, and Social Struggle: A Study of CD." *Midwest Quarterly.* 27 (1987–88): 93–112.

Shepherd, Simon and Peter Womack. *English Drama: A Cultural History.* Cambridge, MA: Blackwell, 1996.

Shilliam, Robbie. "Decolonizing the *Manifesto*: Communism and the Slave Analogy." *The Cambridge Companion to the Communist Manifesto.* Eds. Terrell Carver and Janes Farr. New York: Cambridge University Press, 2015. 195–287.

Siegel, Daniel. *Charity and Condescension: Victorian Literature and the Dilemmas of Philanthropy.* Athens: Ohio State University Press, 2012.

Silver, Harold. *English Education and the Radicals 1780–1850.* London: Routledge, 1975.

Simmons, Clare. *Popular Medievalism in Romantic-Era Britain.* New York: Palgrave Macmillan, 2011.

Simon, Brian. *Studies in the History of Education, Vol. 1: The Two Nations and the Educational Structure, 1780–1870.* London: Lawrence and Wishart, 1960.

Slater, Michael. *Douglas Jerrold 1803–1857.* London: Duckworth, 2002.

Smith, Denis Mack. *Mazzini.* New Haven: Yale University Press, 1994.

Smith, Sheila. *The Other Nation: The Poor in English Novels of the 1840s and 1850s.* Oxford: Clarendon Press, 1980.

Spater, George. *William Cobbett, the Poor Man's Friend.* Cambridge: Cambridge University Press, 1982.

Stedman Jones, Gareth. *Languages of Class: Studies of English Working-Class History, 1832–1982.* Cambridge: Cambridge University Press, 1983.

Stephen, James Fitzjames. "A Tale of Two Cities." *The Dickens Critics*. Eds. George Ford and Lauriat Lane. Ithaca: Cornell University Press, 1961. 38–48.

Stephens, J. R. *Three Sermons Preached by the Rev. J.R. Stephens*. London: n.p., 1839. Gale. Web. May 27, 2016.

Stone, Marjorie. 1991. "Bakhtinian Polyphony in *Mary Barton*; Class, Gender, and the Texual Voice." *Dickens Studies Annual: Essays on Victorian Fiction* 20: 175–200.

Stoneman, Patsy. *Elizabeth Gaskell*. Manchester: Manchester University Press, 2006.

Surridge, Lisa. "Working-Class Masculinities in *Mary Barton*." *Victorian Literature and Culture* 28:2 (2000): 331–43.

Sutcliffe, Marcell Pellegrino. *Victorian Radicals and Italian Democrats*. Woodbridge, Suffolk: Boydell Press, 2014.

Sutherland, Gillian. "Education." *The Cambridge Social History of Britain, 1750–1950*. Ed. F. M. L. Thompson. Cambridge: Cambridge University Press, 2014. 119–69. Nov. 4, 2014. Web.

Taylor, Antony. "Shakespeare and Radicalism: The Uses and Abuses of Shakespeare in Nineteenth-Century Popular Politics." *The Historical Journal*. 45 (2002): 357–79.

"'Some Little or Contemptible War upon her Hands': *Reynolds's Newspaper and Empire*." *G.W.M. Reynolds: Nineteenth-Century Fiction, Politics and the Press*. Eds. Anne Humpherys and Louis James. Burlington, VT: Ashgate, 2008. 99–119.

Taylor, Barbara. *Eve and the New Jerusalem*. New York: Pantheon, 1983.

Taylor, Miles. "Imperium et Libertas? Rethinking the Radical Critique of Imperialism during the Nineteenth Century." *The Journal of Imperial and Commonwealth History*. 19:1 (1991): 1–23.

The Decline of British Radicalism, 1847–1860. Oxford: Clarendon Press, 1995.

Ernest Jones, Chartism, and the Romance of Politics. New York: Oxford University Press, 2004.

[Thackeray, William]. "Half-a-Crown's Worth of Cheap Knowledge." *Fraser's Magazine*. 17 (1838): 279–90.

Thiele, David. "'That There Brutus': Elite Culture and Knowledge Diffusion in the Industrial Novels of Elizabeth Gaskell." *Victorian Literature and Culture* 35:1 (2007): 263–85.

Tholfsen, Trygve. *Working-Class Radicalism in Mid-Victorian England*. New York: Columbia University Press, 1977.

ed. *Sir James Kay-Shuttleworth on Popular Education*. New York: Teachers College Press, 1974.

Thompson, Dorothy. "Ireland and the Irish." *The Chartist Experience: Studies in Working-Class Radicalism and Culture, 1830–60*. Eds. James Epstein and Dorothy Thompson. New York: Macmillan, 1982.

The Chartists. New York: Random House, 1984.

Outsiders: Class, Gender and Nation. New York: Verso, 1993.

"Who Were 'the People' in 1842?" *Living and Learning: Essays in Honour of J.F. C. Harrison*. Eds. Malcolm Chase and Ian Dyck. Brookfield, VT: Scolar Press, 1996. 118–32.

Thompson, E. P. *The Making of the English Working-Class*. New York: Vintage, 1966.

"Mayhew and the *Morning Chronicle*." *The Unknown Mayhew: Selections from the Morning Chronicle*. Henry Mayhew. London: Merlin Press, 1971. 11–50.

Thompson, Noel. *The Market and Its Critics: Socialist Political Economy in Nineteenth Century Britain*. New York: Routledge, 1988.

Thorne, Susan. *Congregational Missions and the Making of an Imperial Culture in Nineteenth-Century England*. Stanford: Stanford University Press, 1999.

Tonna, Charlotte Elizabeth. *The Wrongs of Woman*. New York: Dodd, 1845.

Trevelyan, G. O. *The Life and Letters of Lord Macaulay*. New York: Harper, 1876. Hathitrust.org. Web. June 22, 2016.

Trollope, Fanny. *Domestic Manners of the Americans*. New York: Oxford, 1997.

Jessie Phillips, A Tale of the Present Day. Stroud, Gloucestshire: Nonsuch, 2006.

The Life and Adventures of Michael Armstrong the Factory Boy. Stroud, Gloucestershire: Nonsuch, 2007.

Trollope, Thomas. *What I Remember*. London: Richard Bentley and Sons, 1887.

Tyrrell, Alex. *Joseph Sturge and the Moral Radical Party in Early Victorian Britain*. London: Christopher Helm, 1987.

Uglow, Jenny. *Elizabeth Gaskell: A Habit of Stories*. Boston: Faber and Faber, 1993.

Ulrich, John. *Signs of Their Times: History, Labor, and the Body in Cobbett, Carlyle, and Disraeli*. Athens: Ohio University Press, 2002.

Vanden Bossche, Chris. *Reform Acts: Chartism, Social Agency, and the Victorian Novel, 1832–1867*. Baltimore: Johns Hopkins University Press, 2014.

Vargo, Greg. "*Cobbett's Political Register* (1802–1836)." *Dictionary of Nineteenth-Century Journalism in Great Britain and Ireland*. Eds. Laurel Brake and Marysa Demoor. London: Academia Press and the British Library, 2009. 459–60.

"Literature from Below: Radicalism and Popular Fiction." *Victorian Literature and Culture*. 44:2 (2016): 439–53.

Vernon, James. *Politics and the People: A Study in English Political Culture, c. 1815–1867*. Cambridge: Cambridge University Press, 1993.

Vicinus, Martha. *The Industrial Muse. A Study of Nineteenth Century British Working-Class Literature*. New York: Harper and Row, 1974.

"'Helpless and Unfriended': Nineteenth-Century Domestic Melodrama." *New Literary History*. 13:1 (1981): 127–43.

"Chartist Fiction and the Development of a Class-Based Literature." *The Socialist Novel in Britain: The Recovery of a Tradition*. Ed. Gustav Klaus. Brighton: Harvester, 1982.

Vincent, David. *Bread, Knowledge and Freedom: A Study of Nineteenth-Century Working Class Autobiography*. London: Europa, 1981.

Vinokur, Annie. "Malthusian Ideology and the Crises of the Welfare State." *Malthus and His Time*. Ed. Michael Turner. New York: St. Martin's Press, 1986. 170–86.

von Rosador, Kurt Tetzeli. "Victorian Theories of Melodrama." *Anglia*. 95:1–2 (1977): 87–114.

Wakefield, Edward Gibbon. *The Collected Works of Edward Gibbon Wakefield*. Ed. M. F. Lloyd Prichard. Collins: London, 1968.

Watts, Ruth. *Gender, Power, and the Unitarians in England 1760–1860*. New York: Longman, 1998.

Weaver, Stewart. *John Fielden and the Politics of Popular Radicalism, 1832–1847*. Oxford: Clarendon Press, 1987.

Webb, R. K. *The British Working-Class Reader 1790–1848: Literacy and Social Tension*. London: Allen and Unwin, 1955.

Harriet Martineau: A Radical Victorian. New York: Columbia University Press, 1960.

Weiner, Stephanie Kuduk. *Republican Politics and English Poetry, 1789–1874*. New York: Palgrave MacMillan, 2005.

Weisser, Henry. "The Role of Feargus O'Connor in Chartist Internationalism, 1845–1848." *The Rocky Mountain Social Science Journal*. 6:1 (1969): 82–90.

British Working-Class Movements and Europe 1815–48. Manchester: Manchester University Press, 1975.

West, Shearer. "Introduction." *The Victorians and Race*. Ed. Shearer West. Aldershot: Ashgate, 1996. 1–11.

Wheeler, Michael. *The Old Enemies: Catholic and Protestant in Nineteenth-Century English Culture*. Cambridge: Cambridge University Press, 2006.

Wheeler, Thomas Martin. *Sunshine in Shadow. Chartist Fiction*. Ed. Ian Haywood. Brookfield: Ashgate, 1999 (1849–50).

Wiener, Joel. *William Lovett*. Manchester: Manchester University Press, 1989.

Wilderson, Frank. *Red, White & Black*. Durham: Duke University Press, 2010.

Williams, David *John Frost: a Study in Chartism*. New York: Augustus Kelley, 1969.

Williams, Raymond. *Culture and Society 1780–1950*. Harmondsworth: Penguin, 1958.

The English Novel. New York: Oxford University Press, 1970.

"Radical and/or Respectable." *The Press We Deserve*. Ed. Richard Boston. London: Routledge, 1970. 14–26.

William Cobbett. Oxford: Oxford University Press, 1983.

Wilson, Alexander. *The Chartist Movement in Scotland*. Manchester: Manchester University Press, 1970.

Winch, Donald. *Malthus: A Very Short Introduction*. Oxford: Oxford University Press, 2013.

Woloch, Alex. *The One vs. the Many*. Princeton: Princeton University Press, 2003.

Woodcock, George. "Introduction." *Rural Rides*. William Cobbett. Baltimore: Penguin, 1967. 7–26.

Wyke, Terry. "The Culture of Self-Improvement: Real People in *Mary Barton.*" *Gaskell Society Journal* 13 (1999): 85–103.

Yeazell, Ruth Bernard. "Why Political Novels Have Heroines: '*Sybil*,' '*Mary Barton*,' and '*Felix Holt.*'" *Novel: A Forum on Fiction* 18:2 (1985): 126–44.

Yelland, Chris. "Speech and Writing in the Northern Star." *The People's Charter: Democratic Agitation in Early Victorian Britain.* Ed. Stephen Roberts. London: Merlin Press, 2003. 95–113.

Yeo, Eileen. "Mayhew as a Social Investigator." *The Unknown Mayhew: Selections from the* Morning Chronicle. Henry Mayhew. London: Merlin Press, 1971. 51–95.

Index

CAMBRIDGE STUDIES IN NINETEENTH-CENTURY
LITERATURE AND CULTURE

GENERAL EDITOR: Gillian Beer, *University of Cambridge*

Titles published

CPSIA information can be obtained
at www.ICGtesting.com
Printed in the USA
LVHW011618220219
608476LV00010B/204/P